MAINĀMATĪ :
Sanskrit Inscriptional and Archaeological Study

MAINĀMATĪ :
Sanskrit Inscriptional and Archaeological Study

Bijoy Krishna Banik

BKP

Bharatiya Kala Prakashan
DELHI (INDIA)

First Edition : 2009

Published by **C.P. Gautam**
BHARATIYA KALA PRAKASHAN
3421-A, IInd Floor, Narang Colony, Tri Nagar,
Delhi-110035. Ph. : (011) 32967505, Telefax : 01127393083
E-mail : 3241bkp@yahoo.co.in
Webisite: www. bkp books. com

ISBN : 978-81-8090-233-8

Laser Type Setting by
A-ONE GRAPHICS
Delhi-110088

Printed By :
BDH Printer at Salasar Imaging Systems
Delhi.

Dedicated
to
My Parents

CONTENTS

PREFACE

A proper study of history is based only on two types of mutually complementary sources—literary and archaeological. Literary works give us data that are culturally very significant, but they are often mixed with material, which tends to be less historical and more legendary. The literary material has to be checked, verified and consolidated from archaeological remains and artifacts. So far as the history of the Indian subcontinent is concerned, the importance of Sanskrit language and literature can never be gainsaid. Almost entire archaeological linguistic data for reconstructing our ancient history is preserved in the epitaphs of edicts, pillars and donation copper-plates and even coin-legends which are written in Sanskrit language. Therefore, no study of ancient Indian history can take place without Sanskrit either literary or archaeological.

Maināmatī is a comparatively quite small strip of hilly land but it is extraordinarily rich in archaeological evidences and one of the most important historical and religious centre of Bangladesh. There is a very large assemblage of theruins of Buḍḍhist monasteries. It is in fact a prominent spot for studying the rich heritage of Bangladesh.

Speaking about its richness in archaeological evidences, it will suffice to mention here that from this small strip of hilly land many archaeological brick-structure sites are unearthed (classified into monasteries, large-shrines, administrative sites, hill-top mounds, non-structural sites and water reservoirs etc.), 12 copper-plate grants are found (with 16 from nearby area), and over 200 golden-silver coins and 4 stone images are also excavated. This itself speaks for the historical importance of the area, which was culturally very rich in Bangladesh during 6th to 13th centuries (A.D.).

This area, located in the centre of the Samatāta Maṇḍala, was politically very significant in ancient times, and gave birth to many popular ballads and folk literature. But the political history, the dynastic lineage and the ancient political geography of this area needs to be reconstructed and checked from the archaeological evidences which only can provide the reliable data. A study of this inscriptional material is also expected to help establish a better co-relation between space and time and political situations.

Stray studies of some of these individual archaeological artifacts have found place in some important research Journals. But they do not give us a consistent well-connected study of its entire source-material. This desideratum is intended to be fulfilled in this study. A study of this area will revive the past and will add new dimensions to the history of the present. A historical and cultural study of the archaeological artifacts and inscriptions found in this area is likely to yield very fruitful results. The present study is an attempt in this direction. It aims fulfiling the need of a Complete consistent and comprehensive study of the entire archaeological evidence found in the Mainămatī-Lalmai range in the centre of the Samatāla Maṇḍala and thus adds to and contributes to the general enhancement of the knowledge. No kinds of research project can be successfully completed without wholehearted assistance and cooperation from all concerned. This work is also no exception. I am deeply indebted to a large number of individuals and institutions for their willing assistance and advice in the preparation of my doctoral research.

I find myself lacking in words to express my profound sense of respect and deepest gratitude to Professor Dr. R.I. Nanavati, Director, Oriental Institute, (formerly, Head, Department of Sanskrit, Pali and Prakrit and Principal, Baroda

Sanskrit Mahā-vidyalaya), M.S. University of Baroda. my guiding teacher, for his invaluable guidance and unfailing academic support throughout the course of the present research work, without which it would not have been possible to complete this work. He has not only read the thesis closely, but also made valuable suggestions by discussing several intricate points connected with it. I have always, been provided homely atmosphere in his respectable family at every stage in my foreign days of studies. I shall be ever grateful to him and his family.

I am very grateful to late Professor Dr. R.N. Mehta, (Formerly, Head, the Department of Archaeology and Ancient History, M.S. University of Baroda), a veteran field archaeologist, an eminent historian and a well-known epigraphist, for suggesting the title of my thesis and for valuable guidance in the early stage of my thesis. I wish to express my deep sense of gratitude to Professor Dr. V.H. Sonawane, another veteran field Archaeologist, the then Head, Department of Archaeology and Ancient History, M.S. University of Baroda, for thoroughly checking the archaeological section of my thesis inspite of his heavy schedules. After Professor R.N. Mehta, he constantly encouraged me and gave valuable suggestions, generous help and cooperation at every stage of my project.

I take this opportunity to thank the authorities of the Government of India for awarding me the I.C.C.R. (Indian Council for Cultural Relations) scholarship through High Commission of India, Dhaka. I shall be grateful forever to the Council for giving me the financial assistance and bestowing upon me this opportunity.

I express sincere thanks to all my Departmental teachers, especially. Dr. Uma Deshpande, Dr.. Jaydev jani, Dr. L.M Joshi and Dr. R.K.. Panda for their kind co-operation throughout this research work.

I am extremely grateful to Md. Nazmul Ahshan Chowdhuri, the then Director and Joint Secretary, Muhammad

Abul Hossain, the then Director and Joint Secretary and Md. A.Z.M. Rafiq Bhuiyan, the then Director and Joint Secretary, Directorate of Archaeology, for granting me the necessary leave to pursue this doctoral research and for supplying to me the photographs of the copper-plate grants and archaeological publications.

I gratefully acknowledge the help rendered by Dr. Md. Shafiqul Alam, the then Deputy Director and present Director, Dr. Abdus Sabur Mia, the then Regional Director, Md. Mosharraf Hossain, the then Deputy Director and Shihab-uddin Md. Akbar, Regional Director, Directorate of Archaeology for giving me kind co-operation, encouragement and inspiration for my Doctoral research.

I am extremely grateful and with to offer hearty vote of thanks to Mrs. Lata R. Nanavati for proof-reading thoroughly the entire archaeological portion of my thesis in spite of her heavy duties and providing family atmosphere in her residence in my foreign days.

I deem it a pleasure to record my special and sincere thanks to Lovely Yasmin, Custodian, Directorate of Archaeology, for her keen moral support during the course of my work and for sending important data whenever I needed. I am also thankful to Md. Tauhidunnabi, Chief Photographer, Directorate of Archaeology, for making the photographs.

The thesis would not have seen the light of the day unless there were a facility of the extensive library. I am thankful to the authorities of the Oriental Institute, Smt. Hansa Mehta Library of Baroda, Departmental Libarary of the Department of Archaeology and Ancient History, M.S. University of Baroda and Departmental library of the Directorate of Archaeology, Dhaka University Library, for allowing me to consult numberless books, Journals and Periodicals and manuscripts in their possession. Especially, I would like to offer my sincere thanks to Mrs Alka Patel, the theerLibrarian, Oriental Institute, M.S. University of Baroda for her cordial co-operation to complete my project smoothly.

I would like to express my sincere thanks to a number of friends and individuals who have helped me in one way or another during the course of my study. My special thanks due to Joydev Kumar Saha, Umesh Kumar Tiwari, Hemant Bhatt and Santimoy Dutta, for all their friendly co-operation to me in my carrying out this work.

I am extremely obliged and grateful to my brother and my sisters for their constant encouragement, inspiration and strong moral support during the entire course of my studies. I am also thankful to my wife Swikriti Sarkar and my only son Rik for their kind cooperation and moral support. The successful completion of this huge task reminds me of my parents late Ranajith Kumar Banik and late Bichitra Rani Banik. I am what I am today due to them only. I, therefore, dedicate this work of mine to their sacred and fondest memory.

—Bijoy Krishna Banik

LIST OF ILLUSTRATIONS

PHOTOGRAPHS

TABLES

TRANLITERATION SCHEME OF DEVANAGARI ALPHABET

The following diacritical marks are used in this Thesis

VOWELS

	अ a	आ ā	इ i	ई ī	ऊ u
	उ ū	ऋ ṛ	ॠ ṝ	ऌ ḷ	ए(अे) e
	ऐ(अै) ai	ओ o	औ au	अं(म) aṁ	अः aḥ

CONSONANTS

ह् h	क् k	ख् kh	ग् g	घ् gh	ङ् ṅ
श् ś	च् c	छ् ch	ज् j	झ् jh	ञ् ñ
ष् ṣ	ट् ṭ	ठ् ṭh	ड् ḍ	ढ् ḍh	ण् ṇ
स् s	त् t	थ् th	द् d	ध् dh	न् n
ह् h	प् p	फ् ph	ब् b	भ् bh	म् m
	य् y	र् r	ल् l	व् v	

CHAPTER-I

BRIEF SURVEV OF MAINĀMATĪ, COMILLA

INTRODUCTORY REMARKS

Mainămatī, the name of a village and a union, is a very familiar historic place situated in Burichang Police Station of Camilla district in Bangladesh of southeastern Bengal. It is well known due to its transferable and non-transferable archaeological evidences, which have yielded its extraordinarily rich archaeological wealth. The name Mainămatī is associated with a number of local legends and ballads, which have come to light probably only a few hundred years ago It is located about five miles to the northwest of Comilla town and is a range of small hillocks almost abruptly erupting in the middle of a vast level plain. This range extends for about eleven miles north south from Mainnmti village to Caṇḍī-Murā. Average height of the hills is only 40 feet but some peaks rise up to 150 feet or even a little more. In present times and in the recent past, there were formed a British Army Cantonment, the campus of Pakistan Academy of Rural Development (at present known as BARD), a Rādhā Kṛṣṇa temple of the Tippera peoples, and Muslims mosques and temples, A thousand years earlier there were constructed on this hillock-range a number of monasteries, stūpas, shrines, palaces and religious structures

Mainămatī excavations have uncovered a large number of valuable archaeological artifacts which have thrown a flood of light on the history of the area surrounding these hillocks which was called Samataṭa Maṇḍala from 6th to 13th century A.D

MAP NO. 3

MAP SHOWING THE DISTRICTS OF BANGLADESH

GRAPHOSMAN

The ancient character of the site was first noticed in 1803 A.D. The copper-plate grant of King Raṇavaṅkamalla Harikāladeva was accidentally discovered in the course of constructing the Dhaka-Comilla Highway at Mainâmatī area. Since then, twelve copper-plate grants in all of various dynasties have been found from excavations in this area. Some of them are in good condition and give important political, geographical and socio-cultural data for the southeast part of Bengal during these times. A study of these plates is, therefore, bound to yield very fruitful results. These plates and artifacts have often been studied individually in isolated and stray papers and articles, which are scattered in various journals. But these individual offers do not afford a coherent and comprehensive picture of the area in those times. An attempt is made in this thesis to fulfill this longstanding desideratum by bringing together all available material and trying to co-relate them and create as complete a picture of that society as possible.

SECTION-I

To understand the location of the area of the newly found copper-plates in today's Bangladesh it is necessary to get an idea of the administrative units into which Bangladesh is at present divided.

Bangladesh is bounded on north, west and east by Indian territories, in the south by the Bay of Bengal and in the extreme south-east by Burma. The territories of Bangladesh are divided for administrative purpose into various categories as follows:

Bangladesh consists of six divisions i.e. Dhaka, Chittagong, Shylet, Rajshahi, Khulna and Barishal. These divisions are again divided into districts and districts into Thanas i.e. Police Stations that cover some unions which are actually small groups of villages.

In this way, for example, speaking about the Chittagong Division, it is divided into eleven districts which are named Brahmanbaria, Comilla. Chandpur. Noakhahi, Lakṣmīpur.

MAP NO. 5

MAP SHOWING THE COMILLA DISTRICT OF BANGLADESH

Feni, Chittagong, Cox's Bazar, Khagrachari, Rangamati and Bandar-ban.

It should be noted that the district of greater Comilla originally was a part of the Tippera (Skt. Tripura) State. At the time of the formation of East Pakistan, Tippera was divided into two areas called Comilla and Tippera; Comilla was included into East Pakistan, whereas Tippera went to India.

There are twelve Thanas in this newly formed Comilla district. According to the census of 1974 four subdivisions i.e. Brahamanbaria, Comilla Sadar-south, Comilla Sadar-norlh, and Chandpur constitute the greater Comilla district. This greater district of Comilla which was formerly known as a part of Tippera, lies between 23°-31' and 24°-16' north latitude and 90°-31' and 91°-22' east longitude[1]. The Tropic of Cancer passes at 0°-58' south of the chief city of the Comilla district, called Comilla town. The district is bounded on the north-west by district of Dhaka and Mymensing: on the North-east by greater Shylet; on the east by the state of Tippera (which is a hill area in India); on the south by greater Noakhali and on the west by the main stream of Meghna which separates it from Faridpur Dhaka and Mymensing.

HISTORICAL BACKGROUND OF MAINAMATI

The area of this district of Comilla was acquired in A. D. 1765. In 1790, the district of Comilla came into being as a separate district with the name of Tippera and included the whole of the present Comilla plus the mainland of Noakhali except the Islands, Taluk Amirabad and North Brahmanbaria. Taluk Amirabad was included in it in 1799. In 1811, the adjustment of the boundary between Comilla on the one side and Mymensing and Dhaka on the other was made by making the Brahmaputra and the Meghna as the western boundary of the district. In 1830, the five paragaṇās i,e. Sarail, Daudpur, Haripur, Bejra and Satarakhanda (a bulk of Brahmanbaria subdivision were also transferred from Mymensing to Comilla. In

1960, the subdivision of Nasirnagar, now called Brahmanbaria, was formed and in 1879, the south western Thanas were included in the Chandpur subdivision.

In 1875 Thana Chagalnaiya in the south-east of Comilla and forming the southern division of Chakla Roshnabad, was transferred to Noakhali. When in 1905 (16th October), division of Bengal took place, Comilla went to the new provience of Eastern Bengal and Assam. Finally, decades after, on the lst October I960, the name of the district was changed from Tippera to the more widely known one of "Comilla". At present, there are twelve Thanas in the district of Comilla i.e. Homna, Daudkandi, Murādnagar, Debidwar, Brahmanpara, Burichang, Chandina. Comilla Sadar, Barura, Laksham, Chouddagram and Nangolkot Thana. The area of the newly found copperplates, i.e. that of Maināmatī-Lalmai Hills falls in the Burichang and Comilla Sadar thanas which are bounded on north-west by Brahmanpara, Debidwar, Chandina and Barura Thanas; on the south by Lalsham and Chauddagram Thana and on the east by the western border of Tippera territory (India). According to the census of 1974, there are fifteen unions (and 197 villages) in the Burichang Thana and Maināmatī itself is a union situated in the Burichang Thana. Maināmatī union consists of the following 23 villages: Baje Baherchar, Mainpur/Bagilara, Debpur, Harindhara, Bajehora, Raypur, Kathalia, Sinduriapara, Sharifpur, Kachharitala, Jaipur, Chandsar, Akabpur, Paikpara, Namtala, Binandiarchar, Hossenpur, Sahdaulatpur, Kala-Kachua. Shamaspur, Dakshin Mirpur, Rampal and Śrīpur.

HISTORICAL LEGENDS AND BALLADS OF MAINĀMATĪ

Maināmatī, the name of a village and a union, is very familiar and is situated at Burichang Thana in Comilla district of Bangladesh. This name is associated with a number of local legends and ballads. Probably, the Maināmatī was named to us only a few hundred years ago. Till today, we do not get any historical or epigraphic evidence for the naming of this place as Maināmatī. But the history of it goes back to the remote past and is inseparably connected with the history of the surrounding land which came to the light in our knowledge as Samataṭ a. a historical name indicating a land lying almost level to the seashore.

There are so many ballads, folklores and legends on the name of Maināmatī, the Queen of king Manikcandra, which are popularly sung in Bengal. Queen Maināmatī gave birth to prince Gopicandra. Some of these songs are collected in books like *Gopicandrer-gāna,* Vols-1 and 11 (Pub. Calcutta University), *Gopicandrer Sanyāsa* (Abdul Sukkur Muhammed) and Minachetan (Ed. by N.K. Bhattasali), *Gopicandrer-gāna, Mānikcandrer-gāna* and other such types of edition completed in 17th-18th centuries A.D. mention the name of Rani Maināmatī. We have also found a number of references about ancient places and personalities of ancient Samataṭa area from these legends and ballads. According to Tārānatha[2] and some of these ballads, Gopicandra was a ruler of Mṛkul (now known as Meharkula in Tippera district, at present, Comilla district). Bhattasali thinks that Govinda Candra is identical with king Gopicandra known from some Bengali and Punjabi ballads as well as drama and from the tradition recorded by Tārānatha. This Gopicand is said to have been the son of Tilakcand and the ruler of Mṛkul i.e. the Meharkul paragaṇā of the Tippera District[4]. But now it is known from the epigraphic evidence of the copper-plate of Laḍaha Candra and Govinda Candra that Govinda Candra was the son and successor of king Laḍaha Candra and Queen Saubhāgyadevi. So, it is now clear that Govind Candra and Gopicand are not the same. Sircar indicates that Gopicand was the son of Tilakcand and the younger brother of Śrī Candra of the Candra dynasty of Samataṭa. No historical evidence has been found for this assumption. We have found many copper-plate grants of Candra dynasty but there is no epigraphic proof that Gopicand was the son of Tilakcand though there is a similarity between the name of Tilakcand, the father of Gopicand and Trailokya Candra the father of Śrī Candra. The name of the wife of Trailokya Candra was Śrī Kāñcikā (according to Sylhet plate) and the name of the mother of Gopicand was Maināmatī (according to Gopi Candrer-gana, Vol. 1 & II). But it is likely that the village name Maināmatī has come to light from the name of Queen Maināmatī the mother of Gopicand and the ruler of Mṛkul in eleventh-twelfth century A.D.

APPROACHING THE SITE OF MAINĀMATĪ

In 187I, the road construction act was formed and by the beginning of 20th century, the district Comilla was well furnished with roads.

In 1820, the system of communication was formulated and by the way of this, in 1866, there was only one road i.e. from Daudkandi via Comilla to Chittagong. By 1873, there were in the then greater Comilla district 12 miles of the metalled and 616 miles of uimetalled roads besides the Trunk road. W.W. Hunter[5] reports that by 1876 there was prepared a Trunk road from the Meghna at Daudkandi to Chittagong boundary via Comilla district from east to west. The following roads in the district were important: (1) from Comilla to Noakhali via Laksham, (2) from the river Gumati to Napit bazar, (3) from Napit Bazar to Brahmanbaria, (4) a road leading to the Trunk road in between the Maināmatī-Lalmai Hill ranges to Companyganj on Gumati river, (5) from Comilla to Bibirhat.

By 1969 A.D. Roads and Highways Directorate of East Pakistan had constructed the major roads of Comilla. By 1973, the Zila Board of Comilla constructed the roads of this district. In 1969, Chandpur Municipal Committee maintained 46 short roads. Seven important bus routes were also constructed in this year.

The first Railway line of the district was opened in 1895 by the Assam-Bengal Railway, which proceeds down the east of the district for a distance of about 70 miles. The first Station in the south on this line is Gunabati which lies at the 64 miles from

Chittagong. At present, the Roads and Railways in this district are furnished nicely.

In spite of the improved roads and railways, the most common people of this district used to travel by boat between June and October, when water level in the rivers and canals was high. Steamers, launches and large boats move in the river Meghna throughout the year. The important rivers of this district are the Gumati, the Dakatia and the Titas which are all navigable all the year round by small launches. Besides these, there are numerous Khals (canals) and Bils in this district.

For different purposes, different types of boats are in use and they are known by different names. The most common types are Gach, Kunda. Saranga, Pātam, Mut, Othar, Lakhai and Morkush.

In 1899 A.D the district had only 80 post offices. In 1909, the number rose to 130. By 1961, it was 419 and by June 1970, the total number of post offices in the district had increased to 587 of which, three were Head offices located at Comilla, Brahmanbaria and Chandpur with 48 sub post offices and 536 branch post offices.

By 1967, there were six telephone exchanges in the district at Ashuganj, Akhaura, Brahmanḇaria, Comilla, Daulatganj and Hajiganj. The district had 650 main telephone lines and 190 extension lines. Trunk telephone service has heen introduced throughout the district. There were 33 public call offices situated all over the distiict.

SECTION-II

GEOGRAPHICAL DESCRIPTION

An extraordinarily rich culture of Buddhist period lies in Maināmatī-Lalmai hill range in Comilla district of Bangladesh. The famous Chinese pilgrim Yung Chwang visited Samataṭa in between 635 A.D. and 639 A.D.[6] From Kāmarūpa Yung Chwang went to south and after a journey of 1200 li or 1300 li, reached the country of San-mo-taṭa (Samataṭa). The pilgrim mentioned the name of six countries beyond Samataṭa. One of these is Kiā-mu-laṅg-kia. He indicated that this Kiā-mu-laṅg-kiā is located to the southeast of Samataṭa and near the Bay of Bengal. The name of the place Komalā is noted in the Vayu Pūrāṇa. Most probably, the Komalā of Vāyu Pūrāṇa[8] is same to Kiā-mo-laṅg-kiā of Yung-Chwang. Samuel describes, "Furtlier on to the southeast, on the borders of the Ocean, we come to the country of Kamalanka (Kia-mo-lang-kia)[9]. Dey Nundo Lal has mentioned that Kamalāṅka-Comilla was the capital of Tipper in the sixth century A.D.[10] Cumiingham identified Kiā-mo-laṅg-kiā with the district of Comilla, to the east of the river Meghna and at the head of the Bay of Bengal.[11] So, we can strongly conclude that the present Comilla is the Kiā-mo-loṅg-kiā of Yuang-Chawng.

The district of Comilla was formerly known as Tippera (Skt. Tripura). The district Tipper, according to Webster, "takes its name from the adjoining State of Hill Tipper, to which it was attached formerly. The derivation of the name is uncertain. The state annals show Tripura, grand-son of Yayāti, king of the Seven Continents, whose deeds are chronicled in the Rig Veda, to have been second in the line of the kings, and the name has also been explained as either the "three cities" or the Country of Tripureśvarī. The latter derivation is connected with an ancient legend of Hill Tripura according to which no less than 51 goddesses sprang out of the corpus of Bhagavatī, the wife of Mahādeva, and by some mysterious process dispersed over the face of the world. One of them, Tripureśvarī or the ruler of the three worlds, took up her residence at Udaipur, the former capital of Hill Tippera where a large temple was dedicated to her. This temple ranks as one of the great *Tirthas* or holy shrines which every year attracts thousands of devout pilgrims.

It is, however, possible, perhaps probable, that the name is not of Hindu origin, and the author of the '**Rājmālā**' derives it from the words **Tui-prā,** meaning in the language of the hill

MAP NO. 1

MAP SHOWING THE ANCIENT GEOGRAPHIC POSITION OF BENGAL

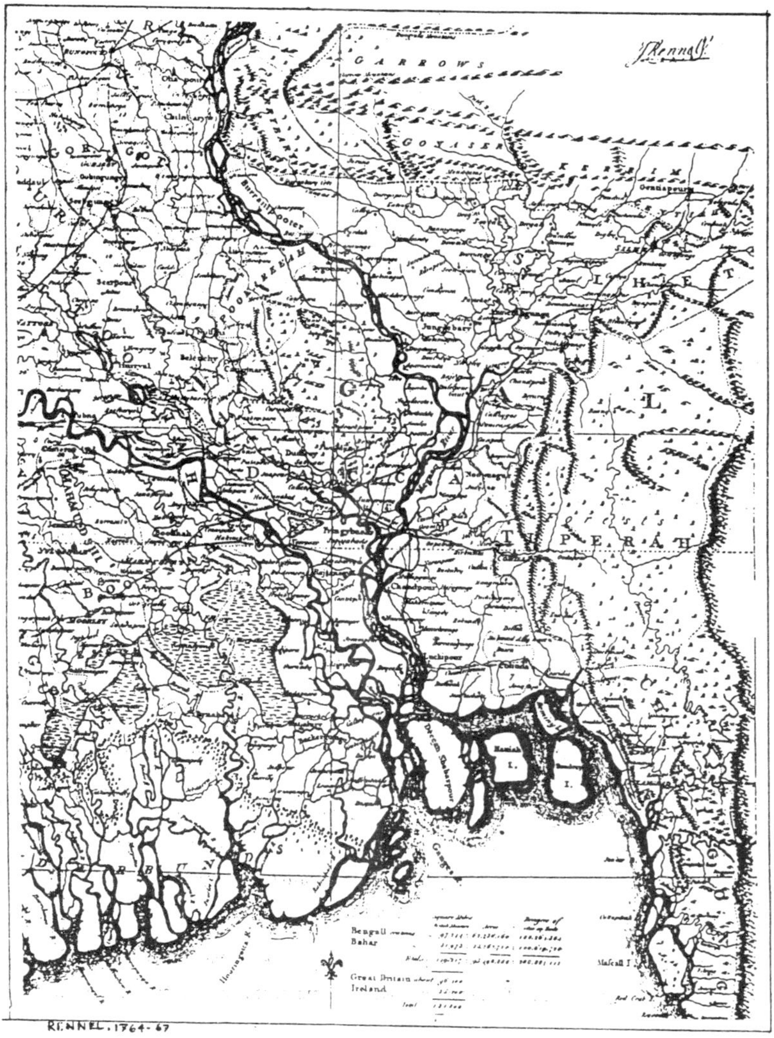

people as the country towards the sea. The hill men themselves pronounce the name Tipra, which would be a natural contraction from either Tui-prā or Tripura and the fact that "Tui-mā", the Meghna, is to this day an object of worship among the Tipperas lends colour to the fonner derivation; but the solutions are at the best plausible guess.

According to the census of 1872, the district of Tippera comprises an area of 2556 square miles and the total population of the district was 14,47,583 persons. In 1951, it comprises an area of 2531 square miles and the total population was 37,92,200 persons. According to the census of 1961. it comprises an area of 2594 square miles and the total population of the Comilla district was 43,88,906 persons, the density being 1,693 persons per square mile. According to the census of 1974[13], the population of the district was 58,19,176 persons and the density per square mile was 2,245 persons.

Geographical history of Comilla district is found in the ancient map of Pargitar. It mentions that Prāgjyotiṣa and Kirātas are located on northward of the southern sea of this area[14]. Roughly, the basin of the river Lohitya was named Prāgjyotiṣa and the area of around the foot of eastern hills was named Kirātas. At present, the river Lohitya is known to us as the river Brahmaputra. The movement of the river is marked in Kirātas. So, it appears that the eastern area of Prāgjyotiṣa i.e., most of the place of Kirātas is the present Comilla district. In the map of Tomas Watters, the movement of the river Titas and Gumati are shown in the area of south-eastern Bengal. In I560, John D. Byaros mentioned the location of "Trapo" in his map. There is no room for doubt that this Trapo is Tripur or present Comilla. In 1665, Syanson D. Ababil mentioned in his map that Trapo is located on the east of Dhaka, on south of Sirot (at present Syhet) and on north of Bengal (i.e. Bay of Bengal). So, it is strongly established that Trapo is Tripura and at present Comilla (part of Tripura).

In 1779, Major Rennel not only mentioned in his map the

MAP NO. 4

MAP SHOWING THE CHITTAGONG DIVISION OF BANGLADESH

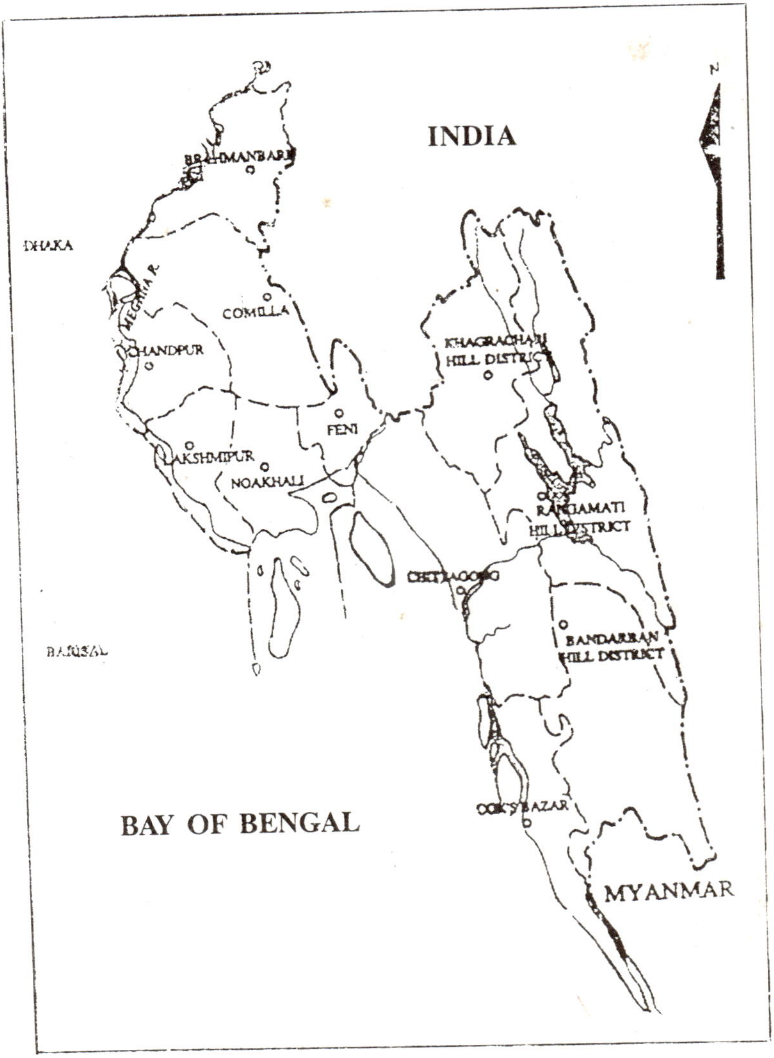

location of Tripura disirict but also marked the proper location of Chandpur and Comilla. Generally, in ancient period, the eastern part of Bangladesh was named after Kirātas. Roughly, the present movement of Meghna River indicates the western limit of this Kirātas, At that time, the river Brahmaputra was known by the name Lohitya and was flowing on about the present course of the river Meghna and went down into the sea i.e. Bay of Bengal. But the sea was not as far as it is today. Kirātas knew the surrounding area of the foot of the hills and the present district of Comilla is located in the midst of it.

In !974, four subdivisions (at present three districts) Brahmanbaria, Comlla Sadar-south, Comilla Sadar north and Chandpur constituted the greater Comilla district. There are 23 Thanas in the greater district of which 6 are in the Brahmanbaria. 5 in Sadar-south, 5 in Sadar-north and 5 in Chandpur district.

There are 96 unions and 1,278 villages in Brahmanbaria district of which 13 unions and 112 villages are in Nasirnagar Thana, 10 unions and 82 villages in Sarail Thana, 24 unions and 413 villages in Brahmanbaria Thana; 15 unions and 355 villages in Kasba Thana; 21 unions and 210 villages in Nabinagar Thana and 13 unions and 106 villages in Bancharampur Thana. There are 81 unions and 1,144 villages in Comilla Sadar North of which 10 unions and 189 villages are in Homna Thana, 22 unions and 405 villages in Daudikandi Thana, 112 unions and 126 villages in Chandina Thana, 16 unions and 136 villages in Debidwar Thana and 21 unions and 288 villages in Muradnagar Thana.

There are 89 unions and 1,819 villages in Comilla Sadar-south of which 15 unions and 197 villages are in Burichang Thana, 12 unions and 361 villages in Kotwali Thana, 20 unions and 500 villages in Chouddagram Thana, 35 unions and 233 villages in Barura Thana, and 27 unions and 528 villages in Laksham Thana

There are 89 unions and 1.413 villages in Chandpur district of which 22 unions and 480 villages are in Matlab Thana. 20 unions and 164 villages in Chandpur Thana,16 unions and

167 villages in Faridganj Thana, 19 unions and 321 villages in Hajiganj Thana and 12 unions and 281 villages in Kachua Thana.

In shape, Ihe district resembles a long and somewhat narrow triangle over 90 miles in length running between the Meghna on the west and the forest clad hills of Hill Tippera (India) on the east, with its base resting on the district of Noakhalī. The country slopes down gradually from the foot of the Tippera Hill (India) towards the west, and there is also a perceptible downward inclination from north to south, which is most pronounced in the north of the district and along the banks of the Meghna. The slope in these two directions is so gradual that it nowhere disturbs the general aspect of the country, which presents an almost continuous flat surface. Its level is broken only by the Lalmai Hills, an isolated range five miles west of Comilla stretching for 11 miles from north to south. There are also outlying spurs from the low forest-clad hills of the Tippera State (India) which here and there fall just within the eastern border. The greater portion of the district is a rice plain, well cultivated and intersected by numerous rivulets, streams and creeks which, in the south and west, are tidal.

The greatest assemblage of ancient Buddhist remains in Bangladesh lies in Mainămatī-Lalmai in the Camilla district It extends for about 11 miles north-south from the Mainămatī villages on the Gumati river in the north and Caṇḍī Murā near Lalmai Railway Station in the south and is about 25 miles in circumference. In its widest parts the ridge is about three miles across and its highest peaks attain a height of 150 feet in a few places, but the average elevation is 40 feet above the plains and 90 feet above sea-level; the highest peaks are Kalir Bazar and Caṇḍī Murā. Like the Barind and Madhupur Tract, this ridge represents a small mass of quasi-lateritic old alluvium. The hill is bounded by the faults on the western and eastern sides. The fault scrap on the east is up-thrown to the west and considerably dissected by drainage channels. On the west there are two parallel faults about a mile apart. Both are up-thrown on the east. The inner fault forms a well-defined valley. The outer (western most) fault has a surface throw in excess of 100 feet at several places. These highlands were formerly thickly wooded with an abundance of wild life, but land-hungry local farmers have now pushed back the forest to the highest points and to the patches of Sal trees on the slopes. Structurally this range is a horst, tilted to the east. The upper part of this horst is composed of oxidised clays and sands of pleistocene age, which rest upon beds of sandy shales, coarse ferrugenous sand stones and mantled clays and sands, probably of the Tipam series. An interesting material that is found all over the place is fossil wood. The eastward deep of the upper deposits are slight, but of the lower deposits are quite steep.

GEOLOGICAL FOUNDATION AND FORMATION

In Geological and land-formation art, it is mentioned as Tippera surface. Most of the areas of this plain land, in rainy season, are under 5 to 25 feet of water. In rainy season, though this land is under water but much alluvium does not settle because the flow of river Meghna does not earn much alluvium. But this sunk soil, due to much wetting, is to be favorable for good tilling.

Geological history of famous Camilla district can not be called very ancient The stone of Miocene age has been found in deep of Lalmai range, which is very ancient stone field of this district. This age can also be mentioned as, 3-3,5 crore years-notmore than this.

Geological formation of most of area of this district has been composed in Pleistocene and Halocene of present age. It is not only for Camilla district but the formation of all Bangladesh also roughly the same. So, Geological history of this district is comparatively new. Geological formation is also not called very complicated.

In view of Geological formation, whole Vaṅga basin has been divided into three parts; the Himalayas stairs of Tetulia on most north-west, is consisted of about all of north Vaṅga to which Indian stairs. Vaṅga stairs of on southeast and southeast regions is to the south The plain land of Tripura range is located to the western side of folded mountains of the eastern side of Vaṅga basin; that means, the position of Comilla district is the eastern side of Vaṅga stairs. From earth-movement and land formation, it can be called that still now an active action is continuing.

From near the middle stage of Turseary era that means, from Miocene Epoch, neatly 40.000 feet alluvium bed, since its starting existence till today, has hccn settle in this region from its bottom of a foundation. The bottom of a foundation of this district has been placed before nearly 3 crore years in Miocene Epoch. In Miocene age i.e nearly 3.5 crore years of the beginning, lower land stone has been discovered in that stratum of the earth of subterranean region of Maināmatī-Lalmai range. in between land alluvial stones have sandstone, shale, melt stone and some beds of time. In different age. time and environment the below stratum of the earth was made by settled alluvium Depth of it is more than 1,700 feet. This layer chiefly consists of shale but sandstone mixed with time, melt stone and sandstone have been decorated in different land stone. It is chiefly consisted of sand stone and shell and its depth is above 3300 feet to 4250 feet. On upper land of Miocene age, two chief layers are found. One of these is Bocabi and another one is Tipam. On layer of upper land stone is Bocabil and its depth is nearly 3,500 feet. Depth of Tipam is nearly 1000 feet on Bocabil. Dupi Tila stone layer of Pliocene Epoch lies on Tipam layer to which depth is near 100 feet. Red soil has been found, of Pleistocene Epoch in Maināmatī -Lalmai range, on Pliocene age i.e. Dupi Tila, which is nearly 1.5 crore years old. Age of Pleistocene Epoch is 10 lack to 20 lack. Red-brown coloured soil has been found in it The soil is soft. Yellow-brown coloured sand is also composed in it The soil of Maināmatī Lalmai range, is composed by red alluvium of Pleistocene Epoch, is reddish-brown or brown coloured. Owing to the monsoon of tropical region, the colour of this alluvium has been changed for more rain falling, temperature and passing of time. Proportion of organic substance of the clay is comparatively poor. It is a repetition of Tripura Hills and is composed by different type of clay which is different than new made alluvium clay of adjacent area Largeiy the bill has been decayed and most of the place of the lower area is covered by bed of new alluvium. For digging adjacent lower land of Hills, subterranean water is found. The soil of this region is covered by Madhupur clay of Pleistocene Epoch, which, is overlain by Dupi Tila formation of Pliocene Epoch. The soil of this region is roughly called reddish-brown or yellow-brown coloured clay or sandy-soil. The existence of Madhupur clay has been observed around the bottom of Mainamatī- Lalmai range. The existence of Madhupur clay is also found from northern Harashpur to southern Kasba and every hilly area of Bangladesh. There are many scattered hillocks from Kasba to south Dattasar, to which, the existence of same kinds of soil is found. There is a hilhangc named Raghunanda from north Harashpur to Saliaji- bazar, to which, is found the existence of soil of Dupitila of Mainamatī -Lalmai hill range.

The soil of the district varies considerably. Close to the hills, the soil even where it is not the old alluvium, partake somewhat of its nature as it continues to receive deposits washed down from them. It is very fine clay which cakes are very hard in the dry season and are capable of being used for the walls of a house. Though in such a wet clithate, it is not often used for this purpose, its character shows itself by the neat ails which form the boundaries between neighbouring cultivated plots. These soils are acidic, low in plant nutrient and droughts. Further away from the hills the soil normally contains a higher percentage of decayed vegetable thater, which renders it more capable of retaining moisture. It gradually passes from a pale yellow clay to the dark soil found in Chandpur Thana which is perhaps some of the richest and most fertile in the sub-continent. There is an abrupt change, which a region is reached which is being curved and remolded by the Meghna and its branches. The soil then becomes more sandy, not necessarily less fertile but of different character. When the level has been depressed, but active channels from the Meghna have not found their way into the depression, long submersion and the action of aquatic plants have sometimes so finely disintegrated the soil that it has become a black mud as treacherous as a quick sand. In some of the beds near Bandiarampur and in Brahmanbaria thana the cultivators have to push themselves about over the soft mud on Plantain-tree stems when engaged in transplanting their boro paddy.

In 1871, brown iron ore was found in the Mamathati - Lalmai hills, but is probably not present in a quantity that is worth working.

There are abundant deposits of various types of sand including silica sand in many districts of Bangladesh of which special mention may be made of the district Comilla, Mymensingh. Syhlct Glass making sand was deposited in heart of old rivers-channels, which was hidden in subterranean region at plain land of around the bottom of Tippera Hills. From interior land formation, it is known till today that there are found six upper folds. From the direction of geological sense these are simple folds and were created in time of third insurgence of Himalayas and mixed up inseparably. These folds are 1. Kachuya 2. Dandkandi 3, Titas 4 Bakharabad 5. Lalmai and 6 Kalatia. And the gas is found from these upper folds in abundance. This gas is accumulated from Titas and Bakharabad folds. Apart from these upper folds, there is an upper fold named Chandpur-Barishal in between Matin and Faridpur region. The width of this fold is nearly fifty miles. Alluvial stone covers its upper side.

With the discovery of gas in Brahmanbaria, the natural gas industry in Bangladesh reached a new dimension. The most significant factor in the composition in that, there is no toxic contents in the Titas gas and does not require purification. The total reserve of gas in the Titas gas field is estithated to be 2.5 billion cubic feet Supply of Titas gas to industries in Dhaka-Narayanganj belt has been started by the beginning of 1968. There is the huge requirement of this gas particularly at

MAP NO. 2

MAP SHOWING THE RIVER SYSTEM OF ANCIENT BENGAL

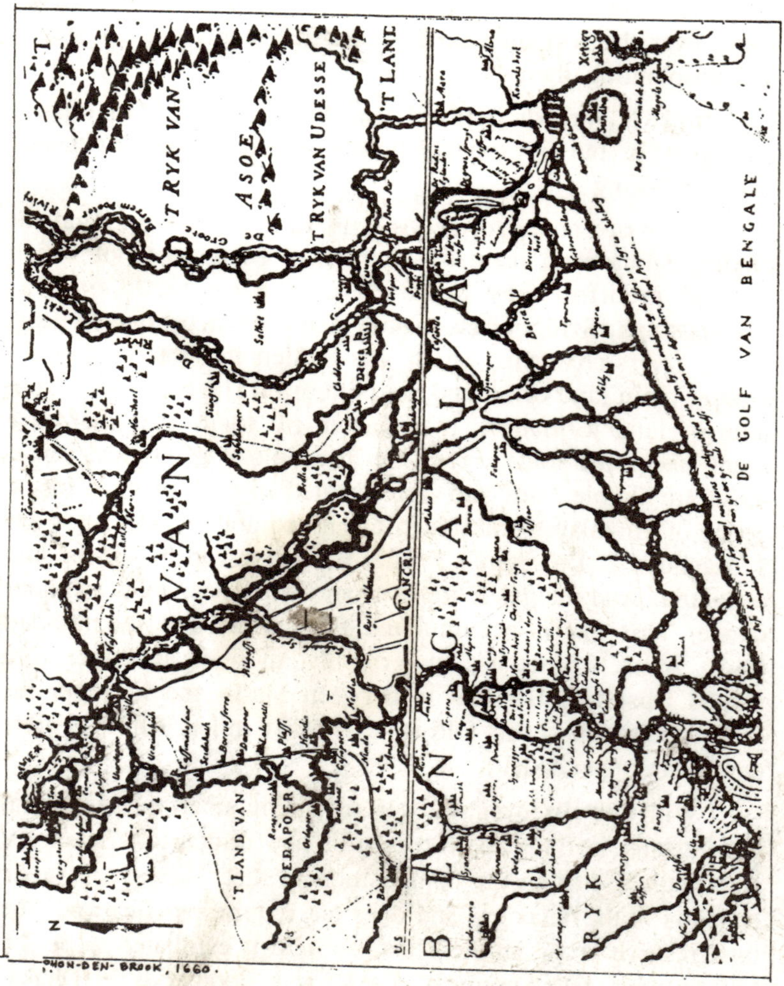

HON-DEN-BROOK, 1660.

Siddirganj, Ashuganj and Ghorasal power plants together with the demand for the fertilizer factory at Ghorasal.

ECOLOGICAL DESCRIPTION

Every where the village sites are well-wooded but the trees are more numerous and luxuriant and their character more tropical in the south-west. The traveller who gilds down the Meghna from Catalpara to Chandpur cannot fail to observe the gradually increasing richness and luxuriance in the growth of palms and other trees. Some of the villagers are buried in variable forests where the stranger may lose his way and looking round from some high place, the horizon is bounded on every side by trees. The Mainãmatī - Lalmai Hills were once densely wooded[15]. At present, an area near Kotbari has been earmarked as a forest belt, though almost the whole of Mainãmatī-Lalmai Hills have been cleared up and cultivation has been extended at foot hills. The Kotbari Range comprises three forest beats i.e Comilla beat in Kotwali P. S., Rajeswar beat in Kotwali P. S. and Choudyagram P S. and Belonea beat in Parshuram P. S. The whole of forest of this region is classified as acquired one. The total area of it in 1972-1973 was 1,901,34 acres[1'']. But the forests were unimportant, and did not yield any revenue to the Government. A list of plants prepared in 1888 shows 49 species of timber trees 56 kinds of uncultivated trees and plants; 71 used in European and 198 in native, medicine. 14 giving oil 7 used in dyeing and 4 used in tanning.

There are practically no wild animals in the district. About 100 years back, there was a good number of barking deer, leopard, tiger, wild hog and various species of wild cat on the Maimathati - Lalmai Hills in general and on the eastern border of the hill in particular. There in at present, jackals in large number in the district and share with, vultures and cows the duties of village scavenger. The mongooses are common, but there are few monkeys and squirrels to be seen. Bird life is luxuriant. Fish eagles kites and brilliantly coloured kingfishers are common. Most of the road side and other trees in the village remain crowded with small birds, golden oriole, erected bulbul, king crows, the crow-pheasant wood packers, sun-birds, sparrows, host of little flycatchers and of course, the ubiquitous mania. At nightfall, the air is resonant with their clamour, and even later the silence is broken by the deep-toned hoot of the horned owl and, alas, by the too insistent note of the coppersmith and the crescendo of the brain-fever bird. The game birds of the district include jungle fowl, wild duck, tea, golden plover, and .snipe, which offered fair sport in the winter months. At present, most of natural environments on geological structural foemation of this district are the donation of river system. From ancient time, numerous rivers and creecks are flowing over this district helping for its formation work. After all, the rivers, from ancient time, are making contributions in natural land formation. Roughly, the five main rivers are flowing over the district of Comilla These are (1) The Tits stream on northern portion in the district, (2). The Gumati stream in the middle portion (3) The Dakatia stream on the middle and south-western portion (4) The small Feni river stream on south eastern portion (5) The Meghna river stream on north-west and near to the western border aiea of the district. Of them, theTitas, the Gumati and the Dakatia have joined in to the Meghna stream. The Meghna and small Feni River fall into the Bay of Bengal. Many sub branch rivers and numerous creeks and marshes have joined into above-mentioned rivers. Most of the sub rivers of this district have been coming out from the Hills of Tripura kingdom of eastern boundary.

There are few Lakes in Comilla district, but the marshes (bells) are numerous and covered an aggregate area of 92 square miles (Hunter's Account of Tippcia 1876). At present, many mashes are thoroughly filled up, the following are most important marshes in the district: (1) Atkopa beel in paragaṇā sarail, area about 1 square mile. (2) Alta, beel in paragaṇā sarail, area about 12 square miles. (3) Bahjuni beel in paragaṇā Sarail area about 14 square miles. (4). Baralla bcci ill paragaṇā

Sarail area about 5.9 square miles. (5) Chantar beel in paragaṇā sarail, area about 2.4 square miles. (6) Kajala beel in paragaṇā sarail, area about 2.1 square miles. (7) Kakai beel in paragaṇā sarail area about 1 square mile. (8) Bara beel in paragaṇā Bardakhar, area about 2.4 square miles. (9) Bandghar beel in paragaṇā Bardakhat, area nearly 1 square mile.. (10) Mondahari beel in paragaṇā Nurnagar, area about 1 square mile, (11) Chandaler beel, area about 2 square miles. (12) Bariyadharer beel, area about 2 square miles. (13) Dakatia and Stabila area aboul 1 square mile. (14) Chhyafullakandi beeL (15) Satbaria beel in Chauddagram Thana. (16) Baidyar beel in Murādnagar Thana and. (17) Baraikuri beel.

The line of Tropic of Cancer is passed over the Camilla district. So the district is fully under tropical tarea. Naturally. Tropical monsoonal clithate is observed here. In rainy season, it rains heavily in the district. Roughly, the winter season of this district is dry. Annual rainfall ranges from 80" to 120". In winter season, the rainfall is very poor. The average temperature is 78.7^0 F. in May month, the average temperature is 86° F.and winter season, in January month k 66^0 F, But, some rimes m April-may months, ihe temperature, is 107° F and December-February months, is 45°F to 42°F. Roughly, the clithate of this district is comfortable and healthy.

NOTES AND REFERENCES

1. Chaudhari, Firoza Begum, C.Z.I., ed. Jakaria, A.K.M, Zela Parisad, Comilla, 1984, p. 2
2. Ramchadran, T. N., "Recent .Archaeological Discoveries along The Maināmatī and Lalmai Ranges, Tippera District, East Bengal", B.C. Law Volume, ed. D,R, Bhanderkar. 1946, Part - II. Poona, p. 214.
3. Sircar, D.C., "Paikpara Vasudeva Image Inscription, " I.C., Vol.-VII, 1940- 41, p. 412
4. Ibid., pp. 412-413
5. Hunter, W.W. S. A. B, Vol.-VI, London, 1876.
6. Wheeler, R.E.M, E.P.F.T.P, 1950, p. 97. and Sircar, D.C., "The

Kailan copperplate Inscription of King Śrīdharana Rāta"; I H.Q. Vol. XXIII, No. 3, 1947, p. 230.

7. Watters, T.Y.T. 1, Vol.- II, 1973, pp. 187-88.
8. Vy. P, II, Ch. v, 369.
9. Beal Samuel, "San-Mo-Ta-Cha (Samataṭa)" B.R.W. W (Iran), pp. 199-200.
10. Dey, Nundo Lal, G.D.A.M.I, 1971, p. 80.
11. Cunningham, Alexander, "Samataṭa", A.G.I. 1924, pp. 576-578.
12. Webster, J.E., E.B.D.G., Tippera, (Allahabad, 1917), p. 1
13. Rabbni Ghlam A.K., M, Secretary, V.P.S., Comilla District, Bangladesh Bureau Statistics, 1974, p. 173.
14. Chaudhuri Firoza Begum, C.Z.I, Zela Parishad, Comilla, 1984. p. 1
15. Smart Robert B, Geographical and Statistical Report on the District of Tippera, (Cal. 1866), p.2
16. Annual Progress Report of Forest Administration in Bangladesh, Forest Directorate, Dacca, 1976, p. 71.

MAP NO. 6

MAP SHOWING THE ARCHAEOLOGICAL SITES ON MAINAMATI-LALMAI HILL RANGE

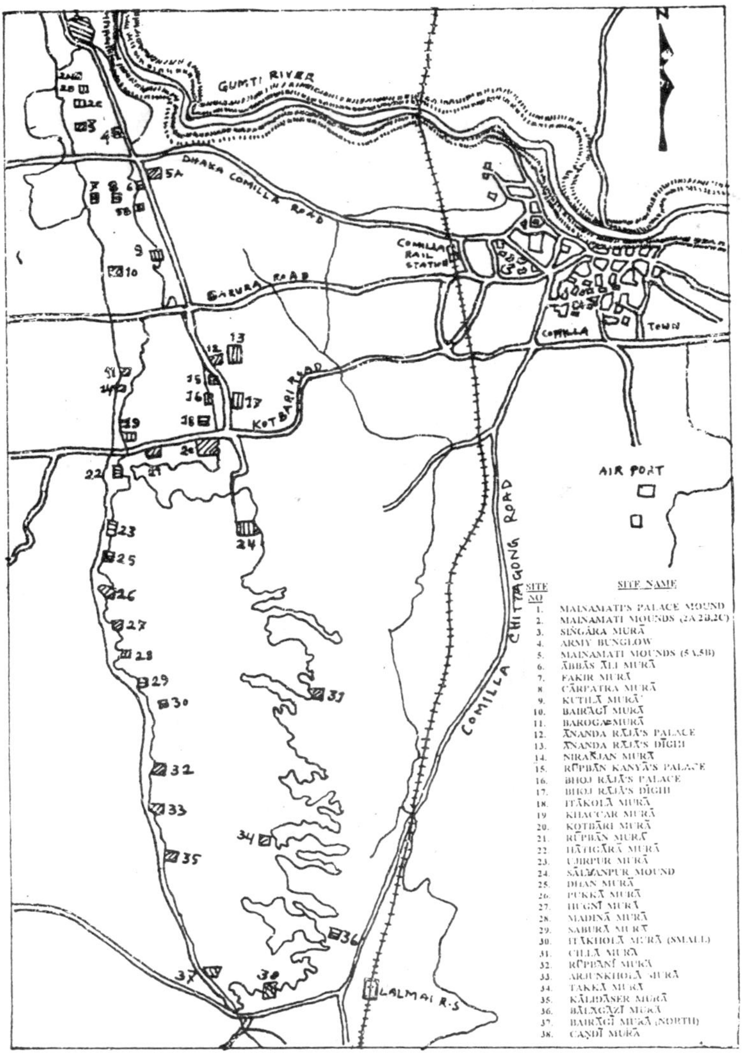

CHAPTER - II

ASSEMBLAGE OF ANCIENT SITES AT MAINĀMATĪ-LALMAI HILL RANGE

INTRODUCTION

Maināmatī is a very familiar name of Comilla district in Bangladesh. This familiar name is associated with a number of local legends and ballads. It is located about five miles to the west of Comilla town and is a range of small hillocks almost abruptly erupting in the middle of a vast level plain. This range extends for about 11 miles north south from Maināmatī village on the Gumati River in the north. The widest part of the range that is about three-miles east-west. Average height of the hills is only 40 feet but some peaks rise up to 150 feet or even a little more. The northern part of the range in locally known as Maināmatī, which merely echos the memory of the queen mother Maināmatī. the real mother of king Govinda Candra. While the southern part is known as Lalmai or Red Mother Earth (Lal-red, mai-thatrri mother) from the red colour (laterite) of the soil. The historical antiquity of this area was noticed in 1803 A.D. after the accidental discovery of a copper-plate of Raṇavaṅkamalla Harikaladeva.

There is a very large assemblage of ancient Buddhist ruins at the Maināmatī Lalmai hill range. These sites were discovered during the Second World War. The British military came to Maināmatī-Lalmai area at a number of points on the flat tops and slopes of these hills for setting up their advance camps. In the first hurried survey, 18 ancient sites were detected. By that time, the brick-hunters and military contractors heavily damaged many sites. After the cessation of the war, the area was regularly surveyed between 1955 to 1957 and a large number of these ruins were brought to light. About 50 of such ancient sites of varying sizes and importance were discovered of which 20 were declared protected by the Department of archaeology of the then Pakistan Government. Six of these sites, namely—Sālvaupur Mound, Ānanda Rāja's Pālace. Kutilā Murā, Rūpban Murā. Itakholā Murā and Cārpatra Murā have been excavated. Trial excavations have also been conducted at the Pālace and temple of Queen Maināmatī, located on the northern tip of the Maināmatī hill. Brief descriptions of the 38 sites together with the 20 protected sites are given below. The remaining 12 sites (out of 50) do not have any structural evidences

SECTION -1

MONASTERIES

1. ARMY BUNGALOW SITE (ST.-4)

This site is located on the western side of Comilla - Debidvar Road and about one-half mile north of the junction with Comilla to Daudkandi - Dhaka road. It was highly disturbed by British military construction during the Second World War and by subsequent construction on the perimeter of the site by the Pakistan Army. It is covered with bushes and trees. The site stretches for about 125 yards from east to west and about 1-40 yards from north to south. The eastern edge is longer than western one. It is nearly 200 yards on a north - south axis. This additional irregular - shaped is on the south - western corner that appears to be of a later date. The surface of the site is uneven. In the centre of the site is a series of cement slabs where the British army had built barracks, which are now removed. The top of the site is about 15 feet high from the surrounding level. The site is a gradually slopes down to the west. Ancient broken bricks, modern bricks and cement are intermixed from the British Period. Pottery is found sparsely over the surface of the site. The military authorities had dug a number of trenches. Old brick walls and pottery were revealed to the depth of *4.5* feet. The configuration of the perimeter wall and the size of the site suggest a monastic site resembling Sālvanan Vihāra.

2. ĀNANDA RĀJĀ'S PALACE: (ST -12)

It is one of the largest archaeological sites, popularly known to the local people as Ānanda Rājār Bāri. After archaeological excavations from 1976 to 1978. the site was discovered as a square monastery enclosing a central shrine of multi angular form the configuration and visible remains, as well as local name, indicate that it is an ancient monastic site.

Location: This big mound is located about a furlong square and one and a half miles to south of Kutilā Murā and four miles to the south west of Comilla and at the eastern side of Comilla of Cantonment Road and is about a mile north of the BARD complex at Kotbari, Comilla Compass bearings from the central structure of Ānanda Vihāra were read as south 10 east to the BARD water tower and north 350 west to the centre of Kotilā Murā. It is situated more than a mile and a half to the north of Sālvan Vihāra. Together with Bhojrājā Vihāra and Rūpbān Kānyā Murā, the two other archaeological sites in its immediate neighbourhood, it forms an interesting group of monuments, which seems to have a significant bearing on the history and the culture of the region. It is more then 650 feet square in size and about 15 feet higher than the plain cultivated land. It was the scene of heavy depredation for bricks during the Second World War. Cart lords of bricks were removed from this mound before action could be taken to check this ancient site.

Structural Description: T.N. Ramachandran who visited this site in 1942 noted that, "the remains revealed, however, on plan a square monastery about a furlong each side, with an arrangement, as at Paharpur, of a central temple with recessed corners and reentrant angles. Probably, the arrangement of the central temple resulted, as at Paharpur, in a cruciform shape with one projecting angle between the arms of the cross"[1].

During his visit, a large number of terracotta plaques were recovered from the central temple enclosure. These plaques were used to decorate the outer face of the walls of the multi angular central temple.

The military contractors, brick hunters and the cantonment builders damaged Ānanda Vihāra. The western and northern wing of the monastery together with its front facade and gateway complex, and the imposing central shrine had been damaged very ruthlessly. These are the most important and significant parts of the great establishment of the monastery. The Department of Archaeology and museums, Bangladesh, has conducted seasonal excavations at the site since 1975. During three seasons work, remains of a huge monastery has been brought to light. The out line of the 624 feet long northern wing and almost the entire western wall of equal length except a little portion which remains underneath the Cantonment road has been fully cleared and exposed. In the middle of the northern wing, the excavation has exposed tire grand 99'-6" long and 45 feet wide projected front facade and monumental gate way complex. The central area of the gateway is arranged in three sections. A 17' -6" long and 7'-6" wide entrance passage with rounded corners opens on to the interior through a 5 feet wide door way which gives access to rectangular hall measuring 30' x 15'. Behind this front hall lies a second hall, 24' x 8'-6", at the same alignment of the cells. Its walls at plinth level and above have decorations of ornamental mouldings, offsets and projections. Much more work remains to be done to clear fully the inner arrangements of the gateway of several periods made more complex by the recent damages and disturbances. From the remains it appears that in the later phases, the front hall of the gateway measuring 28' - 9" x 27' - 6" was added to the main complex. Six monastic cells lying on both sides of the gateway has also been partially dug deeper. In the later periods, these cells were 10 to 12 feet in length and 9 feet in breadth.

The cells are separated from each other by a 5'-6" thick partition wall. The front wall of the cells is 6 feet thick while the back wall is 9 1\2 feet thick- Deep excavation at some places has, however, revealed that the walls were originally 19 feet thick. Possibly, during later repairs and renovations the thickness of the walls was reduced. On the eastern side of the complex, in the area of the front verandah, a flight of six steps was provided in these late phases, apparently for easy communication between higher levels of the verandah and the gateway which itself remained lower on account of constant repairs, restoration and cleaning. A similar arrangement on the opposite, that is western side of the gateway, is reasonably assumed, but has not yet been exposed by excavation.

The discovered facade on three sides was found in very damaged condition up to a considerable depth. However, the extant remains of the back wall, so far unearthed shows that it had five offsets with an half round brick course on top at plinth level and three feet above this rounded brick course, lies another set of offsets marked again by a half round brick course on top. This feature has been discovered to continue on the wall-face on all sides: the west, north, south and east and the same feature has also been found on the facade of the gateway projection. This delightful feature breaks the monotony of the dreary outer facade of the monastery which is absent at Sāl van Vihāra. Excavation at the north-west corner has discovered a part of the Verandah retaining wall, which gives a valuable idea about the interior arrangements during the later phases. From the north-west corner of the two wings, the northern and western walls have been exposed eastward and southward for a considerable distance. It is decorated with moulded ornamental bricks.

The same decorative arrangement has been noticed in the exposed southwestern corner retaining wall of the Verandah, which however, was found in a bad state of preservation.

Stratigraphy: The Stratigraphy of the outer accumulation, which found against the outer face of the monastery, is given below.

Layer-1: Topsoil: grayish sandy silt mixed with brick particles. The top is marked by the present surface with humas and plant roots. The deposit represents wind blown dust accumulated after the site ceased to exist as a living monument and the broken and fallen wall also ceased to fall any more.

Layer-2: Composed of raddish brown soil mixed with fallen brick bats and brick fragments. This is the layer of last fall represented by a great frequency of fallen building material and brickbats.

Layer-2 A : This layer consists of brownish soil with sandy silt and loose soil mixed with brick particles, when the structure was probably more or less stable. This layer is missing at places where a clear pit along the brick wall shows that the monastery was repaired and restored at the next higher stage, that is in layer (2), thoroughly disturbing or, at places, completely removing this layer.

Layer-2 B: Compact brownish soil with great frequency of brickbats and brick concrete.

Layer-3: Hard and compact brownish soil associated with brick particles, and with lesser frequency of brick fragments and brickbats, its bottom resting on a hard concrete formation mixed with fine brownish clay indicating a floor level. Most of the antiquities found in situ outside the monastery came from this level.

Excavation was stopped at the level except where deep diggings were carried out. The work done so far has revealed the outlines of a large 624^2 feet square monastery of the same type as exposed at Sālvan Vihār. It has similar rows of monastic cells, neatly arranged in four- wing around a shrine standing in the centre of a wide, open courtyard. The only one entrance, in the centre of the northern wing, like that of Sālvan Vihār, is set in an imposing front facade with a number of guard rooms symmetrically arranged on the blanks projecting outwards. The structure of this area is so badly damaged. The building remains particularly in the lower levels are well constructed with better materials and are excellently preserved. The establishment appears to have a large number of subsidiary buildings which are yet to be uncovered. However, the archaeologically more important, better preserved and well-stratified cultural remains of the earlier periods in lower levels are still intact and undisturbed, and this has obvious significance in the context of the earlier excavation in Maināmatī. As there was very little scope for systethatic investigation of the earlier cultural remains āt the excavated sites of Sālvan Vihāra, Ānanda Vihāra, Kutil ā Murā, and Cārpatra Murā without destroying their' well preserved monumental structures of later periods which lie on top more or less completely covering the early remains of those sites, this huge site with its ruthlessly destroyed upper levels expected to provide excellent opportunities for extensive deep diggings and intensive investigations of these early remains which may reveal more clearly and adequately the early history and culture of this region.

Comparative analysis: Moreover, although Maināmatī excavations has provided some information about the early history of this area. We have very little information about Śrī Ānandadeva, the third and greatest ruler and almost no knowledge at all about the earlier rulers of this powerful and prosperous eight century Buddhist dynasty of Samataṭa and their times. The family is known from the two recently discovered copperplate grants of Bhavadeva[3], son and successor of Ānandadeva, provides sufficient hints about the greatness of the latter. The Khaḍga and Rāta levels at Sālvan Vihāra and Kutilā Murā have been very insufficiently investigated in few narrow and confṁḍ pits and though the Maināmatī excavations have yielded a number of Khaḍga records: copperplates, coin and sealings, and the only known record of the Rāta kings of Devaparvata was found at Kailān[4], not very far from Maināmatī. The Knowledge of those two early dynasties of

Samataṭa is still very meagre and unsatisfactory. We know almost nothing about their architectural and cultural remains, through the lower levels of the Maināmatī rains are definitely known to belong to their times. It is expected that systethatic digging at Ānanda Vihāra will supply valuable information regarding not only Śrī Ānandadeva and his family, but also the Khaḍga and Rāta dynasties or even still earlier times, about all of which we have so far very little knowledge. Moreovere, the apparent concentration of large and important monuments around Ānanda Vihāra, its central position together with its large size, distinctive architectural features and decorative style makes it one of the most interesting and important monuments. The suggestion by some scholars including R.C.Majumdar and T.N.Ramchandran that the site represents the city of Devaparvata of the famous Paṭṭikeraka Vihāra of ancient records[5], which was situated in the city of that name and generally identified with the Maināmatī ruins[6], is also significant and needs a careful examination. We learn about the existence of this urban settlement (Paṭṭikeraka), undoubtedly same as Paṭṭikera of the later days, for the first time from Laḍaha Candra's Maināmatī plate . It is described by Raṇavaṅkamalla Harikāladeva's Maināmatī plate, quite fittingly, as "adorned with forts and monasteries"[8].

The association of the site with name of greatest of the early rulers of Devaparvata and Paṭṭikera and with myths and legends connected with both the cities makes the investigation even more necessary for the location and identification of these two famous cities of ancient Samataṭa, which rose and fell successively in the same general area. Though the site is very badly damaged, there are sufficient surface indications to suggest its importance in ancient times and it is quite reasonable to think that this monument played a leading role among the Buddhist establishments of Maināmatī-Lalmai and was probably the centre of the last great Buddhist University of Bengal, and for that thatter of the subcontinent, a worthy successor of Taxila and Nalanda.

Antiquities: A number of important antiquities have been discovered from the Ānanda Vihāra excavations which include very few Neolithic stone axes together with some unfinished specimens and raw materials, an imitation type post Gupta gold coin and silver coins; with bull and legend Paṭṭikera, bronze votive images representing the Buddha, Dhyānī Buddhas, Bodhisattvas, four to eight handed varieties of the Buddhist goddess Tāra or Cūṇḍā, bronze replica of votive stūpas, a large number of terracotta plaques, a large number of ornamental bricks containing the usual designs of stepped pyramid, lotus petals, dental edge and a variety of geometric-cum-floral designs and chain motifs either on the flat body on the edge of the bricks, a large number of inscribed terracotta searings with the Buddhist creed formula, a small baked clay tablet with fine representation of goddess Tāra in low relief, clay and baked clay votive stūpas, a few semiprecious stone beads, a number of terracotta beads, a large number of iron nails, complete and broken pots, oil lamps and numerous potsherds.

3. RŪPBĀN KANYĀ'S PALACE (ST - 15):

Location: This mound is situated about a furlong south of Ānanda Rāja's Pālace and north of Bhoja Rāja's Pālace and is adjacent to the western side of the Cantonment Road. It is a slightly raised site built on the flat land at the eastern foot of the hill. Compass bearings from the central raised area gave readings south 560 west to BARD water tower and north 200 west to the central height within Ānanda Vihāra.

Structural Description: There is an evidence of an extensive brick structure, although the configuration of the site has been badly damaged by the erection of modern cement - floored structures (which are no longer standing). The brick hunters plundered many bricks of this site. The mound measures about 450 feet square and is 15 feet high from the surrounding paddy fields. Though highly disturbed, the traces of the central structure and enclosing walls can be made out from the remains of the debris, scattered on the plain surface.

The edifice is a square structure measuring 250 x 250 feet and seems apparently to be a monastery. The eastern side of the mound is higher than the other three sides, which are almost at the level to the cultivated land. The overall dimensions of the site are somewhat smaller than those of the other identified monastery site though not so small as to preclude the possibility of being a monastery.

Anitqities: A stone cubical pillar base showing the design of a Caitya window on each side was found in the centre of the mound suggesting the existence of a stone maṇḍapa or shrine. Terracotta plaques and bricks of various sizes were revealed from this site. One of the large brick measuring 13" x $11^{.1}/_{2}$ x $2^{3}/_{4}$" was disclosed. Though brick depredation was heavy here, traces of a structure, perhaps a monastery with arrangement of central temple and surrounding cells can bee noticed. A few plaques were also recovered which show the semi-divine Yakṣha, the hybrid Kiṁpuruṣha and the wild boar in all its wild majesty.

4. BHOJ RAJA'S PALACE (ST- 16) :

Location: Bhoj Rājār Bāri or Blioj Vihāra is located hardly half a furlong to the south of Rūpbān Kanya's palace and half a mile to the south of Ānanda Rājā's palace. It is also northern side of Itākholā Murā and western side of Comilla town. This mound is locally known as Bhoja Rājār Bāri. The site was also heavily disturbed during the Second World War by the brick hunters and military contractor.

Structural Description: The shape of the mound is square with 600 feet in each side. Its sides are five to ten feet higher than the agricultural land but the middle portion is about 10 feet higher than its sides. During the archaeological survey, damaged portion of some massive brick walls covering an area of 400 x 400 feet was discovered. Here also the walls were built enclosing a square structure, profusely decorated with ornamental bricks and terracotta plaques similar to those found in Ānanda Vihāra and Sālvan Vihāra. From the elevation of the central structure, it appears that the approach to the monasteiy is from the north. An inclined approach leads to the centre of the northern wall, where apparently a gateway opened on to a raised walkway that runs across the interior of the quadrangle to the central shrine. Various changes in the ground level within the enclosed area of the monastery suggest there were other structures. Pottery was found in heavy concentrations under the eastern wall where sand and mud have been excavated to build up the new road that passes nearly. Many pieces of pottery were lying embedded in stratified layers in the banks beside the eastern wall of the monastery. This evidence clearly suggests that it was the dump for discarding pottery. These evidences suggest that this site was probably a Buddhist Vihāra with the shrine in the centre as at Pahārpur, Ānanda Vihāra and Sālvan Vihāra.

5. KOTBĀR1 MURĀ (ST - 20)

Location : This site is situated about a few furlongs west of the Rūpbān Murā and north of Itākholā Murā and south-western side of Comilla town. In 1803, the site was first come to our knowledge during the construction of the Comilla- Kālir Bazar Road and erroneously identified as the remains of a fort. This mound was also heavily damaged during the Second World War by the military contractor and brick plunderer. Compass bearings were taken from the central structure that gave reading of south 84° east BARD water tower and north 7° west Comilla Cantonment water tower.

Structural Description: The diggings for bricks had been very here resulting in virtual obliteration of the structural remains underneath. One such structure had seen by late Ramachandran was a pyramidal temple with reentrant corners of walls and surrounded by rows of cells. He thought that the remains of the site to be a monastery of modest size approxithately measuring 300 feet each sides enclosing a cruciform center temple with approxithately one hundred feet on all sides[9].

Nonetheless, the exterior walls once housed monastic cells

of the same kind as those excavated in Sālvan Vihāra. At these places the brick walls still stand six or seven feet high. The presence of a central shrine is indicated in the center of the monastery where the land is raised approxithately eight feet above the surrounding level. From this central shrine, the entrance to the monastery can be observed. A ramp passes between the two exterior structures, through the north wall, and along a raised path to the central structure within the monastic compound. The exterior structures flanking the entrance are raised three or four feet above. The surrounding agricultural level, though their elevations are difficult to determine because of the road cut at the passes close beside them. These secondary structures are about ten to fifteen yards in radius.

Antiquities: The scattered bricks were found all over the site. Large sized rectangular bricks, 14'' x 9" x 2.75" were profuse here. There was a moderately dense concentration of pottery found along the eastern and southern edges of the exterior walls of the monastery. A few plaques were also reported from here but none could be recovered. One interesting plaque however came from somewhere nearly though the man who brought it could only declare it as from Lalmai hill. The subject of the plaque is a flying Vidyādhara in the violent movement of flight mixed with dance, in which acts the garland that he held in his hand snaps. The upper cloth, necklace, *yagňopavīta, aṅgadas,* brocaded under garment and lotus buds are note worthy decorative features presented on this plaque which would at once classify it among the best productions of the Pāla period.

6. RUPBAN MURĀ: (ST - 21)

Location: The mound is located to the west of Kotbāri Murā and a furlong to the south of Itākholā mound. The mound is also situated in between the BARD and the Bangladesh Rifle's office. The compass bearings of the central mound are south 37° east BARD water tower and north 20° west cantonment water tower. Northern side of the mound meets the Comilla-

Kālir Bazar road in a gentle slope but the other three sides are steep. The mound is about two feet high from the metalloid road. Sometime towards the end of the Second World War, T.N Ramachandran the superintendent of the archaeological section of the Indian Museum toured the hills and apparently opened the top of the main mound at Rūpbān Murā. He reported that it was "a cruciform brick structure resembling in plan, the central Temple of Paharpur and of the Nandangarh temple, with its reentrant angles and recessed comers richly dressed on the out side with carved plaques and moulding bearing interesting designs''[10].

The brick hunters and the military contractor had disturbed the mound, Rūpbān Murā like other archaeological sites of the Mainamti Lalmai range. The vandals for the query of bricks first disturbed it during the Second World War. The British 14th Division Army during the war had built some modern structures over the northern side of the mound whose foundations are still traceable. The mound also suffered badly during the Liberation War of Bangladesh when Pakistan army dug a number of trenches at various points of the mound. The mound is approxithately 400 feet long and 400 feet width.

The excavation of the site was started in 1984 and was continued for 6 months. The next two years (i.e. 1984 and 1986), it was repeated for 4 to 5 months in every year. A small-scale excavation was also earned out in 1992 in order to expose the boundary wall of the temple and that of the gate way complex of the monastery

Structural Description: The excavation have brought to light the structural remains of a Buddhist establishment consisting of a medium sized temple together with a stūpa and a square structure in front and a small monastery. Both, the temple and monastery discover three phases of building activity. Out of the three different phases of the temple, the first (earliest) phase has been exposed partly, the second fully and the third superficially. In the above mentioned two phases the temple was cruciform in plan but nothing could be ascertained about the third phase. Layout of the first and second phases of the monastery has been exposed fully while the remains of the third phase could be traced in a restricted area. In the first phase the monastery was square and larger while in the second and the third phases it became oblong and smaller.

Temple: Only a small portion of the temple structure of the first phase could be exposed since it is mostly covered by tlie second phase structure. From the exposed remains, it seems that this temple was built in a cruciform plan with four image chambers. The central square of the cross has been partly exposed with its each face measuring 24 feet. But the arms of the cross along with the image chambers are found to be totally destroyed. From the remains of the arms and the four faces of the central square of the cross the width of the image chambers (4 feet) could be ascertained. A small portion of the ambulatory passage and the exterior wall of this temple have been exposed at places. The exterior walls could be discovered to a distance of 15 feet northward and southward from the central square unit. In the southern side the wall has been found to a depth of 3 feet from its surviving top. It is 3 feet wide. A portion of the ambulatory passage, laid in brick dust, was encountered along the inner face of this wall at a depth of 20" from the top of the floor of the second phase temple. It appears that the later builders raised the floor of the temple to 20" while rebuilding the temple. Probably the temple was cruciform in plan with its arms measuring 62 feet long. Probably the approach was from the eastern side as appeal's from the later temple.

The second rebuilding phase stands on a cruciform platform with image chamber. The entire structure was provided with an ambulatory passage engirdled by an exterior wall. The length of this temple arm to arm, is 90 feet. During this phase, the temple was extended further and was built over the ruins of the earlier one. The cruciform platform was also enlarged. The extended portion of the larger platform was built separately on four sides of the earlier platform up to its surviving heights. The builders of the second phase seems to have removed the bricks from the walls of the image chambers and the exterior walls of the first phase structure (up to the certain level) and reuse them.

While renovating this temple initially, the arms of the cross were extended up to the exterior wall on the western, northern and southern sides. In order to provide an uninterrupted ambulatory passage all around the temple there fore 3 feet area of the outer wall along its inner side was reduced. 2.5 feet also reduced the lengths of the arms of the cross, so that the ambulatory passage was widened to 5.5 feet. The image chambers were provided with brick pedestals excepting the middle one to the east, which had a stone pedestal. Images were placed along the back walls of the chambers. It appears that the images were removed from their original places at a later stage except the Buddha image, which was left in the place. A few bronze pieces, probably fragments of bronze sculptures, were found on the pedestals of northern and southern chambers. It is likely that in the central chamber of the eastern side a colossal stone image and in other chambers bronze images were installed. Sidewalls of the image chambers were provided with corbelled niches probably for keeping lamps of rituals.

The main approach to the temple of this phase measuring 12 feet wide was provided in the middle of the eastern exterior wall. No flight of steps could be traced here for they were badly damaged and obliterated. But the remains of the projected arms indicate that the lower portion of the approach path was an infilling of earth mixed with debris. The flight of steps might have been built above that level. The approach to the shrine was built after the construction of the exterior wall, as there is no bondage between the two. Only the projected arms of the approach could be traced which measured 3 feet wide. As the monastery was built to the east south east of the temple. The main gateway of the temple was provided to its east. While the gateway of the monastery to its north. In addition to the main entrance to the temple, smaller entrances were provided in front of the image chambers on other three sides. The entrance of the eastern side is 9 feet wide. While on the other sides they are 3 feet. Moreover eight small openings were provided at various points in the exterior wall for admitting light and air into the temple.

The temple of the third phase has not survived. It is difficult to reconstruct its plan or other architectural features. It was built over the remains of the second phase. The only traceable remains were the damaged walls over the remains of northern and eastern image chambers and a part of the derefict structure overlying the central unit.

Stūpa: An octagonal Stūpa was built 39 feet east of the temple over a square base measuring 15 feet by 15 feet. The Stūpa survives to a height of 3 feet from the square base and is enclosed by 2 feet thick wall. There is a circumambulatory passage between the stūpa and its enclosure wall. It is 2.5 feet wide. Strati graphically, it appears that the stūpa is related to the second phase of building activity at the site.

Square Structure: A Square structure was found 35 feet northward of the octagonal stūpa. It is discovered in a highly damaged condition with only its base surviving. Its architectural feature could not be clearly made out. Complete bricks were used at the edge while broken bricks were used in the center. It survives up to a height of 2.5 feet.

Enclosure: An enclosure wall was provided on four sides of the temple complex (temple stūpa and square structure) that wall is 4.5 feet wide. An opening 4 feet wide was kept in the southern aim of the enclosure. Another opining 4 feet wide was accommodated in the northern extended wall. This extension enclosed the entire gateway complex of the monastery. Only the base of the enclosure wall survives.

Monastery: The monastery is located 100 feet east - south east of the temple. There is also found three building phases. The layout of the establishment in the beginning was oblong, measuring 115 feet N-W and 83 feet N-S but during the construction it was further extended towards south by about 42 feet and this extension gave the monastery almost a square shape.

Several distinguishing features are noticeable in the original plan of the Vihāra and its later extension. In all 24 monastic cells have been exposed in the entire Vihāra. Of these 15 cells have been exposed in four wings of the original part and in three wings of the extended part of the Vihāra. The cells are unequal in size. In the original monastery, each of the cells shows a doorway with the average width of 4 feet, which opens on the common verandah that runs round the entire courtyard. It is noted that there was no verandah in the extended part in front of the cell. The verandah is 7.5 feet wide. The thickness of the retaining wall is 334 feet. The first oblong open courtyard measures 47.5 feet E - W by 17.5 feet N - S the second courtyard too is oblong and it measures 67.5 feet by 11.5 feet.

Some important architectural features of monastery have also been noticed during excavation. These include a staircase, a drain, platforms, niches and bricked doorways.

Stratigraphy: The cross trenches one running E-W and the other N- S were sunk through the middle of the temple area. The latter one includes a deep trench on the southern end. A few cross trenches were also laid in the monasteiy area in different direction i.e., N-S and E-W Besides these, deep digging was conducted in several points of the monastery like the monastic cells courtyard, verandah and the gateway complex. In both the temple and the monastery areas undisturbed natural soil was encountered. Some variations were noticed between the two areas. Minimum number of layers and floors were encountered in the monastery area viz layers 1A, IB, 2, 2A, 3,4,5,6, and 7 of these layers 3,4,5 and 6 were overlaid by floors. All these layers and floors were not uniform in every trench or cell whereas some layers and floors were found missing.

Antiquities : Excavation at Rūpbān Murā have discovered more than five hundred antiquities, including a colossal stone image of standing Buddha, five Gupta imitation debased gold coins, three silver coins with Paṭṭikera legend, two bronze images, a hoard of bronze ingots, a large number of terracotta plaques, ornamental bricks carved with slepped pyramid, lotus petal, dental edge motif, a variety of geometrical cum - floral designs and chain motifs, earthen oil lamps, earthen weights, sprinklers tops, red ochres, iron nail and various other miscellaneous minor objects of every day use. Most of the antiquities, e.g. stone Buddha, almost all the terracotta plaques and ornamental bricks were collected from the temple area whereas other antiquities like coins, bronze images and other objects of everyday use were recovered from the monastery area. A small quantity of pottery has been recovered from the monastery area. Except a few oil lamps no complete pots were found. They are fragments of rim, neck and base of different household wares such as pitcher, bowl, saucer, lid, sprinkler and oil lamps. The shards are very in colour and texture. Most of them are pale red and a few are deep ash coloured. Thin textured shards are common and medium textured are few while heavy textured shards are totally absent. Some shards bear herringbone decorations, reticular and incised lines.

Chronology: Though a large number of cultural materials have been found from the site but no epigraphic records could be salvaged from here. In the absence of datable evidence, it is difficult to establish any absolute chronology of this establishment However, on the basis of the iconographic parallels, legends of the coins, and the themes displayed in the terracotta plaques, a relative chronology of the site can be arrived at. The colossal Buddha and the coins referred to above are dated to 7th century AD Whereas the terracotta plaques represent a time span from 7th / 8th century to 12th century. Thus the Buddha image could be placed in the first phases of the temple and was probably reinstalled in the temple of the succeeding phase. The copper - plates recovered from the locality indicate its earliest date to the 7th century during the rule of the Khaḍga dynasty. On the basis of the above finds, the antiquity of the site could be placed to 7th century, which also corroborates the available paleographic evidences.

Discussion: The excavation at the site has revealed a four-faced cruciform temple and a detached monastery. Both, the temple and the monastery reveals three phases of building activities, although the relationship between two could not be well established. A comparative study between the temple and the monastery provides some interesting and identical feature. The excavation of the temple reveals that the temple was smaller in the first phases and larger in the second phase. Similarly the original monastery might have been smaller in size and became larger in the second phase, as a result of its extension to the southern side. In the extended part (probably second phase) the walls were initially wider and then their breadth was reduced by abandonment of some portion of those walls as observed at the temple.

On the basis of the above evidence, it is presumed that the smaller temple and smaller original monasteiy might have been contemporary while the larger temple and the larger (extended) monastery might have been rebuilt simultaneously in the second phase. During this rebuilding phase the builders might have restored to similar slipshod plan in the temple as well in the monastery. So finally they had to change the alignments of both the monuments in then: respective portions in order to achieve the desired shape and size. If so, the third phase of the temple corresponds to that phase of the monastery.

Conclusion: From the structural remains so far exposed at the site it may be concluded that both, the temple and the monastery, presents an unusual feature in the monastery architecture. Provision of two inner courtyards is also another exceptional feature. From the architectural feature, numisthatic evidences, iconographic parallels and the themes depicted in the terracotta, art the Buddhist establishment may be dated to 7th century A.D.

7. SĀLVAN MOUND (ST - 24):

The Sālvanpur mound is the earliest dated site in the Maināmatī - Lalmai hill range, still now. Excavations of this site, had been started since 1955 by the Department of Archaeology, have discovered remains of a 550 feet square Buddhist monastery. After the excavation it was renamed Sālvan Vihāra owing to its proximity to the Sāl forest in the west.

Location of the site: The ancient and famous archaeological site, Sālvan Vihāra is located almost at the middle of the Maināmatī - Lalmai hill range of Comilla district. Near about a mile to the south-east of Rūpban Murā is Sālvan Vihāra which is situated to the south-west of Comilla town and western side of Railway line.

Structural Description: The site is consisted of four distinct parts: a central shrine, minor buildings within the courtyard, an enclosing quadrilateral containing monastic cells, and a subsidiary shrine outside the monastery walls.

The front gate of the big monastery was approached from the north by a 174 feet long and 3.5 feet wide a brick path. The gateway of the monastery is 74 feet wide. There is an entrance hall (measuring 32 by 23 feet) is flanked by guardrooms. From the entrance hall, a short series of steps lead to the inside of the monastery courtyard. The boundary wall of the monastery, which also serves as the back wall of the monastic cells. It is 6 feet high and 16.5 feet thick. The cells, separated from each other by 5.5 feet thick walls, were provided with 3.5 feet wide door passages, which opened to a 8.5 feet wide verandah. The big monastery, consisting of 115 monastic cells, was built around a spacious courtyard with a cruciform shrine in the centre. From the verandah the 115 cells of the ground floor of the monastery can be entered. It has only one entrance that is in northern wing of the monastery. 5.5 feet separate the cells. approxithately 12 by 12 feet, partition walls, many of which have small corbeled niches. The entrances of the cells were probably closed by wooden door. So many things were found in the brickwork of the doorways. The cells are almost uniform in size with the exception of which measures 6.5 feet by 10 feet.

In the four Corners were staircases to the roof. The remain ruins of the boundary wall of the monastery are surviving only 4 to 6 feet high. So it is difficult to ascertain whether the roof provided a second storey of walls and rooms or not. The excavators of the site supposed that the roof was supported on heavy wooden beams and was made of concrete stiffened with crushed brick. There is no known analysis. with the favour of this supposition.

A few subsidiary structures have exposed in the courtyard of the monastery. One of them, a large pillared hall with two attached chambers was found at the south -east corner of the courtyard. It seems to have been the community-dining hall of the monastery in its later stages. A large number of potsherds and utensils discovered in its vicinity in association with ashes and charcoal pieces strongly suggested its use during the third period of occupation.

Another subsidiary structures in the courtyard including two small shrines were discovered on the western side of the central shrine. The larger one of these facing east is rectangular in shape, surrounded by a specious *Pradakṣīṇā path,* it consists of a rectangular hall in the front and a small cell behind on the west. The smaller one is a square structure with recessed corners, each containing three decorated brick pillars are circular shape. The smaller one of these two structures has been found on the southwestern side of the central shrine as a Stūpa.

The Central Shrine: In the centre of the courtyard of the monastery is located a large shrine, built originally in the form of a cross-oriented to the cardinal point of the compass. Four periods of re-buildings have been found in the shrine. The ground plan of the first period has been clearly exposed. It was cruciform in shape. From arm to arm, the shrine stretched 170 feet. From its ground plan, some scholars think that the shrine attained a considerable height. From its disclosed structure, it is difficult to guess whether it rose up into roof. A 7 feet wide *Pradakṣīṇā path* permitted the devotee to perambulate the central shrine and visit each of the smaller shrines in the projecting amis, facing to the cardinal points. A big bronze pedestal of an image has been found from the western cell of the central shrine. So it is easy to say that every cells of the central shrine contained big image or images of Buddha. Entire basement wall of the central shrine was well decorated with terracotta plaques and ornamental bricks, which are found in Situ in the south-western projection, and in some places of the eastern basement wall. According to Alam, these terracotta plaques faithfully illustrate the flock art of the period. Antelopes, pigs, monkeys, horses, elephants, peacocks, swans, snakes and men in fighting poses, depicted all the discovered plaques. The rebuilding of the structure changed the plan from cruciform to oblong measuring 110 feet, east to west, by 168 feet, north to south with a 30 feet square pillared hall in the centre and the principal cell or the main prayer chamber accommodated at the back on south side. A procession path surrounding the hall and the principal cell also connected with other cells on east and west. There is a number of steps leading to an entrance hall in front of the pillared pavilion from the north into approach to the shrine. The drastic change in the plan has not been related to other developments at the site. As the first construction of the shrine antedates the monastery by nearly a century, according to Rashid, the change in plan of the shrine may have coincided with the construction of the surrounding monastery. The significance of the shift in plan is difficult to evaluate, but the early cruciform resembles. The great shrine at Paharpur in the Rajshahi district, and some of the shrines at Pagan in Burma and Kalasan in Central Java, while the later rectilinear plan modified it to resemble Buddhist and Hindu shrines in Bihar. The central shrine at Sālvan Vihāra is actully not one but several structures, built successively in different periods and on different plans. They provide interesting evidence of gradual transformation of the traditional Buddhist architecture and of its merging into that of the Hindu temple. There are eight rooms, four on the east and four on the west of the hall, and the main prayer chamber located on the south. These rooms were provided with wooden doors and niches and were perhaps used by the priests.

The north-western shrine: Another small shrine has been discovered at the north-western side of the Sālvan Vihāra. It is located outside of the monastic courtyard. At present, the shrine is 12 feet high from the surrounding level. It is approachable from the east by a flight of 10 steps leading to a terrace in front of the Sanctum. A 6.5 feet wide Verandah runs around the sanctuary and also served as an ambulatory path. It is originally roofed on round pillars. The walls of the shrine are of considerable thickness in the corner form the only decoration of this shrine. It is very difficult to explain why the side of the big monastery erected this small temple.

Deep diggings have revealed four repair and rebuilding phases in the monastery. The large number of artifacts were found from the first phase, which undoubtedly indicates that the monastery was thickly populated in its early years. The antiquities include important objects like copper-plates, silver ingots, a large number of bronze images of Buddha and other Buddhist Gods and Goddesses, oil lamps, decorated lids and earthen wares, storage jars etc., were also discovered from tin's phase. Earthen cooking pots in Situ on fireplaces and in association with charcoal and ashes were discovered from a number of cells. This indicates that the monks used to cook their food inside the cells and that there was no community kitchen in the earliest period.

In the second period, filling the floors and door passages with bricks and new cells were constructed without changing the original plan raised the plinth level. The period is also characterized by the frequency of earthen pots, big storage jars and other household objects but less in number in comparison to the first period.

In the third period the plan of the cubicles were not thoroughly changed but some minor adjustment were made. Antechambers were added in the back walls of some cells, brick platforms were placed on the floors and staircases were constructed in the corner rooms. With the exception of a few ornamental bricks and terracotta plaques no other important antiquities were discovered from this period.

Remains of the 4th or the last occupation period are found only in the western half of the northern side of the monastery where the cells were rebuilt after reducing the thickness of the back wall from 16.5 feet to 10 feet and thus the cells and verandah were pushed backwards. No antiquity was found in these cells.

Date of Sālvan Vihāra: A large number of artifacts were found during excavation besides the structural remains of this large monastery. These include copper plates silver and gold coins, bronze images of Buddha and other Buddhist deities, bronze caskets, bronze utensils and other metal objects, terracotta seals and sealings, pottery', terracotta plaques and array of various other objects accumulated over the centuries. Amongest these various antiquities, the copper plates are the most valuable historical documents. Total eight copper plates were discovered from this site. Most of the artifacts are now on display in the Maināmatī museum, Comilla. The scope of work does not permit a detailed discussion of the antiquities nor it is possible as the detailed report of the excavations has not yet been published. However for fixing a date of the monastery some important antiquities are discussed below in brief.

Out of the eight copper-plates from Sālvan Vihāra only two plates are found in comparatively good state of preservation. One of them has brought to light for the first time a new powerful royal dynasty of south east Bengal, viz, the Devas, who seems to have come to power in the closing year of the 7th century or in the early years of 8th century A.D. But others, discovered from the same occupation level, received less attention due to their decayed and highly damaged conditions- One of these is a badly creaked large plate. The text of this highly incrusted plate is illegible though an inscription on the obverse running the length of the plate can be seen and faint lines on the reverse suggest that the text continue on the back. A beautiful seal 3.5 inches in width and 4.75 inches in height is fixed on top of the plate. The upper half of the seal bears a recumbent bull facing proper right below which is a singular incised name, which has been read as *"Mahārājā Śrī Vuinayaguptasya"*[n] As the appearance of the seal and the style and direction of the writing on the plate all closely resemble the published Gunaighar copperplate of Vainyagupta. The published plate of Vinyagupta was found in Gunaighar about eighteen miles north west of Commila City and about the same distance from Sālvan Vihāra. It was issued from the camp of victory at Kripura and was dated 188 in the current era (which, the editor took to be the Gupta, era and which gives a date of 508 A.D.). While there is no reason for linking the Āśrarma Vihāra of the Gunaighar copper plate with the Sālvan Vihāra. It is significant that an inscription of the same king occurs at Sālvan Vihāra. The presence of this plate suggests that the nucleus of the Sālvan Vihāra can be dated back to the reign of Vainyagupta at the beginning of the sixth centure A.D and that the territory around the hills was under his administration. Another possibility suggested by Mr. Morrision is that the peculiar early form of the central shrine was related to the worship of Ārya Avalokiteśvara of the Gunnaighar copper plate[11].

The next three copper plates from Sālvan Vihāra resemble each other closely and were also recovered from the early phase of the monastery. These plates were issued by the Khaḍga king Devakhaḍga and Bālabhaṭṭa who are already known to us from the Ashrafpur copper plate inscription found thirty miles north east of Dhaka, approxithately forty two miles from Sālvan Vihāra. The presence of these three plates of the Buddhist king whose capital was at Jayakarmantavasaka (probably the present day Baḍakāmtā),[13] strongly suggest that the Khaḍga kings endowed Sālvana Vihāra with land - grants for its maintenance. The date of Khaḍga dynasty' is well established by the accounts of Seng-Chi a Chinese pilgrim who visited Samataṭa in or about 671 A.D when Rājārājā Bhaṭṭa (identified with Bālabhaṭṭa), son and successor of Deva Khaḍga was rulling. Assuming the standard of twenty years for each ruler and that Balabhaṭṭa was half way through Ins reign when Seng-Chi came to Samataṭa Mr. Morisson has dated the copper-plates between 641 and 671 A.D and as the plate came from the earliest phase of the monastery he has suggested that the occupation of the monastic quadrangle may be tentatively dated to the reign of Deva Khaḍga (circa 641 661 A.D.). The tentative dating of Morission is century or more earlier then the date suggested by Harunur Rashid, the principal excavator.

Rashid attaches more importance to the Deva copper plates. As many as four copper- plates of the Dava kings have been recovered from the monastic cells. The first one came from the earliest phase and was issued by Ānanda Deva and endorsed his successor Bhava Deva. The remaining three plates were recovered in badly damaged condition but the seals on their top and occasional legible lines enough to identify them as Deva inscriptions. The earlier published copper plate of Bhava Deva[14] recovered from this area and these copper -plates have proved beyond doubt the existence of the independent Deva dynasty in South -East Bengal.

Dani has suggested an eight-century date for this copper -plates[15]. The Sālvan Vihāra copper-plates of the Devas (not yet published) do not bear any proof of the transfer of property to a large Buddhist establishment like the Sālvan monastery.

TABLE NO - 1
MONASTERIES

Sl. No.	Name of the Mound	Dimensions in feet		Area in square feet	Present height in feet	Finding Structure	Finding antiquites	Excavated/Unexcavated	Present Name	Detation
		N-S	E-W							
1.	Army Bungalow (ST.-4)	140	125	17,500	15	Brick Wall	Pottery, old bricks	Unexca-	-	-
2.	¶nanda REja's Palace (ST-12)	208	208	43,264	15	Wall Gateway, cells, shrine, courtyard.	Pottery, Iron nails, Terracotta plaques Neolithic stone axes, gold coins, silver coins, bronze votive images, votive stpu. brick, sealings, terracotta beads.	Excavated	¶nanda Vihara	8 Hi-0th century A.D.
3.	Rnpban Kaiiya's Palace (ST-15)	80	80	6400	15	enclosing wall central shrine	A stone cubical pillar, terracotta, plaques, bricks, pottery	unexcavated	Rupban Kanya's Vihara	-
4.	Bhoj Raja's Palace (ST-16)	200	200	40,000	10	Enclosing wall, central shrine gateway.	Pottery bricks.	unexcavated	Bhoj Vihara	-
5.	Kotbari Mura (ST-20)	100	100	10,000	8	Pyramidal temple, walls, cells	Pottery, bricks terracotta plaques	unexcavated	Kotbari Vihara	-
6.	Rupban Mura (ST-21)	400	400	1,60,000	60	Temple, StÊpa Enclosure, Monastery	Stone image, gupta imitation gold coins, silver coins, bronze image, tngols, terracotta plaques, ornamental bricks	Excavated	Rupban Mura	7th century A.D.
7.	Salvanpur Mound (ST-24)	183	183	33,489	12	Central shrine, enclosing wall, cells, minor buildings within the courtyard, subsidiary slirine.	Pottery, bricks terracotta plaques, copperplates, silver coins, terracotta seals and sealings, gold ornaments. Bronze images oil lamps, lids, earthenware, siorage jars, cooking pot.	Excavated	Salban Vihara	7th-8th century A.D.

But earlier published Bhava Deva plate mentions the transfer of land to a Viharika, a small monastery situated in or around the Mainămatī hill. In addition to the copper- plates there is one short terracotta sealing that says simply *"Śrī Bhavadeva Mahā Vihāra Ārya Bhikṣu Saṅghasya."* [16] This can be translated as the order of the noble monks of the monastic establishment of Śri Bhavadeva. The implication would be that the monastery was constructed or at least generously supported by Bhavadeva. Similarly the distribution of the Deva inscription through the three periods of the monastic quadrangle suggests that the dynasty supported the foundation after the Khaḍgas and that some of the inscriptions were of sufficient importance to be preserved through the various disasters and rebuilding that the institution experienced. The date of the Deva dynasty is not fixed but in the judgement of A.H Dani, who examined the inscriptions for his study of Indian paleography. These are to be placed in the eight century[17]. Rashid suggests that Ānandadeva and his successor Bhavadeva built the monastic quadrangle some time during the eighth century though this would make the presence of the Vainyagupta and Khaḍga plates anomalous and so further supporting evidence is needed. The architectural features of the monastery strongly support the 7-8th century date as it closely resembles the well known Paharpur monastery which was built in the late eighth or early ninenth century. The copper- plates of earlier dynasties were probably connected with some earlier establishment in the area and were preserved by the inthates of the Sālvan Vihāra, built on a larger scale at a later date.

The available evidences from the inscriptions suggest a time span from the early sixth century through the eight-century for the building and use of the central shrine and monastic quadrangle at Sālvan Vihāra. Subsequent rebuilding led the excavator to suggest that the structure was in use until the wall in to the period of the Candra dynasty in the eleventh century or later . In the absence of a systethatic documented report on the excavation, his interpretation for this must be accepted.

Among the more important finds at the site were three hoards of gold and silver coins found inside clay pots buried beneath an early floor level. The first hoard contained three gold coins, one of Candragupta 11 (376 -415 A.D.), one an imitation Gupta coin, and the third, a coin of the Devas. The second hoard contained 52 silver coins in three different denominations, while the third pot held 172 silver coins of the largest denomination only. Both the second and third hoard contain the same kind of coins, which bear on the obverse recumbent bull with the legend Paṭṭikara or Lalitakerah Dharmavijay and on the reverse trident surmounted by images of the sun and moon. These coins are the first major finds of high quality silver currency in the delta that can be dated between the Gupta and early Muslim periods. Their number, associations, find-spot and other available evidences indicate that these coins were issued locally by a sufficiently powerful and prosperous dynasty of Samataṭa most probably, Śrī Ānandadeva of Deva dynasty. Detail description has given in chapter IV study of coins.

SECTION - II

LARGE SHRINES

1. ĀBBĀS ĀLI MURĀ (ST-6):

This mound is located on a low prominence rising above the agricultural lands on the eastern side of the hills, fifty yards south west of the new cantonment school that faces onto the Eastern Boundary road (south of its intersection with the Comilla Daud Khandi road). It is twelve to fifteen feet above the land to the east and covers an area of about 25 yards north-south and 30 yards east-west. Many broken bricks and pottery were collected from surface of the site. Judging from the lay of the land and the configuration of the site, the entrance was from the east and from the location, orientation, and size, this mound appears to be a shrine like Cārpatra Murā and Kutilā Murā.

Supporting this view are the dimensions of the site (25 yards north-south x 30 yards east-west) and of the enclosed area, which falls within the size range of other shrines.

2. CĀRPATRA MURĀ (ST-8):

Location : The mound Cārpatra Murā, is located to the western side of Comilla town, southern side of Dhaka-Comilla road, and near to the Kutilā Murā and Brigade Headquarters of the Bangladesh Regiment. It is nearly 35 feet higher man the surrounding agricultural land. Excavation on this mound has completely exposed the remains of a big temple complex.

Structural Description: A salvage operation at Cārpatra Murā during a military construction work exposed the remains of an interesting shrine. Later on, the Department of Archaeology excavated it. It was found in a highly disturbed condition. The ground plan of this temple complex, measuring 105 feet from east to west and 55 feet from north to south. The approach to the shrine was from the east through a large gateway brick - paved path that led into a spacious hall. The roof of the hall was supported on four massive brick pillars. The pilgrims were led into the cell on its western side by a covered passage. In its present condition, it is not possible to explain the shape of superstructure. Compared to the Buddhist shrine farther south at Kutilā Murā, this one is small and sparsely decorated. There is little in the way of ornamental brick - work evident. However, the site contained an abundance of pottery and most important four inscribed copper plates. Hence it was renamed as Cārpatra Murā. Three of these copper-plates were issued by rulers of the Candra dynasty (i.e. Laḍalha Candra Deva and Govind Chandra Deva) and one by a later ruler, Śrī Vīradharadeva later Deva dynasty.

Datation: From the structural remains, which clearly indicate its function, and from all the copper plates which state that property is being transferred " to the God Śrī Laḍaha Mādhava Bhaṭṭākra. " We can be reasonably sure that this is the shrine dedicated to that God. Laḍaha Candra carried out the installation of the image of Śrī Laḍaha Mādhava according to the statement in this first inscription. It is not known if the shrine was first built at that time. All that is certain that property was transferred to provide support for the worship of this deity during the reign of Laḍaha Candra, (i.e. beginning of 11th century) and that a further grant of property was made during the reign of Vīradharadeva, who can be placed in twelfth or thirteenth century[20]. Therefore, it is strongly suggested that the shrine was likely to have been used in between 11th to 12th century AD

3. KŪTILĀ MURĀ (ST-9):

Location: Kūtilā Murā site is situated to the western side of Comilla town and southern side of Dhaka - Chittagong highway and about three miles north of Sālvan Vihāra in Maināmatī-Lalmai hill range. The layout of three principal stūpas and a number of subsidiary stūpas have been exposed in 1956. It is an interesting stūpa complex. A massive boundary wall encloses all. This site is also situated on the hilltop. Kūtilā Murā is an extensive mound about a furlong square. Fossil wood specimens were picked up in this area.

Structural Description: The excavated shrine named Kutilā Murā includes three stūpas constructed on a common plinth is located on the top of a low hill on the eastern side of hills facing the plains. A massive boundary wall decorated with recessed panels encloses the entire structural complex. The three principal stūpas are found side by side and are surrounded by other stūpas and structures spread over an area, measuring about 280 feet from north to south and about 225 feet from east to west. The main three stūpas are approached from the east by a wide staircase that ascends in three stages and crosses a massive wall and to three rectangular entrance halls. The dimension of northern hall could not be accurately measured due to its highly damaged condition. The southern hall measures 5T-6" x 37'-9" and the central one 55'-5" x 45'-7". The three main stūpas, in north-south alignment with their square bases are behind the entrance halls. The measurement of these stūpas are respectively 39'-9", 36'-10" and 47'-7" from north to south. The square bases support circular drums and hemispherical domes. The height of the central one is 10 feet from plinth level. The three main stūpas here probably represent the three jewels of Buḍḍhism : Buddha, Dharma and Saṅgha. The ground plan of the middle stūpa was laid in the form of a Dhannacakra (wheel of the law). A deep central shaft and the spokes represent the hub by brick walls, which have formed eight cells or box chambers. Inside the central shaft and the box-chambers, hundreds of enshrined miniature stūpas and untaked clay searings were found. From these, a number of broken pieces of stone sculptures in soft grey stone have salvaged. These depict, in high relief, figures of the Buddha and Bodhisattvas seated on lotus throne and attended by lay worshippers. The other two stūpas, representing the Buddha and the Saṅgha are made of solid brick masonry, each with a deep central shaft, which also contained a large number of clay mainature stūpas and terra-cotta sealings. The outer faces of the drums of these stūpas have been discovered with a number of small corbelled niches, intended perhaps, receptacles for oil lamps. Other nine stūpas have been found behind the three principal stūpas (Tri-Ratna Stūpas) i.e. on the west of these nine, six small stūpas are built on a common platform and aligned in north-east direction. Two slightly bigger stūpas are found on both ends of this group of stūpas. A remains of another stūpa was also found near the southwest comer of southern most stūpa of the Tri-Ratna group. Super structures of these stūpas are completely damaged. In the plan, they are round with square bases ranging in size from 27 square feet to approxithately 15 square feet. A number of miniature clay stūpas were found from inside the deep shaft in the center of these stūpas.

Two of the stone statues discovered in side the stūpa shaft, representing the *Dharmacakra,* bear some inscriptions on their pedestals. Paleographical they may be dated around seventh century A.D. and thus the *Tri-Ratna stūpa* may also be tentatively dated to that period. It should, however, be noted that the shrines of Kutilā Murā show three distinct phases of repairs and rebuildings. In the first phase, mere were probably two entrances, one almost in the middle of the eastern wall and the other near the northern end of the small wall. In the second phase the eastern boundary wall was pushed back-wards and the one entrance was provided in the middle. The three oblong halls in front of the stūpas were also extended in the second phase. These were enclosed within circumambulatory passages. There is also an antechamber at the back of the southernmost hall, which indicates that the halls also served the purpose of shrines and images of Buddha or Bodhisattvas were once installed therein for worship. Remains of the third period of the shrines are visible only in the oblong hall in front of the middle stūpa and in the eastern boundary wall. A number of fireplaces discovered at the back of the main stūpas probably belonged to the latest phase of the shrines perhaps those were built later for cooking food for large gatherings. The other artifact was a single gold coin recovered from upper level of this site. It was belonging to the last Abbasid Caliph, Abu Ahmad-Al Mustassim B'illah (1242-1258 A.D.)" . While the inscribed statues give a seventh century date for the use of the shrine, the single Abbasid coin is not sufficient to establish that shrine was in active use until the middle of the thirteenth century. A later visitor to the area could easily have dropped such a coin. From the remains of different periods we may conclude that the shrines at Kutilā Murā were in active use for a long period beginning from seventh century to at least thirteenth century A.D.

4. ITĀKHOLĀ MURĀ (ST-18)

Location: This Itākholā mound is situated at the northern side of the Kotbāri Road and two hundred yards to the south of Bhojarāja's palace and south-western side of Comila town. It is a big mound covered by thick vegetation. The brick hunters also disturbed this mound. Scattered ancient bricks are still noticeable all over the mound. Compass bearings from the central mound were south 32° east BARD water tower and north 25° west Cantonment water tower. The mound stands an estithated 60 feet above the natural ground level, though this is difficult to estithate because of the curvature of the hill upon which it is built.

The excavation of the site was started in 1986 and ended in 1992 for span of 3 to 4 months each year. It had exposed the structural remains of Buddhist temple together with the stūpa and Vihāra. The temple was built once more. It reveals five phases of building activity. Two phases of building activity of Vihāra are also traced. The comparative analysis of the phases of building activity of both the temple and the monastery appears that the monastery was built at the third phase of building activity of the temple.

Structural Description: First phase of building activity of the temple: A large structure measuring 43' x 43', has been exposed of the first phase of building activity. An image chamber, measuring 8' x 7' is found in the eastern wall of this large structure. The first phase is covered by the second phase structure. A stone image is discovered in the third phase. The image is not removed from the third phase image chamber. Due to this, the archaeological inquiry is stopped here. The measurement of the temple together with residential area is 111^{1}- 6"x 43". The temple has a small ambulatory passage, measuring 136-^{1}6"x 82-^{1}0". Some pestholes are traced on the circumambulatory path. It appears that the roof covered the temple, probably, dry straw. Mud was used as mortar in the structure. So, it was usual for surviving the structure from the rain. There is an open ground all around the temple. It is also bounded by another wall measuring 182'-10 "x 162-'0". It is 6'0" width. Two architectural evidences have been found in north-east and south-east corner of the outer surrounding walls. Both these structures measure 13' x 13'. There is a hole, measuring 3' x 3', in the middle of both the structures. It is not clear why it was dug. A floor is also traced in the first phase of building activity.

Second phase of building activity: Ground plan of the first phase is remains more or less the same in second phase. During this time, external sides of both the walls of the main passage of the image chamber were widened. In the first phase, it was 5'-0" wide and in the second phase, it is 8'-3". The passage, measuring 12'-6", in between the walls, is not changed. A large vessel and its fragments have been recovered from the second phase floor of the temple. This time, the most worth mention change is that the outer surrounding walls were reduced from 6 feet to 5 feet. Two bends and panel decoration were included on the external face of the outer boundary walls. It is noted that there is no decoration in any portion of the structure except the above-mentioned decoration. The size of the panel is very small and no terracotta plaques have been found in the excavation of the temple area. Besides this, the main temple wall measuring about 16/17 feet, has been discovered undisturbed condition without any decoration. So it appears that there is no decoration on the structure of the Itakhola Murā.

Third phase of building activity: The worth mentions change of the temple area brought into the third phase of building activity. There was a provision for residential area for the monks in the first and second phase. It was totally closed in the third phase. At this time, external sides of both the walls of the main passage of the main image chamber were widened. In the second phase, it was 8'-3" and in the third it is ll'-3". A small group of image chambers were made on the remains of residential area. A Dhyānī Buddha Akṣobhya image has been found in this phase. It is established on 7 feet high from the floor of first phase, on 5 feet high from the floor of second phase and on 3 feet high from the floor of third phase. Besides this, a two feet high platform together with an arched drainage was made in front of the Dhyānī Buddha. Same structures have been found in north-east and south-east corner of external boundary, which was found in second phase. Twelve re-built floors have been traced in the eastern main passage of the main temple. It appears that this passage was used heavily by the devotees.

Fourth phase of building activity: Ground plan of the whole temple had been changed in this phase of building activity. At that time, 43 feet square main temple had been extended up to 57 feet to the north south. Two-image chambers had been added in each extended portion of the temple. At the same time, front image chambers had been closed. Both the walls of the main passage of the temple had been widened up to 13'0". The arched drainage platform of 3rd phase of building activity raised in the 4th phase and it was changed as an attractive second altar. Most probably, a cruciform Stūpa was made on the Western side of the temple and inner side of the external boundary wall. Moreover, three more stūpas are traced on the eastern side of the external boundary wall and near to the staircase of boundary wall. They were protected by a slightly raised.

Fifth phase of building activity: Both the walls of the main passage of the temple had been widened again in the 5th phase of building activity. At this time, a new altar is included on the cruciform stūpa, which is located on the western side of the temple. Another two stūpas were built in between the three stūpas of the 4th phase and staircase of outer boundary wall and both the side of the eastward staircase of outer boundary wall. It is noted that there is no decoration on the body of the main temple but panel decoration is seen on the body of the outer boundary wall. A large number of decoration is seen on the body of the each exposed temple and stūpa. But Itakholā temple is an exceptional one.

Itakholā Viharā: The east-faced Itakholā Vihāra is located to 160 feet due north of the Itakhola temple. It is 130' long and 130' wide. A road was essential for direct communication in hetween the temple, stūpa and Vihāra. However no passage of communication is traced. The Vihāra is established on 7/8 feet height from the temple and stūpa. The only way of

TABLE NO - 2
LARGE SHRINES

Sl. No.	Name of the Mound	Dimensions in feet		Area in square feet	Present height in feet	Finding Structure	Finding antiquites	Excavated/Unexcavated	Present Name	Detation
		N-S	E-W							
1.	Abbas Ali Mura	25	30	750	15	Entrance	Bricks, Pottery	Unexca-valed	May be Shrine.	-
2.	Catpatra Mura	55	105	5,775	35	Entrance, Four massive brick pillars, hall rooms.	Four copperplates, bricks, pottery.	Excavated	Temple complex	llth-12th century A.D
3.	Kutila Mura	280	225	4,6800	10	Massive boundary wall, stircasee ntrance halls	Bricks,pottery,sealings, miniature stupas, Stone sculptures, oil lamps, fireplaces, gold coins.	Excavated	Slupa complex	7th-13th century A.D
4.	Itakhola Muia	150	150	22,500	10	Temple, stupa and small Vihara	Brick, pottery, eight metaled images, coins, terracotta plaques, gold balls.	Excavated	Illakhola Vihara	6th-7th century A.D.

communication of both the establishments is from the 80 feet height to direct eastward plain land. It appears that the temple is earlier than Vihāra. Only 2/3 phases of building activity are traced in the Vihāra establishment The foundation of the Vihāra is higher than the temple. It is noted that a group of image chambers were made on the residential arrangement of the monks in the 3rd phase of building activity. Therefore, the residential arrangement has been transferred to another place in last three phases of building activity of the temple. Actually, there are no phases of building activity in between the two establishments. So it appears to be that the monastery was made in the third phase of building activity of the temple and the monks were rehabilitated in the monastery from the residential area of the temple.

First phase of building activity of the Vihāra: A courtyard, measuring 54' x 54', is discovered in inner side of the Vihāra. Surrounding walls of the courtyard are 3'-2" wide. A well, not brick-built, is traced on the north-eastern corner of the courtyard. It is dug up to 25 feet from the top and at this level, it is stopped due to the brake down of the margin of the wall. This type of well is found on the hilltop in the small monastery for the first time. Probably, a staircase was in the middle of the western wing of the courtyard. A metaled floor is also found in the monastery. A verandah is traced around the courtyard. It is 8'-9" wide. The boundary wall measuring 130' x 130', consists of 19 small chambers in every wings. The opening of these small chambers is toward the verandah. The divider wall of the chambers is 5 to 7.5 feet wide. Front wall and back wall are 6 feet and 8'-3" feet accordingly.

Second phase of building activity: The ruins of the first phase are found on the metaled floor of the same phase that is found still now, it is uncertain how the establishment destroyed. The bricks were removed for reuse from the ruins. Due to this fact, the 3 feet thick layer of broken bricks, brick-dust, and mud mortar are traced. Second phase of building activity is established on this layer. The width of Verandah is reduced to

6" from 8'-9". Some pestholes are found on the wall. At that time, watch room of the main gate was closed and a wall was built there. A chamber of western wing is to be turned as a cash chamber in the second phase of building activity. Three gold balls were found in an earthen vessel in the cash chamber. These balls are now deposited in the local treasury. From this Vihāra. those artifacts were discovered, amongst them, eight metal images, coins, ornamental terracotta plaques etc., are especially important. It appears that there were another phases of building activity in the second phase of the monastery. From the discussion and analysis of the temple, it appears that the establishment of the temple is the beginning of architectural activity of the Mainãmatī-Lalmai area.

SECTION - III

ADMINISTRATIVE SITE

1. PALACE AND TEMPLE OF QUEEN MAINĀMATĪ (ST-1):

The mound containing the palace and temple of Queen Mainãmatī lies on the northern most limits of the Mainãmatī hill and north-western side of Comilla town. Present Gumati river flows to the eastern side of the mound. This slightly elevated flat-topped site, otherwise known as the Rānīr Bungalow, spreads over an area of 700 feet by 600 feet. Excluding the comparatively lower western part and a transverse extension at the north-western corner, the main mound is square with about 550 feet in each sides. It is 40 feet high from the surrounding agricultural land.

The Pakistan Department of Archaeology during the 1965-66-excavation season had completed test excavation. Four trenches exposed parts of a perimeter wall of fired bricks. These were excavated to the depth of thirty-five feet. A 11'-6" thick boundary wall that runs 510 feet from north to south and 500 feet from east to west. A 14 feet wide passage, built into the northern enclosure wall, seems to have provided access to the inner area. Other trenches exposed a number of brick structures in the interior of the flat hilltop. The configuration of the site, with its broad approach way from the south and the evidence of a strong gateway, as well as massive walls, led the officer in charge of the excavation during the 1965-66 season, Ranajith Kumar Sarma, to suggest that the site was a fortress. Adding to the evidence is the popular- name for the site, Maināmatī Mandir. The word Maināmatī is a proper name and the second word specifies the nature of the structure dwelling, palace, or temple; the connotation is that it is a special dwelling place for either the nobility or the gods. Since Maināmatī is not the name of a goddess, the name of the site may be translated as the palace of Maināmatī. The final element of the name, Mandir, occurs nowhere else in the whole range of hills, which indicates the uniqueness of the site in popular perception.

We found the inscriptions issued from Devaparvata. It was described in two ways. The earliest, that of Śrīdhāraṇa Rāta dated second half of the 7th century A.D, states that Kṣīroda River surrounded Devaparvata in which elephant's bathed and innumerable boats floated.[22]

The inscription of Bhavadeva, dated in eighth centuiy, was found in Sālvan Vihāra excavation. The description of Devaparvata and the river scenes are greatly amplified in this inscription. It indicates that Devaparvata has a raised mound and a temple that reaches upward as if to touch the sky. There are other literary allusions suggesting a location on a height of ground.[23]

It is clear that the palace is situated on a hill, possesses lofty buildings. It is protected with boundary wall and is washed by the river Kṣīroda. N.K. Bhattasali found literary and administrative references, though he gives no details, to an old watercourse known as Kṣira, which branched off from the Gumati and ran along the eastern side of the Maināmatī-Lalmai hills where it joined another stream at the southern top of the hills.

Searching for traces of this old river course, nothing was

TABLE NO - 1
MONASTERIES

Sl. No.	Name of the site		Dimensions in feet		Area in square	Present height in feet	Finding Structure	Finding antiquites	Excavat-ed/Unex-	Present Name	Detation
			N-S	E-W							
1.	MainEmatI Mounds. (ST-2)	2A	-	-	Small	10	-	Bricks- Pottery, Broken bricks	Unexa cavaled	-	-
		2B	-	-	"	8	-				
		2C	-	-	"	10	-				
2.	Mainamiati Mounds. (ST-5)	5A	-	-	"	10	-	"	"	-	-
		5B	-	-	"	10	-				
3.	Fakir Mura (ST-7)		30	20	600	12	-	"	"	-	-
4.	Bairagi Miira (ST-10)		20	20	400	8	-	"	"	-	-
5.	BarogacMura(ST-II)		20	20	400	10	-	"	"	-	Bricks are same of tlie Salvan Vhara,
6.	Niranjan Mura (ST-I4)		20	20	400	7	-	"	"	-	"
7.	KhaccarMura (ST-19)		20	20	400	6	-	"	"	-	"
8.	HatiGaraMura(ST-22)		20	20	400	10	-	"	"	-	"
9.	Ujipru Mura (ST-23)		350	250	87,500	15	-	"	"	-	Anand & Bhoj Raja's type Bricks
10.	Dhan Mura (ST-25)		14	20	280	5	-	"	"	-	Salvan Vihara. lypc Bricks
11.	Pukka Mura (ST-26)		20	20	400	20	-	"	"	-	"
12.	Hugni Mura (ST-27)							"	"	-	"
13.	Madina Mura (ST-28)		26	20	520	4	-	"	"	-	"
14.	Salvan Mura (ST-29)		20	15	300		-	"	"	-	"
15.	Itakola Mura (ST-30)		18	20	360	3	-	"	"	-	"
16.	Cila Mura(ST-3I)		125	100	12,500	10	-	"	"	-	"
17.	Rupbani Mura(ST-32)		20	23	460	20	-	"	"	-	"
18.	Arjuna Kliola Mura(ST-33)		-	-	-	4	-	"	"	-	"
19.	Kalidaser Mura (ST-35)		-	-	-	5	-	"	"	-	"
20.	Bairagi Mura North(ST-37)		25	25	625	3	-	"	"	-	"
21.	Caiidi Mura (ST-38)		500	200	1,00,000	15	-	"	"	-	8th-12th century A.D

found within a quarter of a mile of the southern tip. However the old Kṣira River cut past the northern tip of the hills and drained down the western side of the hills towards the south and extensive deposits of sand were found below this mound in a broad track-heading south. About four miles south the track was about one hundred yards in breadth and at least fifteen feet deep. Furthermore, the specific designation of the inscriptions suggest a small site. It is called Kumāramātyādhikaraṇa or "the administrative office of the prince minister "in Śrīdharana Rāta plate, [24] while the Bhavadeva inscription says that the order was issued from *Devaparvata avasthitasrimaj-Jayaskandhāvarit,* or from the blessed camp of victory established at Devaparvata". In one case, Devaparvata is called an administrative office, and in the other, a "Camp of Victory", a conventional designation for a royal residence. Thus, the description of Devaparvata as an executive office and a camp of victory lying beside the river Kṣīroda (which can be located at northern tip of the hills), gives grounds for identifying Rānīr Bungalow Mound (ST-1) as Devaparvata.

The earliest use of the site will not be known until the excavations are completed and reported for the present, the evidence consists of the inscription and the pottery. The earliest reference to Devaparvata occurs in the Śrīdharaṇa Rāta plate, dating second half of the 7th century A.D, and since the Bhavadeva plate is of the eighth or early ninth century. The site was in use at these two points in time and quite Possibly for the intervenine two centuries.

SECTION - IV

THE HILL-TOP SMALL MOUMDS

1. MAINĀMATĪ MOUNDS (ST-2):

No.-2A: This mound is located on a hillock by the western side of Comilla-Brahmanbaria road and only a furlong or so north of Dhaka Chittagong Road. It is about 30 feet high from the surrounding agricultural land. The central portion is higher than the sides. Northern and western sides are steep but the eastern and southern sides are gradually descending down. At present, the mound is covered with grass and small trees. It is unexcavated.

No.-2B: It is situated to the south of Maināmatī Mound No.-2A. This Mound is only a few feet high from the plain land. It is close to the Dhaka Chittagong Trunk Road. Narrow road runs north to south through this mound eastern edge of the mound is higher than the other sides. It is also covered with grass and bushes. It is unexcavated site.

No.-2C: This site is very close to mound No.-lA and its southern side is very close to the Dhaka-Chittagong Trunk Road. There are found ancient bricks and potsherds on the surface of the mound. It is also unexcavated.

2. MAINĀMATĪ MOUNDS (ST-5)

No.-5A: This site is situated to the west of the Brigadier's Bungalow and is approachable by an unmetalled road from the metalled cantonment road which runs south to north following the eastern slope of the Maināmatī hill. It is not a big mound but about 100 feet high from the surrounding paddy field. The top of the mound is almost flat. Bushes and small trees now cover this mound.

No.-SB: This mound is located to the southern side of Maināmatī mound No.-5A and is close to the Cantonment Road. Northern portion is higher than the other sides but a few new constructions by the Military have reduced its area. The southern slope extends up to the Brigadier's Bungalow.

3. FAKIR MURĀ(ST-7):

This mound is situated about 150 yards directly east of Cārpatra Murā and southern side of Dhaka-Comilla Road. The measurements of the area are 30 yards north south and 20 yards east west on the top of a low hill. Some broken old bricks and a few fragments of pottery were found from this area. It is about 50 to 60 feet high from the surrounding ground level. Dense bramble bushes cover the site. Moreover, the hill had been hollowed out during the Second World War for the construction of amunition store and debris further obscured older remains. The name supplied by a resident suggests that the hill was associated with a religious ascetic.

4. BAIRĀGI MURĀ (ST-10):

This site is located on the highest hill on the south-western corner of the Lalmai hills and one-third of a mile from the Caṇḍī Murā bazar. This small mound is six feet high and is approxithately 20 yards in diameter. The hole of the hilltop has been brought under cultivation. Ancients broken bricks are distributed on the hill. No other antiquities have been found from this mound.

5. BAROGAC MURĀ (ST-11):

This site is located on the edge of the western range of the top of the hill and western side of Ānanda Vihāra. It is cone shaped mound rising about six feet above the hill plateau. The mound is roughly circular and measures about 20 yards in diameter with a depression in its center. Bushes and grass cover the mound. Many bricks and brick bats have been found from the surface of the site. These are of the same appearance as the Sālvan Vihāra bricks. The site takes its name from a large tree (baro-large,gac-tree).

6. NIRAÑJAN MURĀ (ST-14):

This mound is located on the crest of the western hills and western side of the Rupbān Kanyā Vihāra. The diameter of the circular ruins is approxithately 20 yards. It is nearly seven feet high from the surrounding ground level. Ancient broken bricks have been found over the surface of the mound. These type of bricks found at Sālvan Vihāra. No other artifacts were found.

7. KHACCAR MURĀ (ST-19):

This site lies on the western edge of the range and western side of Itākhola Murā and northern side of Kotbāri Road. It is roughly round in shape with a diameter of 20 yards. It is about six feet high above the surrounding ground level. Top of the site has a slight depression. Old broken bricks are found on the surface of the mound. Local people reported that the site had been given its name because the Army grazed Mule (Khaccar) on the hilltop when the area was the part of the British Cantonment.

8. HĀTI-GĀRĀ MURĀ (ST-22):

Location: It lies on the west of Kotbāri and southern side of the Comilla-Kaliibazar Road. Grass and creepers cover it. From the top of the site, compass readings were taken south 88° west to the BARD water tower and north 13° west to the Comilla cantonment boundary pillar number 43(C.B.P. No.43)

Structural Description: It seems to be an undisturbed site. The Hatigara Murā site consists of the ruins of a brick structure that formed a cone-shaped mound on the top of the prominent hills. It measures approxithately 20 yards north to south and the same distance east to west This mound is about 40 feet high from the surrounding cultivated land. Numerous broken ancient bricks of the type found at Sālvan Vihāra were scattered over the crest of the hill as well as being concentrated on the raised part of the site. A slight pression is marked the center of the site. No other cultural materials could be found.

9. UJIRPUR MURĀ (ST-23):

Ujirpur site is located about one mile west of the Sālvan Vihāra and to the western edge of the Maināmaṭī hill. It lies also in between the Hatigārā Murā and Pukkā Murā a mile to the south west of Kotbari. The mound measures 350 yards × 250 yards and 100 feet high from the western paddy field. It is gradually slope towards the west. It seems to be intact. Some ancient bricks have found on the surface of the mound. Ordinary bricks of various sizes and potsherds, some with designs as at Ānanda Rāja's palace and Bhoja Raja's palace mounds, were also noticed.

10. DHAN MURĀ (ST-25):

This mound is located on top of one of the hills on the western side of Maināmatī- Lalmai hill range. It lies on northern side of Pukkā Murā and northwestern side of Sālvan Vihāra. It is cone-shaped mound and is about five feet high above ground level. The mound measures approxithately 20 yards north to south and 14 yards east to west. On the top of the mound a pit about 4 feet deep had been dug, revealing bricks of the Sālvan Vihāra type, lying in layers as though they had once formed a part of a wall. No other cultural material was found on the site.

11. PUKKĀ MURĀ (ST-26):

Location: This small circular mound is situated about one mile to the south of Ujirpur Murā and on the western fringe of the hill range. Compass readings of north 470 east to the BARD water tower and directly north to the Cantonment water tower were recorded. It is covered with grass and herbs.

Structural Description: This smaller circular mound, is in cone shaped on the top of one of the hills, measures 20 yards north to south and same east to west. It is more than 100 feet high from the western agricultural land. Eastern portion of the mound is under cultivation but less disturbed. On the eastern slope and continuing eastward from the crown of the hill, thin scatters of tiny potsherds were collected. It is apparent that bricks of Sālvan Vihāra type form part of the mound.

12. HUGNĪ MURĀ (ST-27):

This site is located directly one-half mile south of Pukkā Murā and western edge of the hilltop of the Maināmatī-Lalmai hill range. The grass and bushes cover it. A few scattered sherds of pottery and fragments of bricks have been found on the southern face of the hill. It marks a former building site at Hugnī

Murā. A brick has been recovered from the site measures 19 to 20 inches in length. Hundreds of them are now buried under the earth where the men were working. A few brickbats are visible in nearby bushes. No other artifacts were discovered. The mound is apparently of little archaeological interest.

13.MADINĀ MURĀ (ST-28):

It is on top of the western edge of the Maināmatī-Lalmai hill range and southern side of Hugnī Murā. The apex of the hill was covered with a mound of tumbled bricks. It is three to four feet high above the ground level. The mound measures 20 yards east to west and 26 yards north to south. There is a depression in the center of the mound due to brick hunting. Various sizes of old bricks have been revealed from this site. Similar bricks are also found in Sālvan Vihāra. No other cultural material was discovered.

14. SABURĀ MURĀ (ST-29):

This mound is located on the western edge of the Lalmai hills and southern side of Madinā Murā containing brick remains. The mound measures an area 20 yards north to south and 15 yards east to west. The centre of the mound has depression in the middle, while there was a profusion of bricks on the hilltop. No other cultural materials were traced here.

15. ITĀKHOLĀ MURĀ-SMALL (ST-30):

This site lies on the top of the hill on the western edge of Lalmai range and southern side of Saburā Murā. It was covered with bushes. Heaps of old broken bricks were observed among the bushes in an area about 18 × 20 yards. It was three feet high from the ground level. The name of the site indicates that it is a place where bricks (Ita) and fields (Khola) are to be found.

16. CILĀ MURĀ (ST-31):

The mound is situated about three miles south-east of Sālvan Vihāra and on the eastern side of Maināmatī -Lalmai hill range. It is a small mound and is only 10 feet high from the surrounding paddy fields. The area is about 125 × 100 square yards. It is noticed that pottery and bricks are profusely scattered on the surface of the mound. A fragment of a stone image was here. This fragment suggests that this mound may be a temple.

17. RUPBANI MURĀ (ST-32):

Location: The site is located about 5 miles south-west of Sālvan Vihāra, four miles to the south-east of Pukka Murā and three quarters of a mile south of Adinā Murā. Rūpbānī Murā is a hill topside on the western edge of the Maināmatī- Lalmai hill range. The mound measures 400 × 250 square yards, and about 150 feet high from the western paddy field and adjacent to the Nalua village. Compass bearings taken from the center of the site gave readings of north 100 east on the BARD water tower and north 90 west on the highest part of the Adinā Murā mosque

Structural description: The site is covered with grass and shrubbery. It seems to be that the brick ruins stretched about 23 yards from east to west and about 20 yards from north to south. The site rose to two separate elevations, one on the east and the other to the west. The general elevation of the built-up portion could not readily be determined. The center of the site was marked by a depression, around which exposed bricks and part of a brick wall were observed. The mound is intact and is of sufficient promise.

Antiquities: Bricks of various sizes and potsherds were visible on the surface. No trace of any other cultural materials could be found.

Legends: Local people reported that the name of the hill was derived from a Muslim beauty by the name of Rūpbānī who retired to the hill. She was known as the daughter of an important ruler in the area. No further details were available from the people.

18. ARJUNAKHOLĀ MURĀ (ST-33):

This mound is located on the hill top on the western edge

of Lalmai range. This site is about one and one-quarter miles north of Caṇḍī Murā bazar and southern side of Rūpbānī Murā. This mound has been dug up and brought under cultivation. The brick fragments that interfered with cultivation were collected and piled up around the trees and stūpa on the hilltop. These types of bricks were found at Sālvan Vihāra. No other artifacts were discovered.

19. KĀLIDĀSER MURĀ (ST-35):

This site lies on a hilltop on the western side of the Lalmai range. It is southern side of the Arjunkholā Murā and is about three-quarter of a mile north of Caṇḍī Murā bazar along the footpath running beside the western foot of the hills. Scattering of Sālvan Vihāra type bricks found at the western foot of the hill that had been carried down in an earth slide from the top of the mound several years earlier. About 200 feet southwest of the western foot of Kālidāser Murā, part of a broken brick wall was found and exposed in an old drainage channel. No other antiquities were discovered.

20. BAIRĀGĪR MURĀ (ST-37):

Location: The mound is located about one mile northwest of Kutilā Murā and to the west of the Mainamatī Hills. The size and elevation of the mound is difficult to determine since it is overgrown with waist bushes. It is also on the top of the hills. Compass bearings taken from the center of the mound gave the following readings—north 80 west cantonment water tower and south 300 east BARD water tower.

Structural Description: Luckily this mound has been saved from the contractors in their search for bricks at the time of Second World War. The scattered broken bricks marking the site stretches in diameter. A pit had been dug near the highest point of the site. A disturbed structure of a wall had been found in the pit up to a depth of five feet. The sizes of the bricks were of the Sālvan Vihāra type. It appears to be promising for scientific excavation.

Legend: The local people say that the hill was named Bairāgī because of its association with some reputed saint who has lived on its top.

21. CAṆḌĪ MURĀ (ST-38):

The site, Caṇḍī Murā, is located to the southern edge of Lalmai hill, south-west of Lalmai Railway station and about two miles south-east of RupbanT Murā .The mound is very near to Comilla -Barura Road. It is very high and extensive mound. The mound is almost 100 feet height and 500 × 200 square yards extent.

The two temples measure twelve feet square and rise to a height of about fifteen feet on the top of the mound, are side by side, facing west, each having an entrance from the west. Scattered bricks found here and there on the mound. The structures of these temples have been cracked of due to the penetration of roots of the trees. The bushes and trees cover the mound. Besides the standing temple structures, there is a brick boundary wall whose remains can be traced that encloses an area thirteen yards by fifteen yards. This is called Caṇḍī Murā after the name of Caṇḍī for whole a temple is constructed on its top.

There is a another small mound measuring five yards by ten yards, northern side of the two temples. Another mound has been found about thirty five yards to the north east of second mound. It measures ten yards by fifteen yards. Both of these mounds are enclosed by the boundary wall, are covered with broken bricks of the same type that were found in Sālvān Vihāra.

More than these shrines the archaeologist is attracted by the large number of potsherds and bricks found in area as at Ānanda Rāja's and Bhoja Rāja's palaces and Rūpbānī Murā mounds. Fossil wood abounds in this area. At the eastern foot of this mound is a tank from which were recovered some years ago two images of black basalt which are now worshipped in the temple of Caṇḍī. One represents Mañjūvara, a variety of

Mañjūśrī Bodhisttva and an emanation of the five Dhyānī Buddhas, who is highly placed in the Mahāyanist pantheon. The second was an image of Sūrya, a Hindu deity. Both are judged by Ramachandran to resemble sculpture of the Pāla period, which covers four centuries, from the middle of the eighth to the mid twelfth. When the images from Caṇḍī Murā are compared with published studies of Bengal sculpture, both images appear to have been carved in the late Pāla period, about the 11th or 12th century[26]. Clearly the existing structures have consistently been used for religious devotions, though the images installed in the buildings have varied.

A temple of Caṇḍī from which the mound is known as Caṇḍī Murā seems to have once stood at this site. Only deep excavation can reveal the fact and may throw further light on the *Paṭṭikere Caṇḍīvarabhavane Caṇḍī* of Aṣṭasahasrikā Prajñā Paramita, dated 1015 A.D., now in the Cambridge University Library

SECTION - V

NON-STRUCTURAL SITES

1. SINGĀRA MURĀ (ST-3):

This mound is situated to the western side of Army Bungalow, and northern portion of Maināmatī-Lalmai hills. This site is 100 to 150 yards north of the Comilla to Daudkhandi road, about one-half mile west of its junction with the Comilla-Debidvar road. The ground of this site is level with land on the eastern, northern and southern sides, and drops away to an excavated water tank to the west. It was very much disturbed by the modern construction and is now under cultivation. A huge number of ancient broken bricks and potsherds were scattered over the surface of the site.

2. TĀKKĀ MURĀ (ST-34):

This site is located on the eastern side of the Lalmai hills and in between the Cillā Murā and Balagazir Murā. It is a large flat area covered with broken bricks, though there is no evidence of architectural remains or any built-up area. This site was heavily disturbed by the activities of the Burma Oil Company drilling crews, who reportedly sank a test hole in this location.

3. BĀLĀGĀZĪR MURĀ (ST-36):

The mound is located about 6 miles southeast of Sālvan Vihāra and south-east corner of Lalmai range and about a mile to the north-west of Lalmai Railway Station. It is a low uneven mound of irregular configuration stretching 125 yards from east to west and approxithately the same distance north to south. The mound is 5 to 10 feet high from surrounding level. On the eastern slope of the mound are found an old brick wall and many scattered broken bricks. The surface of the mound is thickly covered with potsherds. It was reported that a Muslim warrior about 250 had seized the land years ago and when his descendants left, potters occupied the site, accounting for the dense distribution of potsherds.

SECTION-VI

WATER RESERVOIRS

1. ĀNANDA RĀJAR DĪGHI (ST-13):

This Dighi (tank) is located directly on the eastern side of the monastery, Ānanda Vihāra. It lies an estithated 100 yards east of the eastern wall of the monastery. It is a large excavated and embanked water reservoir. The rectangular tank embankment ran for 500 yards from north to south and 200 yards from east to west, enclosing an area in excess of 20 acres. The embankment still stood 20 to 25 feet above the exterior ground level, while part of interior dropped to 25 feet below ground level and may have deeper, for water covered part of the interior. No antiquities were found nor any reported by the local people.

2. BHOJ VIHĀRA DĪGHI (ST-17):

This site is located due east of the Bhoj Vihāra. It is a large excavated and embanked water reservoir. This Dīghi (tank) is estithated 125 yards distance from the eastern wall of the monastery. The tank is approxithately square, stretching 300 yards on both its north-south and east- west axes. The inside of the tank had been dug. It is difficulty to determine the original depth. At present, the thick embankment is 15 to 20 feet high above the surrounding ground level, though it is breached in various places. No cultural materials were found on the embankments or on the parts of the interior that were searched. The local people were asked if any thing had been found in the interior of the tank, they replied that they knew nothing.

SECTION-VII

THE HISTORICAL RELATIONS OF THE SITES OF MAINĀMATĪ

No evidence has been, correctly found the peoples who lived in Mainamatī-Lalmai area. But the assemblage of the ancient and archaeological sites show its ancient historic relation with the present. Above fifty sites are traced in Maināmatī-Lalmai hill range. Out of fifty, thirty-eight brick structures were traced and the Department of Archaeology, Bangladesh, excavates some of them. A number of archaeological findings have been recovered from those sites. It is known to all from Gunaighar copperplate grant of Vainya Gupta that there was a Buddhist monastery in somewhere of Comilla district by the time of Vainya Gupta. Maināmatī copperplate grant of Vīradhara Deva of 13th century indicates that 17 patakas of land were granted to the illustrious lord Vāsudeva. From the 6th century A.D. to 13th century A.D, there was a practice to donate temples and Buddhist monasteries. Due to this fact, an extraordinary rich culture was developed in Maināmatī-Lalmai hill range. The greatest assemblage of ancient Buddhist remains in Bangladesh lies in Maināmatī hill range.

From the sixth century through the thirteenth, two major historic phases can be distinguished. The construction and successive enlargement of Buddhist Monasteries and the inscriptions of Vainyagupta, Śrīdharana Rāta, the Khaḍgas and the early Devas marked the first phase. The inscriptions in form to us that it was dated from the beginning of the sixth century to the end of the eight-century A.D. The second phase may be defined by the structure of smaller temples and by the Candra and later Deva dynastic inscriptions. The inscriptions range from the beginning of the tenth century to the and of the thirteenth century A.D.

In the first phase, there is a good evidence that they built a large Buddhist centre in Maināmatī region. A large number of artifacts were found during excavation in various sits. These include copper-plates, silver and gold coins, bronze images of Buddha and other Buddhist deities, bronze caskets, bronze utensils and other metal objects, terracotta seals and sealing, pottery, terracotta plaques and a number of various other objects accumulated over the centuries. Out of the seven copper-plates from Sālvan Vihāra, one of the themes has been found in first occupation level, received less attention due to its decayed and highly damaged conditions. But a beautiful seal, bears recumbent bull below which is a single line of inscription, which has been read as "Mahārāja Śrī Vainya Guptasya". As the appearance of the seal and the style and direction of the writing on the plate all closely resemble the published Gunaighar copper-plate of Vainyagupta. This Gunaighar is eighteen miles distance from Sālvan Vihāra. This Gunaighar-plate was dated in 508 AD. The presence of the Sālvan Vihāra plate of Vainyagupta suggests that the Sālvan Vihāra can be dated back to the reign of Vainyagupta at the beginning of the sixth century AD.

Two gold coins are belonging to the imperial Guptas in the earliest date. One of them, found from Sālvan Vihāra, depict on its obverse an uncaparisoned horse infront of a bent post placed on reverse a female figure. This has been identified as Aśvamedha coin of Samudrā Gupta (c.335-375 AD).

Three hoards of gold and silver coins were found inside clay pots buried beneath an early floor level. The first hoard contains one of Candra Gupta II (376-415 A.D.) and two of imitation Gupta coins. The second hoard contained 52 silver coins and the third hoard contains 172 silver coins. Both second and third hoard contains the same kind of coins. There were found a dozen of post-Gupta imitation Archer type of gold coins from Sālvan Vihāra. According to the legends on the coins, this most probably were issued by the early Deva rulers of Sathataṭā Maṇḍala. A large number of silver coins were found from Maināmatī excavations of Sālvan Vihāra and Ānanda Rāja's Place Mound with the legends of Paṭṭikera from the evidences and their large number, association and findspot, the coins were issued by the powerful and prosperous ruler of Samataṭa most probably Śrī Ānanda Deva of Deva dynasty.

From the evidence of the coins it has come to light that Sālvan Vihāra and Ānanda Vihāra were the constructions and successive enlargements of Buddhist monasteries, which may be dated in 6th to 8th century A.D. From the preliminary examination and the excavation reports, there were traced seven large monasteries named Army Bungalow Vihāra, Ānanda Vihāra, Rupbānkanya Vihāra, Bhoj Vihāra, Kotbari Vihāra, RupteruiVihāra and Sālvan Vihāra. These seven large monasteriescould be dated in sixth to eighth centuries A.D. when Buddhist religion, political and socio-cultratural relations where in prosperous and increasing position in Buddhist world only in Maināmatī area but also in all over the ancient India.

In the second phase, the 10th to 13th cenruty, Maināmatī-Lalthati area lost its political autonomy for a time and the support for the monasteries fell away as Vaiṣṇava shrines gained in their place. The ninth century is in dark position till today for the lack of authentic informations. The copper-plate grants of Candra transferring property in Samataṭa Manndala were issued from Vikramapura forty miles to the west from Maināmatī. The Candra were the rulers of Vaṅga, Vaṅgāla, Candrdvipa,

Samataṭa and Harikela region. But their principal seat was in Vikramapura. It seems to appear that the Candra rulers neglected Devaparvata, Kripura, Vasantapura and Karmanta. By the time of Candra kings, the size of the buildings and the bugets were reduced. It is noted that the amount of the danated lands was also reduced. The Maināmatī grants of Laḍaha Candra were recored the lands for the small shrines. The grant of Govinda Candra was recorded the land for small shrine. The grant of Roṇavaṅkamalla Harikāla Deva was recorded the land for small monasteres. And the Viradhara Deva grant was recorded land for the small shrine. So, no evidence has been found in second phase for the large establishment in Maināmatī-Lalmai hill range till today.

An interpretation of the rains in the Maināmatī-Lalmai hill range has been built up. The representation of thirty-eight brick shructure has been given in this chapter. Most of their functions were identified, using criteria of size, configuration, and location. It was argned that the early indenpedent rulers with Maināmatī hills had been generous supporters of the large Buddhist monasteries and the from the time of the Candras when Samataṭa was incorporated for a time in a large kingdom patronage was less generous and directed to the Vaiṣṇava shrine, Brahmans and small Tāntric monastry. From the discussion of the above mentioned sites, it has come to light that gthe ruīns of Maināmatī-Lalmai hill range were mostly used for the religious purpose from 6th to 13th century A. D.

NOTES AND REFERENCES

1. Ramchandran, T.N, "Recent Archaeological Discoveries along the Maināmatī and Lalmai Ranges,Tippera District." B.C. Law Volume, ed. D.R. Bhanderkar,Part-II,Poona,1946, p. 220.
2. The exposed northern wing measures 624 feet. The western wing has also been exposed except the south -west corner, which lies under metaled road. There fore its exact measurement cannot be ascertained at present.
3. The copper plate inscriptions of Śrī Bhavadeva of the early Deva

dynasty are known: 1. Maināmatī plate of Śrī Bhavadeva, year 12, unpublished and (2.) A. S. B, Calcutta plate of Śrī Bhavadeva of Devaparvata, year 2, published by D.C. Sircar, J.A.S.B.L, Vol.-XVII, No.-2, 1951, p. 83.

4. Sircar, D.C., The Kailan copperplate Inscription of Śrīdharana Rāta of Samataṭa, I.H.Q, Vol.- XX1II, 1947, pp. 121 f.
5. Bhattasali, N.K., in H.B, ed. R.C. Majumdar, Vol.-11, p. 217.
6. Bhattasali,, N.K, Iconography, P. II.7. Dani, A.H, P.A, No. 3, pp.2 3, 44; J.V.R.M, Vol.-5. 1976-77, pp. 53-4.
8. Bhattasali, N.K., Iconography, p. II; 1 HQ, Vol.- IX., p. 282 ff, V.R.S.M, NO-5, Rajshahil, p. 10 ff.
9. Ramchandran, T.N., B.C. Law Volume, ed. D.R. Bhanderkar, Part-II, Poona, 1946, p. 225
10. Ibid, p. 225.
11. Barrie, M. Morrison, L.C.C.E.B, New York, 1977, p. 22
12. Ibid, p. 24.
13. Bhattasali, N.K., IBBS, pp. 4, 6, 10.
14. Sirkar, D.C., J.A.B.L, XVII, 1951.PP 83-94
15. Dani, A.H, IP, Oxford, 1963, p. 135.
16. Khan, F.A., Maināmatī, p. 31
17. Dani,A.H., L.P., Oxford, 1963, p. 119.
18. Rashid, H, E.H.S.E.B, p. 110.
19. Ramachandran, T.N., "Recent Archaeological Discoveries along the Maināmatī and Lalmai Ranges, Tippera District", in B.C. Law Volume, Ed. D.R. Bhandarkar, Part-2, Poona : The Bhandarkar Oriental Researcher Institute, 1946, p. 229.
20. Barua, B.M. and Chakravarti, P.B., "Meher Plate of Dāmodaradeva", E.I, Vol.- XXVII, 1947, p. 183.
21. BLK, Vol.-1, No.-1, Dhaka, January, 1975, p. 58.
22. Sircar, D.C., The Kailan copper-plate inscription of King Śrīdharana Rāta of Samataṭa", I.H.Q, Vol.-XXI1I, 1947, pp. 221-41 and Bhattasali, N.K., "The new Kailān plate of Śrīdharana Rāta", I.H.Q, Vol.-XXII, 1946, pp. 169-71.
23. Sircar, D.C., "Copper plate inscription of King Bhavadeva", J.A.S.L, Vol.-XVII, 1951.pp. 83-94.
24. Sircar, D. C., I.H.Q, Vol.-XXII, 1947, p. 222.
25. Sircar, D. C., "Copper plate inscription of King Bhavadeva". J.A.S.L, Vol.-XVII, 1951, p. 93.
26. Bannerjee, J.N., "Religion: Iconography", in H.B, ed. Majunder, R.C., The University of Dacca, 1943, 1: 469-70 and plate 22; also Bhattasali, N.K., I.B.B.S, 1929, p. 170 and Plate-6a.

CHAPTER - III

ASSEMBLAGE OF SANSKRIT INSCRIPTIONAL COPPER-PLATE GRANTS AND IMAGES OF MAINĀMATĪ AND NEARBY AREAS

INTRODUCTION

Maināmatī excavations have unearthed a large number of antiquities, which are valuable artifacts for reconstructing the historical co-relations in the time and space of this area. For reconstructing such historical co-relations, epigraphs are the most dependable and inforthative sources. Various types of epigraphs are recovered from Maināmatī-Lalmai hill range, which include copperplate grants, coins, stone image inscriptions, terracotta seals and sealing etc. The copperplate grants discovered from Maināmatī are twelve in all. Some of these were unearthed during actual excavations on the sites. Seven copperplate grants have been found from Sālvan Vihāra, four grants from Cārpatra Murā and one was accidentally found from Dhaka-Comilla Highway area when the work of digging the earth for road construction was going on. Out of the seven copperplate grants from Sālvan Vihāra, five are heavily corroded and impossible to decipher. The remaining two also are only partly deciphered due to corrosion by Kamala Kanta Gupta [vide-bibliography]. Out of the four copperplate grants from Cārpatra Murā, A.H Dani deciphers three. S.B.Bhattacharjee deciphers the remaining one. H.T. Colebrooke deciphers the one found during the highway construction.

Seven other epigraphs- three copper-plate grants of Śrī Candradeva (Candra dynasty) and four stone image inscrip tions-which are found not actually from the area under study but from a nearby area are also included here in this chapter because they provided good material for reconstruction of the dynastic chronology and historical co-relation of the ruling dynasties of Samataṭa Maṇḍala.

The Sanskrit texts of all of these copperplate grants and stone image inscriptions (along with some corrections, independent translation and my own comments) are included here.

SECTION-1

THE MAINĀMATĪ COPPER-PLATE OF SRI LADAHA CANDRADEVA

Introduction

This copper- plate was traced accidentally in a mound known as **Cārpatra Murā** ('the mound of the four plates') in 1954 A.D. This mound is located on the western side of Comilla town, southern side of Dhaka-Comilla road, near the Kutilā Murā and Brigade Headquarters of the Bangladesh Regiment. It is now deposited in the custody of the Directorate of Archaeology, Bangladesh.

This is a single plate inscribed on both the sides. It bears a seal attached to the top from which it projects about and causes a break in the middle of the first four lines on the obverse and first two lines on the reverse. In line 55 i.e. line 24 on reverse the seal, attached to the top, is described as the *Dharmacakra Mudrā* or the 'Emblem of the Wheel of Law[1]. If consists of a number of concentric circles. The innermost is in the upper part, which represents a wheel flanked on two sides by two small antelopes. It is well known that this type of representation is found in the copper plate of Pāla. The margin of

PLATE NO. 1

MAINAMATI COPPERPLATE GRANT OF LADAHA CANDRADEVA OBVERSE

the seal is marked by a beaded border, which goes around the overhead projection. There are forty-one beads excluding those on the projection, which has ten extra beads. The space of the seal has been divided into two parts by a line of inscription. It reads *ŚrīLaḍaha Candra Devah.* The lower portion of the seal has a floral motif. The inscription consists of 62 lines of which 31 are engraved on the obverse and 31 on the reverse.

The text begins with benedictory *"Oṁ Oṁ namo bhagabate Vdāsudevāya"* then 9 verses praise the origin and the ancestors and then in 10 verses are described the birth, victories, glory and religious performances of the donor king **Laḍaha Candra;** the prose protion that follows describes the exact location and area of the gifted land with markers of the boundaries and indication of authorities and powers over the land of gift and then five benedictive and imprecatory verses; the plate ends with the indication of the date of donation and witness.

The donee is **Laḍaha Bhaṭṭāraka** with reference to **Vāsudeva Bhaṭṭāraka.** The purpose is of achieving merits and fame for his parents and himself. The date is 30th day of the month **Jyaiṣṭh** in the Sixth regnal year of the king.

The characters are of the type of Northern **Nāgari,** which is allied to the orthography variety found in the copper-plates of the later Pālas and current in North-eastern India towards the close of the tenth and beginning of the eleventh century A.D. Some differences noticed in the characters of the Candras and Pālas are stylistic, depending upon different hands or school. They do not show any regional variation between the character of North and East Bengal. The language is Sanskrit. There are altogether 24 verses, which are composed in a variety of meters viz. ***Vasantatilaka, Śārdulavikṛḍita, Upajati, Anuṣṭubh, Visamavrṭṭa, Sikharini, Sragdharā*** and ***Puspitagra.***

TEXT

श्रीलडहचन्द्रदेवः

[१] ओम् ओम् नमो भगवते वासुदेवाय।।

ज्योतिस्तुषारशिशिरं च्युतमत्रिनेत्रा-
[२] च्चन्द्रः स तत्क्षणमभूवनैकदीपः।
वङ्शस्ततः प्रववृते पृथिवीप[३]तीनां
सारोत्तरश्च सरलश्च समुन्नतश्च ।।१।।
विश्वोपकारस्य परो[४]विधाता
धर्म्यात् पथश्चाच्युत एव जात्या।
महेश्वरश्चाजननादतो (ऽ) भूद्-
देवत्रयात्मे[५]व स चन्द्रवङ्शः ।।२।।
तस्याभ्युन्नतिशालिनः प्रचयिनो वङ्शस्य मुक्तामणिः
ख्यातः क्ष्मावलयैकना[६]यकतया त्रैलोक्यचन्द्रो नृपः।
अक्षुद्रः परिशुद्धिमानपशतत्रासः सुवृत्तो गुण-
ग्राह्यः पुण्य[७]तमो बभूव जगतः प्रीत्यै च भूत्यै च यः।।३।।

सम्पाद्यते प्रतिनरश्रुतिपावनीभि-
रद्यापि यस्य गुणिनो[८]गुणसङ्कथाभिः।
आनन्दबाष्पभरमन्थरपक्ष्मचक्षुः
पर्युल्लसत्पुलककञ्चुकमङ्मङ्गम्।।४।।

तस्मात् म[९]हावनिभृतां शरणादनन्त-
भोगास्पदात् समकरादुदधेरिवेन्दुः।
श्रीचन्द्र इत्यजनि काञ्चनकान्ति[१०]चौर-
स्तन्वन् श्रियं जगति काञ्चन काञ्चनेयः।।५।।

प्राग्ज्योतिषेश्वरवधूजनलोचनानां
बाष्पव्ययव्रतम[११]खण्डितमाततान।
गौडावरोधवनिताधरपल्लवानि
चक्रे च यो विगलितस्मितकुड्मलानि।।६।।
राज्ञस्त[१२]स्य पवित्रितोभयकुलः कल्याणचन्द्रः सुतः
प्रख्यातो विमलोज्ज्वलैस्त्रिभुवनालङ्कारभूतैर्गुणैः।
जात्या[१३]धर्ममयो महावनिभृतां तुङ्गैः शिरोभिर्धृतः
सद्भिः सेव्यतमः प्रवाह इव यस्त्रैस्त्रोतसः पावनः।।७।।

[१४]म्लैछीनान्नयनेषु येन जनितः स्थूलो[ऽ]श्रुकोशव्ययो
गौडीनां स्मितचन्द्रिकाविरहिणः सृष्टाश्च वक्त्रेन्दवः।
[१५]आतस्तार निजैर्यशोभिरमलैरष्टावनष्टोदयै-
र्यश्चैताः शशभृत्करैरिव घनत्यागप्रकाशैर्दिशः।।८।।

लक्ष्मी[१६]रिवात्यन्तमनोज्ञरूपा तस्यानुरूपा पुरुषोत्तमस्य।
प्रिया तदाराधानकेलिकल्या कल्याणदेवीति शुभा ब[१७]भूव।।९।।

कुन्तीव सत्यवाचं रुद्राणीवात्मजं महासेनम्।
सूते स्म लडहचन्द्रं सा खलु देवी महार्हगुणम्।।१०।।

दिव्यो दु[१८]न्दुभिरुन्ननाद ननृतुर्विद्याधरश्रेणयः
पुष्पञ्च त्रिदिवात् पपात मधुकृत्क्वाणोर्मिवाचालितम्।
जाते यत्र व[१९]वुः सुखाश्च मरुतस्ताश्च प्रसेदुर्दिशो
देवी दूरमुदश्वसत् किमपरं सार्द्धं समुद्रैश्च भूः।।११।।

काष्ठां प्रापदहोभि[२०]रेव परमां विद्योपविद्यासु यः
क्रूरान् यश्च षडान्तरानिव शतं बाह्यानजैषीद् अरीन्।
भर्तुर्यस्य च रञ्जितास्त्रि[२१]भुवनोद्गीतैर्गुणानां गणै-
र्गीश्च श्रीश्च वसुन्धारा च वशगास्तिस्त्रो(ऽ)प्यभूवन्निमाः।।१२।।

प्रयुज्य तांस्तान् गुणवान् गुणा[२२]न् यो
महाफलं वृद्धिमवाप्य चैषाम्।
भोक्ता च गोप्ता च नयैकचक्षु-
रभूद् भुवः सागरमेखलायाः।।१३।

लक्ष्मीमूर्जि[२३]तविक्रमो बलिज्यप्रख्यातवीर्योदय-
श्चक्रे यः पुरुषोत्तमो निजगुणैस्तैस्तैरनन्यानुगाम्।
अङ्गेष्वर्पयिता[२४]न्च भूतिमनत्रां कामं विजेता च यो
दुर्गायाः करमग्रहीद् गिरिभुवो भूतेशतामास्थितः।।१४।।

योऽन्तर्मग्नश्च पारं पर[२५]ममुपगतश्चाशु विद्यानदीनां
दोष्णा यः ख्यातवीर्यो जगदवनमहानाटिकानायकेन।
क्षोणीभृन्मौलिमालाप[२६]रिमलसुरभीभूतपादाब्जरेणु-
र्यश्चानन्यातपत्राम् अकृत वसुमतीम् अप्रयासाद् अहोभिः।।१५।।

वाराणस्यामयासीत् सहगी[२७]स्सुतया शम्भुनाध्यासिताया-
मस्नासीत् तत्र गाङ्गे पयसि गतमलः स्वान् अतर्प्पीत् पितृंश्च।
पाणौ पाणौ द्विजानामथ[२८]कनकमदात् तस्य को वेत्ति संख्यां
संख्यावान् एक एव त्रिभुवनतिलकः क्ष्मापतिर्धिक् तदन्यान्।।१६।।

PLATE NO. 1

MAINAMATI COPPERPLATE GRANT OF LADAHA CANDRADEVA REVERSE

साक्षाद् अक्षतधीर[२९]यष्ट दशभिर्यत्राश्वमेधैः स्वभूः
श्रीकण्ठः सह दुर्गया प्रमुदितो याम् अध्यवात्सीत् स्वयम्।
गङ्गाक्षालितपापपङ्कवि[३०]शदां तामेत्य वाराणसीं
सस्नौ च प्रददौ च कोशमखिलं धर्मानुरागो नृपः।।१७।।

सुखं स्नात्वा कृत्वा तदनु पितृसन्तर्प्प[३१]णविधिं
विधिज्ञः सम्भेदे शुचिपयसि गङ्गायमुनयोः।
द्विजानां तर्षार्त्तिं घनकनकधारावितरणान्
महाभूतः सो-

TEXT

REVERSE SODE

[१]भूच्छमयितुमलं भीष्मचरितः।।१८।।

स्थानेऽत्रैव सुरापगा च यमुना चात्रेव विस्पन्द[२]ते
सोप्यत्रैव युगक्षयाखिलजगद्धन्यैकसाक्षीवटः।
तस्यात्रैव च कीर्त्तिवल्लभनृप[३]स्याकल्पदानं जनाः
सत्यं विस्मयघुण्डमानशिरसः के वा न रोमाञ्चिताः।।१९।।

स्वस्ति स खलु श्रीविक्रमपुरसमा–

[४]वासितश्रीमज्जयस्कन्धावारात् परमसौगतो महाराजाधिराज श्रीकल्याणचन्द्रदेवपादानुध्यातः परमेश्वर प–

[५]रमभट्टारकमहाराजाधिराजः श्रीमान् लडहचन्द्रदेवः कुशली।। पौण्ड्रभुक्तान्तःपाति। समतटमण्डले ।

[६]श्रीपट्टीकेरके। फुल्लहडासम्बद्धस्वसीमावच्छिन्नपादोनषड्-द्रोणप्रमाणजम्पावणीभूमौ। तथा डोल्लवा

[७]यिका सं पूर्वेण द्रीर्घिका पश्चिमार्धसूपकारवोरक-बुद्धनन्दीग्रामभूमि-पश्चिमान्तारोपितकीलकाः सी

[८]मा। दक्षिणेन बलेश्वरवद्‌र्धकिवोरकभूम्युतरालिः। गोविन्दोञ्चमदक्षिणपाडश्च सीमा। पश्चिमेन ओडगो-

[९]धानिकाभूमेः पूर्वालिगोधानीभूमेर्दक्षिणसीमाल्यारोपित-कीलकघणारव-भूमेर्दक्षिणसीमालिपूर्व-

[१०]सीमालयः सीमा। उत्तरेण जयलम्भग्रामीयदक्षिणालिः सीमा। एवं चतु:सीमावच्छिन्न बिन्दुद्वयाधिक-काकत्र

[११]योपेतपञ्चयष्ठिसहितपादोनपञ्चद्रोणान्विताष्टपाटकप्रमाणवप्पसिंहवोरकग्रामे च। तथा गुप्तिना-

[१२]टन सं। पूर्वेण बुड्‌ढिगङ्‌गिणी सीमा। दक्षिणेन करवत्तीवोरकोत्तरालिः सीमा। पश्चिमेन वग्गूरभोगभूमेः पश्चि-

[१३]मदण्डालिः सीमा। उत्तरेण शङ्‌करभट्टारकभुज्यमानभूमेर्दक्षिणवद्दिकार्द्धः सीमा। एवं चतु-स्सीमावच्छिनवग्गुर-

[१४]भोग। धृतिपुरहट्टिकासमेतकाकाधिकनवद्रोणोपेतपाटकत्रयभूमिप्रमाण महादेवग्रामे च समुपग-

[१५]ताशेषराजपुरुष राज्ञी राणक राजपुत्र राजामात्य महाव्यूहपति मण्डलपति महासान्धिविग्रहिक। महासे-

[१६]नापति। महाक्षपटलिक। महासर्व्वाधिकृत। महाप्रतिहार। कोट्टपाल। दौस्साधसाधनिक। चौरोद्धरणिक। नौ-

[१७]बल। हस्त्यश्वगोमहिषाजाविकादिव्यापृतक। गौल्मिक। शौल्किक। दण्डपाशिक। दण्डनायक। विषयपत्यादीनन्यां-

[१८]श्च सकलराजपादोपजीविनोऽध्यक्षप्रचारोक्तान्निहाकीर्त्तितान्। चाटभटजातीयान्। जनपदान्। क्षेत्रकरांश्च-

[१९]ब्राह्मणोत्तरान् यथार्हं मानयति बोधयति समादिशति च। मतमस्तुभवताम्। यथोपरिलिखितभूमिरियं ग्रामद्व-

[२०]यञ्च। स्वसीमावच्छिन्नं। तृणपूतिगोचरपर्यन्तं। सतलं। सोद्देशं। साम्रपनसं। सगुवाकनालिकेरं। सलवणं। सजल-

[२१]स्थलं। सगर्तोषरं। सदशापराधं। सचौरोद्धरणं। परिहृतसर्वपीडं। अचाटभटप्रवेशं। अकिञ्चित्प्रग्राह्यं। समस्तरा-

[२२]जभोगकरहिरण्यप्रत्यायसहितं अस्मत्कारित-श्रीलडहमाधवभट्टारकाय। विधिवदुदकपूर्वकं कृत्वा। पुण्येऽ-

[२३]हनि। भगवन्तं वासुदेवभट्टारकमुद्दिश्य मातापित्रोरात्मनश्च पुण्ययशोऽभिवृद्धये। आचन्द्रार्कक्षितिसमका-

[२४]लं यावत्। भूमिच्छिद्रन्यायेन श्रीमद्धर्म्मचक्रमुद्रया। ताम्रशासनीकृत्य ढौकितमस्माभिः। अतो भवद्भिः सर्वैरनु-

[२५]मन्तव्यं भाविभिरपि भूपतिभिर्भूमेर्दानफलगौरवाद् अपहरणे महानरकपातभयाच्च दानमिदमनुमोद्या-

[२६]नुपालनीयम्। निवासिभिः क्षेत्रकरैश्चाज्ञाश्रवणविधेयीलूय यथोचितप्रत्यायोपनयः कार्य इति।

[२७]भवन्ति चात्र धर्मानुशंसिनः श्लोकाः।

भूमिं यः प्रतिगृह्णाति यश्च भूमिं प्रयच्छति।
उभौ तौ पुण्यकर्माणौ नियतं स्वर्ग्गगामिनौ ।।२०।।

[२८]षष्ठिं वर्षसहस्राणि स्वर्गे मोदति भूमिदः।
आक्षेप्ता चानुमन्ता च तान्येव नरकं वसेत् ।।२१।।

स्वदत्तां परदत्तां वा यो हरेत वसुन्ध[२९]राम्।
स विष्ठायां कृमिर्भूत्वा पितृभिस्सह पच्यते ।।२२।।
बहुभिर्वसुधा दत्ता राजभिस्सगरादिभिः।
यस्य यस्य यदा भूमिस्तस्य तस्य [३०]तदा फलम् ।।२३।।
इति कमलदलाम्बुबिन्दुलोलां
श्रियमनुचिन्त्य मनुष्यजीवितञ्च।

सकलमिदमुदाहृतञ्च बुद्ध्वा

न हि पुरुषैः परकी[३१]र्त्तयो विलोप्याः ॥२४॥

श्रीमल्लडहचन्द्रदेवपादीय सम्वत् ६ ज्यैष्ठदिने ३० महासान्धि नि अनु महाक्ष नि॥

Translation of the Text

Line-1. ***Oṁ Oṁ*** Salutation to Loard **Vāsudeva.**

Verse-1. The light cool as snows, fallen from the eye of **Atri,** became, that very moment, the moon----- the unique lamp of the world. From that started the genealogy of the kings (literally the lords of the earth) who were strong straightforward and high.

Verse-2. Therefore, that line of **Candra** was of the form of the triad of gods- viz. the greatest **Vidhātā** (= Creator and Lord Brahma) of the obligation of the world, by birth **Acyuta (=undeviated** and Lord **Viṣṇu)** from the religious path and Maheśvara **(the great master and Lord** Śiva) from the (line of its) origination.

Verse-3. There existed, for the joy and wealth of the world, king **Trailokya Candra** who was the crest jewel of that genealogy (always) growing and resplendent with rise, who was well-known as the only leader of the circle of earth, who was not small, had great purity, was dispeller of hundreds of terrors, of good character, attracted by (good) qualities and most auspicious.

Verse.4. Even today, the talks of the qualities of whom, the qualified person, purifying the ears, make every limb of everybody robbed by intensely rising horripilation with eye-lids slow due to the heavy tears of joy.

Verse-5. From him, who was the refuge of the great rulers and the abode of infinite enjoyments, was born **Śrī Candra**, like the moon out of the ocean full of crocodiles, who was the thief of the luster of gold and who added some indescribable beauty to the gold (itself)

Verse-6. And who made the vow of the shedding of tears for the eyes of the ladies of the lord of **Prāgjyotiṣa** uninterrupted, and made the sprouts of the lower lips of the ladies of the harem of Gauḍa (king), with the buds of smiles dropped.

Verse-7. The son of that king was **Kalyāna Candra**, who sanctified both the families (i.e. paternal and thaternal), who was famous for his pure and bright qualities, which were the ornaments of the three worlds. He, by birth of the nature of ***Dharma***, was held on the high heads of the great kings and was the most resortable by the good people, like the pious Gangetic stream.

Verse-8. Who created a large flow of the mass of tears in the eyes of **Mleccha**-women and rendered the moon-faces of the **Gauḍa**-women bereft of the moon-light of smile, and who spread these eight directions with his never-diminishing spotless fames like the rays of the moon bright on account of the dispersal of clouds.

Verse-9. The auspicious **Kalyānadevī** of extremely beautiful form was his beloved queen worthy of him, like **Lakṣmī of Puruṣottama**, and (always) agreeable to the acts pleasing him.

Verse-10. Like **Kunti** to **Yudhiṣṭhira** (lit. one whose speech is always true), or like **Rudrāṇī** to the son **Mahāsena**, that queen indeed gave birth to **Laḍaha Candra** of invaluable qualities.

Verse-11. At whose birth, there sounded a divine drum, danced the lines of **Vidyādharas**, flowers made noisy by the waves (groups) of humming bees were strewn from heaven, pleasing breezes blew, and the directions became cheerful and, what more, the very goddess Earth heaved a long sigh (of happiness) alongwith its Oceans.

Verse-12. Who attained highest level in (various) sciences and sub-sciences in a few days only, and who won over hundreds of cruel outer enemies as the six inner ones; and pleased with the group of qualities of which lord- sung in the three worlds all these three - the speech, the glory and the earth - became obedient (to him).

Verse-13. Who, possessing good qualities and with a singular eye to polity, having applied those appropriate qualities, and having obtained its great fruit i.e. enrichment of those (qualities), became the enjoyer and protector of the earth girded by oceans.

Verse-14. Who, with his brilliant prowess (or steps) and with his rise of strength well-known through his victory of the strong (enemies or King Bali), the best among man (or lord **Puruṣottama**) with his excellent qualities, made the (fickle) royal glory (or, **Lakṣmī**) not going to any one else, and who bestowed faultless glory upon **Aṅga** (Country) (or applied ashes to his limbs) and conquered **Kāma (rūpa** Country or Lord **Kāmadeva**), collected taxes from the people of unapproachable mountain lands, (or, held the hand of **Durgā**, the daughter of the Mountain), thus attaining the position of the Lord of beings (kingship or Śhiva-hood).

Verse-15. Who, as soon as he dipped into, reached quickly the other end of the rivers of sciences, who is well-known for prowess by his hands—the hero of the great drama called 'Protection of the World', and who, the dust of whose lotus-feet is scented by the fragrance of the garlands of the heads of Kings, made the earth effortlessly in a few days without any other parasol.

Verse-16. He went to **Vārānasī**- the abode of lord **Śambhu** with the daughter of the Mountains, bathed there in the **Gangetic** waters, and with his sins removed, performed obsequies for his forefathers; then gave away gold in the hands of the Brahmins, who would know their numbers? Only he, the wise, the crest-jewel of the three worlds is the lord of the earth. Fie upon others!

Verse-17. Where lord Self-Born (Brahma) of uninhibited intellect performed in person ten **Aśvamedha** sacrifices and wherein lord **Śiva** himself resides joyfully with **Durgā**; having come to that **Vārānasī** purified with mud-like sins washed away by the **Ganges**, that king having love for religion bathed (in the Ganges) and gave away his entire treasure.

Verse-18. Having bathed happily and performed thereafter the obsequious ceremony in the pure waters of the confluence of **Gaṅgā** and **Yamunā**, and by distributing thick streams of gold that knower of ceremonies,

REVERSE

the great person of staunch character, only was enough to appease the pains of thirst of the Brahmins .

Verse-19. in this place only flows the river of Gods (i.e. **Gaṅgā**)and here only ripples the **Yamunā**; even that **Banyan** tree, the blessed witness of the entire universe at the time of the end of an age. is here only; and the unimaginable gifting of that fame-loving king also is here only; really, which people would not turn their head in wondrous horripilation?

3-5 Hail, from his illustrious "Camp of Victory", situated at **Vikramapura**, ***Parameśvara*** (the great lord), ***Paramabhaṭṭāraka*** (the great warrior), ***Mahārājādhirāja*** (the overlord of the great kings), the illustrious **Laḍaha Candra Deva**, meditating upon the feet of the ***Paramasaugata*** (the great follower of ***Sugata*** i.e. Buddha), ***Mahārājādhirāja*** **Śrī Kalyān Candra Deva**, is hale and hearty.

5-6 Under **Pauṇḍrabhukti** (**Pauṇḍra** proviśnce), in **Samataṭa Maṇḍala** (**Samataṭa** Division), at **Śrī Paṭṭikeraka** (name of the city), connected with **Phullahadā** (probably name of an area or nearly village), in the thatter of the land of **Campāvan** measuring five and three-fourths of dronas separated by its own boundaries;

6-8 And connected with **Dollavāyikā**, on the east, the boundary (of the donated land) is pinned by the western part of the village (inhabited) Supakaras (cooks), **Voraka** (scribes), **Buddhists** and Nandis and western half of the Dīrghika (tank);

8-10 on the south, the southern boundary is surrounded by the land of **Baleśvara**, **Varddhaki** (carpenters), **Voraka** (scribes) and **Govindoñcama**;

10 on the west, the boundary is demarcated by the southern and eastern boundaries of the land of **Ghanārva** marked by the southern boundary of **Godhanī** (pasture land of cows) and eastern boundary of **Oḍa-Goghānī** (pasture land of cows of **Oḍa**);

10 On the north, the boundary is (marked by) the southern ridge of the village of **Jayalambha**;

10-11 Thus separated by four boundaries; measuring eight ***Pātakas,*** four and three-fourth Droṇas together with five ***Yaṣṭhis,*** three ***Kākas*** and two ***Vindus*** in the village (named) **Vappasiṁha** (inhabited by) **Voraka** (scribes);

11-12 And connected with **Guptināṭana**, on the east, the boundary is (demarcated by) the **Buḍḍhi-gaṅginī**;

12 on the south, the boundary is the northern ridge of **Karavatti Voraka**;

12-13 on the west, the boundaries demarcated by the land enjoyed by **Vaggura** is the western ridge;

13 on the north, the boundary is the southern half of the **Vaddika** of the land enjoyed by the lord **Śaṅkara**;

13-14 Thus separated by four boundaries and the enjoyment of **Vaggura**, along with the market **Dhrtipura**; the land measuring three Pāṭakas, nine Droṇas and a **Kāka** in the village **Mahādeva**;

14-15 duly honours, informs and orders all those that are present viz. ***Rajapurum*** (royal servants), the Queen, ***Kānakas***[1] (the feudal kings), ***Rājaputras*** (royal princes), ***Rājādmātyas*** *(royal* ministers), ***Mahāvyūhapati*** (the great general), ***Maṇḍalapati*** (the governor of Division), ***Mahāsāndhivigrahika*** (high minister of war and peace or minister of foreign affairs)

15-16 ***Mahā-senāpati*** (the commander in chief), ***Mahākṣ apaṭalika*** (accountant general), ***Mahāsarvvādhikṛta*** (chief superintendent), ***Mahāpratihāra*** (high chamberlain), ***Koṭṭ apāla*** (protector of a fort), ***Dauḥsādhasādhanika*** (officer in charge of difficult jobs, probably intelligence duties), **Cauroddharaṇika** (police official),

16-17 engaged officer-in-charge of fleet, infantry, elephant corps, cavalry, cows, buffaloes, goats, sheep, etc., ***Gaulmika*** (military or police officer), ***Saulkika*** (customs officer), ***Daṇḍapāśika*** (officer entrusted with the punishment of criminals), ***Daṇḍa-nāyaka*** (Judge),

17-19 Officer-in-charge of **Viṣaya** (district) and all other servants of the king mentioned in the list of the ***Adhyakṣas*** (Department) but not specified here, the people of the class of ***Cāṭas*** and ***Bhaṭas,*** countrymen, the tillers of the land and best among the Brahmins;

19-20 Be it known to you that this land as described above within the two villages as separated by its own boundaries, along with the grass, puti-plants and pasture lands, with low and high lands, with mango and jack-fruit trees, with betelnut and coconut trees,

20-21 with salt, with water and land, with pits and barren tracts, with tolerance of Ten crimes, with police protection, immune from all kinds of forced labour. not to be entered by ***Cāṭas*** and ***Bhaṭas,*** not to be taxed at all,

21-22 along with all the income such as taxes and gold enjoyed by the king-

22-24 is presented by us to Lord Śrī **Laḍaha Mādhava**[2] caused to be made by us ceremoniously after doing the water rite, on this auspicious day, having address the Lord **Vāsudeva** for the increase of the merit and fame of his parents and his own self, as long as the Sun, the Moon and the Earth endure, according to the law of ***Bhūmicchidra,*** by means of a copper-plate charter and affixing the illustrious ***Dharmacakra*** seal;

24-26 Therefore it should be approved by all of you. This gift should be approved of and protected by the future kings also considering that gift of land entails enormous merit and its taking away, the fear of falling into the great hell. The inhabitants and the peasants should be obeyed and all dues that are proper should be paid.

27 There are also verses in praise *of Dharma* in this thatter:

Verse-20 One who accepts the land, and one who gifts the land are both (persons of) meritorious deed, both will definitely go to heaven.

Verse-21 The giver of the land enjoys in the heaven for sixty thousand years; the interrupter and his supporter would live in hell for so many years.

Verse-22 He, who snatches away the land given by his ownself or by others, is rotten with his forefathers having become a worm of the dung.

Verse-23 Many kings like **Sagara** etc. have donated land; whoever is the master of that land at a certain time obtains the fruit at that time.

Verse-24 Therefore, having thought wealth and human life to be as fickle as a drop of water on a petal of lotus, and having understood all the sayings above, the persons should not efface the fames (i.e. good deeds) of others.

31 On the 30th day of **Jyaiṣṭha** of the 6th regnal year of ***Śrimad Laḍaha Candra Deva***. Approved by ***Mahā Sāndhivigrahika***. Approved by ***Mahākṣa-Paṭalika***.

THE MAINĀMATĪ COPPER-PLATE OF ŚRĪ LAḌAHA CANDRADEVA

Introduction

The copper-plate no.2 of Śrī **Laḍaha Candra** was also discovered accidently in a mound known as **Cārpatra Murā**, in 1954 A. D. This mound is situated in the **Maināmatī-Lalmai** hill range, on the western side of Comilla town, southern side of Dhaka-Comilla road, near the Kutilā Murā and Brigade Head-quarters of the Bangladesh Regiment. This plate is now preserved in the custody of the Directorate of Archaeology, Bangladesh.

This is a single plate inscribed on both the sides. A round seal is attached to the top of the middle of the plate. Due to this seal, there is a break in the middle of the first three lines on obverse and first one line of the reverse. In line 22 on reverse, the seal, attached to the top, is identified as the ***Dharmacakra Mudrā,*** This ***Dharmacakra Mudrā*** symbolizes the Buddhist faith. It is also the emblem of the wheel of law. It consists of a number of concentric circles. The innermost is in the top. It shows a small wheel flanked on two sides by two antelopes. This type of wheel is found in the **Pāla** copperplates. This seal has been divided into two parts by a small line of inscription. It is deciphered as ***Śrī Laḍaha Candra Devaḥ,*** The lower most part of the inscribed line is a floral motif. Out of the concentric circles and lower part of the seal is also the floral motif. The margin of the seal is decorated by 41 beads and projection by ten extra beads. The inscription consists of 60 lines of which 30 are engraved on the obverse and 30 on the reverse.

The text beginning with benedictory "***Oṁ, Oṁ namo Bhagavate",*** is same as that of plate no. 1 of **Śrī Laḍaha Candra Deva.** There are total 24 verses described on the plate and they are verbatim the same as in the plate no. 1 of **Śrī Laḍaha Candra Deva.** The only difference is about the limits on the land donated and the date. End of the plate indicates the date of donation and the witiness. The date of donation is 30th day of the month of ***Aṣāḍha*** in the Sixth regnal year of the king.

We are therefore printing only the prose text of this copperplate in Sanskrit and the English translation of the prose portion and request the readers to refer to the text and translation of the verses in the first plate of Śrī **Laḍaha Candra Deva**.

TEXT REVERSE

स्वस्ति स खलु

[६] श्रीविक्रमपुरसमावासितश्रीमज्जयस्कन्धावारात् परमसौगतो महाराजाधि-राजश्रीकल्याणचन्द्रदे

PLATE NO. 2

MAINAMATI COPPERPLATE GRANT OF LADAHA CANDRADEVA REVERSE

[७]वपादानुध्यातः परमेश्वरपरमभट्टारकमहाराजाधिराजः श्रीमान् लडहचन्द्रदेवः कुशली॥

[८]श्रीपौण्ड्रभुक्त्यान्तःपाति-समतटमण्डले। पेरनाटनविषय सं। पूर्वेण मायुपाटकावस्थित-लोकनाथ-

[९]भट्टारकीयशासनभूमेः पश्चिमालिः सीमा। दक्षिणेन लोकनाथभट्टारकीयशासनभूमेरेवोत्तरालिः

[१०]सीमा। पश्चिमेन ब्राह्मणदेववोरकग्रामीयपूर्वान्तः सीमा। उत्तरेण कंसाराकद्दपोलकग्रामीयदक्षि-

[११]णखातः सीमा। एवं चतुः सीमावच्छिन्नोनत्रिङ्श(=द)ष्टाधि कसार्द्धद्रोणोपेताष्टपाटकप्रमाण-सुरवोरक ग्रामे।

[१२]समुपगताशेष-राजपुरुष-राज्ञी-राणक-राजपुत्र-राजामात्य-महाव्यूहपति-मण्डलपति-महासान्धि

[१३]विग्रहिक। महासेनापति। महाक्षपटलिक। महासर्व्वाधिकृत। महाप्रतीहार। कोट्टापाल। दौस्सा-

[१४]धसाधनिक। चौरोद्धरणिक। नौबल। हस्त्यश्वगोमहिषाजाविकादिव्यापृतक। गौल्मिक। शौल्कि-

[१५]क। दण्डपाशिक। दण्डनायक। विषयपत्यादीनन्यांश्च सकलराजपादोपजीविनोऽध्यक्षप्रचारोक्तान्निहाकीर्त्ति

[१६]तान्। चाटभटजातीयान्(।)जनपदान्। क्षेत्रकरांश्च ब्राह्मणोत्तरान् यथार्हं मानयति बोधयति समादि

[१७]शति च। मतमस्तु भवताम्। यथोपरिलिखित ग्रामो(ऽ)यं स्वसीमावच्छिन्नः। तृणपूतिगोचरपर्यन्तः सतल-

[१८]सोद्देशः साम्रपनसः सगुवाकनालिकेरः सलवणः सजलस्थलः सगर्तोषरः। सदशापराध सचौ

[१९]रोद्धरणः परिहृतसर्वपीडः अचाटभटप्रवेश। अकिञ्चित्प्रग्राह्यः समस्तराजभोगकरहिरण्यप्र

[२०]त्यायसहितः। श्री-पट्टीकेरकेऽस्मत्कारित-श्री-लडमाधवभट्टारकाय। विधिवदुदकपूर्वकं कृत्वा।

[२१]पुण्येऽहनि। भगवन्तं वासुदेवभट्टारकमुद्दिश्य मातापित्रोरात्मनश्च पुण्ययशोऽभिवृद्धये-

[२२]आचन्द्रार्कक्षितिसमकाल। यावत्। भूमिच्छिद्रन्यायेन। श्रीमद्धर्म्मचक्रमुद्रया। ताम्रशासनीकृत्य।ढौ

[२३]कितोऽस्माभिः। अतो भवद्भिःसर्वैरनुमन्तव्यः भाविभिरपि भूपतिभिर्भूमेर्द्दानफलगौरवाद् अपह-

[२४]रणे महानरकपातभयाच्च दानमिदमनुमोद्यानुपालनीयम्। निवासिभिः क्षेत्रकरैश्चाज्ञाश्रवणवि

[२५]धेयीभूय यथोचितप्रत्यायोपनयः कार्य इति। भवन्ति चात्रधर्मानुशंसिनः श्लोकाः।

भूमिं यः प्रतिगृह्णा[२६]ति यश्च भूमिं प्रयच्छति।
उभौ तौ पुण्यकर्माणौ नियतं स्वर्ग्गगामिनौ ।।२०।।

षष्ठि वर्षसहस्राणि स्वर्गे मोदति भूमिदः।
[२७]आक्षेप्ता चानुमन्ता च तान्येव नरकं वसेत् ।।२१।।
स्वदत्तां परदत्तां वा यो हरेत वसुन्धराम्।
स विष्ठायां क्रि(कृ)मिर्भूत्वा[२८]पितृभिस्सह पच्यते ।।२२।।

बहुभिर्वसुधा दत्ता राजभिस्सगरादिभिः।
यस्य यस्य यदा भूमिस्तस्य तस्य तदा फलम् ।।२३।।

[२९]इति कमलदलाम्बुबिन्दुलोलां
श्रियमनुचिन्त्य मनुष्यजीवितञ्च।
सकलमिदमुदाहृतञ्च बुद्ध्वा
न हि पुरुषैः[३०]परकीर्त्तयो विलोप्याः ।।२४।।
श्रीलडहचन्द्रदेवपादीयसम्वत् ६ आषाड दिने ३० महासान्धि नि अनु महाक्ष नि।।

TRANSLATION OF REVERSE

5-7 Hail, from his illustrious 'Camp of Victory', situated at **Vikramapura,** ***Parameśvara*** (the great lord), ***Paramabhaṭṭāraka*** (the great warrior), ***Mahārājādhirāja*** (the overlord of the great king), the illustrious **Laḍaha Candra Deva,** meditating on the feet of the ***Paramasaugata*** (the great follower of ***Sugata*** i.e. Buddha), ***Mahārājādhirāja*** **Śrī Kalyān Candra Deva,** is prosperous.

8 Under **Śrī Pauṇḍrabhukti (Śrī Pauṇḍra province)** in **Samataṭa Naṇḍala** (**Samataṭa** Division),

8-9 And (connected with) **Pernāṭana Viṣaya (Pernāṭana** District), on the east, the boundary (o donated land) is the western boundary of a royal grant of land of lord **Lokanātha** situated in **Māyupāṭaka;**

9-10 on the south, the boundary is the northern boundary of a royal grant of land of **Lokanātha**;

10 On the west, the boundary is the East End of the village **Brāhmāṇadeva Voraka** (scribes)

10-11 on the north, the boundary is the southern trench of the village of **Kaṁsārakoddapolaka**;

11 thus demarcated by the four boundaries; measuring eight Pāṭakas and thirty-seven and a half dronas, in the village **Sura-Voraka**.

12-13 duly honours, informs and orders all those that are present viz. ***Rājapuruṣa*** (Royal servants), the Queen, ***Rāṇakas*** (the feudal kings), ***Rājaputras*** (Royal princes), ***Rājamātyas*** (Royal Ministers), ***Mahāvyūhapati*** (the great general), ***Maṇḍalapati*** (the governor of division), ***Mahāsāndhivigrahika*** (High minister for war and peace or minister of foreign affairs);

13-14 ***Mahāsenāpati*** (the commander-in-chief), ***Mahākṣapaṭplika*** (Chief accountant), ***Mahāsarvvādhikṛta*** (Superintendent of all works), ***Mahāpratihāra*** (High chamberlain), ***Koṭṭapāla*** (Protector of a fort), ***Dauḥ-***

sādhasādhanika (officer-in-charge of difficult jobs, probably intelligence duties), ***Cauroddharaṇika*** (Police official),

14-15 engaged officer-in-charge of fleet, infantry, elephant corps, cavalry, cows, buffaloes, goats, sheep, etc., ***Gaulmika*** (military or police officer), ***Saulkika*** (customs officer),

15-16 ***Daṇḍapāśika*** (officer entrusted with the punishment of criminals), ***Daṇḍanāyaka*** (Judge), officer-in-charge of ***Viṣaya*** (district) and all other servants of the king mentioned in the list of the ***Adhyakṣas*** (Department) but not specified here, the people of the class of ***Cāṭas*** and ***Bhaṭas,*** countrymen, the tillers of the land and best among the Brahmins;

17-18 Be it known to you that this land as described above within the two villages as separated by its own boundaries, along with the grass, puti-plants and pasture lands, with low and high lands, with mango and jackfruit trees, with betel nut and coconut trees, with salt, with water and land, with pits and barren tracts, with tolerance of Ten crimes,

18-19 with police protection, immune from all kinds of forced labour, not to be entered by ***Cāṭas*** and ***Bhaṭas,*** not to be taxed at all,

19-20 along with all the income such as taxes and gold enjoyed by the king-

20-23 is presented by us, at **Śrī Paṭṭikeraka**, to **Lord Śrī Laḍaha Mādhava**[3] caused to be made by us ceremoniously after doing the water rite, on this auspicious day, having addressed to the Lord **Vāsudeva** for the increase of the merit and fame of his parents and his own self, as long as the Sun, the Moon and the Earth endure, according to the principle of ***Bhūmicchidra,*** by means of a copper-plate charter and affixing the illustrious ***Dharmacakra*** seal;

23-25 Therefore it should be approved by all of you. This gift should be approved of and protected by the future kings also considering that gift of land entails enormous merit and its taking away, the fear of falling into the great hell. The inhabitants and the peasants should be obeyed and all dues that are proper should be paid.

25 There are also verses in praise *of **Dharma*** in this thatter:

Verse-20 One who accepts the land, and one who gifts the land are both (persons of) meritorious deed, both will definitely go to heaven.

Verse-21 The giver of the land enjoys in the heaven for sixty thousand years; the interrupter and his supporter would live in hell for so many years.

Verse-22 He, who snatches away the land given by his ownself or by others, is rotten with his fore-fathers having become a worm of the dung.

Verse-23 Many kings like **Sagara** etc. have donated land; whoever is the master of that land at a certain time obtains the fruit at that time.

Verse-24 Therefore, having thought of wealth and human life as fickle as a drop of water on a petal of lotus, and having understood all the sayings above, the persons should not efface the fames (i.e. good deeds) of others.

30 On the day of **Aṣāḍha** of the 6th regnal year of **Śrī Laḍaha Candra Deva**. Approved by ***Mahāsāndhi-vigrahika***. Approved by ***Mahākṣapaṭalika.***

MAINĀMATĪ COPPERPLATE OF

SRI GOVINDA CANDRA DEVA

Introduction

This copper plate of **Śrī Govinda Candra Deva** was traced accidentally in a mound known as Cārpatra Murā in 1954 A.D. It is located in the **Mainšmatī-Lalmai** hill range, on the western side of Comilla town, southern side of Dhaka-Comilla road, near the Kutilā Murā and Brigade Head-quarters of the Bangladesh Regiment. This plate is in a good condition. Presently, it is in the custody of the Directorate of Archaeology, Bangladesh.

This also is a single plate inscribed on both the sides. It bears a seal attached to the middle of the top and causes a break in the middle of the first three lines on the obverse and of the two lines on the reverse. In line 19 the seal is described as the ***Dharma Cakra Mudrā***. This ***Dharma Cakra Mudrā*** symbolizes the Buddhist faith. It is also the emblem of the wheel of law. It consists of a number of concentric circles. The innermost small circle is in the top. It shows a small wheel flanked on two sides by two gazelles. This type of characteristics of wheel is found in the Pāla Copper-plates.

The projected circle is divided into two parts by a small line of inscription, which is deciphered as ***Śrī Govinda Candra Devaḥ***. The lower part of the inscribed line is a floral motif Five petals of lotus decorate lower part of the seal, i.e. out of the concentric circles. The margin of the seal is furnished by 41 beads. The projection is furnished by 10 more beads. The inscription consists of 58 lines of which 29 are engraved on the obverse and 29 on the reverse.

It begins with ***"Oṁ Svasti"***. Then there are 16 verses of genealogical praise mentioning in highly ornate language, the benediction (1), the origin of the royal lineage (2-3), King **Śrī Candra** (4-5), King **Kalyāna Candra** (6-7), King **Laḍaha Candra** (8-9), and his queen **Saubhāgyadevī** (10) and finally King **Govinda Candra** (11-16). The prose portion describes the demarcations of the donated land with usual orders to royal officers and finally five verses praising donations and deprecating its snatchers.

Strongly, the plate is not dated. There is space if the donor wanted to inscribe it. But he has chosen not to. One can only guess at the reasons for this. The plate ends with two ver-

PLATE NO. 3

MAINAMATI COPPERPLATE GRANT OF LADAHA CANDRADEVA OBVERSE

tical strokes, some space, a circle, and some space again and finally two vertical strokes again. **Dani** says, "It is difficult to say whether this circle has any numerical value". We aver it has none; it has only decorative value.

The characters are of the type of Northern **Nāgari** which is allied to the alphabet found in the copper-plates of the latter **Pālas** and current in North-eastern India towards the close of tenth and first half of the eleventh century A.D.There are only small of differences between the inscriptions of Candras and there of **Pālas**. The letters are very stylistic, depending upon different hands or school. They do not show any regional variations between the character of North and East Bengal. The language of the inscription is Sanskrit. There are altogether 21 verses which are composed in a variety of metres viz. ***Indravajrā, Sārdulavikṛiḍitaṁ, Vasantatilaka, Śikhariṇi, Anuṣṭubh, Puṣpitāgrā, Upajāti.***

TEXT

OBVERSE SIDE

श्री गोविन्दचन्द्र देवः

[१]ओम् स्वस्ति

निःश्रेयसाप्या(=या)स्तु जिनो जनाना-

मनुत्तरं शर्म्म करो[२]तु धर्म्मः।

संघोऽप्यघं हन्तु तयोः प्रभावा-

दुत्तीर्णसंसारमहास[३]मुद्रः ॥१॥

यदद्भुतं निर्गतमत्रिनेत्राज्-

ज्योतिः प्रकृत्या शिशिरं सितञ्च।

सो[४]ऽभूत् क्षणात् सुन्दरकान्तिरिन्दु-

रानन्दनो लोकविलोचनानाम् ॥२॥

तस्य प्रजाप्रीतिकरोद[५]यस्य

दिशान्तमःखण्डनपण्डितस्य।

क्रमात् प्रवृद्धः सरलः सुपर्वा
समुन्नतश्च प्रससा[६]र वङ्गः ।।३।।

वागीशाधिकधीरखण्डितमहीरक्षाधिकारव्रतः
प्रत्यत्विप्रतिपादिते[७]प्सितफलः कल्पद्रुमो जङ्गमः।
श्रीचन्द्रः शरदिन्दुसुन्दरमुखो विद्यावधूनां पति(:)
[८]जातस्तत्र पवित्रितोभयकुलः क्षोणीभुजामग्रणीः ।।४।।

येनाजौ द्विषतां गणः सुर[९]वधूसङ्गोत्सवैर्योजितः
पात्रं मित्रजनः कृतश्च धवलच्छत्रस्मितानां श्रियां।
लोकानां[१०]परिपालने च भरणे चात्यन्तबद्धोद्यमः
ख्यातो यश्च सशैलसागरमही पर्यन्तपा[११]च्छैर्गुणै।।५।।

तस्मात् क्षीरनिधेरिवेन्दुभवने तत्रोत्सवैकप्रसू-
र्दूरोल्लासिकलाकलापनि[१२]लयः कल्याणचन्द्रो नृपः।
यस्त्यागेन बलिर्द्विषद्भयकृता रामः प्रतापेन यो
यः स[१३]त्येन युधिष्ठिरो बलवता शौर्येण यश्चार्जुनः ।।६।।

येनासौ द्विगुणीकृतः पतिवधादु[१४]द्वेजितानां घनैर्
म्लेच्छीनान्नयनाम्बुभिर्विगलितैः लौहित्यनामा नदः।
येनाजौ ग[१५]जवाजिपत्तिबहुलां सेनां गृहीत्वा बलाद्
गौडानामधिपः कृतश्च (सु)चिरं लज्जावनम्रा[१६]ननः ।।७।।

तस्मादजायत सुतः श्रुतशीलशाली
कौलीनभीरुहृदयः सदयः प्रजा[१७]सु।
विद्याधरैः कनकशैल इवाधिगम्यः
सर्वोत्तरो लडहचन्द्र इति क्षितीन्द्रः ।।८।।

[१८]ययौ वाराणस्यां सुरसरिति सस्नौ च बहुशः
शतं वारानर्थिष्वथ कनकवृष्टिञ्च वि[१९]दधे।
कवित्वात् पाण्डित्याद्दिशिदिशि च यः कीर्त्तिमनघां
वितेने शत्रुशस्त्रीनिधुवनकलो[२०]च्छेदचतुरः ॥९॥

देवस्य तस्येन्दुसमानकान्तेः
सौभाग्यदेवीति महानुभावा।
शिवा शि[२१]व(स्येव) हरेरिव श्रीः
प्रियङ्करा प्राणसमा प्रिया(ऽ)भूत् ॥१०॥

सा सुप्रशस्ये(ऽ)ह्नि शुभे मुहूर्त्ते
परीतम[२२]ङ्गैश्शतराजचिह्नैः।
मुखश्रिया निर्जितमण्डचन्द्रं
गोविन्दचन्द्रं सुसु(=षु)वे सुखेन ॥११॥

भूते जन्मनि तस्य[२३]पुष्पमपतद्दिव्यं महीमण्डले
सामोदः शिशिरः शनैर्म्मरुदवादासन् प्रसन्ना दिशः (।)
वीणा[२४]वेणुमृदङ्गनिस्वनमयं शृङ्गारचेष्टामयं
तत्तल्लास्यकलामयं पितृपुरं सान्तःपुरञ्चाभ[२५]वत् ॥१२॥

ईशस्तस्य पिता शिवा च जननी सो(ऽ)भूत् स्वयं शक्तिमान्
लोको(ऽ)यं धृतिमानजायत म[२६]हासेनस्य तस्योद्भवात् (।)
विद्याः शैशव एव तेन दिवसैरल्पैः सुखं शिक्षिताः
स्वभ्यस्तो[२७]गजवाजिवाहनविधिर्ज्ञाताश्च सर्वाःकलाः ॥१३॥

PLATE NO. 3

MAINATMATI COPPERPLATE GRANT OF GOVINDA CANDRADEVA REVERSE

मूर्त्तो धर्म्म इति क्षमानिधिरिति त्राता प्रजा[२८]नामिति
श्रेय: पात्रमिति श्रियां वसतिरित्युद्दामधामेति च (।)
क्षोणीन्द्र: परिकीर्त्यते प्र[२९]तिदिशं प्रत्यालयं प्रत्यहं
सानन्दं सकुतूहलं सपुलकं लोकै: स एक: परं ।।१४।।
आखण्डलस्ये

TEXT

REVERSE SIDE

[१]व विकस(=स्व)रा श्री:
प्रचण्डरश्मेरिव चण्डमोज:।
तस्यास्तु भूमण्डलम[२]ण्डनस्य
मृकण्डसूनोरिव दीर्घमायु: (।।) १५।।

शिवं स्वयम्भू: सृजतु प्रकामं
हरि: श[३]रीरस्थितिमादधातु(।)
विपक्षसंहारमुदारकीर्त्ते-
र्ग्गोविन्दचन्द्रस्य हर: करोतु ।।१६।।
स खलु श्रीवि

[४]क्रमपुरसमावासित श्रीमज्जयस्कन्धावारात् परमसौगतो महाराजाधिराज: श्रीलडहचन्द्र-

[५]देव-पादानुध्यात: परमेश्वर: परमभट्टारको महाराजाधिराज: श्रीमान् गोविन्दचन्द्रदेव:

[६]कुशली श्रीपौण्ड्रभुक्त्यन्त:पाति समतटमण्डले पेरनाटनविषय सं साहरतलाके पाटक-

[७]द्वयभूमौ। समुपगताशेष-राजपुरुषराज्ञीराणकराजपुत्रराजामात्यमहाव्यूहप-

[८]ति मण्डलपति महासान्धिविग्रहिक महासेनापति महाक्षपटलिक महासर्व्वा-

[९]धिकृत महाप्रतिहार कोट्टपाल दौःसाधसाधनिक चौरोद्धरणिक नौवलह-

[१०]स्त्यश्वगोमहिषाजाविकादिव्यापृतक गौल्मिक सौ(शौ)ल्किक दण्डपाशिक द(ण्ड)नाय-

[११]क विषयपत्यादीनन्यांश्च सकलराजपादोपजीविनो(ऽ)ध्यक्षप्रचारोक्तानिहा-

[१२]कीर्त्तितान् चाटभटजातीयान् जनपदान् क्षेत्रकरांश्च ब्राह्मणोत्तरान् यथार्-

[१३]हं मानयति बोधयति समादिशति च मतमस्तु भवतां यथोपरिलिखिते भूमि-

[१४]रियं स्वसीमावच्छिन्ना तृणपूतिगोचरपर्यन्ता सतला सोद्देशा साम्रपनसा सगु-

[१५]वाकनालिकेरा सलवणा सजलस्थला सगर्त्तोषरा सदशापराधा सचौरो-

[१६]द्धरणा परिहृतसर्व्वपीडा अचाटभटप्रवेशा अकिञ्चित्प्रग्राह्या समस्तराज

[१७]भोगकरहिरण्यप्रत्यायसहिता नट्टेश्वरभट्टारकय पुण्येऽहनि विधिवदुद-

[१८]कपूर्व्वकं कृत्वा भगवन्तं शिवभट्टारकमुद्दिश्य मातापित्रोरात्मनश्च पुण्ययशो-

[१९]भिवृद्धये।। आचन्द्राक्र्कक्षितिसमकालं यावत् भूमिच्छिद्रन्यायेन श्रीमद्धर्म्मचक्रमु-

[२०]द्रया ताम्रशासनीकृत्य प्रदत्ताऽस्माभिः अतो भवद्भिः सर्वैरनुमन्तव्यं भाविभिर-

[२१]पि भूपतिभिर्भूमेर्दानफलगौरवादपहरणे महानरकपातभयाच्च दानमि

[२२]दमनुमोद्यानुपालनीयं निवासिभिः श्रेत्रकरांश्चाज्ञाश्रवणविधेयीभूय यथोचि-

[२३]तप्रत्यायोपनयः कार्य इति। भवन्ति चात्र धर्म्मानुशंसिनः श्लोकाः।।

भूमिं यः प्रतिगृ[२४]ह्णाति यश्च भूमिं प्रयच्छति।
उभौ तौ पुण्यकर्म्माणौ नियतं स्वर्ग्गगामिनौ ।।१७।।

षष्ठिं वर्षसह[२५]स्त्राणि स्वर्ग्गे मोदति भूमिदः।

आक्षेप्ता चानुमन्ता च तान्येव नरकं वसेत् ॥१८॥

स्वदत्तां पर[२६]दत्तां वा यो हरेत वसुन्धराम्।
स विष्ठायां कृमिर्भूत्वा पितृभिः सह पच्यते ॥१९॥

वहुभिर्वसुधा[२७]दत्ता राजभिः सगरादिभिः।
यस्य यस्य यदा भूमिस्तस्य तस्य तदा फलम् ॥२०॥

इति कमल[२८]दलाम्बुबिन्दुलोलां
श्रियमनुचिन्त्य मनुष्यजीवितञ्च।
सकलमिदमुदाहृतञ्च बुद्धवा
[२९]न हि पुरुषेः परकीर्त्तयो विलोप्याः ॥२१॥

Translation of the Text

Obverse

Line-1. *Oṁ* Welfare (to all)!

Verse-1 May **Jina** (Lord Buddha) be for the weal of the people. May Dharma give highest bliss to all and the may **Saṅgha** also, which has owing to influence of these two (i.e. **Jina and Dharma**) crossed the great Ocean of this world, destroy sins.

Verse-2 That wondrous light which came out of the eyes of sage **Atri**[4] and which is cool and white by nature, turned that very moment into the moon of beautiful lustre pleasing to the eyes of the people.

Verse-3 In the order of the rise of that (i.e. the moon and the royal lineage) joyous to the people, and expert in destroying the darkness of the directions, the **Vaṅga** (country) prospered and extended straight and coherently to preeminence.

Verse-4 There was born **Śrī Candra,** pre-eminent among the kings, of intellect greater than that of the lord of **Vāl,** having a vow of authority to protect the entire earth, who, the mobile desire-yielding tree, quickly accomplished the desired fruit, having the face as beautiful as the autumnal moon, lord of the ladies of learning, who purified the families of both (paternal and thaternal)

Verse-5 Who, in the battlefied, united the group of enemies with the festivals of the company of divine ladies, and made the friend-folk a receptacle of the (royal) glories smiling with white umbrellas[5], and (who was) extremely attentive ***(baddhodymaḥ)*** in the protection and nourishment of the people, and who was well-known by his pure qualities to the ends of this earth along with its mountains and oceans.

Verse-6. From him , like moon from milky Ocean, was born king **Kalyāna Candra**, the source of only joy to the eyes, the abode of the group of **Kalas**(digits or arts) risen high, who was(like) king **Bali** in (the quality of) sacrifice, who was Rāma by his valour creating fear in enemies, who was **Yudhiṣṭhira** in truth and **Arjuna** in the forceful prowers.

Verse-7. Who redoubled this great river called **Lauhitya** by the thick (flow of) tears shed from the eyes of the **Mleccha**-women distressed by the killing of their lord; and who made the lord of the **Gauḍas** low-faced by shame by having forcefully made captive his great army of elephants, horses and foot-soldiers in the battle-field for a long time.

Verse-8. From him was born a son called **Laḍaha Candra**, the highest of Kings, shining with wisdom and character, afraid at heart of popular censure and kind towards subjects, approachable like a golden mountain by the learned (or like Mountain Meru approachable only by **Vidyādharas**);

Verse-9. Who went to **Vārānasī**, and bathed in the divine river many times, then hundreds of times bestowed golden shower upon the supplicants, and who spread his spotless fame in all directions with his poetic genius and scholarship and who was clever in snapping up the carnal arts of the females of his enemies.

Verse-10. Like Śiva of lord Śiva and Śrī (i.e. **Lakṣmī**) of lord **Viṣṇu, Saubhāgyadevī** of great demeanor was the beloved (queen) of that lord of moon-like lustre, loved by him like his soul and always doing what he liked.

Verse-11. On an auspicious day and in an auspicious hour, she happily gave birth to **Govinda Candra** who was endowed with limbs possessing hundreds of royal signs, and who won the orb of moon with the luster of his face.

Verse.12. When he was born, divine flowers fell on the earth, pleasing and cool wind blew slowly, the directions were bright, and capital of his father with its femalefolk, his harem became over-flowing with delicate arts full of the sounds of lutes, flutes and drums and full of artistic (lit erotic) activities.

Verse-13. His father was lord **Śiva**, his mother **Śiva**, and he himself was **Śaktimān** (i.e. **Kārttikeya**). By the rise of that (king) of great army, this world become reposed, the sciences were learnt by him with ease in child-hood only within a few days and he was well studied in the science of elephants, horses, carriages and (he) learnt all the arts.

Verse-14. Only this single King is praised in every direction, in every house, everyday by people with joy, with eagerness, with horripilation as ***Dharma*** incarnate, as the ocean of tolerance, as protector of the subjects, as an object of welfare, as the abode of riches, and as unrestrained luster;

Verse-15. May the brightening glory of **Indra**, the severe luster of the sun and the long life of the son of (sage) Mrkanda be for him who is the ornament of the circle of earth.

Verse-16. Of this **Govinda Candra** of wide fame, may Lord self-born produce profuse bliss, may **lord Hari** bestow steadiness of his body and Lord **Hara** destroy (his) opponents.

3-6 Hail, from his illustrious "**Camp of Victory**," situated at **Vikramapura**, **Parameśvara**, **Paramabhaṭṭ āraka**, **Mahārājādhirāja**, the illustrious **Govinda Candra Deva**, meditating upon the feet of the ***Parama Saugata, Mahārājādhirāja*** **Śrī Laḍaha Candra Deva** is hail and hearty.

6-7 Under **Śrī Pauṇḍrabhukti** in **Sathataṭā Maṇḍala** connected with **Peranāṭana Viṇaya** at **SahaRātalāka** in the thatter of two pātakas of land;

7-9. Duly honors informs and orders the entire group of ***Rājapuruṣa, Rājñi, Rāṇakas, Rājaputra, Rājamātyas, Mahāvyūhapati, Maṇḍalapati, Mahāsnd' hivigrahika, Mahāsenāpati, Mahākṣapaṭalik, Mahāsarvvādhikṛta, Mahāpra-tihāra. Koṭṭapala, Dauḥsādhasādhanika Cauroddhraṇika,***

9-11. Engaged officer-in-charge of fleet, infantry, elephant corps, cavalry, cows, buffaloes, goats, sheep, etc. ***Gaulmika, Saulkika, Daṇḍapasika, Daṇḍanāyaka,***

11-12. Officer-in-charge of ***Viṣaya*** and all other servants of the king mentioned in the list of the ***Adhyākṣas*** but not specified here, the people of the class of ***Cāṭas*** and ***Bhaṭas,*** countrymen, the tillers of the land and best among the Brahmins;

12-17. Be it known to you all that this land as mentioned above within the SahaRātalaka as demarcated by its own boundaries, along with the grass, puti-plants and pasture lands, with low and high lands, with mango and jack-fruit trees, with betelnut and coconut trees, with salt, with water and land, with pits and barren tracts, with tolerance of Ten crimes, with police protection, immune from all kinds of forced labour, not to be entered by ***Cāṭas*** (cheats) and ***Bhaṭas*** (soldiers), not to be taxed at all, along with all the income such as taxes and gold enjoyed by the king.

17-19. To **Naṭṭeśvara Bhaṭṭāraka** after doing the water rite, on this auspicious day, having addressed to the **Lord Śiva Bhaṭṭāraka** for the increase of the merit and fame of his parents and his own self;

19-20. As long as the Sun, the Moon and the Earth endure, according to the law of ***Bhūmicchidra,*** by means of a copper-plate charter and affixing the illustrious ***Dharmacakra*** seal; is presented by us.

20-23. Therefore, it should be approved by all of you. This gift should be approved of and protected by the future kings also considering that gift of land entails enormous merit and its taking away, the fear of falling into the great hell.The inhabitants and the peasants should be obeyed and all dues that are proper should be paid.

23. There are also verses in praise of ***Dharma*** in this thatter:

Verse-20 One who accepts the land, and one who gifts the land are both (persons of) meritorious deed, both will definitely go to heaven.

Verse-21 The giver of the land enjoys in the heaven for sixty thousand years; the interrupter and his supporter would live in hell for so many years.

Verse-22 He, who snatches away the land given by his own self or hy others, is rotten with bis forefathers having become a worm of the dung.

Verse-23 Many kings like **Sagara** etc. have donated land; whoever is the master of that land at a certain tune obtains the fruit at that time.

Verse-24 Therefore, having thought of wealth and human life as fickle as a drop of water on a petal of lotus, and having understood all the sayings above, the persons should not efface the fames (i.e. good deeds) of others.

THE MAINĀMATĪ COPPERPLATE OF RANAVANKA MALLA SRIMAT HARIKALADEVA

Introduction

This copperplate was found towards the end of the year 1803. When the repairing work of the highway, through the mainathati hills, was going on and accidentally, the workers of that area got the plate at the time of digging earth in the district Tippera (at present the district of Comilla), about five miles to the west of the town of Comilla. It was found in good condition and was in the cusody of the Asiatic Society of Bengal.

This is a single plate inscribed on one side only. The plate measures about 11" × 9", it bears an arch, and inside it is a crown, at the top of the plate which measures about 2" in height. This delineation probably shows the symbol of the Royal dynasty. The sides of the plate have a gentle curvature, The inscription consists of 24 lines. The size of the letter in about 1/4".

The plate is in the praise of the donor **Dhādi-Eba,** horse officer, of king **Raṇavaṅkamalla.** The inscription opens with *"Oṁ"* Then there are 9 verses of which first verse praises one **Hedi-Eba** whose son **Śrī Dhādi-Eba** is described in three elegant verses (i.e. 2,3 and 4). Dhadi-Eba is the chief officer of the king **Raṇavaṅkamalla** (5). then the small monastery of Goddess **Durgottārā**, the city of Paṭṭikera, 20 dronas of donated land in the village **Bejakhaṇḍa** (6), the fame of the donor (7), request for the protection of the donated land to the future king (8), one **Medini-Eba** (9), and the date of donation of the land are 1141s year of the **Saka Era** that is the 17th regnal year of the king (Line 22-24).

The characters are of the type of proto-Bengali. The l language is Sanskrit. The last three lines, where tha date of the copperplate grant is mentioned, are in prose. The epigraph consists of nine verses employing seven different metres i.e. ***Mandākrāntā, Vasantatilaka, Drutavilambita, Śārdula-vikṛīḍita, Anuṣṭubh, Mālini and Sragdhārā.***

PLATE NO. 4

MAINAMATI COPPERPLATE GRANT OF RANAVANKAMALLA HARIKALA DEVA OBVERSE

TEXT

ONLY OBEVERSE

[१]ओम्

तस्मिन्नुच्चैरमलिनकुले विश्वविख्यातकीर्त्ति-
र्विद्याधारः परमसुकृ[२]ती मण्डनम्पण्डितानाम्।
ख्यातः श्रीमानजनि स महान् हेडिएबाभिधानो
यस्य[३]स्वच्छे व्यचरदनिशम्मानसे धर्महंसः ।।१।।
तस्मादभूदमलकीर्तिकलावितानः
[४]श्रीमानमात्यतिलको मनुजामलेन्दुः(।)
द्रष्टा शशी तमिति यस्त्रुटिवृद्धिशाठ्या-
[५]ल्लज्जारजीश्वयधु(?)मानिव सविभाति ।।२।।
अविरहात्स महाश्वनिबन्धिकः परम[६]तत्त्वमहत्त्वमधिष्ठितः(।)
रुचिररीतिषु नीतिषु गीष्पतिः सहजधर्मसु कर्मसु [७]शोभते ।।३।।
दानध्यानमहोदधिः प्रविचलच्चित्तैककारागृहं
तप्त्वास्वादतृ(?)षा[८]मयः कतिदयाधारः परप्राणिनां।
धर्म्मस्यातुलकेलिसद्म सुकृती गुप्तैकयो[९]गीश्वरः
सो(ऽ)यं श्रीधडिएब एक उद्रभूदानन्दचन्द्रो भुवि ।।४।।
यस्यैवाश्वनिबन्धि[१०]को(ऽ)यमभवत् क्षोणीन्द्रचूडामणे-
स्तस्य श्री रणवङ्कमल्लनृपतेर्लीलापि लोको[११]त्तरा।
आक्रामद्भिरितस्ततस्त्रिजगतीं यत्तद्यशोभिः सितैः
प्रासाद्रे(=दे)ऽपि नि[१२]जे सहस्तनयनो जातोऽवनीनामितः ।।५।।
दुर्गोत्ताराविहारी रुचिरविर[१३]चिता पट्टिकेरानगर्यां
ये ये धर्मस्य कामं मुकुटविरचनाप्रक्रियेवाभि[१४]भाति।
ग्रामेऽस्यै वेजखण्डे निजसरलहृदा विंशतिर्द्रोणभूमि-
र्दत्ताचन्द्रा[१५]र्कमास्तामतिविमलयशः शस्यसम्यक् कृषिश्च ।।६।।
युक्तस्तदस्य कीर्तेर्य[१६]त् सर्वत्र भवति भ्रमः।
दत्ता दक्षिणचितेन चतुः सीमेति भूः स्वयम्।।७।।
हं [१७] हो बोधत भाविभूमिपतयो यत्ताम्रपत्राङ्कुरं
युष्मानश्वनिबन्धि[१८]को(य)मधुना कृत्वाञ्जलिं याचते।
पालया भूमिरियं न वा कतिपयद्रोणे[१९]न राज्यस्थिति-
र्धिग्दैन्यं विधवेव सा वसुमति यस्या[२०]न प्रीयात् पतिः ।।८।।

सहजगुणमहिम्ना यद्यपीयं स्वभावा-
दति विलसति गुप्ता वंशजानां[२१]प्रशस्तिः।
विमलकुलगुणौघैर्गाढमाकृष्यमाणः
प्रकटयति तदित्थं [२२]मेदिनीएब एषः ॥९॥
शकनृपतेन(र)तीता अब्दाः ११४१ रणवङ्क-
[२३]मल्लश्रीमत् हरिकालदेवपादानां सप्तदश सम्वत्सरेऽभिलिख्य-
[२४]माने पत्राङ्केनापि संवत् १७ सूर्यगत्या फाल्गुन दीन(द्रि) २६ (।)

Translation of the Text

Verse-1 In that high and pure family there was born a great gentleman called **Hedi-Eba,** the repository of learning, highly meritorious, ornament of **Pandits**, well-known and in whose pure mind, there always swam the swan of **Dharma**.

Verse-2 From him was born the honorable, crest of ministers spreading the canopy of the spotless fame, the pure moon among men; having seen him, the moon appears having the shame and the swelling of dropsy under the pretext of waning and waxing.

Verse-3 That chief officer of the horses, continuously stationed in the greatness of the Supreme Element, the master of the worlds, always shines in the polities of charming courses and in the activities of the ***Sahaja*** cult.

Verse-4 Then there arose this **Dhādi-Eba**, the only joyous Moon on the earth, who was a great ocean of charities and austerities, the prison house of the fickle mind, full of thirst for the experience of the Supreme, support for numberless, compassion over the other animals, the incomparable pleasure-house of **Dharma**, the meritorious and a master ascetic privately.

Verse-5 And even the graceful sports of the king Raṇavaṅkamalla, the crest-jewel among the kings, whose chief horse officer he was, were extra ordinary, for wide glories attacking all the three worlds here and there made even the thousand-eyed god (i.e., Indra) (though seated) in his own palace made to bow down on earth.

Verse-6 The small monastery of (Goddess) **Durgottārā** is beautifully created in the city of Paṭṭikera and very much shines like the process of creating crown of this ***Dharma***. For that monastery, the land of 20 dronas, in this village **Bejakhaṇḍa**, was given by him with his simple heart. May his very pure fame stay till the Sun and the Moon shine and may the farming of corns also be proper.

Verse-7 It is proper that his fame wanders in all directions as he has himself donated the land with four boundaries with an honest mind.

Verse-8 Ho! Kings of the future, may you mark the writing of this copper-plate; this horse-officer requests you now with folded hands that this land should be protected as the steadiness of a kingdom is not dependent upon a few dronas: Fie upon such miserliness; widow is that earth whose master is very small (at heart).

Verse-9 Even through this praise of the descendant of this family naturally shines brilliantly, protected by the greatness of their natural Virtues, yet this **Medini-Eba**, attracted intensely by multitude of the qualities of the pure family, thus announces:-

22-24 That 1141 years of the Saka king have passed away when this is being written in the 17th year of the honourable Raṇavaṅkamalla lord Śrī Harikala Deva, whereby, even numerically the year 17, according to solar calender, this 26th day of Phalguna.

MAINĀMATĪ COPPERPLATE OF SRI VIRADHARA DEVA

Introduction

This copperplate was discovered in a mound known as

Cārpatra Murā in 1954A. D. This mound, **Cārpatra Murā**, is situated on the western side of Comilla town, southern side of Dhaka-Comilla road, near the **Kutilā Murā** and Brigade Headquarters of Bangladesh Regiment. The plate was found in a good condition. It is now in the custody of the Directorate of Archaeology.

This is a single copperplate engraved on both the sides, measuring about 11" by 9". It bears a seal projecting about 1" to the top of the middle of the plate on both the sides. In line 8 on the obverse, the seal, attached to the top, is described as the ***Śrīthat Viṣṇu Cakra Mudrā***. It presents a wheel flanked on two sides by two symbols of conch. The seal consists of one outer circle and eight thin spoke-like motif arms around two internal circles. It represents the ***cakra*** of lord **Viṣṇu**. At the end of the text, on the reverse, is engraved a figure of a running dog. This grant consists of 23 lines of which 11 are engraved on the obverse and 12 on the reverse. The size of the aplhabets is 3/8" on the obverse and 1/2" on the reverse.

The text opens with name of **Śrī Laḍaha Mādhava.** It is the form of lord **Vasudeva.** Altogether 17 patakas of land were donated for the increase of merit and fame of the doner King **Śrī Vīradhara Deva** and his parents. The donated lands are situated in **Samataṭa Maṇḍala** of **Pauṇḍravarddhanabhukti.**

The character of the script is proto-Bengali and the language is Sanskrit. It has a very small text, entirely in prose and contains no panygyric verses in the beginning nor imprecatory verses in the end.

TEXT

OBVERSE

[१] श्री लडहमाधवाभिधान श्री वासु-

[२] देव भट्टारकाय श्रीमता श्री वी-

[३] रधरदेवेन पुण्येऽहनि विधिव-

PLATE NO. 5

MAINAMATI COPPERPLATE GRANT OF VIRADHARA DEVA OBERSE

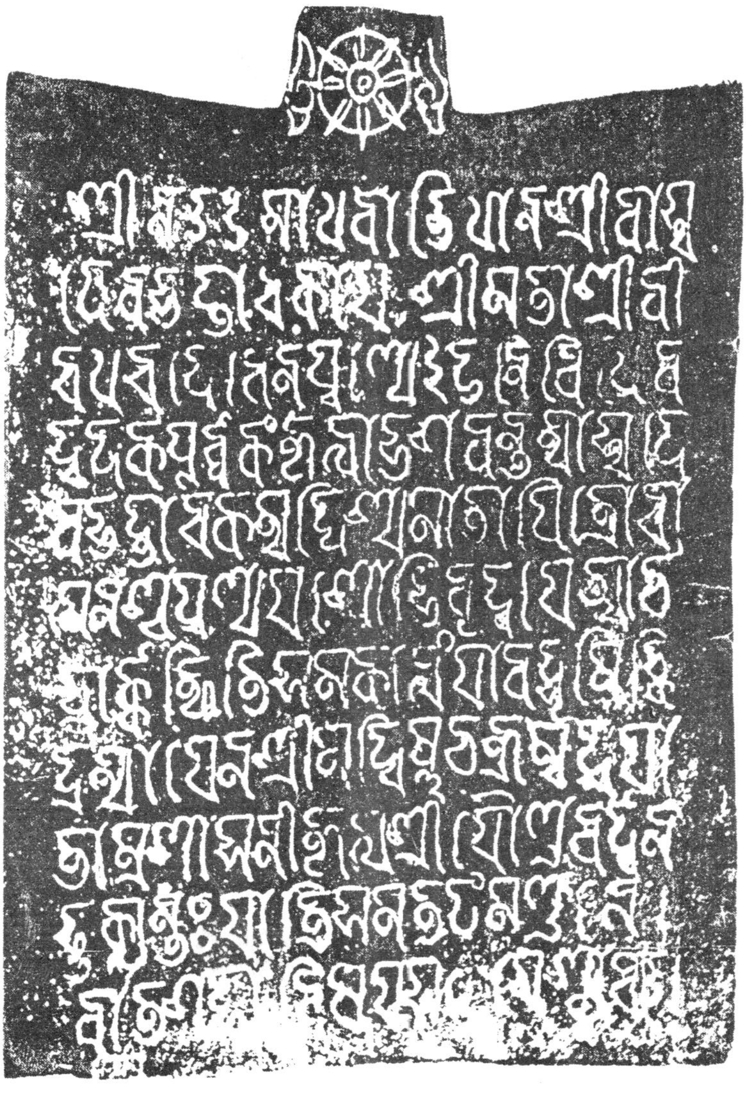

[४] दुदकपूर्वकं कृत्वा भगवन्तम् वासुदे-

[५] व भट्टारकमुद्दिश्य मातपित्रोरा-

[६] त्मनश्च पुण्ययशोभिवृद्धये आच-

[७] न्द्राक्र्क क्षितिसमकालं यावत् भूमिच्छि-

[८] द्रन्यायेन श्रीमत्विष्णुचक्रमुद्रया

[९] ताम्रशासनीकृत्य श्रीपौण्ड्रवर्द्धन

[१०] भुक्तान्तःपाति समतटमण्डले

[११] वातगङ्गा विषय सं मेश्वावर्त

TEXT

REVERSE

[१२] अधवसा ग्रामयोः हट्टघट्टतरबलजम

[१३] लक्षं गुवाकादिसमेतद्वादशपाटकाः ग-

[१४] ङ्गामण्डलविषयसं नारोराके हट्टादि

[१५] समेत पञ्च पाटकाः एवं हट्टादि समे

[१६] त सप्तदशपाटकभूमिः स्वसीमावच्छिन्ना

[१७] तृणपूतिगोचरपर्य्यन्ता सतला सोद्देशा साम्र-

[१८] पनसा सगुवाकनारिकेला सलवणा सजल-

[१९] स्थला सगर्त्तोषरा अचाटभटप्रवेशा अकि-

[२०] ञ्चित्प्रग्राह्या समस्तराजभोगकरहिरण्य-

[२१] प्रत्यायसहिता प्रदत्तेति यत्र भूयाज्ञा

[२२] अनया ताम्रफली १ श्रीमत् वीरधरदेव

[२३] पादीय सम्वत् १५ कार्तिक दिन ९

TRANSLATION OF THE TEXT

1-3 For the illustrious Lord **Vāsudeva** (in the form of) **Śrī Mādhava** by name by honorable **Śrī Vīradharadeva,** on this auspicios day.

3-6 having made it over ceremonially first with water, hav-

PLATE NO. 5

MAINAMATI COPPERPLATE GRANT OF VIRADHARA DEVA REVERSE

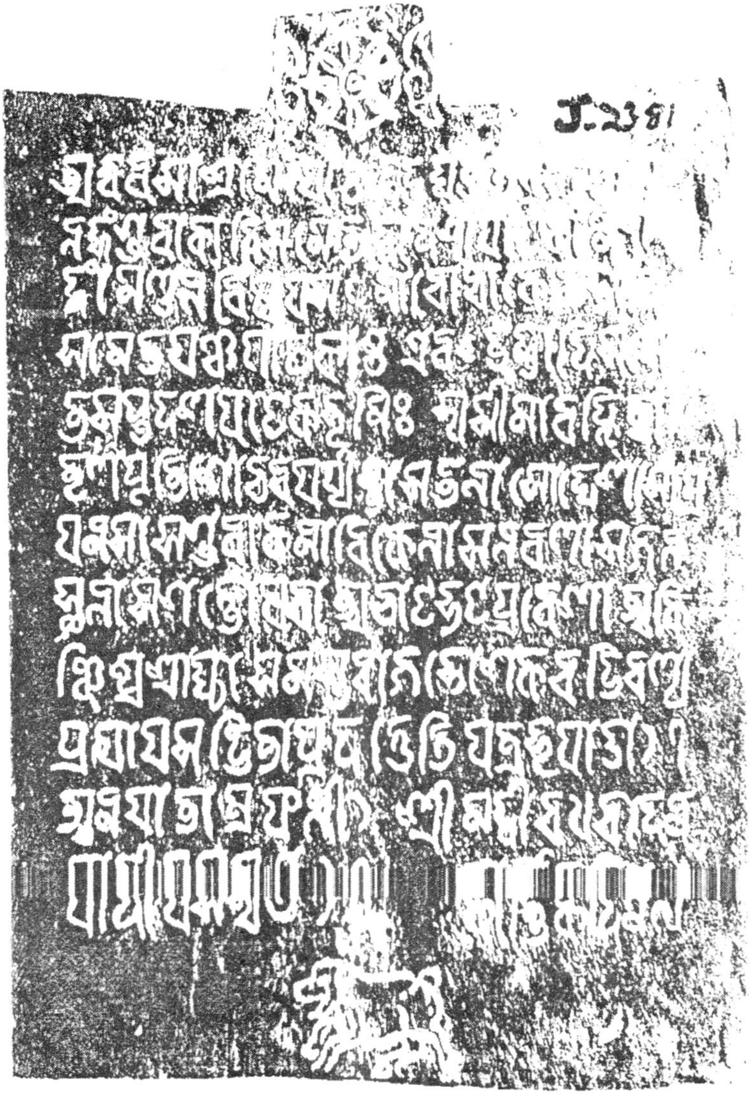

ing directed it to the God Lord **Vāsudeva,** for the growth of the merits and fame of his moter-father and his own self.

6-9 Up to the time of (the existence of) the earth, the sun and the moon, on the principle of the bhumicchidra (land from which no income is taxed, a hole in the entire land, a land from which all royal command is withdrawn), having copper-plated the order with the seal of the disc of Lord **Viṣṇu,**

9-13 the land of twelve patakas together with betel-nut trees etc. and not taking into accont (the income) arising out of market places, water-landings, groups of boats etc. in the villages **Meśvāvarta** and **Adhabasā** connected with the area of **Vataganġā** in Division of Samataṭa falling in the province os Śrī **Pauṇḍra-varddhana,** (and)

13-15 five patakas together with (the income of) markets etc, in (the village) **Nārorāka** connected with the area of **Gaṅgā Maṇḍala-**

15-16 thus the land of seventeen-patakas together with (the income of their) market-palaces etc,

16-19 demarcated by its own limits, up to the (lands of) grass-weeds-grazing fields, with their low and high areas, with their mangoes and jack-fruit trees, with their be-tel-nut and coconut trees, with their salt, water-places, with its pits and barren lands,

19-20 not to be entered by government officers and soldiers, not to be taken anything from, is granted,

20-23 together with its entire royal entertainment taxes, gold and income to which end, by this, (this) single copper-plate is taken to be the letter of order, (for the) 17 (Pāṭ akas) today the ninth day of Kārtika of the 15th regnal year of **Śrī Vīradhara Deva.**

SECTION-II
RAMPAL COPPER-PLATE OF SRĪ SRĪ CANDRA DEVA

Introduction

This copper-plate was found in the village of **Pañcasār,** near the village **Rāmpāl** of the **Munshigunj** district in the possession of one Yadunāth Banik in 1913 A.D. by **Rādhāgovinda Basāk** who purchased it from him on behalf of the Verendra Research Society. According to the historical background, the village **Rāmpāl** is well known to the historian. It is one and a half-mile distance from the village of **Pañcasar.** So, it seems that the original findspot of the copperplate must be somewhere in **Rampal.** It is now in the possession of the Society's Museum at **Rajshahi.**

This is a single plate incribed on both the sides, The plate measures about 9 1/2" × 8". A seal must have been attached to the top of the plate. It must have projected about 2 3/4". The seal is now broken away and lost irrecoverably. The breakage makes a half round gap in the middle top of the plate and breaks the first for lines on the obverse and the first two lines on the reverse. The seal is describad as the **Dharma Cakra Mudrā** in line three on the reverse. edges of the copperplate are raised into rims. The inscription consists of 40 lines of which 28 are engraved on the obverse and only 12 on the reverse, The size of the letters is about 1/4".

The text begins with benedictory "***Oṁ Savasti***", followed by verse in honour of **Jina** (e.e. buddha), **Dharma** and also indirectly of ***Samgha.*** It then mentions, the name of **Purṇa Candra** of **Rohitagiri** (2), his son **Suvarṇa Candra** (4 and 4), his son **Trailokya Candra**; who was the king of **Harikela** and who became the king of **Candradvīpa** (5), who was the king of **Harikela** and who became the king of **Candradvīpa** (5), his beloved queen **Śrīkāncana** (6), their son **Śrī Śrī candra** (7), and his victorious and glories (8). Thus eight verses describe the origin, the ancestors, birth and the victorious glory of the donor king, **Śrī Candra Deva.**

The prose section starts from the line 14. It mentions the

location of the granted land in the village of **Nahākāṣthi** in the **Nānya Maṇḍala** of the **Pauṇḍrabhukti**. This document was issued from his camp at **Vikramapura**. It rcords the grant of one **pataka** of land. The done was **Sāntivārika Pitavāsa Gupta Śarman** who belonged to **Śāndilya gotra**. This land was granted in the presence of all royal officers. The prose portion ends in the line 34.

There are five benedictory and imprecatory verses after the prose portion on the obverse of this grant. The peculiar thing about this plate is that it bears no date of donation of the doner king **Śrī Candra Deva.**

The characters are of the type of Northern **Nāgari.** There is a close similarity between the writing of this plate and that found in the copperplates of the later Pālas. The laguage is Sanskrit. There are altogether 13 vrses, which are composed in a variety of metres viz. ***Vasantatilaka, Śārdulavikṛīḍita, Upajāti, Anuṣṭubh*** and ***Puspitāgrā.***

TEXT OBVRSE

[१] ओम् स्वस्ति।

व[न्द्यो] जिनः स भगवान् करुणै(क)पात्रं

धर्म्मो(ऽ)प्यसौ[२]विजयते जगदेकदीपः।

यत्सेवया सकल एव महानुभावः

सं[३]सारपारमुपगच्छति भिक्षुसङ्घः ।।१।।

चन्द्राणामिह रोहितागि(रि)भुजां वङ्शे[४] विशालश्रियाम्

विख्यातो भुवि पूर्णचन्द्रसदृशः श्रीपूर्णचन्द्रोऽभवत्।

अर्च्चा[५]नाम्पदपीठिकासु पठितः सन्तानिनामग्रत-

ष्टङ्कोत्कीर्णनवप्रशस्तिषु जयस्तम्भेषु ताम्रेषु च ।।२।।

बुद्धस्य यः श[६]शकजातकमङ्कसंस्थं

भक्त्या बिभर्त्ति भगवान् अमृताकराङ्शुः।

PLATE NO. 6

RAMPAL COPPERPLATE GRANT OF SRI CANDRADEVA OBVERSE

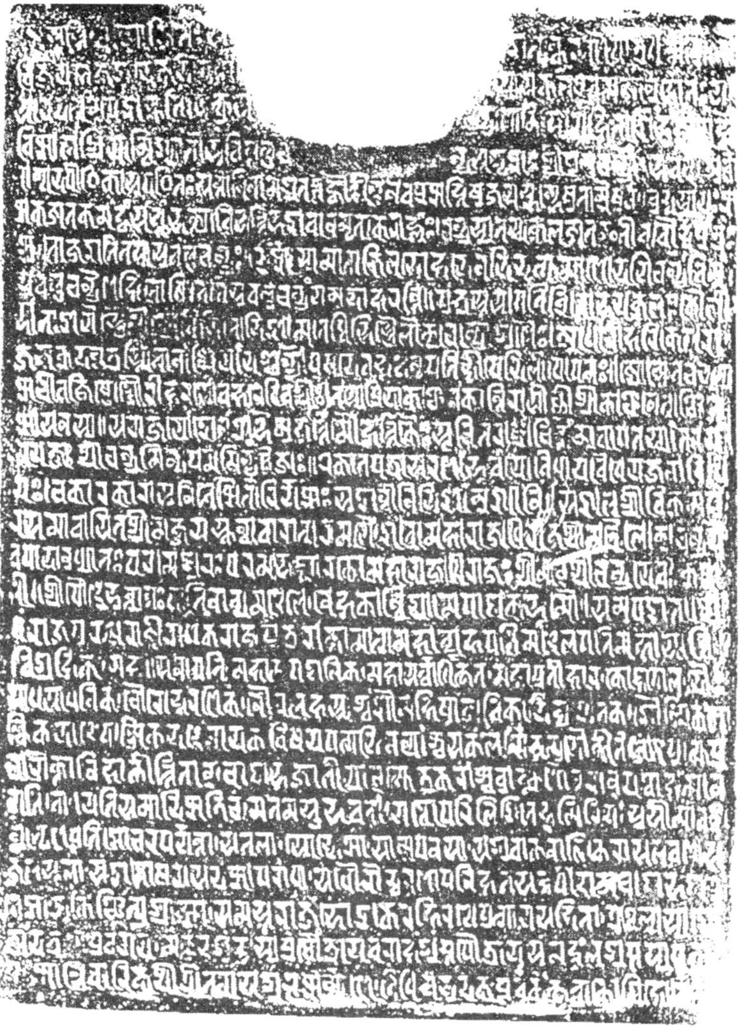

चन्द्रस्य तस्य कुलजात इतीव बौद्ध(:)
पुत्र:[७]श्रुती जगति तस्य सुवर्णचन्द्रः ।।३।।
द[र्शे](ऽ)स्य माता किल दोहदेन
दिदृक्षमाणोदयि चन्द्रबिम्बं।
[८] सुवर्णचन्द्रेण हि तोषितेति
सुवर्णचन्द्रं समुदाहरन्ति ।।४।।
पुत्रस्तस्य पवित्रितोभयकुलः कौलीन[९]भीताशयै-
स्त्रैलोक्ये विदितो दिशामतिथिभिस्त्रैलोक्यचन्द्रो गुणैः।
आधारो हरिकेलरा[१०]जककुदच्छत्रस्मितानां श्रियां
यश्चन्द्रोपपदे बभूव नृपतिर्द्वीपे दिलीपोपमः ।।५।।
ज्योत्स्नेव चन्द्रस्य[११]शचीव जिष्णो-
र्ग्गौरी हरस्येव हरेरिव श्रीः।
तस्य प्रिया काञ्चनकान्तिरासी-
च्छी(च्छ्र)काञ्चनेत्यञ्चित[१२]शासनस्य ।।६।।
स राजयोगेन शुभे मुहूर्त्ते
मौहूर्त्तिकैः सूचितराजचिह्नं(।)
आवाप तस्यां तनयं[१३]नयज्ञः
श्रीचन्द्रमिन्द(न्दू)पममिन्द्रतेजाः ।।७।।
एकातपत्राभरणां भुवं यो
विधाय वैधेयजनाविधे[१४]यः।
चकार कारासु निवेशितारि-
र्यशःसुगन्धीनि दिशां मुखानि ।।८।।
स खलु श्री विक्रमपु-

[१५]रसमावासित-श्रीमज्जयस्कन्धावारात् परमसौगतो महाराजाधिराजः श्रीमत् त्रैलोक्यचन्द्रदे-

[१६] वपादानुध्यातः परमेश्वरः परमभट्टारको महाराजाधिराजः श्रीमान्

PLATE NO. 6

RAMPAL COPPERPLATE GRANT OF SRI

CANDRADEVA REVESE

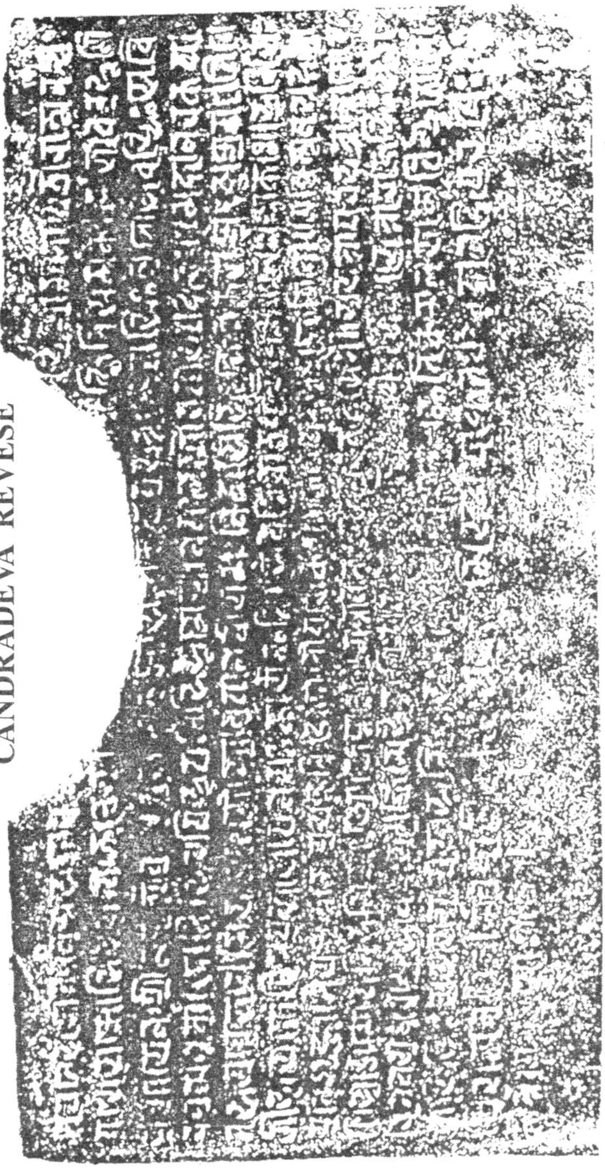

श्रीचन्द्रदेवः कुश-

[१७]ली।। श्रीपौण्ड्रभुक्त्यन्तःपातिनान्यमण्डले। नेहकाष्ठिग्रामे पाटकभूमौ।। समुपगताशे-

[१८]ष-राजपुरुषराज्ञीराणक-राजपुत्रराजामात्य-महाव्यूहपति-मण्डलपति-

महासान्धि-

[१९]विग्रहिक।महासेनापति। महाक्षपटलिक। महासर्व्वाधिकृत। महाप्रतीहार। कोट्टपाल। दौः-

[२०]साधसाधनिक।चौरोद्धरणिक।नौवलहस्त्यश्वगोमहिषाजाविकदिव्यापृतक। गौल्मिक। [शौ]-

[२१]ल्किक[।]दण्डपाशिक[।]दण्डनायक[।]विषयपत्य(त्या)दि(दी)नन्यांश्च सकल राजपादो(प)जीव(वि)नोऽध्यक्षप्र-

[२२]चारोक्तानिहाकीर्त्तितन्।चाटभ(ट)जातीयान् क्षेत्रकरांश्च ब्राह्मणोत्तरान् यथार्हं मान-

[२३]यति बोधयति समादिशति च। मतमस्तु भवतां। यथोपरिलिखितभूमिरियं। स्वसीमावच्छी(च्छि)-

[२४]न्ना। तृणपूतिगोचरपर्यन्ता। सतला। सोद्देशा। साम्रपनसा। सगुवाकनालिकेरा सलवणा स-

[२५]जलस्थला सगर्त्तोषरा सदशापराधा। सचौरोद्धरणा परिहतसर्व्वपीडा अचारभटप्र-

[२६]वेशा अकिञ्चित्प्रग्राह्या। समस्तराजभोगकरहिरण्यप्रत्यायसहिता। श(शा)थ(ण्डि)ल्यस्य गो-

[२७]त्राय त्र्य[र्षि]प्रवराय। मक्कडगुप्तस्य प्रपौत्राय वराहगुप्तपौत्राय सुमङ्गलगुप्तस्य पुत्रा-

[२८]य । शान्तिवारिक श्रीपीतवासगुप्तशर्म्मणे। विधिवदुदकपूर्वकं कृत्वा कोटिहोमे(ङ्)ग-

TEXT

REVERSE SIDE

[२९]तवते भगवन्तं बुद्धभट्टा(र)कमुद्दिश्य मातापित्रोरात्मनश्च।

[३०]पुण्ययशोभिवृद्धये। आचन्द्रार्क्कक्षितिसमकालं यावत्। भूमि(च्छि)-

[३१]द्रन्यायेन।श्रीमद्धर्म्म(च)क्रमुद्रया ताम्रशासनीकृत्य प्रदत्ताऽस्मभिः[।]अतो भवद्भिः सर्वै-

[३२]रनुमन्तव्यं।भाविभिरपि भूपतिभिर्भूमेर्दानफलगौरवादपहरणे महानरकपा-

[३३]तभयाच्च दानमिदमनुमोद्यानुपालनीयम्[।]निवासिभिः क्षेत्रकरांश्चऽ (आ)ज्ञाश्रवणविधे-

[३४]यीभूय (य)थोचितप्रत्यायोपनयः कार्य इति। भवन्ति चात्र धर्म्मानुशंसिनः श्लोकाः।।

भूमिं यः [३५]प्रतिगृह्णाति यश्च भूमिं प्रयच्छति।

उभौ तौ पुण्यकर्म्माणौ नियतं स्वर्ग्गगामिनौ ।।९।।

षष्ठिम्व[र्ष]सहस्त्रा।।[३६]णि स्वर्ग्गे मोदति भूमिदः।

आक्षेप्ता चानुमन्ता च तान्येव नरकं वसेत(त्) ।।१०।।

स्वदत्तां परदत्तां वा यो ह[३७]रेत वसुन्धराम्।

स विष्ठायां क्रि(कृ)मिर्भूत्वा पि[तृ]भिः [सह पच्यते] ।।११।।

बहुभिर्व(सु)धा दत्ता राजभिः सग[३८]रादिभिः[।]

यस्य यस्य यदा भूमि[स्त]स्य तस्य तदा फलम् ।।१२।।

इति कमलदा(द)(ला)म्बुबिन्दुलोलां

[३९]श्रियमनुचिन्त्य मनुष्यजीवितञ्च।

सकलमिदमुदाहृतञ्च बुद्ध्वा

न हि पुरुषैः पर[४०]कीर्त्तयो वि(लो)प्याः ।।१३।।

Translation of the Text

Line-1 ***Oṁ*** Bliss!

Verse-1 Obeisance to that lord Jina (i.e. Buddha), the singular receptacle of compassion. Even this religion ***(Dharma)*** the only lamp of the world becomes victorious, by following which the entire high-minded ***Saṅgha*** of monks goes to the end of this world.

Verse-2 In the line of die Candra kings of **Rohita** Mount of wide glory, there was Śrī **Pūrṇa Candra** like the full moon well-known on earth, who first among those possessing progeny, was mentioned on the pedestals of idols in the fresh panegyrics carved with chisels, on victory-pillars and copper-plates.

Verse-3 As he was born in the family of that **Candra** who the lord with the nectar-like rays bears with devotion the ***Śaśa-jātaka*** of lord **Buddha** in his lap (or in his mark), his Buddhist son was well-known in the world as **Suvarṇa Candra**.

Vcrsc-4 His mother had a longing *(=dohadit-desirse* of a pregnant woman) to see the rising orb of the moon on the no-moon night, which was satisfied by a golden moon (orb of full moon artificially created from gold). Hence (they) call him "**Suvarṇa Candra**".

Verse-5 His son was **Trailokya Candra** who purified both the families (i.e. paternal and thaternal), afraid at heart of popular censure, well-known in the three worlds by his good qualities- the guests of directions, who was the support of the royal glories smiling with the royal umbrella having the symbol[6] of the kings of **Harikela** and who became a **Dilipa**-like king in the island having '**Candra**' as its penultithate word.

Verse-6 Like the moon-light of the moon, like **Śaci** of **Jiṣṇu** (i.e. **Indra**), like **Gauri** of **Hara** and **Lakṣmī** of **Hari**, **Śrīkāñcana** of golden hue was the beloved of him whose reign was moving (i.e. progressing).

Verse-7 He, the knower of polity and possessing **Indra**-like brilliance, obtained in her at an auspicious hour, in the ***Rājayoga***[7], a son (named) **Śrī Candra** comparable to moon and in whom royal signs were suggested by the astrologers.

Verse-8 Who, not to be guided by foolish persons, having put the enemies in jails and having made the earth decorated by a single umbrella, made the faces of the directions fragrant with his fame.

14-16 From his illustrious "Camp of Victory", situated at **Vikramapura**, ***Parameśvara, Paramabhaṭṭāraka, Mahārājādhirāja***, the illustrious **Śrī Candra Deva**, meditating upon the feet of the ***Paramasaugata, Mahārājādhirāja*** **Śrī Trailokya Candra Deva**, is hale and hearty.

17. Under **Pauṇḍrabhūkti**, in **Nānya Maṇḍala** , at the village of **Nehākāṣṭhi**, in the thatter of one ***Pāṭaka*** of land;

17-18. Duly honours, informs and orders all those that are present Viz.,***Rājapuruṣa, Rājñi, Rāṇakas , Rājaputras, Rājathatyas, Mahāvyukapati, Maṇḍalapati, Mahāsāndhivigrahika,***

19-22 ***Mahāsenāpati, Mahākṣapatalika, Mahāsarvvddhikrta , Mahāpratihāra, Kottapala, Dauḥsādhāsādhānikā, Cauroddhraṇika,*** engaged officers-in-charge cf fleet, infantry, elephant corps, cavalry, cows, buffaloes, goats, sheep, etc., *Gaulmika, Saulkika, Daṇḍapasika, Daṇḍanāyaka,* officer-in-charge of *Viṣaya* and all other servants of the king mentioned in the list of the *Adhyakṣas* but not specified here, the people of the class of *Cāṭas* and *Bhatas,* countrymen, the tillers of the land and best among the Brahmins;

22-26 Be it known to you that this land as described above demarcated by its own boundaries, along with the grass, puti-plants and pasture lands, with low and high lands, with mango and jack-fruit trees, with betelnut and coconut trees, with salt, with water and land, with pits and barren tracts, with tolerance of Ten crimes, with police protection, immune from all kinds of forced labour, not to be entered by *Cāṭas* and *Bhaṭas,* not to be taxed at all, along with all the incomes such as taxes and gold enjoyed by the king-

26-31 is presented by us to *Santivārika* Śrī Pitavasāgupta Śarman[9], who is the great grandson of Makkaḍa Gupta, grand son of Varāha Gupta and son of Sumaṅgala Gupta, belonging to the Sāṇḍilya gotra and Pravara[10] of the three Ṛṣis, has undergone the *Kotihoma*[11] (ceremony or who has attended or performed a crore of oblations), after doing water rite, having addressed the lord **Buddha Bhaṭṭāraka** for the increase of the merit and fame of his parents and his ownself, as long as the Sun, Moon and Earth endure, according to the law of *Bhūmicchadra,* by means of a copper-plate charter and affixing the illustrious *Dharmacakra* seal.

31-34 Therefore it should be approved by all of you. This gift should be approved of and protected by the future kings also considering that gift of land entails enormous merit and its taking away, the fear of falling into the great hell. The inhabitants and the peasants should be obeyed and all dues that are proper should be paid.

34 There are also verses in praise of *Dharma* in this thatter:

Verse-9 One who accepts the land, and one who gifts the land are both (persons of) meritorious deed, both will definitely go to heaven.

Verse-10 The giver of the land enjoys in the heaven for sixty thousand years; the interrupter and his supporter would live in hell for so many years.

Verse-11 He, who snatches away the land given by his ownself or by others, is rotten with his forefathers having become a worm of the dung.

Verse-12 Many kings like Sagara etc. have donated land; whoever is the master of that land at a certain time obtains the fruit at that time.

Verse-13 Therefore, having thought of wealth and human life as fickle as a drop of water on a petal of lotus, and having understood all the sayings above, the persons should not efface the fames (i.e. good deeds) of others.

KEDARPUR COPPER PLATE OF SRĪ SRĪ CANDRADEVA

Introduction

This copper plate was discovered in the course of digging a trench at the village of **Kedarpur** in the district of **Madaripur** in 1919 A.D. N. K. Bhattasali soon noticed the plate. He got it for the Dhaka Museum, now called the National Museum, Dhaka.

This is a single plate inscribed on one side only. It is 8.5" long and *$7^1/_2$"* wide. It bears a seal on the top of the plate. The projection of this seal is about $2^3/_4$". Due to the attachment of the seal on the top, it makes a break in the middle of the first two lines, only on the obverse. The seal consists of a number of concentric circles. It is . divided into two parts by a small line of inscription, which reads Śrī Srf Candra Deva. On the upper part of the small inscription, there is a decorated motif of a wheel flanked on two sides by two deer. This type of wheel is also traced in the Pāla copper-plates. Lower part of the seal contains floral motif. The inscription consists of 18 lines. The size of the letter is about *3/10"*. It is an incomplete grant.

The text opens with auspicious *Om Svasti* followed by verses in honour- of Jina, *Dharma* and *Saṅgha* (1), then Pūrṇa Candra (V-2), his son Suvarṇa Candra (V.3),his son Trailokya Candra (V-4,5) and his son Śrī Candra (V-6,7). Then, lines 16-18, mention the illustrious "Camp of Victory" situated at Vikramapura.

The characters are of a type of Northern Nagari, which is closely related to the alphabet of the Pāla copperplates. The language is Sanskrit. There are altogether seven verses, which are composed in various metres like *Vasantatilaka, Anuṣṭubh Śārdulavikrīḍita, Upajāti, Indravajrā* and *Sragdhārā.*

PLATE NO. 7

KEDARPUR COPPERPLATE GRANT OF SRI CANDRADEVA OBVERSE

TEXT

श्री चन्द्रदेवः

[१]ओम् स्वस्ति
वन्द्यो जिनः स भगवान् करुणै(क)पात्रं
[२]धर्म्मो(ऽ)प्यसौ विजयते जगदेकदीपः।
यत्सेवया[३]सकल एव महानुभावः
संसारपारमुपगच्छति भिक्षुसङ्घः ॥१॥
पूर्ण[४]चन्द्र इति श्रीमानासीन्नासीरजं रजः।
यस्यो(---)मातपत्रमपत्र[५]पाः ॥२॥
नाग्नौ विशुद्धो न तुलाधिरूढः
किन्तु प्रकृत्यैव युतो गरिम्णा।
तथापि क[६]ल्याणसुवर्णकल्पः
सुवर्णचन्द्रस्सुकृती ततोऽभूत् ॥३॥
पुण्यावलोकः परलो[७]कभीरो-
र्लोक्यः समाश्वासितजीवलोकः
त्रैलोक्यसंकीर्त्तितपुण्यकीर्त्तेः
त्रै[८]लोक्यचन्द्रोऽस्य बभूव पुत्रः ॥४॥
चतुःपयोराशिसमाप्तपृथ्वी-
जयाभिलाषो वि[९]षयेष्वलुब्धाः।
युद्धेषु निस्त्रिंङ्शलवाजलेन
यो वैरिवह्निं स(=श)मयाञ्चकार ॥५॥
[१०]श्रीमान् श्रीचन्द्रदेवः समजनि तनयस्तस्य सद्वर्त्मबन्धोः
क्रूरारम्भे स(द)यालुः[११]परगुणमुखरो दोषवादैकमूकः(।)
प्रेक्ष्यः पीनो गुणानां निधिरिति [१२]विषयासक्तिपक्षाद्विपक्षे
यस्मिन्नाधत्त वेधा श्रियमतिरभसादर्थतो ना[१३]मतश्च ॥६॥
स्पृष्टः पार्थिवपांसुदोह(द)रसश्लाघाघन(=नै)दि(र्दि)ग्गजै-
र्नेत्राणामनिमे[१४]षतः परिहृतो दूरेण वृन्दारकैः(।)

केशेष्वप्सरसामपूर्व्वपलितभ्रान्तं [१५]समारोपयन्

सन्तानो रजसां रणेषु जयिनो यस्य द्युमार्ग्गं गतः ।।७।।

[१६]स खलु श्री विक्रमपुरसमावासित-श्रीमज्जयस्कन्धावारात् परमसौगतो

[१७]महाराजाधिराजः श्रीत्रैलोक्यचन्द्रदेवपादानुध्यातः परमेश्वरः प-

[१८]रमभट्टारको महाराजाधिराजः श्रीमान् श्रीचन्द्रदेवः कुशली।।

Translation of the Text

Line-1 ***Om*** Bliss!

Verse-1. Obeisance to that lord **Jina** (i.e. buddha), the singular receptacle of compassion. Even this religion (**Dharma**), the only lamp of the world becomes victorious, by following which the entire high-minded ***Saṅgha*** of monks goes to the end of this world.

Verse-2. There was one respectable (king called) **Pūrṇa Candra** the dust raised by whose army-front....... the umbrella by the (enemies) without shame (?).

Verse-3. From him was born the meritorious **Suvarṇa Candra** who though not purified by fire and not ascending the scales, still was naturally endowed with dignities like the auspicious gold.

Verse-4. Of him who was afraid of the other world, and whose fame was well praised in the three worlds was born a son (called) **Trailokya Candra** having noble appearance, handsome and in whom the living world found consolation;

Verse-5. Who, possessing desire to win over this earth bounded by four oceans and not greedy of worldly objects, extinguished the five of his enemies in the battles by the water of creeper-like sword.

Verse-6. Of that friend of good path, was born a fortunate son **Śrī Candra Deva,** who was compassionate in cruel activities, eloquent about others' qualities, and absolutely silent in mentioning their faults, handsome, strongly built, treasure of qualities, opposed to the side of worldly enjoyments, in whom lord Brahma placed the goddess Lakṣmī very forcefully both in spirit and in name (letters).

Verse-7. Of whom the victorious, the continuum of dust (raised) in the battles and rising on the heavenly path was touched by the quarter-elephants intensely happy at the joy of longing for the dust of the king (being fulfilled), was avoided from distance by gods due to the non-winking of their eyes, and which created an unprecedented confusion of white hair in the hair of nymphs.

16-18. From his illustrious "Camp of Victory" situated at Vikramapura, *Paramesvara, Paramabhaṭṭāraka, Mahārājādhirāja,* illustrious Śrī Candra Deva, meditating the upon the feet of the *Paramasaugata, Mahārajādhirāja* Śrī Trailokya Candra Deva, is hale and hearty.

MADANPUR COPPER-PLATE OF SRI SRICANDRA DEVA

Introduction

This copperplate was discovered in the village **Madanpur**, near the old and famous village of **Sabhar**, under Dhaka district, in June 1946, when earth was being dug out for the foundation of a wall on the land belonging to one **Sekh Newajuddin**. The village Madanpur is situated about 15 miles north-west of the Dhaka city. The plate was found in a fair state of preservation. Unfortunately, the left corner of this plate was cut away by the illiterate worker of the foundation-wall, probably for testing its metal out of greed for gold.

This is a single plate engraved on both the sides. The plate is $8^1/_4$" long and 6.5" wide. It bears a seal attached to the middle of the top, measuring about $4'/_2$" × $3^1/_4$" and causes a break in the middle of the first three lines on the obverse only. It consists of four concentric circles and is divided into two parts by a small-inscribed line which reads ***Śrī Śrī Candra Devah***. There is a small wheel, on top of this inscribed line, flanked by two antelopes. The wheel consists of eight spokes. Lower part of the inscribed line is a floral motif. The basement of the seal also shows a floral motif. According to the other plate of Śrī Candra, we know this seal as a *Dharma Cakra Mudrā,* It may be noted that seals of this types were also attached to the top of the copper charters of Buddhist Pāla kings of Bengal. The edges of this plate are raised into rims on the obverse, evidently for the preservation of the writing. It consists of altogether 42 lines of which 23 lines are engraved on the obverse and 19 on the reverse. The style of the writing is excellent, the alphabet in all lines being almost of uniform size, which is about $1/_4$".

The text opens with auspicious *Oṁ Svasti*. It is followed by 8 verses in praise of the predecessors of the royal donor. First verse praises Jina, ***Dharma and Saṅgha***. It then mentions the name of Śn" Pīrṇa Candra, like the full moon on earth, of **Rohita Mount** (V-2), his son **Suvarṇa Candra** (V.3-4), his son **Trailokya Candra**, who was the support of the kings of Harikela and who, became the king of **Candradvīpa** (V-5), his beloved queen **Srī Kāñcana** (V-6), their son **Śrī Candra** (V-7), his victories and glories (V-8). Thus, eight verses indicate the origin, the ancestors, birth and the victorious glory of the donor king **Śrī Candra Deva**.

The first prose portion begins from line 17 and ends in 29. The illustrious Camp of Victory of the king was situated at **Vikramapura**. The location of the donated land is in the (village of) Vāṇḍāriyaka in the **Yola Maṇḍala** of **Pauṇḍraibhukti**. Total measurement of the donated land is not clear because of the breakage of the plate. The remaining portion of the plate mentions only 8 drons of land. The land was donated, with reference to the **Lord Buddha Bhaṭṭāraka**, doing water rite for the increase of the merit and fame of the donor's parents and himself.

After this prose portion, there are 6 verses describing the genealogy of the donee, honourable **Sukra Deva**. Three ancestors of this by name **Mākha, Rāma** and Dhruva (V-9) are mentioned. From the line of these Brahmins, was bom Mahā Deva (V-10), his son **Varāha** (V-ll), Ms son **Hari** (V-12) and his son, the donee **Sukra Deva** (V-13,14).

Again, there is a prose portion in lines 36-37 which contains a request to the future kings to protect the land otherwise, there is the fear of falling into the great hell.

After this prose portion, there are three benedictory and imprecatory verses. After all, it has mentioned the date of donation i.e. 44 regnal year of the donor king Śrī Candra, on the 28th day of the month **Mārga Śrī** ṣa.

The characters are the type of Northern **Nāgari which** is allied to the alphabet found in the copper-plates of the latter Pālas and current in North-eastern India towards the close of tenth and beginning of the eleventh century A.D. The language is Sanskrit. There are altogether 17 verses of various metres viz. *Vasantatilaka, Sārdulavikrīḍitaṁ, Upajāti, Upendravajrā, Anuṣṭubh* and *Puṣpitāgra*.

TEXT

OBVERSE

[The first eight verses are the same as those of the Rampal Copperplate. Hence they are omitted here]

स खलु श्रीविक्रमपुरसमावासित-श्री

[१८][मज्जय]स्कन्धावारात् परमसौगतो महाराजाधिराजः श्रीत्रैलोक्यचन्द्रदेवपा

[१९][दानुध्या]तः परम(मे)श्वर[ः पर]मभट्टारको महाराजाधिराजः श्रीमान् श्रीचन्द्रदे

[२०][वः कुश]ली(।।)श्रीपौण्ड्र[भु]क्तयान्तःपाति योलामण्डले वंगसागर सं भाण्डारियके

[२१]---ष्टाधिकाष्टद्रोणभूमौ समुपगताशेष-राज्ञीराणक-राजपुत्र-

[२२][राजपु]रोहितमहासान्धिविग्रहिक। महासेनापति। महासामन्त।

[२३][महाधर्म्मा]ध्यक्ष मह(हा)सर्व्व(र्व्वा)धिकृत। महातन्त्राध्यक्ष। महापीलुपति। गोष्ठ[क]

PLATE NO. 8

MADANPUR COPPERPLATE GRANT OF SRI CANDRADEVA OBVERSE

TEXT

REVERSE SIDE

[२४]पति अर्द्धनौवाटक। नौवाटक। दुस्साध्यसाधनिक। गोमहिष्यजा[ध्य]-

[२५]क्षानन्यांश्चानुक्तान् व्रा(ब्रा)ह्मणोत्तरान् मानयति वो(बो)धयति। वदति आ[दि]श-

[२६]ति च। भूमिरियं। स्वसीमावच्छिन्ना। सोद्देशा। सगुवाकनालिकेरा। साम्रप

[२७]नसा।सगर्त्तोषरा। अचाटभटप्रवेशा। द्रअकिञ्चिद्ग्राह्या। सदशापराध(।)

[२८][स]प्रजा अगस्त्या-तृतीयायां स्नात्वा विधिवदुदकपूर्वकं कृत्वा भगवन्तं बुद्ध[भट्टा]-

[२९]रकमुद्दिश्यमाता[पि]त्रोरात्मनश्च पुण्ययशोऽभिव(वृ)द्धये

[३०]माखरामध्रुवाकारा [यज्ञी]याः सोमपितिमः(पीथिनः)।

भूमिदेवाः किलाभूवन(न्) सुख्यातप्रवरत्रयाः ।।९।।

तदन्वये[३१][समुत्प]न्नो महादेव इति द्विजः(।)

देवेष्विव महादेवो भूदेवेषु व(ब)भूव यः ।।१०।।

श्रुतिक्रतुपृ(प्रि)य[३२]रस्तस्य वाराहाख्यः सुतोऽभवत् ।

हरेरादिवराहस्य सालोक्यं प्रेत्य योऽगमत्।।११।।

धरा[३३][ध]रसमक्षे यः साक्षाद्धर इवापरः(।)

हरो नामाभवत्तस्य तनयो विनयान्वितः ।।१२।।

भावि[त][३४]वार्धकस्त्रय्यामार्य्यस्सज्जनवासवः।

यदुकः क्रमुकः श्रीमान् शुक्रदेवो(ऽ)भवत्त[तः] ।।१३।।

[३५]एकदेशभवस्तस्मै स्मितपूर्व्वाभिभाषिणे

श्रीमते शुक्रदेवाय श्रीचन्द्रनृप[तिर्द][३६]दौ ।।१४।।

तद्भवद्भिरनुमोदनीया भाविभिरपि भूपतिभिर्भ(भू)मिदाने महाफल-[गौरवात्]हरणे[च महा]-

[३७]पातकदर्शनादनुप(पा)लनीयेति।। भवन्ति चात्र धर्म्मानुर्शसिनः श्लोकाः।।

भू[मिं यः प्रतिगृ][३८]ह्णाति यश्च भूमि प्रयच्छति(।)

उभौ तौ पुण्यकर्म्माणौ नियतं स्वर्ग्गगामिनौ।।१५।।

[स्वदत्तां][३९]परदत्तां वा यो हरेत वसुन्धरा(म्)।

स विष्ठायां कृमिर् भूत्वा पितृभिः सह [पच्यते] ।।१६।।

[४०]इति कमलदलाम्बुबिन्दुलोलां

श्रियमनुचिन्त्य मनुष्यजीवितञ्च।

स[कलमिदमु][४१]दाहृतञ्च वु(बु)ध्वा(द्धवा)

न हि पुरुषैः परकीर्त्तयो विलोप्याः ।।१७।।

श्रीश्रीचन्द्र[देवपादीय]

[४२]सम्वत् ४४ मार्ग्गदिने २८ मा सा नि अनु नि महा[क्ष]।।

Translation of the Text

17-20 from his illustrious "**Camp of Victiory**" situated at **Vikaramapura, *Parameśvara, Paramabhaṭṭāraka, mahārājādhirāja,*** the illusrious **Śrī Candra Deva,** meditating upon the feet of the ***Paramasaugata, Mahārājādhirāja* Śrī trailokya Candra Deva,** is hale and hearty.

20-21 Under **Puṇḍra-Bhukti**, in **Yolā Maṇḍala,** connected with **Vaṅga sagara** at **Vāṇḍāriyaka ....** eight dronas....... of land.

21-25 (He) duly honours, imforms and orders all the officers together viz, Queen, ***Rāṇakas, Rājaputras, Rājapurohitas*** *(royal priests),* **Mahāsāndhivigrahika, Mahāsenāpati, *Mahāsāmanta*.** (the great feudatory prince), ***Mahādharmmādhykṣa*** (the supreme officer ofreligionthatter),**Mahāsarvvadhikrita, Mahātantradhykṣ a** (the chief officer of administration), **Mahāpilupati** (chief of Agriculture), **gosthakapati** (chief of husbandry), **Ardhanauvataka** (semi-ferry stations), **Nauvataka**[12] (ferry-stations) **dusadhyasadhanika,** engaged officer-in-charge of cows, buffaloes and goats and all other servants of the king mentioned in the list of the Adhyakas but not specified here, and best among the Brahmins.

25-27 Be it known to you all that this land demarcated by its own boundaries, along with high lands, with mango and jack-fruit trees, with betel nut and coconut trees, with pits and barren tracts, with tolerance ot Ten crimes, not to be entered by **caṭas** and **bhaṭas**, not to be taxed at all.

28-29 after bathing and doing water rite, having addressed to the Loārd Buddha Bhaṭṭāraka for the increase of the merit and fame of his parents and ownself.

Verse-9 There were indeed three well-known Brahmin ancestors called[11] **Māktha, Rāma** and **Dhruva** who performed sacrifices and were partakers of Soma.

Verse-10 There was born in that line a Brahmin called Mahādeva, who was among **Brahmin** as **Lord Mahādeva** among gods.

Verse-11 His son was called Varāha who loved Vedic sacrifices, and who. after passing away, attained the world of Hari (in the form of) **Ādi Varāha**.

Verse-12 His son was Hari by name and endowed with culture who was like another lord **Hara** incarnate before the king.

Verse-13 From him was bom honourable **Sukradeva** who had attained thaturity in the three **Vedas**, who was noble, best among good people, and who was **Yaduka** (?)and Kramuka[14](?).

Verse-14 King Śrī **Candra**, who belonged to the same country (as that of the donee) gave (the gift of this land) to that honourable **Sukradeva** who (always) spoke with a smile.

36-37 Therefore it should be approved by all of you. This gift should be approved of and protected by the future kings also considering that gift of land entails enormous merit and its taking away, the fear of falling into the great hell. There are also verses in praise of *Dharma* in this thatter:

Verse-15 One who accepts the land, and one who gifts the land are both (persons of) meritorious deed, both will definitely go to heaven.

Verse-16 He, who snatches away the land given by his own self or by others, is rotten with his forefathers having become a worm of the dung.

Verse-17 Therefore, having thought of wealth and human life as fickle as a drop of water on a petal of lotus, and having understood all the sayings above, the persons should not efface the fames (i.e. good deeds) of others.

41-42 The 44 regnal year of Śrī Śrī Candra Deva and the 28th day of themonth *Mārgaśirṣa*[15].Approved by *Mahāsāndhivigrahika* and approved by*Mahākṣapaṭalika*.

SECTION-III

IMAGE INSCRIPTIONS OF KHAḌGA AND CANDRA DYNASTIES

Introduction

A large number of images are found in Eastern Bengal. Most of them are of gods like Viṣṇu, Śiva, Śūrya, Sakti, and Buddhist male and female divinities. The images of Viṣṇu and Śiva are the most numerous in numbers among those that are found in all over Bangladesh. It shows that Vaisnavism and Saivism were very popular during the Pre-Muslim period. Two powerful Brahmanical families of kings i.e. Varmmanas and Senas ruled over southeastern Bengal. The Varmmanas were worshippers of Viṣṇu and the Senas were the worshippers of Sūrya and Siva.

Here are described only four inscription images of Sarvvāni, Nartteśvara, Sūrya and Vasudeva.Vāsudeva is the incarnation of God Viṣṇu and Narttesvara is the Supreme Dancing form of Siva. Two of them were found in Comilla district, one in Noakhali and one in Munshiganj. The district of Comilla and Noakhall were under Samataṭa Maṇḍala and Munshiganj widely known as Vikramapura, was the "Camp of Victory" of the Candra dynasty.

DEULBADI ŚARVVĀNI IMAGE INSCRIPTION

The image of Sarwāni has been found in a small village of Deulbadi under Chauddagram Thana in the district of Comilla. It is located at about 14 miles southeast south of Comilla town.

The image is about 20 inches in height and rather heavy. A portion of the top proper left of the rim is missed. It has eight arms. The proper left four hands hold the thunderbolt, the bell, the bow and the shield from the bottom to upwards respectively. The proper right hands hold the conchshell, the goad, the sword and the wheel from the bottom upward respectively. Two maids are on her two sides. The goddess stands on a lotus-seat on the back of a sitting lion. The thin sheets of gold covered the image. It is the pious work of queen Prabhāvatī, the wife of Devakhaḍga.

The image inscription mentions the names of three generations of Khaḍga dynasty viz. Khaḍgodyama, his son Jatakhaḍga and his son Deva Khaḍga. This genealogy of the Khaḍga dynasty is also mentioned in the copperplate grants of Deva Khaḍga[16].

It shows that Prabhāvatī, queen of Deva Khaḍga, caused the image of Śarwāni to be covered with gold leaves out of reverence for the goddess. The Ashrafpur grants inform us that Deva Khaḍga was a donor of land to Buddhist monasteries. The queen Prabhāvatī and their son also followed the characteristics of Deva Khaḍga. The Khaḍgas were Buddhists but they showed great devotion to the Hindu gods.

The characters of the script have a similarity with the Gupta, Rāta and Nātha scripts of Estern Bengal. Laskar suggests that the plates of Deva Khaḍga are dated the 8th or 9th century A.D. R.D Banerji suggests on palaeographical grounds and is inclined to push the date still further forward[17]. On the basis of the Khaḍga plates, the accounts of Seng-chi, I-tsing

PLATE NO. 9

DEULBADI SARVVANI STONE IMAGE INSCTIPTION

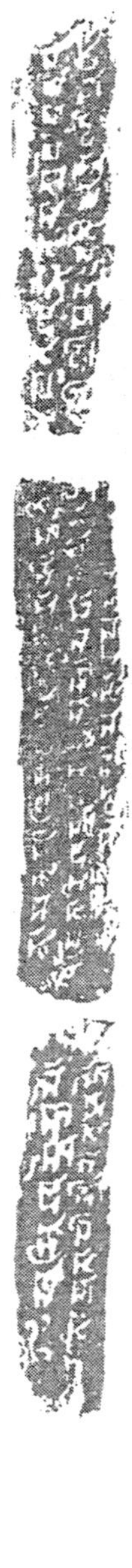

PLATE NO. 10

BHARELLA NARTTESVARA STONE IMAGE INSCTIPTION

and Yuand-Chwang and the comparative study of the other plate of Eastern Bengal, this image inscription can not be dated after 7th century A.D. It may be dated 3rd quarter of the 7th centuray A.D. The text is compased of two metres i.e. Upajāti and Anuṣṭubh.

Text of the Inscription

[१]ओम् स्वस्ति-

खड्गोद्यमो नाम नृपाधिराज-

स्तत्सूनुरासीद् भुवि जातखड्ग:(।)

तदात्मजो दानप[२]तिः प्रतापी

श्रीदेवखड्गो विजितारिखड्ग:। (॥)

राज्ञस्तस्य महादेवी महिषी श्रीप्रभावती(।)

स(श) र्व्वाणीप्रतिमां[३]भक्त्या हेमलिप्तामकारयत्॥

Translation of the Text

Om! Hail!

There was a lord of the kings named Khaḍgodyama. His son on earth was Jata Khaḍga. His son was Śrī Deva Khaḍga who was liberal (lit. master of charities), powerful and who conquered the swords of the enemies. The chief queen of that king, queen Śrī Prabhāvatī, caused this image of Śarwāni to be covered by gold through devotion.

BHARELLA NARTTESŚVARA IMAGE INSCRIPTION

The image of Narttesvara was recovered in the village of Bharella of Debidvara Thana in the district of Comilla. The village is situated about 5 miles west of Maināmatī-Mandir of Maināmatī-Lalmai hill range. It was found when a tank was being dug.

The image of Naṭarāja Śiva was made of black stone. The image was broken to pieces by a fanatic Fakir. It is originally a large image. It had twelve hands. All the proper right hands are missing. The god with a left hand shows the Añjali pose. This hand was above the crest of the god. Lower portion, below the knee, is missing. Two of the proper left hands are broken. One of the proper left hands forms the Añjali pose. Another holds the tail of a snake. The other two have the skull and the Trident A figure of Kārttikeya is represented in the left upper corner. The image is properly ornamented. The pedestal of the image is inscribed with a long inscription. The inscription is in two lines in four sections. The third and the longest section has lost some letters.

Narttesvara means the Supreme Dancer. This pose of Śiva is extremly interesting as found in eastern Bengal. The dancing form of Śiva is particularly found in Sauthern India. But how the special form of Śiva came to Eastern Bengal is not known to us. It is generally believed that there is no **Narttesvara** form of Śiva in north and west Bengal. Roughly, in **Vaṅga** and **Samataṭa** area, the image of **Narttesvara** were recovered.

The language of the inscription is Sanskrit The characters of the scripts are of the north-eastern variety. The inscription mentions the name of a king, **Laḍaha Candra**. Maināmatī inscription of Laḍaha Candra indicates that he was the king of at least **Samataṭa Maṇḍala and** Vaṅga. The image was made in the 18th regnal year of king Laḍaha Candra Deva.

TEXT OF THE INSCRIPTION

PART-I

[१]ओम्

श्रीमल्लडहचन्द्रदेवपादी-

यविजयराज्ये अष्टा[दश- (।)

---कृ]ष्ण चतुर्दश्यां तिथौ

बृहष्प(स्प)तिवारे पुष्यनक्षत्रे। (।।)

कर्म्मान्तपाल-श्रीकुसुमदेव-

सुत: श्री भावुदेवकारित (।)
श्रीनर्त्तेश्वरभट्टा[रक--
--]चन्द्रगत्या आषाढदिने १४।।
खनितञ्च रातकेन सर्व्वाक्षर:

PART-II

[१]खनितञ्च श्रीमधु
[२]सु(सू)दनेनेति।।

TRANSLATION OF THE TEXT

PART-I

Om! on Thursday the 14 Dark Tithi, and the constellation Puṣya, in the 18th regnal (year) of the victorious kingdom of the illustrious Laḍaha Candra Deva. Śrī Kusuma Deva was the mayor of Karmmānta. (His) son, Bhāvu Deva, caused to be made (the image) of illustrious lord Nartteśvara ----. And all the letters engraved by Rātaka.

PART-II

Also engraved by Śrī Madhusūdana.

KULKUDI SUN-GOD IMAGE INSCRIPTION

The image of Sun-God was actually discovered from the island of Hatia in the district of Noakhali, i.e. in the mouth of the Meghna river on the northern coast of Bay of Bengal- It was collected by the progenitor of Guha family of Kulkudi in the Gosairhat Thana of the District of Sariatpur. From that time the image was worshiped by that family.

The image is made of black stone. It is an excellent specimen of East-Bengal Icons. The God stands on lotus pedestal, holding in his two hands two full-blown lotuses, which rise just above the shoulders. It represents a smiling face and the head is surrounded by a halo. The neck, ear, wrist and waist are ornamented properly. The feet and lower part of the legs are closed by high boots.

Two miniature female figures stand by two sides of the God's feet. To the proper right of the God, a fat-bellied bearded man is carrying pen and inkstand in his hands. To the proper left, a female figure stands with a sword.

Four females figurs, on both the sides of the God represent shooting attitude with bow and arrows. Beneath the pedestal, the seven horses are pulling a single wheel ' car of the God. The eleven other Ādityas, in miniature form, exactly like the Sun-God, are presented on both the sides within circles. Six of them are on proper left and five of them on proper right. The sixth circle on proper right, a female figure is holding a lotusstalk in the right hand and a Kamuṇḍala in the left. The Matsya Purāṇa has mentioned the iconographic description of Sūrya (Sun-God).(Chap-261,p.902) which exactly fits in with this image of Sun-God. This type of Sūrya image is very rare in any other region of India.

The inscription is in a single line in four sections on the pedestal just below the seven horses of the Sun-God. The characters of the script are of the proto-Bengali style of the early 11th century A.D. The laguage of inscription is Sanskrit.

TEXT OF THE INSCRIPTION

[१]श्री लक्ष्मि(क्ष्मी)दि(दी)नकारी(रि)त(।)भट्टारक-
श्रीगोविन्दचन्द्रदेवपा-
दीय सम्वत् १२ फाल्गुन
दिने १९।

TRANSLATION OF THE TEXT

(The image of the Sūrya) caused to be made by Śrī Lakṣ midīna in 12th regnal year of the lord Śrī Govinda Candra Deva on 19th day of the month of Phālgun.

PAIPARA VĀSUDEVA IMAGE INSCRIPITION

The image of Vasudeva was found in the village of Paikpara of Tangivadi Thana in the District of Munshiganj when an old tank was being execavated.

PLATE NO. 11

KULKUDI SUN-GOD STONE IMAGE INSCRIPTION

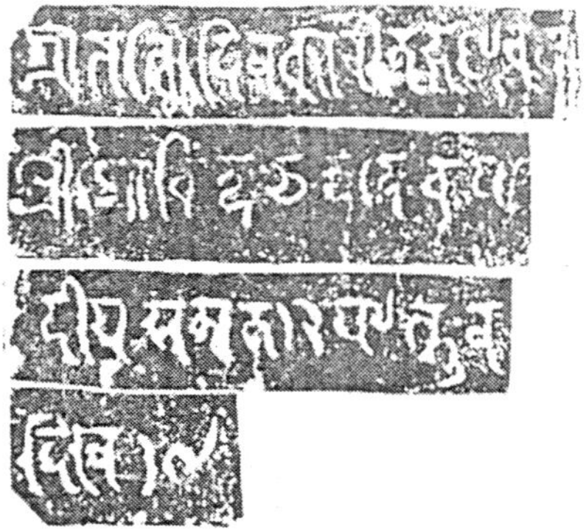

PLATE NO. 12

PAIKPARA VASUDEVA STONE IMAGE INSCRIPTION

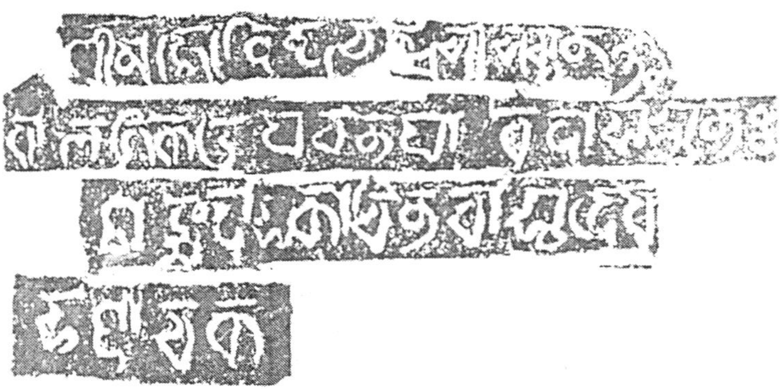

The image is about 4 feet in height. It is just an ordinary image of Viṣṇu. The god Viṣṇu has four hands in which he holds Śaṅkha (conch shell), Cakra (wheel), Gadā (Mace) and Padma (Lotus). His head, neek, hand, waist and legs are properly ornamented. He sands on a lotus, which is born by Garuḍa, the Vhicle of Viṣṇu sitting in a kneeling positon. The god flanked on two sides by two Goddesses, Sarasvati, and the goddess of culture to his left and Lalkṣmī the Goddess of beauty and wealth to his right. There are five miniature figurs in, standing and sitting positions on the pedestal and four miniature animal representations are depicted on the edges of the background surface of the image. Two Vidyādharis are represented in flying attitude-holding gralands in their hands. It has the Kṛttimukha sign at the top of the background space.

The inscription is in four lines each line being made up of three sections with the exception of the fourth line, which is is finished, in a single line. The languge is Sanskrit. The inscription is in prose form. The characters of the script are similar to the script of the Kulkudi image inscription. The image was made after elven years of Kulkudi image. Both of the images were issued from the kingdom of **Govinda Candra Deva** who ruled over sathatata in the elventh century A.D.

TEXT OF THE INSCRIPTION

[१]श्रीमद्गोविन्दचन्द्रस्य सम्वत् २३

[२]बालजिक उपरत पारदास सुतः

[३]गङ्गदास कारित वासुदेव

[४]भट्टारक

TRANSLATION OF THE TEXT

The image of the Lord Vāsudeva caused to be made by **Ganga Dasa**, son of the expired **Balajika Paradasa**, in the 23rd year of illustrious Govinda Candra.

NOTES AND REFERENCES

1. *Rāṇa-Corruption* of *Rajan* (cf. M. Monier Williams, A Sanskṛit-English Dictionary, p. 875, Col-3), Hence the diminutive *Rāṇaka* should mean a small king, a feudatory Lord.
2. It appears that king Laḍaha Candra caused to be made an image of Lord Vāsudeva or Mādhava which is referred to as Laḍaha Mādhava after the name of the king who got it made and placed in a temple.
3. Refer to fn. 2 above.
4. Dani translates *atrinetrāt* as "not emanated from the three-eyed God (i.e. Śiva)". This is not correct. Purāṇas describe moon as having emanated from the eyes of sage Atri (c.f. Bhagavata-Purana, 9.14.2-3). Otherwise, the moon in the sky can never be dissociated from Śiva. The bard of Govinda Candra has no reason to refer to Siva even indirectly, since the king is a staunch follower of Buḍḍhism as shown in the very first verse.
5. Dani's translation is wrong. He translates "who was made by his friends the object of " etc. Actually, by the force of **ca** in line **b,** the passive subject yena is to be supplied in this line also from the previous one.
6. ***Kakuda***—The word commonly known as *Kakud,* but about the form *Kakuda,* Apte.V.S. (The Student's Sanskrit-English Dictionary, Delhi, 1987, p. 127, Col.-1) says "According to Pāṇini V.4.146-147, *Kakud* is the form to be substituted for *Kakuda* in adjective or *Bahuvrihi* compounds", therefore, *Kakuda* is the word in this compound.
7. Certain conjunctions of constellations, day and hour are supposed to forecast certain good or bad things. They are called *Yoga. Rājayoga* suggests royal achievements.
8. **Śantivarika**—a peculiar word, perhaps the title conferred upon **Śrī Pitavasagupta Śarman.** The word *Śanti-udaka* is known in Śanskrit literature. It means the water for appeasement of miseries, the propitiatory water. If Santivarika is a title, it must mean a person whose blessed water must have been considerded very efficacious for propitiatory purposes.
9. *Sarman*—Prosperous; an affix added to the name of a Brahmin. Apte, V. S., The Practical Sanskrit-English Dictionary, 1995, p. 910, Col-3.
10. *Pravara,* "A Muni or noble ancestor who contributes to the credit

of a particular goṭra or family". Apte, V.S., op. cit. p. 668, Col-1 and 2.

11. *Koṭihomena* (?) *Gatāvate*— "to one who has gone in (or at) a crore of oblations". The adjective shows that this Brahmin was continuously engaged in large and great sacrifices, and must have been very reputed and continuously in demand for the performances of such sacrifices.
12. *Nauvāṭaka—Nau* boat means of water transportation. *Vāṭaka*-enclosure, garden, plantation, the site of a house, op. cit., p. 939, Col-1. *Nauvāṭaka* should therefore mean an enclosure or a place (on waterfront) where boat-services are available. Therefore it can be translated as a Ferry-station. The word *Ardha-nauvāṭaka*-presents some difficulty. Does it mean that part of that waterfront place was used for transportation and the other part for domestic purpose? In that case, it would be translated as we have done.
13. *Ākara—Ākaraṇa* 'inviting, calling'.
14. *Kramuka*—a betelnut tree (!). R.G. Basar takes Yaduka, Kramuka and Sukradeva to be the three sons of Hara, but the consistent use of singular forms of all adjectives and the verb-form go against this interpretation. Basar also has not made any comment on his peculiar gramthatical interpretation throughout his article. Vide "Madanpur Plate of Śrī Candra: Year 44", by R.G Basar, E.I., Vol.-28, 1949(Pub-1952), pp. 51-58. We acknowledge we are unable to translate these two words as adjectives of **Sukradeva**.
15. *Mārgakaḥ—The* month called *Margaśīrṣa*. Apte, V.S., op.cit., p. 75S, Col-3.
16. Laskar, G.M., "Ashrafpur copper-plate grants of Devakhaḍga", M.A.S.B., No.-1, 1906, pp. 85-91
17. Banerji, R.D., "The Pālas of Bengal", M.A.S.B., Vol.-V, No.-3, p. 67

NOTES OF THE MAINĀMATĪ COPPER-PLATE(1)OF LADAHA CANDRA DEV:

VERSE:

२०,२१,२२,२३ = अनुष्टुभ्,

२४ = पुष्पिताग्रा

पंक्ति = ३४-३८ गद्य, पंक्ति = ६२ गद्य।

NOTES OF THE MAINĀMATĪ COPPER-PLATE(2)OF LADAHA CANDRA DEV:

VERSE:

१,४,५,६ = वसंततिलका, २,९,१३ =उपजाति, ३,७,८,११,१२,१४,१७,१९ =शार्दूलविक्रीडितम

१० =विषमवृत्त, १५,१६ =स्रग्धरा, १८=शिखरिणी, २०,२१,२२,२३ =अनुष्टुभ्, २४ = पुष्पिताग्रा

पंक्ति=५-२५ (Reverse)गद्य, पंक्ति=३० (Reverse) गद्य।

NOTES OF THE MAINĀMATĪ COPPER-PLATE OF GOVINDA CANDRA DEV:

VERSE:

१,२,३,१०,११ =इन्द्रवज्रा, १५,१६ =उपजाति,४,५,६,७,१२,१३,१४ = शार्दूलविक्रीडित
८ = वसंततिलका,९ =शिखरिणी,१७,१८,१९,२० =अनुष्टुभ्, २१ =पुष्पिताग्रा
पंक्ति =४-२३ (Reverse)गद्य, पंक्ति=२८-२९ (Reverse)गद्य।

NOTES OF THE MAINĀMATĪ COPPER-PLATE OF RANAVANKAMALLA HARIKALA DEVA:

VERSE:

१ = मन्दाक्रान्ता, ३=द्रुतविलम्बित, ४,५,८ =शार्दूलविक्रीडित

२ =वसंततिलका, ६ = स्रग्धरा, ७ =अनुष्टुभ्, ९ =मालिनी

पंक्ति =२२-२४ गद्य।

NOTES OF THE MAINĀMATĪ COPPER-PLATE OF VIRADHARA DEVA :

पंक्ति = १.२३ गद्य।

NOTES OF THE RAMPAL COPPER-PLATE OF SRI CHANDRA DEVA:

VERSE:

१,३ =वसंततिलका,४,७,८ =उपजाति,२,५ =शार्दूलविक्रीडित

६ =इन्द्रवज्रा,९,१०,११,१२ = अनुष्टुभ्, १३ = पुष्पिताग्रा

पंक्ति = १४-२७ (Obverse) गद्य, पंक्ति =(Obverse) गद्य

NOTES OF THE KEDARPUR COPPER-PLATE OF SRI CHANDRA DEVA:

VERSE:

१= वसंततिलका,३, ५=उपजाति, ७=शार्दूलविक्रीडितम

४= इन्द्रवज्रा, २= अनुष्टभ्,६= स्रग्धरा

पंक्ति= १६-१८(Obverse)गद्य

NOTES OF THE MANDANPUR COPPER-PLATE OF SRI CHANDRA DEVA:

VERSE:

९,१०, ११, १२, १३, १४, .१५, १६=अनुष्टुभ्, १७=पुष्पिताग्रा

पंक्ति = १४-२७ (Obverse)गद्य, पंक्ति=२४-२९, ३६-३७, ४१-४२ (Reverse)गद्य।

CHAPTER-IV

ARCHAEOLOGICAL FINDINGS OF MAINĀMATĪ

INTRODUCTION

The Maināmatī excavations have discovered a large number of valuable archaeological findings. It has thrown a flood of light on the history of Samataṭa Maṇḍala from 6th to 13th centuries A.D. As many as 400 specimens of gold, silver and copper coins of various types and sizes were found. Except a few, all of them 'were recovered from an early occupation level of the monastic cells of the Sāl van Vihāra. A large number of terracotta plaques in various designs were recovered from Maināmatī-Lalmai hill range. These specimens of terracotta plaques were mostly found in loose conditions from Sālvan Vihāra, Kutilā Murā, Ānanda Vihāra, and Cārpatra Murā excavations. These plaques represent the popular folk art of Bangladesh. Huge quantity of pottery was recovered from archaeological sites of Maināmatī- Lalmai area. Most of them were found from the first and second construction and reconstruction level of Sālvan Vihāra. A large number of Bronze images and two stone images were found from this area. It is worth remembering that there are no rocks and good stone to be found in Maināmatī - Lalmai hill range and even in Bangladesh. Due to these artifacts, the Maināmatī-Lalmai hill range is well-known among scholars. These artifacts of varied types the objects of the everyday life of the people- inform us about the culture and civilizational tendencies of these people.

HISTORICAL RE-CONSTRUCTION ON THE BASIS OF INSCRIBED COINS

Ancient coins are one of the most important sources for the archaeologist for the reconstruction of history. Nearly two hundred years ago, the historical information about the South Eastern Bengal was almost nil. In 1803 A.D., a copper plate was accidentally found on Maināmatī hill range and the history started revealing itself to the scholars. The first regular excavation was started in 1955 on this hill range. From Maināmatī excavations we have recovered over 400 specimens of gold, silver and copper-coins of various types and sizes. Except a few, all of them were discovered from an early occupation level of the monastic cells of the Sālvan Vihāra. The vast majority of these are silver coins.Gold coins are few in numbers. These coins are important as some of them represent the earliest coins found from stratigraphical levels in this region. The large number of silver coins represent the local culture and tradition, and are therefore, more important and valuable. The gold coins include five Gupta, three Khaḍga, a dozen post Gupta "imitation" type and one Abbasid specimens[1].

Two gold coins belong to the imperial Guptas of the earliest date. One of them, found from Sālvan Vihāra depicts on its obverse an uncaparisoned horse bent infront of a post placed on an ornamental pedestal and on the reverse a female figure. This has been identified as Aśvamedha coin of Samudrāgupta (c. 335 - 375 A.D.) on the basis of the motif and a short legend inscribed on the reverse[2].

The other three Gupta coins are found amongst a hord from another cell of Sālvan Vihāra. One of them represents the well-known Lakṣmī and Archer type coins. This has been identified as a coin of Candra Gupta II (c. 376-415 A.D.). The coin is not in a good state of preservation. Yet it is distinguished by the purity of its metal and the artistic excellence of its style. The Lakṣmī and Archer type coins, characteristically Indian in style

FIGURE NO. 1 GOLD COINS

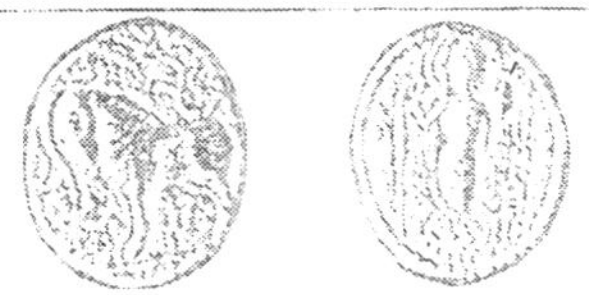

1. Aśvamedha gold coin of Samudragupta, Sālvan Vihāra

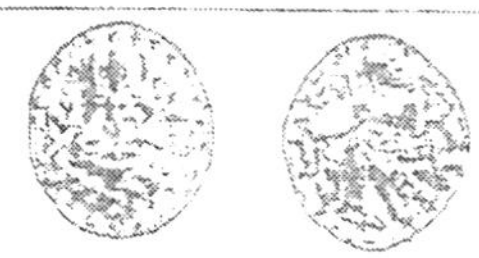

2. Gold coin of Candra gupta II, Sālvan Vihāra

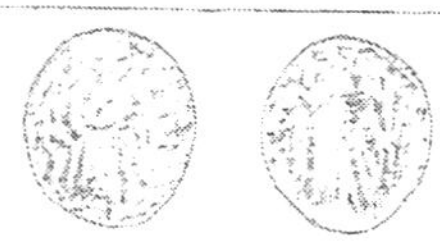

3. Gold coin of Gupta dynasty, Sālvan Vihāra

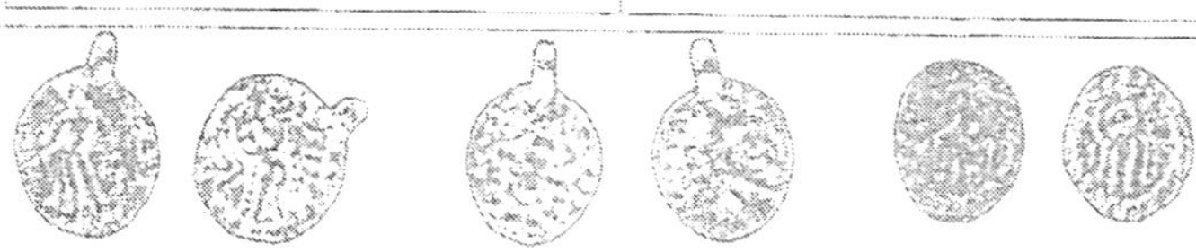

4. Post-Gupta imitation gold coinsof Khadga dynasty, Sālvan Vihāra

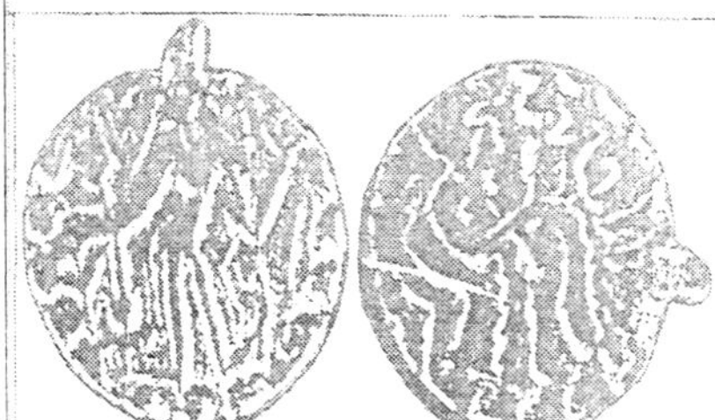

5. Post-Gupta imitation gold coin, Ānanda Vihāra

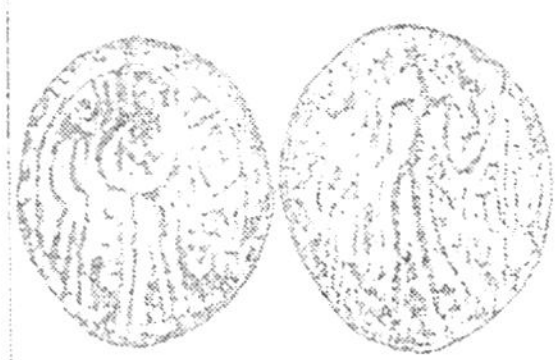

6. Post-Gupta imitation gold coin, of Deva dynasty, Sālvan Vihāra

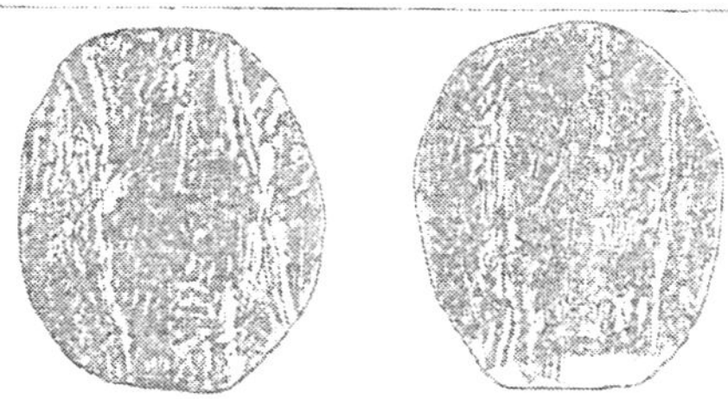

7. Abbasid gold coin, Kutiā Murā

FIGURE NO. 2 SILVER COIN

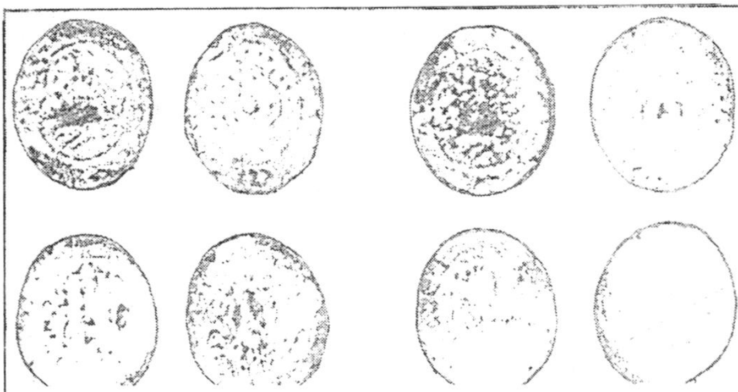

1.Mainamati silver coins, Sālvan Vihāra

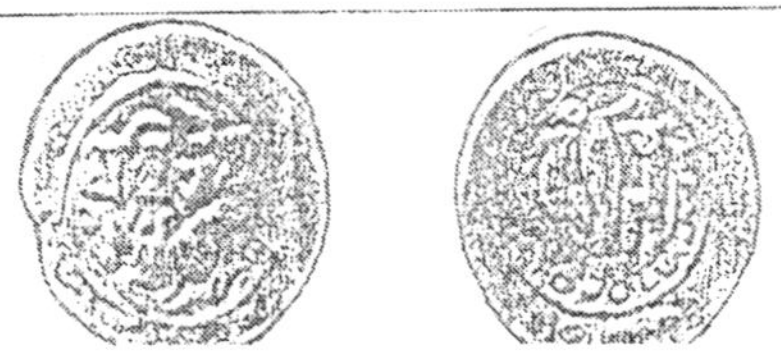

2. Mainamati silver coins, Ànanda Vihāra

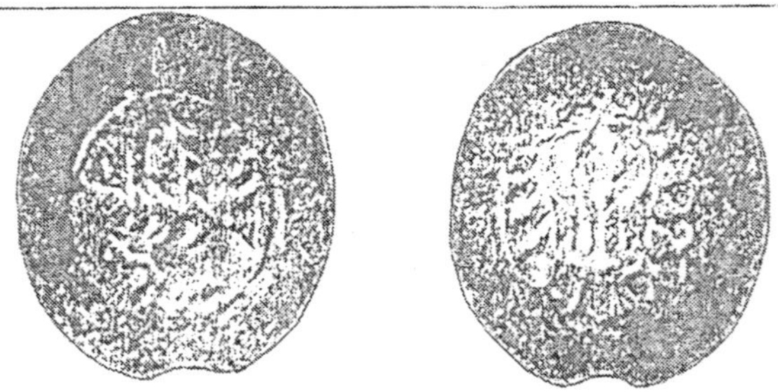

3.Mainamati silver coins, Ānanda Vihāra

and designs, remain an exclusive model for the gold currency of Eastern India for more than three centuries.

Three gold coins, with characteristics similar to the above mentioned coins of Candra Gupta II (c-376 - 415 AD) which are recovered from Sālvan Vihāra are imitations. Two of these coins with another adulterate-metaled-coin belong to Bālabhaṭ ṭa who was probably a prince of the Khaḍga dynasty[3].

These Archer type imitation gold coins found from Sālvan Vihāra are the most interesting. There is a legend on the coins, which has been rendered as *Śrī Vaṅgāla Mṛgāṅka*. These coins are associated with three other gold coins of the Khaḍga dynasty and six golden earrings from Sālvan Viliara. The legend. *Śrī Vaṅgāla Mṛgāṅka* is also found on the top of the Ānandadeva copper plate of Sālvan Vihāra, Maināmatī. *Śrī Vaṅgāla Mṛgāṅka* was probably the royal title of the Deva rulers. If both the readings are correct then we may conclude that the coin was issued by one of the early Deva rulers in imitation of the Gupta coins. These beautiful imitation coins indicate the prosperous condition of the South - Eastern Bengal under the Devas.

Another gold coin recovered from Kutilā Murā excavation in 1957 belongs to the last Abbasid Caliph Abu Ahmed Abdullah Mustaasim Billah (1242-1258 A.D.). It was found in a good state of preservation though it was very thin. The discovery of this coin may indicate good trade relations between the Arab countries and Samataṭa during the pre-Muslim period.

The prosperous condition of Samataṭa is particularly noticed by the recovery of a large number of silver coins from the interior cells of the Sālvan Vihāra. Here 224 silver coins were found from two hoards. All of them bear an image of crouching Bull on the obverse and of Trident, Sun and Moon on the reverse. The portion above the Bull contains two types of legends: In some it is 'Paṭṭikera[1].in others it is 'Lalitakera Dharma Vijaya'. Except these legends all the coins are identical in every other detail. It is to be noted that eight silver coins have been found in Sylhet and adjacent to the north eastward of Comilla district. All of them have a single line of inscription. David W MacDowell read, the legend of these eight silver coins as Yārikṛtya'[4] But Dani A.H., later on, read as 'Paṭṭikera' and ascribed them to the Candra rulers of East Bengal[5]. All of them are similar to the silver coins of Maināmatī.

Now, we know Paṭṭikera to be a city in the Samataṭa Maṇḍala[6]. It could also be a district. But we hardly know anything about any city called Lalitakera. The difficulty is aggravated by the presence of the words "Dharma" and "Vijaya" alongwith it Lalitakera could possibly be a city like Paṭṭikera. But what do we take "Dharma-Vijaya" to mean ? Is it a name of any person ? Or does it suggest some event of religious significance occuring in a city ? Or could it mean that the whole city of Lalitakera embraced some religion, possibly Buḍḍhism, and coins were issue to mark that event? We are at present in no position to make any definite or even positive statement in this regard.

Phayre has described some Arakanese[7] coins. Dani[8] feels that'' in type, fabric and also in some of the coin legends there is a close similarity between them (i.e. The Arakanese silver coins and Maināmatī silver coins bearing the"Lalitakera Dharma Vijaya'legend). Is this an indication to suggest some sort of relationship between the Arakanese Candras and the Candras of South-East Bengal? At least the present copper plates[9] do not hint at this at all". So far Dani appears to be correct. But at another place he suggests that these coins must have been issued by the Candra kings of South East Bengal.[10]

But this seems to be in contradiction of the available facts:

(1) The Candra dynasty ruled over South-East Bengal during 900 to 1050 A.D. According to Dani,[11] however, the coins are found in the archaeological layers of 7th-8th century. The coins thus seem to belong to an era, which was earlier than that of the Candra dynasty.

(2) Even the Pālaeography of these coins indicates an age prior to the Candra dynasty Era[12].

(3) The images of Trident, Sun, Moon, and Bull etc, all indicate to the Hindu religion of the issuing king preferably his Śaiva leanings.

(4) Silver coins of similar type have been found from the earlier phase of Ānanda Rāja's Pālace excavation.

The overlord of this area in the 7-Sth century was the great king Ānanda Deva. The Mainamatī copper-plate of Ānanda Deva is also found from the same place of excavation of Sālvan Vihāra from where the coins are found. The copper-plate indicates the date of Ānanda Deva is 7th - 8th centuries and the coins are also found from the archaeological layers of the same period. Therefore, very likely, Ānanda Deva of Deva dynasty was the issuer of these coins. Even the ancestors of Candra kings must have been present at that time, but they must have been very minor, insignificant royalty, and could not have issued the currency, particularly costly currency like silver coins,

From all these evidences and the large number of their occurance, their association and find-spot a strong indication that the coins were issued by some powerful and prosperous ruler of Samataṭa, probably, Śrī Ānanda Deva of Deva dynasty.

Two other coins, one silver and one gold, are of great interest as these belong to the Abbasid rulers of Baghdad. Both are inscribed with the Muslim creed in Kufic Arabic[13]. The silver coin found from the early level of the Sālvan Vihāra is in a damaged condition. It is undecipherable.

Very few copper coins are discovered in Mainamatī excavations, which include a unique post Gupta "imitation" specimen.

The discoveiy of various types of coins and some gold ornaments from Mainamatī excavations indicate the prosperity of the Buddhist Vihāras in those days. It appears that these

FIGURE NO. 3 TERRACOTTA PLAQUES

1. Buddha seated in Vajrāsana
2. Makara mukha
3. Semi-divine
4. Kinnara
5. Kinnari
6. Gandharva
7. Kimpurusa
8. Vidyādhara
9. Stupā

coins must have been given as donations to the Vihāras by the devotees.

HISTORICAL RE-CONSTRUCTION ON THE BASIS OF TERRACOTTA PLAQUES

A Large number of terracotta plaques in various designs recovered from Mainamatī- Lalmai hill range belong to the early Deva dynasty (C. 7th-8th century A.D.). Most of these were found in loose conditions from Sālvan Vihāra , Kutilā" Murā, Ānanda Vihāra and Cārpatra Murā excavations. These plaques are now on display in Mainamatī Museum, Comilla. All these plaques are fashioned out of fine alluvial clay.

It is well known that there are no rocks to be found in the Mainamatī - Lalmai hill range, and in fact, in the whole of the Bangladesh. The local artists had, therefore, of necessity to fall back upon the alluvial clay, modelling for giving expression to their art. The fact is that the terracotta plaques found in the Mainamatī - Lalmai area are the oldest specimens of this art in the entire Bangladesh area, it also autothatically follows that these plaques are not influenced by the stylistic or thethatic peculiarities of the plaques from other areas of Bangladesh. In other words, the plaques found in this area are the oldest specimen among those in Bangladesh and possess very individual characteristics entirely uninfluenced by the style of plaques from other areas; in fact, these specimen appear to have exercised strong influence upon later models found in the other areas of Bangladesh.

The themes of the terracotta plaques are drawn from the daily life of the people, from all creations of God and nature in their various stages of activity, emotion, movement etc. This art shows clearly the popular folk-art of that period. Divine and semi-divine beings, hybrids, **flying Gandharvas, Apsarases, Kinnaras and Kinnaris, Kiṁpuruṣas, Vidyādharas and Yakṣ as** among the demi-gods, mythical creatures and composite animals, men, women and children either engaged in various activities of life or at rest, warriors, archers, acrobats balancing bodies on their hands, musicians with their instruments. **Makaras** and **Kṛttimukhas**[14], dancers, sages, and ascetics, monkeys and apes, birds, beasts, fish, animal fables, flowers and plants, and domestic and family studies are represented with all their local and ethical characteristics.

Among human beings, these plaques show the creative mind of the artists depicting warriors in action with dagger and shield, with sword and shield, threatening attitude with dagger for killing tiger and archers with bow and arrow etc, offering interesting thateril for study. Besides these, flying female figures, amorous couples, piper and acrobats are fairly common.

Among animals, lion, wild boar, horse, antelope, ram with a flying scarf, monkey, elephants, crocodiles and Kṛttimukhas, are popular. The lions are depicted in majestic style. Running horses are good specimen of naturalistic representations. The crocodile and fish represent the aquatic world. Kṛttmukhas, decorating the corners of building, represent two crouching lions with double bodies on both sides of the corner

Snake is represented in a few plaques. One plaque in the southern basement of the wall of the central shrine of Sālvan Vihāra depicts a small mongoose fighting a big hooded snake. This plaque shows the natural movement of the two natural enemies.

Among birds, peacocks and swans (Rājhaṅsas) are represented in many plaques. A swan holding a string of pearls and another eating a stem of lotus are highly artistic. Another plaque shows a lady seated with her right hand resting on her thigh and left hand touching her head as bemoaning attitude. This would recall a familiar Indian mode of expression of grief or pensiveness.

A large number of plaques representing plant and flowers are also found from different sites of this area. Various forms of lotus have been depicted. Besides the conventional lotus there are representations of full- blown lotuses with bud,

FIGURE NO. 4 TERRACOTTA PLAQUES

1. Warrior with dagger and shield.
2. Warrior with sword and shield

3-4. Threatening attitude with dagger for tiger killing 5. Archer
6. Flying female. 7. Acrobat. 8. Piper

with a bird on its top (lotus symbolizing moon and Sun.) and so on.

A number of terracotta plaques depict **Buddha, Stūpa, Triratna, Makarmukha, Semi-Divine** and unearthly figures including **Kinnari, Gandharva, Vidyādhara, Kiṁpuruṣa, Yakṣa** and a composite animal with a bird's beak on a crocodile's head. Semi-Divine beings, such as **Kinnara** with human head and bird's body and wings, **Kinnara** with human body and horse-head, **Gandharva** as a celestial musician, playing a **ḍamaru** and **Gandharva** (or perhaps a human being) beating time on a pitcher and **Vidyādharas** hovering in the sky with garlands in their hands from the subjects treated on a number of terracotta plaques recovered from the central mound of Bhoj Vihāra, Sālvan Vihāra and Anada Vihāra.

A plaque showing the Buddha seated in *Vajrāsana* with right hand in *Bhumisparś a* attitude and another representing Padmapani seated in *Mahāraja-līlā pose* with Kuṇḍalas in the ears, braided hair in curls, right hand resting on the ground and left holding lotus by its stalk are the best specimens of the heretic religious art of Bengal prevalent under the Pālas. Representations of the demi-gods form the majority. Vidyādharas are depicted on three best specimens. A Vidyādhari forming part of a Vidyādhara couple hovering in the sky forms the subject thatter of yet another plaque that reminds one of the Gupta style of art. While **Vidyādharas** are human, the Gandrvas and **Kinnaras** are hybrid in character. Certain texts describe a **Kinnaraas** one with human figure and head of horse,. or horse's body and the head of a man. Other texts draw a distinction between **Kinnara** and **Kiṁpuruṣa** by ascribing horse-head and human body to the **Kinnara** and human head and horse body to the **Kiṁpuruṣa**[15].

The Mainămatī plaques represent the popular folk art of Bangladesh with little or no direct relation with any other art. Their features recur in reliefs from Paharpur, Mahāsthan, Sabhar and many other sites lying scattered all over Bangladesh

FIGURE NO. 5 TERACOTTA PLAQUES

1. Traditional Lion
2. Wild boar
3. Two horses
4. Antelope
5. Ram
6. Monkey
7. Elephant
8. Crocodile
9. Krttimukha
10. Krttimukha

and approxithately datable to the 8th-9th centuries A.D. Since the Mainamatī reliefs are undoubtedly earlier in date and since the Paharpur series and others show some definite development in technique and style, this remarkable art may have originated in this region under the patronage of the well-known Buddhist dynasties of Samataṭa. These crude, light-hearted unreflective works, deep-rooted in the folk art of Bangladesh represent an indigenous style with a distinct local character and development. It is an uncouth but vigorous style, often heavy and lacking in knowledge but is, nevertheless, expressive in a naive and direct fashion.

This exceptionally rich plastic art of Bangladesh reflects a faithful picture of the prevailing social and cultural life of the people. We can also get a clear idea about their religious practices, their mode of life, dress, ornaments, etc.

HISTORICAL RE-CONSTRUCTION ON THE BASIS OF POTTERY

It is well known that pottery is the most important artifact and is most widely distributed among the sites. For a good study, it is essential to collect sherds systethatically from all the sites. Pottery has been recovered from sixteen of the 38 sites located in or immediately adjacent to the Maimanati-Lalmai hill range. The pottery was collected under varying conditions, but always with the intention of producing a representative sample at each location. After washing, drying, sorting and numbering, these representative samples were prepared for the study. Various representative types of pottery were found from only two or three of sixteen sites. Four types of common pottery (i. e. pink, pale brown, reddish yellow and light gray) were found from each of the sixteen sites. Besides these another type of pottery (i.e. chalky gray, fine reddish yellow, thick dark gray, corded brown) is also found at some sites. Large numbers of pottery are found from large structural sites, which are older in age. Smaller numbers are found from small sites, which are later. The study of pottery thus suggests periods of construction and usage.

FIGURE NO. 6 TERRACOTTA PLAQUES

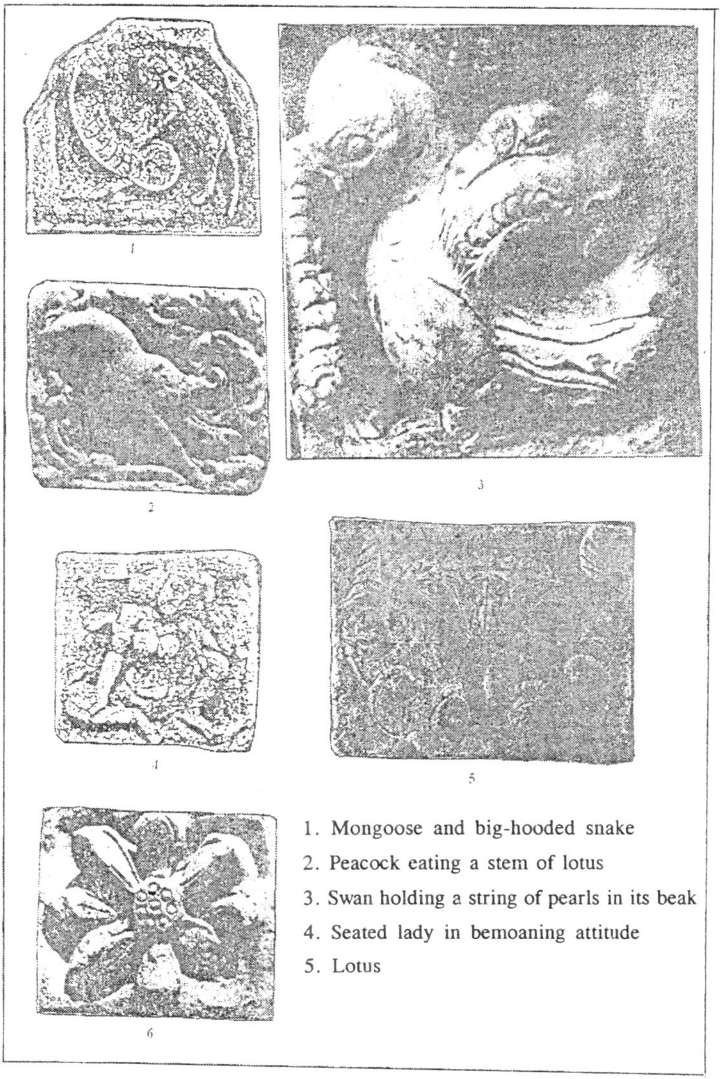

1. Mongoose and big-hooded snake
2. Peacock eating a stem of lotus
3. Swan holding a string of pearls in its beak
4. Seated lady in bemoaning attitude
5. Lotus

FIGURE NO. 7 POTTERY AND BRICKS

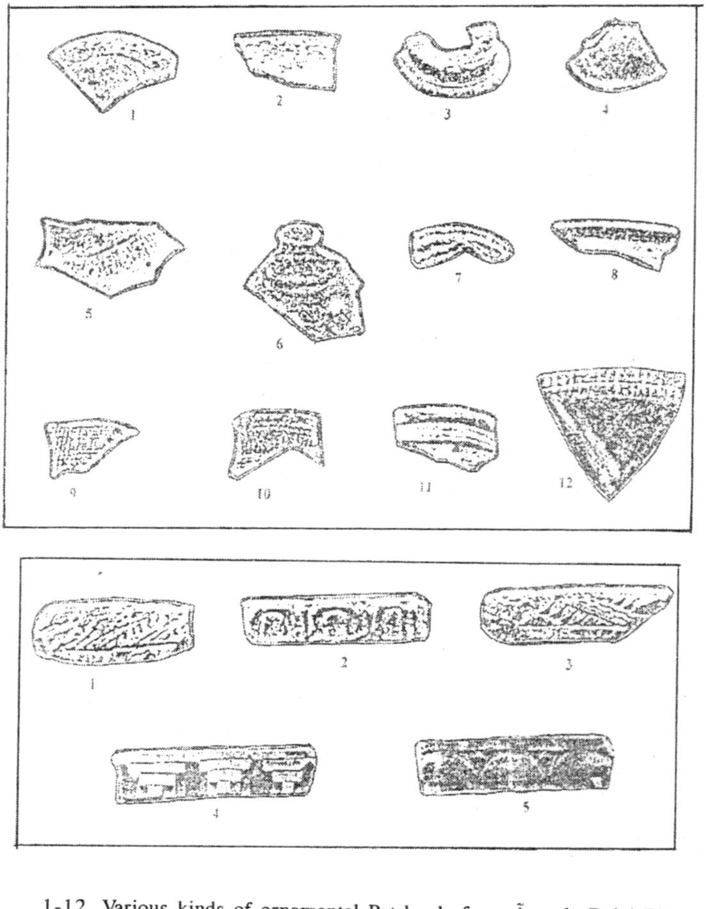

1-12 Various kinds of ornamental Potsherds from Ãnanda Rājā' Place, Bhoja-Rājā's Palace, Kutilā Murā and Sālvan Vihāra.

1-5 Ornamental bricks from Mainamati-Lalmai hill range

The large monastic sites i.e. Sālvan Vihāra (ST. 24), Bhoj Vihāra (ST. 16) Ānanda Vihāra (ST. 12) and Rupban Murā (ST.21) were built early. Sālvan Vihāra apparently continued to be in intensive use for a longer tune than the other large monasteries. The Pālace site i.e. Queen Maināmatī's Pālace Mound (ST. 1), had a long period of active use and was probably contemporaneous with all of the other structural sites. Other large shrines Cārpatra Murā (ST. 8) and Abbas Ali Murā (ST. 6) were probably later in construction and use. There are not enough grounds for dating the hill top sites.

HISTORICAL RE-CONSTRUCTION ON THE BASIS OF ICONS

A. Bronze Images

Large numbers of bronze images are found from Maināmatī area. It has been brought to light that brick hunters recovered seven pots containing hundreds of votive images of Buddha in bronze from Rupān Murā. Later on only thirteen of these could be recovered from them. All the images represent Buddha in ***Bhumisparśa Mudrā*** and are very small in size. The height of these tiny images is about 2" to 14". The monographic details and workmanship of these images are similar to those of the inscribed votive bronzes recovered from Jhewaiy in Chittagong District, assignable to the ninth-eleventh centuries A. D[16]". A large number of bronzte images were also recovered from the excavations carried out in Sālvan Vihāra. All of these represent Buddha, Bodhisattva and Tārā. Among the discovered images, ***Dhyānī* Buddha** is found in *Bhūmisparśa Mudrā* i.e. right hand is in earth-touching attitude and left on the lap. Three images of Buddha **Amitābha** are found in ***Dhyānīmudrā*** seated on lotus. **Bodhisattva Padmapani** is found sitting a cross-legged posture on lotus. **Bodhisattva Mañjūśrī** is found sitting in stretched-legs attitude attended by two deities and *Dhyānī* Buddha on the top. Another type of **Avalokiteśvara** is found in *Lalitāsana* seated on lotus. There are also found eight handed **Mahāpratisāra** and four handed Tārā seated on lotus

FIGURE NO. 8 BRONZE IMAGES

1. Votive miniature Images of Buddha in Bhumisparśa Mudrā
2. Buddha in Bhumisparśa Mudrā
3. Buddha Amitabha in Dhayānī Mudrā
4. Bodhisattva Padmapāni in Bhumisparśa Mudrā
5. Manjusrī in stretehed legs
6. Avalokiteśvara in Lalitāsana
7. Eight-handed Mahāpratisara seated on Lotus

with stretching right leg and left folded on right lap. Eight-handed Mahāpratisara is very interesting. Images of Avalokiteśvara are also found in *Lalitāsana* and *Varadamudrā*. Image of Buddha surrounded by 8 other deities is found in *Bhumisparśamudrā* seated on lotus.

The composition of Mainãmatī bronze images shows a peculiar regional or local characteristic feature probably, because of the freedom adopted by the local artists. It is also to be noted that all the sculptures represent *Tāntric* gods and goddesses. Tāntric Buddhist images, belonging to 8th and 9th centuries, are rare even in the great Buddhist centres like Bodh Gaya, Kukrihar and Nalanda[17]. Among the *Tāntric* gods and goddesses, some of the Mainãmatī bronze images appear to be earlier in date.

B. Stone Images

There are no rocks and good stone to be found in the Mainãmatī-Lalmai hill range and all over in Bangladesh. Therefore, only two stone images have been discovered from the central stūpa of Kutilā Murā. But no other stone images were found from any other sites of Mainãmatī-Lalmai hill range, including the excavated sites. These two stone sculptures are made from soft gray stone.They are made probably by some local artist. Stone images of similar type were also found from the surrounding places of Mainãmatī-Lalmai hill range. All the images indicate the spiritual faith and feelings and the distinctive characteristic of the art and culture of southeast Bengal i.e. Samataṭa. Both of the discovered images are of Avalokiteśvara. In one of these images, groups of miniature Buddhas, Bodhisattvas and other deities surround the central image of lord Avalokiteśvara. The pedestal of the images is depicted with devotees on the sides. Avalokiteśvara with his attendants is seated on lotus above the pedestal. The entire lotus has long lotus stalks. Another image is also decorated with miniature attendants. Both the images bear short inscriptions in the central part of their pedestals. On palaeographical consideration, the sculptures have been dated to

FIGURE NO. 9 BRONZE IMAGES

1. Four handed Tara in Bhumisparśa Mudrā and Varada Mudrā
2. Avalokitesvara in Lalitāsana and Varadā Mudrā
3. Buddha in Bhumisparśa Mudrā surrounded by 8 other deities
4. Stupā

FIGURE NO. 10 STONE IMAGES

1. Stone image of Avalokiteśvara, Murā

2. Stone image of Avalokiteśvara, Kutilā Murā

the 7th century A.D . The style, decoration and ornamentation of both these images indicate a close relation with the Gupta art. It is to be noted that the influence of Gupta art was strong in Bengal throughout the 7th century A.D. But the local artists of Samataṭa tried to give a personal stylistic expression to their art.

MINOR OBJECTS

A large number of minor objects have been recovered from Maināmatī area. Terracotta objects, toys, beads, net sinkers, small figurines, a large number of ornamental bricks in various sizes, earthenware, pots, oil lamps and utensils, semi-precious stone beads, buttons, red ochre, weights, grinding stones, bronze relic caskets, bronze and copper vessels, gold and silver ornaments, bronze bangles, circular pieces of silver ingots, iron nails, glass and shell objects and fossilized wood have been recovered from Maināmatī-Lalmai area. All these minor objects throw good deal of light on the life style of the contemporary people of this region.

NOTES AND REFERENCES

1. Rashid, M.H., "The Maināmatī Gold coin", B.L.K, Vol.-1, No.-1, Dhaka January, 1975, pp. 41-58.
2. Ibid, pp. 47-48.
3. Alam, A.K. M. Shamsul, Maināmatī, Dhaka, 1982, p. 55
4. MacDaowall, David, W. N. C., Vol.- XX, I960, pp. 229 -34.
5. Dani, A.H., "Coins of the Chandra Kings of East Bengal", J.N.S.I. Vol.- XXIV, 1962, pp. 141-42.
6. Paṭṭikera - The name Paṭṭikera is mentioned on the copper-plate of Śrī Laḍaha Candra Deva and Raṇavaṅkamalla Harikala Deva. It was the city in Samataṭa Maṇḍala under Pauṇḍrabhukti.
7. Phayre, A.P., Coins of Arakan of Pegu and of Burmah : Numisthatic Orientation, pp. 28-29.
8. J.N.S.I., Vol.- XXIV, 1962, pp. 141-142; and P. A. No. 3, p. 27.
9. Maināmatī Copper-plates of Laḍaha Candra Deva and Govinda Candra Deva.
10. Dani, A.H., J.N.S.I., Vol.-XXIV, 1962, pp. 141-142.

11. Dani, A.H., P. A., No.-3, 1966, pp. 27.
12. Alam, A.K.M., Shamsul, Mainamatī, 1982, p. 59.
13. Ibid, p. 59
14. The Scholars (Vide: B.A., 1979, p. 79) refer to this terracotta as *'Kṛttimukha'* but this seems unusual. *Kṛtti* means 'skin of an antelope or tiger, used by sages or their pupils to sit upon for study[1] (cf. Amarakoṣa. II, 7.46, Śabdakalpadruma, Vol.-II, p. 176, Dictionaries of M. Monier Williams, p. 304 and V.S. Apte, p. 371). The word *Kirtti* seems to have been used here in its etymological sense (from Krt-'Cut' meaning a devouring animal, a carnivore; it is noteworthy in this connection that the head in these terracotta strongly resembles that of a lion or a tiger. Hence, *Kṛttimukha* 'tiger-head.')
15. Vacaspatya, Bhagavata Purāṇa, Book VII, Chapter 20; but Viṣṇu-dharmottara (Book III, Chapter 42, and Verses 13-14) recognizes two classes of Kinnara- one with horse body and human head and the other *vice versa*. But the Manasara, which is a standard work on this subject, describes the Kinnara as 'a being with legs of animals, upper body like that of man' face with Garuḍa features, arms provided with wings, the crown decorated lotus etc.
16. Ramachandran, T.N., "Recent Archaeological Discoveries along the Mainamatī and Lalmai Ranges, Tippera District." B.C. Law Volume, ed. D.R. Bhandarkar, Part-11, Poona, p. 225.
17. Banerji, R.D., "Eastern Indian School of Medieval Sculpture", ASI, NS, Vol.-XLVIL, Delhi, 1933, p. 99; and A.K.M. Shamsul Alam, Mainamatī, p. 66.
18. Khan, F.A., Mainamatī, p. 29.

CHAPTER-V

HISTORICAL CO-RELATION OF THE RULING DYNASTIES OF SAMATAṬA

INTRODUCTION

For the historical reconstruction, the epigraphs are the most dependable and inforthative material. Literary works also describe historical facts but unless they are substantiated and corroborated by epigraphic evidences (like copper plates, coins, epigraphs etc.) they can not be completely relied upon for historical reconstruction. Also for most of the dynasties we do not get contemporary literature. And whatever information we get from the so called historical works like Purāṇas and Epics can form only preliminary and very vague historical data, more likely than not to be changed or up turned or given up with the findings of epigraphical information. So, practically, inscriptions are the only reliable materials for the reconstruction of the dynastic lineage and ancient historical geography. We are here directly concerned with south- eastern Bengal or more exactly Samataṭa Maṇḍala. When the inscriptions are found in any hill range or adjacent land they are grouped by their affinities and compared with each other as well as with inscription from other as places in the Bengal delta. They show the characteristics of the hill site, historical and political change of the governments, geographical references, religious relationship and cultural status of the different periods and dynasties. The most important problem is to identify the place names

MAP NO. 7

MAP SHOWING THE FINDSPOTS OF VARIOUS COPPERPLATE GRANTS

that are found in the inscriptions. From the data of the inscriptions regarding place names, only a rough framework about geographic situation of the ruling dynasties can be reconstructed. It is also difficult to define exact boundary of the villages, and the administrative centers, which are mentioned in the grants. The co-relation between space and time on the basis of political variations is very important for dating the different periods of the dynasty.

There are a total of 28 inscriptions related to the Maināmatī Lalmai hill range or the adjacent area. They are discussed here for co-relating their data about the ruling dynasties of Samataṭa Maṇḍala. Twelve plates, out of 28, are recovered from Maināmatī Lalmai area itself and rests were unearthed from the nearby areas. The only one inscription of Lokanātha of which geographic associations is not clearly mentioned in this grant is described here. But it was reported that it was found somewhere in the Tippera district. In the following pages the description of above mentioned plates are present chronologically.

TABLE NO.-4

FIND-SPOTS OF THE VARIOUS GRANTS

1	Vainya Gupta A	Gunaighar	Debidvar	Comilla
2	Vainay Gupta B	Maināmatī	Burichang	Comilla
3	Deva Khaḍg A	Ashrafpur	Raipur	Narshingdi
4	Deva Khaḍg B	Ashrafpur	Raipur	Narshingdi
5	Deva khaḍg C	Maināmatī	Burichang	Comilla
6	- Khadg A	Maināmatī	Burichang	Comilla
7	Bālabhaṭṭa	Maināmatī	Burichang	Comilla
8	Lokanātha	-	-	Tippera
9	Śrīdharana Rāta	Kailan	Caṇḍīna	Comilla
10	Ānanda Deva	Maināmatī	Burichang	Comilla
11	Bhava Deva A	Maināmatī	Burichang	Comilla
12	Bhava Deva B	-	-	Comilla
13	- Deva A	Maināmatī	Burichang	Comilla
14	- Deva A	mainathati	Burichang	Comilla
15	Śrī Candra A	Pancasar(Rampal	Munshiganj	Munshiganj
16	Śrī Candra B	Kedarpu	Gosairhat	Shriyatpur

17	Śrī Candra C	Dhulla	Singair	Manikganj
18	Śrī Candra D	Edilpur	Gosairhat	Shriyatpur
19	Śrī Candra E	Madanpur	Sabar	Dhaka
20	Laḍaha Candra	Maināmatī	Burichand	Comilla
21	Laḍaha Candra	Maināmatī	Burichand	Comilla
22	Govinda Candra	Maināmatī	Burichand	Comilla
23	Harikala Deva	Maināmatī	Burichand	Comilla
24	Dāmodara Deva A	Mehar	Saharasti	Chandpur
25	Dāmodara Deva B	Sobharampur	Burichang	Comilla
26	Dāmodara Deva C	Nasirabad	-	Chittagunj
27	Dasaratha Deva	Advadi	Munshiganj	Munshiganj
28	Viradhara Deva	Maināmatī	Burichang	Comilla

SECTION-I

RULERS OF SAMATAṬA AND GEOGRAPHIC REFERENCES IN INSCRIPTIONS

1. Vainya Gupta A

This copper plate was discovered at Gunaighar village, while carried out mud from a tank, about 18 miles to the north west of the Comilla town, a mile and a half to the south-west of Debidvar Thana (police station) It is 10.5 inches long and 6.5 inches width without a rim and is fairly thick. In the middle of the proper right of the plate an oval shape seal is affixed and a bull recumbent facing proper right. The legend on the seal read as *Māhārājā Śrī Vainya Gupta*. The plate is very corroded. It is written on both the sides but not full on the reverse. It consists of 31 lines in which 23 lines on the obverse and 8 lines on the reverse. It bears a number of cut marks of hitting. It was dated in numerical symbols. The last line of the grant is expressed as " *Saṁ 100 80 8 possyādi 20 4*". Such type of writing style can be easily indicated to the Gupta Era. The letters as well as the symbols mostly agree with those of the Gupta period. Therefore, we can say that the grant was issued, on 24th day of the month of Pauśa in the year of 188 Gupta Era, i.e. 508 A.D, from Kripura, which is not identified. The language of the plate is Sanskrit. The subordinate Mahāraja Rudradattā presented the request for an endowment of the Avaivarttikā congregation of monks belonging to the Āśrama Vihāra, dedicated to the Ārya Avalokiteśvara, and headed by the Ācāryya Sāntideva. This Vihāra was then in course of construction by the king Rudradatta on behalf of that Ācaryya Śāntideva. The boundaries of the lands are separated by five parcels of uncultivated land to be held as a tax-free perpetual endowment. The total measure of lands is eleven Pāṭakas situated in Uttara Maṇḍalika. It means, most probably, the northern side of Samataṭa Maṇḍala. It, therefore, seems that the lands were located near the find spot of the plate. Two plots out of the five were situated in the village named Gunikagrahara. The plate was found in the village Gunaighar near- Maināmatī Lalmai hill range. Most probably, the village Gunikagrahara identifies with present Gunaighar. None of other place names can be identified yet. The ruler's order was given to his principal minister, the Mahāraja Vijayasena, who made it known to three prince ministers. The minister of peace and war, Naradatta, recorded the endowment. There is, a particular interest, is the reference to the donated land being situated in the northern Maṇḍala of the Kingdom. Bhattacharya mentions that the main kingdoms of Vainya Gupta with the Headquarters were probably situated in the southern part of the District[1]. The land is further located by a reference to the fields belonging to another monastery, the Mahāvihāra, and to a temple didected to Pradyumneśvara, the god of love. The endowment was intended to maintain the worship of the Buddha and to repair the cracks in the monastery, implying a brick structure.

The mentioned name of the government officers show an imperial bureaucratic government but the concentration of the officers is in the hands of a few" persons, and the absence of any reference to a local government such as was found in the Gupta inscriptions further to the west, suggests that Vainya gupta's rule was limited both in territory and trained administrators. For example, Vijayasena was designated not only as a messenger and principal feudatory but also as " The High chamberlain the officer in charge of elephants, the president of five Law court officers and president of city Governors."[2]Naradatta functioned both as the minister in charge of peace and war and as the principal scribe of the government[3].

2. Vainya Gupta B

This plate was discovered at the lowest level of Sālvan Vihāra excavation. The plate is approxithately of the same size as Vainy Gupta- A plate, measures about 10.5 inches in length and 6.5 inches in breadth. It is highly corroded and not in a good state of preservation. A seal is attached on the proper right measure 3⁵/g inches by 4⁵/g inches on its face. It bears an emblem of a recumbent bull facing proper right with a single inscribed line underneath. A number of latters could be read whose location in the line led to its reconstruction as *Mahāraāja Śrī Vanya Guptasya*. This inscribed line of the seal could be confirmed closely to that of the Vainya Gupta A plate inscription. No other information is available from this plate due to its corrosion.

3. Deva Khaḍga A

This plate was found at Ashrafpur village under Raipur police station. The village Ashrafpur is situated in 38 miles north, north-west from Comilla town and 30 miles north-east from Dhaka. The plate is 10 inches long and 61/2 inches wide. It bears a seal on the top of the middle. The image of a recumbent bull is depicted on the seal. It faced proper left. A single line of inscription was inscribed below the image of the bull. It reads as *"Śrīthat Devakhaḍga"*. It was recorded in the seventh regnal year, . which through the identification of one of Devadhadga's successors with the ruler of Samataṭa during the visit of Chinese pilgrim in 671 A. D.; can be plausibly dated in the raid-seventh century[4]. This copperplate grant was issued from Jayakarmant. It has been identified with the modern Badakamta, which lies five miles due west of Mainathatl Mandir and one-third of a mile north of the Daudkandi road. Nine pāṭ akas and Ten dronas of land were donated to the royal preceptors. Saṅghamitra, who apparently was the head of four Vihāras and Viharikas (large and small monasteries). The exact location of the land has not been Identified, but references to Peranāṭana also occur in the second Laḍaha Candra plate suggesting that the land lay close to the hills where born dynasties were ruled. Puradasa, a devout worshipper of the Buddha[3], wrote the order. The references to large and small monasteries indicate a sacred complex. It is particularly significant that two of the remaining Khaḍga plates were discovered from Sālvan Vihāra excavation. So, it appears that the location of the donated land may be some where in Maināmatī-Lalmai hill range. Also of interest was the occurrence of the name Saṅghamitra, which appeared as that of a poet in the anthology of Sanskrit poetry collected by the abbot Vidyākara[6] in the eleventh century. If these are the references of the same person, then it is an evidence of an accomplished poet who also was the head of four monasteries and occupied an important position at the Khaḍga court. Judging from the inscription, the Khaḍgas were rulers of limited territory.

4. Deva Khaḍga B

This plate was found in association with the Deva Khaḍga A plate at Ashrafpur village under Raipur police station. It is a small plate, measuring ?$^1/_2$ inches long and 6 inches broad. The grant was issued from the same centre, Jayakarmanta. The same type of seal was attached on the top of the middle of the plate. The grant was memorialized in favour of the name of Devakhaḍga. But his son, Rajaraja, granted the land. The account of Six pāṭakas and Ten droilas of land was transferred to the monastery. Śrī Yajñavarman executed the grant. The grant is very similar to that of the Deva Khaḍga A plate.

5. Deva Khaḍga C

This plate was recovered from Sālvan Vihāra excavations. It is very badly corroded. The measurement of this plate is 10 inches long and 8 inches wide. A seal was attached on the top of the middle of the plate. An image of a recumbent bull is depicted on the seal. The direction of the bull is facing the proper left. A single line of inscription is engraved below the image of the bull. It read as *"Śrīthat Deva Khaḍga"*. In the twenty-seventh line, there was a reference to the prince (Rajputra) Śrī Balabhata. Nothing more is known from this plate[7] .

6 - Khaḍga D

This plate was discovered with Deva Khaḍga C plate in Sālvan Vihāra excavation. It is ?'$^1/_2$ inches long and 6 inches width. A seal was fastened in the top of the middle of the plate. It is also very badly corroded. No information could be granted from this plate[8].

7. Bālabhaṭṭa

The copperplate of Balbhatta was recovered from Sālvan Vihāra excavation. This is a single plate engraved on both the sides. It is 13$^1/_2$ inches long and 10$^1/_4$ inches width. A corroded and damaged round seal is attached to the top in the middle of the plate. It projects about 2$^3/_8$ inches. It appears that a single line of legend was inscribed on it. But it is absent at present. It might be destroyed due to corrosion. The copperplate contains 35 inscribed lines on the obverse and 11 inscribed lines on the reverse. Thus in all there are 46 lines in the grant. It was badly encrusted and the extent of the writing could not be clearly determined. The names of "Khaḍga" (L-3), *"Svāmi Devakhaḍga"* (L-12) and donor "Rājaputra Bālabhaṭṭa" (L-20) are read clearly in the document. The family of the Khaḍga kings belonged to *Kanvasakha* of Yajurveda. The father of Svami Devakhaḍga was simply a *Parameśvara*. The wonderful Mahābhogaśrama, eight viharas adorned with large number of white coloured "Caityas" were mentioned in the plate. 28 pāṭakas of land were granted from the capital city, Devaparvata and this gift were made for Lord Buddha. **Dharma** and Saṅgha and also for *Nuvakarmas*. The dutaka of the grant, Śrī

Yajñavarmana was a devout worshipper of Buddha. Bālabbaṭṭa's dates would fall in the last quarter of 7th century but before the Deva rulers of the eighth century.

8. Lokanātha

This plate was found somewhere in the Tippera district of SouthEastern Bengal. It is lo$^1/_2$ inches long and ?^{1}/2 inches width. Four Corners of the plate is missing. It is very badly corroded. The letters of some places are quite effaced and in others partly effaced. Owing to corrosion, decipherment of the plate is very difficult. The upper portion of the plate is comparatively thicker than the lower portion. The plate is very heavy owing to the weight of the heavy seal attached to the middle of its proper right. The seal bears an image of the goddess Lakṣmī or Śrī, standing on a lotus pedestal and flanked by two elephants pouring libations from two jars lifted by their trunks. Two attendants seated cross-legged at the two sides of Lakṣmī. It is round in shape with a diameter of 4 inches. The reverse is depicted by a full-blown lotus. Beneath the Gajalakṣmī, there is a legend read as *Kumāramātyadhikaraṇasya,* The second legend reads as *Lokanāthasya.* It is on the smaller seal affixed on the right side of the image impression of Lakṣmī. It appears that the legend *Loknāthasya* is veiy similar to the seal found on the plate of Śrīdharaṇa Rāta from Kailan. The plate is not in a good state of preservation. It is inscribed on both the sides. It consists of 57 lines of which 26 lines on the obverse and 31 lines on the reverse. The characters of the script belong to the northern class of letters of the 7th century A. D. The letters of this plate are similar to the Banskhera[9] and Madhuban[10] plates of Mahārājā Harṣha, the plates[11] of the time of Sasanka-Raja, and the plates[12] of king Bhaskaravarmanadeva of Kāmarūpa. Dr. Bhoch[13] remarks that the plate is written in characters of the 9th or 10th century A. D. approxithately. But the writing style, of this plate is not appeared as in 9th or 10th century A. D. So, the plate appeal's to be dated in 7 th century A. D. The language of the copper-plate inscription is Sanskrit. The form of the document is very peculiar. It begins with an address in prose. It has mentioned the account of the history of Loknātha's family.

This document was issued thorough *Sāndhivigrahika* Prasantadeva by King Lokanātha. The donee was *Mahāsāmānta* Pardosasarman who made an application through King's son, prince Lakṣmīnatha. The plots of lands were granted in the forest region in the Suvvuṇga Viṣya. Pradosaśarman desired to construct a temple for estolation of an image of Ananta-Narayana. The amount of lands allotted individually and, in some cases, jointly, is also clearly mentioned in the document. First King's name of the plate is partly effaced which ending in the word nath comes from the good family of the Sage Bharadvāja. The next King Srīnathā (son of -natha) was a feudatory ruler acquired much fame in the field of battle. His son, Bhavanatha, was religious minded. Wife of his brother's son. Gotradevi, gave birth to a worthy son, Lokanathā. The significant fact is mentioned in verse 9, that a king named Jivadharaṇa made over his won Viṣaya (district) and army without engaging in further battle to Lokanātha. Son of Loknātha is prince Lakṣmīnātha.

The grant recorded in the 44 regional years in the month of Phālguna and given to Pradosasarman for accuring of merit to his parents and to himself and to Bhagavan Ananta-Narayana, and to the Brahmins.

9. Śrīdhārna Rāta

This plate was traced at Kalian village, 18 miles SouthWest of Comilla and 13 miles due west of the Lalmai Railway Station, under the Caṇḍīna Police Station of Comilla district. The proper right of the plate is broken.

It shows that the finder cut the plate due to his curiosity and was gone to goldsmith for testing whether it is gold or not. Or it was cut accidentally while digging the earth. The plate is 10 7_2o inches long and 8" $/_2$o inches broad with lettering inscribed lengthwise and the scale marked on the proper right. The seal is circular in shape with a diameter of $4^1/2$ inches; but there is a projecting knob at its outer end. The seal is depicted by the goddess Lakṣ mī standing on a full-blossomed lotus and flanked by two elephants pouring libations. Below the elephants are the figures of two devotees. It is very similar to the seal discovered on the plates of Lokanātha and Maruṇḍanatha[14]. There are two inscribed lines below the Gajalakṣmi read as 1. *Śrīthatsathatatesvara-padanudhyatasya* and 2. *Kumaramdtyadhikaranasya.* Another line, afterwards embossed horizontally on the seal just to the right of the figure of Lakṣmī, reads *Śrī ŚrīdharanaRātasya,* It is also noted that the Tippera grant of Lokanātha also mentions a line reading *Kumarathatyadhiharanasya.* The names of Lokanātha and Śrī dharana Rāta were written on the seals indicate that they had countersigned the original document afterwards incised on copperplate. The signature of the king was essential for the documents. Although it was only rarely reproduced on the plates on which charters were afterwards copied, because the latter bore the royal seal indicating the king's sanction. Local rulers of ancient Bengal, however, usually issued charters with their own seals and without any counter signature of the ruler of the country. The importance attached to the counter signature by Loknātha and Śrīdharana Rāta may suggest that they were feudatory rulers risen to an almost independent status and that they were eager to demonstrate their absolute authority over particular regions in defiance of the overlord[15].

The plate is not in a good state of preservation. Some portions of the plate are very corroded. It is engraved on both the sides. It consists of 19 lines of which 28 lines on obverse and 21 lines on the reverse. The language of the record is Sanskrit prose and verses.

The date of the grant is mentioned as "on the seventh *tithi* of the bright half of the month of Sravan in the eighth year of the sovereignty over Samataṭa and many other countries, which has been received from the grace of the feet of the father," i.e. in the eighth regnal year of the king Śrīdhārana of Samataṭa[16]. Comparative study of the Tippera grant of Lokanātha and Kailan grant of Srī dharana Rāta indicate that Jivadharana Rāta, father of Srī dharana Rāta, was a contemporary of Lokanātha. Lokanātha appears to have flourished about the third quarter of the seventh century A. D. So, it may be suggested that Śrīdharana Rāta is roughly dated in the third or fourth quarter of the seventh century A. D.

The charter was issued from Devaparvata under Samataṭa Maṇḍala. The minister for peace and war, Jayanatha, requested that 25 patakas of land be distributed as endowment in the following fashion - $4^1/_2$ patakas to a Buddhist monastery, 13 patakas to thirteen Brahmins, and 7 $^1/_2$ patakas to be held by Jayanatha. The entire land lay within the administrative districts of Guptināṭ ana and Pātalāyika under the jurisdiction of the prince minister of Devaparvata. A later plate, one of Laḍaha Candra's also transfers property in Guptināṭana. There is no further information about the monastery or Brahmains relevant for this study.

10. Ānanda Deva

The copper-plate grant of Ānanda Deva was recovered during the excavation at Sālvan Vihāra along with some other plates. It is a single copper-plate grant engraved on both the sides. It measured $10^5/_8$ inches by $8^1/_8$ inches. A seal is attached to the top middle of the plate. It projects about 4 $/_4$ inches. The seal of *Dharmacakramudrā* was engraved on it. Below this representation, it bears a legend real as *"Śrī Vaṅgāmrgaṅksya"* (the moon of Vaṅgāl). This plate contains of two documents. The first one is of Ānanda Deva, which consists of 37 lines on the obverse and 5 lines on the reverse. An another endorsement of Bhavadeva was engraved on the reverse, which consists of 9 more lines. Thus there are in all 51 lines in two documents. The plate is not in a good state of preservation. Many portions of the inscription are indistinct and illegible.

The royal pedigree opens with Śantideva followed by his son Vīradeva. Vīradeva's son by Somadevi was Ānanda Deva.

Ānanda Deva was a Dvija (twice born) by birth. Vasantapur was the newly constructed capital and Devaparvata might be the old capital city Ānanda Deva had to abandon old Capital City due to the invasion of a strong enemy force. This document was issued in the 39th year of the reign of Ānanda Deva. Probably, it was the latter part of his reign. His son Bhava Deva issued the second document on the reverse of this copperplate in the second year of his reign. It was issued from Devaparvata. So it appears that the old capital situated at Devaparvata was regained within a short period either by Ānanda Deva himself or by his son Bhavadeva.

The donor of the land was *Paramasugata Parameśvar Paramalohaṭṭāraka. Māhārājadhirāga* Srī Ānanda Deva.in total 7½ patakas of land was donated for the temple, built probably by the donee Jalabhuti. The land was situated within Peranāṭana Viṣaya under world famous Samataṭa. A short history of Jayabhuti and his forefathers is beginning from Pusyabhuti. Pusyabhuts son Somabhuti left his native land Oḍḍayana and at first settled in Maghadha, from where he again migrated to Bengal. Somabhuti was rewarded and settled probably as a feudatory chief by Samācaradeva at Sālihradapattana. Somabhuti's son was Sikharabhuti, his son was Ratnabhuti, and whose auspicious born eight issue was Jayabhuti. It is noted from the Ghugrahati and Nalanda copper-plates of Samācaradeva dated in 6th century A. D. Mahārājādhirāja Samācaradeva was contemporary of Somabhuti, and Somabhuti's great grandson Jayabhuti was a contemporary of the donor king Ānanda deva. So, the king, Ānanda deva may be dated in last quarter of the 7th century or beginning of the 8th century A. D, Divakara was the *Mahāpratihāra* and *Dutaka* of the grant. The grant was dated 39th regnal year- on the 12th day of Bhādra.

11. Bhavadeva A

This grant was recorded on the vacant space of the reverse of the Ānanda Deva copper-plate grant. There are in total 14 lines on the reverse side of which 9 lines were engraved in Bhavadeva A grant. This grant was issued from Devaparvata (the illustrious camp of victory). Bhavadeva was designated by *Parameśvara Paramabhaṭṭāraka Mahārājādhirāja*. His father was *Paramasaugtata* (the most devout worshipper of Lord Buddha) *Mahārajādhirāja* Ānandadeva. The dutaka of this grant was *Mahāsamantadhipati* Srī Nandadhara. He places the prayer of Jayabhuti to the king. The donees of both the documents of this plate are Jayabhuti. It appears that Jayabhuti was one and the same person of both the grants. Three patafekas of land were donated in Peranāṭ ana Vaiṣaya by the king in connection with a Vihārika (small monastery) probably established by Jayabhuti, in the name of Tri-ratna i.e. Buddha, Dharma and Sahgha. The land was granted on the 13th day of the month of Bhadra of the 2nd regnal year of the king, Bhavadeva. Bhavadeva may be dated in 8th centuryA.D.

12. Bhavadeva B

The findspot of this inscription is unknown. But it was found in somewhere of the Tippera district. The inscription was written on both the sides of a single copperplate. It is $11^1/8$ inches by $8^7/_8$ inches. A round seal was attached to the top, measured $2^1/^4$ inches in diameter. It bore a *Dharmacakra Mudrā,* which flanked by two deer. The wheel is endowed with a pedestal below and an umbrella above. There is a single line inscribed below the wheel. It reads as *Śrī Abhinava-mrgāṅka.* At the bottom of the seal there is the emblem of a full-blown lotus with a lotus bud on a curved stalk on either side. The face of the seal is encircled by a depression beyond which, is a raised rim. A circle of beads decorates this rim. This beaded border is encircled by another rim. The plate is very badly corroded. There are altogether 64 lines of writing, 34 on the obverse side and 30 on the reverse side of the plate. This inscription was issued from Devaparvata situated in somewhere of Maināmatī-Lalmai hill range. The language of the inscription is Sanskrit.

The grant mentions the king named Viradeva. Viradeva's son was Ānandadeva and Ānandadeva's son and successor was Bhavadeva. The donor king, Bhavadeva is designated as a *Paramasaugata* (i.e., a devout worshipper of Buddha), *Parameśvara, Paramabhaṭṭāraka* and *Mahārajadhirāja*. He is also said to have meditated on (or to have been favoured by) the feet *of Mahārājādhirāja* Ānanda deva who was his father and predecessor. The name of the grandfather of applicant is not clear due to corrosion of the plate. Applicant's father's name is Ādityadāsa and applicant's name is Vibhutidasa was an official of the king who had great confidence in the former. Vibhutidasa approached *Mahāsamanta* Nandadhara with a request to submit his prayer to the king Bhavadeva. King Bhavadeva was requested by *Mahāsāmāntadhipati* Nandadhara to make a grant of 7½ palatakes of land in favour of the Ratnatraya of the Vendathati-Viharika. The expression of *Ratnatraya* indicates the Buddhist trinity of Buddha, Dharma and Saṅgha. The expression Vendathati-Viharika, probably, means the Buddhist monastery located in an area called Vendathati. The 7½ patakas of land is divided in four different plots. The 2½ patakas of land is situated at Vahakakhanda in Vendathati within the Peranāṭana Viṣaya. The other three plots, probably, situated in the same Viṣaya. The ruler, Bhavadeva, instructed Nandadhara to execute the transfer of property and transfer was recorded by Brahmadasa on the copper-plate.

The grant was recorded in the second regnal year of the king, on the 18th day of the solar month of Vaisakha. The characters belong to the East Indian variety of the Northern Alphabet and may be assigned on palaeographic grounds to the seventh or eighth century A.D. A study of the characters of the Kailan plate of Śrīdharana Rāta, Tipperaplate of Lokanātha[17] , Ashrafpur plates of Devakhaḍga suggests that the characters of the copper-plate of Bhavadeva may be assigned to a date later than that of Lokanātha, Śrīdharana Rāta and the Khaḍga kings Devad Khaḍga and Rājarāja, all of whom flourished in the later half of the seventh century. So, the king, Bhavadeva, may be dated in the eighth century A. D.

13. - DEVA (?) A

This inscription[20] was recovered during excavation at Sālvan Vihāra. The measurement of the plate is $16^3/_4$ inches long and 10¼ inches width. It was engraved on both the sides. It had 34 lines on the obverse side and 19 lines on the reverse. A seal is attached to the top center of the plate. The seal bears *Dharmachakra Mudrā* flanked by two deer, as on the other Deva plates. The plate is very badly corroded. No other information is available from the plate.

14. -DEVA(?)B

The Deva B plate[21] was discovered during the Sālvan Vihāra excavation association with the Deva A plate. It is a small plate measuring $5^1/_2$ inches long and $2^3/_4$ inches width. The plate consists of 20 lines on the obverse and 6 lines on the reverse. The *Dharmacakra Mudrā* was affixed on the top of the middle of the plate. Two deer flank it, as on the other Deva plates. This plate is also highly corroded. No information is traced from this plate also.

15. Śrī Candra A

The copperplate of Śrī Candra A was found in the village of Pancasar of the Munshigunj district in the possession of one Yadunath Banik. But the original findspot of the plate appears to have been somewhere in Rampal, one and half a mile from the village of Pancasar where it was recovered in course of digging the land. This is a single plate engraved on both the sides. It is $9^1/2$ inches long and 8 inches width A seal is attached on the top middle of the plate. It projects about $2^3/_4$ inches. The seal is engraved by *Dharmacakra Mudrā,* which is flanked by two deer. This is the emblem of the wheel of Law. Such type of seal is affixed on the seal of the Pāla copper-plate. The border of the seal is highly decorated. There is a lenged, below *Dhamacakra Mudrā* which reads as Srī Candra Devah. The plate consists of 40 lines of which 28 lines on the obverse and 12 lines on the reverse. The size of the letters is ¼ inches.

The inscription describes the genealogy of Candra family. It mentions that one Purṇa Candra, was born in the family. His son was Suvarṇa Candra. His son, Trailokya Candra, was the supporter of Harikela, and become king in Candradvīpa, which may be identified with Bakergunj. The wife of Trailokya Candra was Śrī Kāncan gave birth a son named Śrī Candra. He was designated with *Paramasaugata Paramesvara Paramabhaṭṭraka Mahārājādhirāja.*

The grant records one pataka of land at the village of Nehakasthi in the Nanya Maṇḍala of the Pauṇḍrabhukti. This grant was issued from Vikramapura. The Donee was the *Śantivarika* Pitavāsagupta Śarman. He was the great grandson of Makkadagupta, grandson of Varahagupta and son of Sumaṅgalagupta. They belonged to the *Śāṇḍilyagotra* and the *Pravara* of the three *Ṛṣis.*

The characters are a type of Northern Nagari. It is similar to the Copper-plates of the later Pālas. The language of the inscription is Sanskrit. The inscription did not mention the date of donation. According to palaeographic consideration, it may be dated in 10th century A.D.

16. Śrī Candra B

The copper-plate of Śrī Candra B was recovered from the village of Kedarpur situated in the present Shariyatpur district. It is a single plate inscribed on one side only. It is an incomplete grant. The plate is 8½ inches long and 7½ inches width. A seal is attached to the top of the centre of the plate, which is circular in shape. The seal is engraved by *Dharmacakra Mudrā* which is flanked by two deer as on the Śrī Candra A plate. A single line of inscription is below the *Dharmacakra Mudrā.* It reads as Śrī Śrī Candra Devah. Beneath the inscribed line is floral motif as decoration. The plate consists of 18 lines engraved on the obverse. The language of the plate is Sanskrit. The donor king Śrī Candra was designated by *Parama Saugata Paramesvara Paramabhaṭṭāraka Mahārājādhiraja* is evidently of the same as Śrī Candra A plate. This plate was also mentioned the genealogy of the Candra family from Purṇa Candra to Śrī Candra as like as Śrī Candra A plate. This plate is not mentioned the date of donation and donated land. The grant was issued from Vikramapura. The characters of the inscription are thoroughly same as like as the Śrī Candra A plate. So, it may also be dated in the 10th century A.D.

17. Śrī Candra C

The copper-plate grant of Śrī Candra was found at Dhullā in the district of Manikganj. It is a single plate. The measurement of the plate is $8^5/_8$ inches in length and 7¼ inches in breadth. A seal was affixed at the top of the middle of the plate. It is 3 inches in length and 2¾ inches in breadth. The well-known *Dharmacakra Mudrā* is engraved on the seal. Two deer flank it. The circular' surface of the seal is 2¼ inches in diametre. The plate consists of 47 lines, of which 23 lines on the obverse and 24 lines on the reverse. Many portions of the plate are badly corroded.

This plate is also given the genealogy of Candra family. Purṇa Candra was born in the family and originated from Rohitagiri may be identified with Maināmatī-Lalmai hill range. It is also menitoned that Purṇa Candra's son Suvarṇa Candra became a Buddhist. His son Trailokya Candra was a powerful King. He is compared to Dilip. He was made himself as the lord of Candradvīpa, which may be identified with Bakergunj, is sainted in present Barishal Division. He was the support of Hirikela king. Harikela may be identified with the present Sylhet division, which is situated to the north-eastward of Comilla town. Trailokya Candra's queen Śrī Kancana gave birth to Śrī Candra. In this grant, Śrī Candra was designated as the imperial titles *Paremaśvara Paramabhaṭṭāraka Mahārājādhirāja*. Trilokya Candta was designated as *Parmasaugata Mahārājādhiraj*. So, it shows that both of them were independent rulers and Trailokya Candra was the first independent ruler of Candra family. The grant was issued from Vikramapura identified with present Vikramapura near Dhaka City.

The five plots of land were granted by this document. The first plot of land, measured 4 halls, was situated at a village named **Durvāpatra** in Khediravilli Viṣaya of Vallimunda Maṇḍala under Paudrabhiikti. The second plot of land, measured 3 halls, was situated in an area named, probably, Nondiyajo- Jayastara. It may be situated in same Viṣhaya. The third plot of land, measured 3 halls, was located in the village of Tivaravilli in the same area. The fourth plot of land measured 2 Halas and 6 drones were situated in a village named **Parkaḍimuṇḍa** in **Ikkadasi Viṣaya** of the **Yolā Maṇḍala**. The fifth plot of land, measured 7 halls, was situated in the village named Mulapatra. It may be situated in Yola Marietta. Altogether 19 Halas and 6 dronas of land were granted by the king. The donee *Santivarika* Vyasaganga Sarman was a Brahmin. He belonged to the *Vardhakausikagotra* and the *Kaṇvasākhā*. He was the great grandson of Nandaganga and son of Vibhuganga. The lands were granted for performing four homes in connection with a rite called *AdbhutasdntL* The king in the name of Lord Buddha made the grant for the increase of merit and fame of his parents and himself.

The grant was recorded on the 18th day of month *Asvina* in the 8th regnal year of donor king, in presence of all royal officers those were mentioned on the other copper plate grants of Śrī Candra Deva.

The language of the grant is Sanskrit. The characters of the grant are resembled with the inscription of King Śrī Candra, those were found at Rampal and Kedarpur. All these three grants were issued from Vikramapura on palaeographic consideration, the Buddhist king Śrī Candra, who belonged to the Candra dynasty, ruled over South East Bengal, flourished in the 10th century A. D.

18. Śrī Candra D

This plate was found at Edilpur in Shariyarpur district. It is about 8 inches long and 7 inches width. A seal was affixed on the top of the plate. *Dharmacakra Mudrā* engraves it. as like as other plates of Śrī Candra. It is a single plate inscribed on both the sides. The grant consists of 36 lines. The prose portion of the record states that it was issued from Vikramapura by the *Paramasaugata Parameśvara Paramabhaṭṭāraka Mahārājādhirāja* SrfCandradeva who meditated on the feet of his father, the *Mahārājādhirāja* Trailokya Candra deva.

The king Śrī Candra donated a piece of land. It was situated in village of Leliyā in the Satatapadmavati Viṣya of KumāRātalāka Maṇḍala.

The language of the grant is Sanskrit. The characters of the scripts are evidently same of the others grants of Śrī Candra. So, this grant also may be dated in 10th century A. D.

19. Śrī Candra E

This copper-plate grant of Śrī Candra was discovered in the village of Madanpur, near the old famous village of Sabhar in the district of Dhaka. The village, Madanpur is situated about 15 miles north-west of the city of Dhaka. It was found while the earth was being dug for the foundation of a wall.

This is a single plate engraved on both the sides. The measurement of the plate is 8¼ inches in length and $6^1/_2$ inches in breadth. It bears a seal attached to middle of the top. It is about $4^1/_2$ inches by $3^1/_4$ inches. *Dharmacakra Mudrā* such as engraves the seal found on the other copper-plates of Śrī Candra. The inscription consists of 42 lines of which 23 lines on the obverse and 19 lines on the reverse. It is written in Sanskrit language. It may be noted that the first 8 verses of this plate are identical with the 8 verses of the Kampala plate of Śrī Candra.

The historical informations are found in this plate. The first verse describes with devotion to the Buddhist "Three Jewels" i.e., Buddha, Dharma and Saṅgha. King Śrī Candra was designated by the royal title, *Paramasaugata Parameśvara Paramabhaṭṭāraka Mahārājādhirāja*. The ruling Candra dynasty was originated from a locality of Rohitagiri is identified with Maināmatī-Lalmai hill range. This grant is also mentioned the genealogy of Candra dynasty. From this inscription, it appears that the first nobleman in the dynasty, named Purṇa Candra, became very famous; his name could be "read on the pedestals of images and (stone) pillars of victory and copper-plates in which new epigraphs were inscribed." Such type of description is interpreted in verse 2 of this inscription. Purṇa Candra's illustrious son, Suvarṇa Candra, was known in the world as Buddha. So, it appears that, he was the first in the dynasty to embrace Buḍḍhism. But Purṇa Candra and Suvarṇa Candra were not described as a king. Son of Suvarṇa Candra, Trailokya Candra, was mentioned in all the records, became the first independent king. Most probably, Vikrampura was his capital. He was the king of Candradvīpa and was the supporter of Harikela king. Candradvīpa was known as Bakla Candradvīpa in mediaeval period. Bakla Candradvīpa[22] comprised within its boundaries, some portion of the modem districts of Bakerganj, greater Khulna and greater Faridpur. Trailokya's wife was ŚrīKāñcana who gave birth to her illustrious son Śrī Candradeva.

Moreover 8 drones of land was granted to a Brahmin, named Sukradeva. This land was situated in a locality called *Vaṅgasāgara-sambhaṇḍāriyaka* in **Yola Maṇḍala** under Pauṇḍrabhukti. Sukradeva was the son of Hara, grandson of Varāha and great grandson of Mahādeva who himself was born in the family of three *Somapitin* Brahmins named Makha, Rāma and Dhruva, having the three well-known *pravaras*. This copper-plate grant was issued from Vikramapura. The land was dedicated to the name of Lord Buddha, according to law of *Bhūmicchidra,* dully-touched water, for the increase of merit and fame of donorking's parents and himself. The grant was recorded in presence of all royal officers and approved by the *Mahāsāndhivigrahika* and *Mahākṣapaṭalika* as like as the other grants of Śrī Candradeva.

The grant was recorded on 28th day of month of *Marga-Śīrṣa* in the 46th regnal year of King Śrī Candra Deva. The characteristics of this inscription are resemblance to other inscriptions of Śrī Candradeva. So, this grant also may be dated in 10th century A. D.

20. Laḍaha Candra A

This copper-plate of Laḍaha Candra A was found accidentally in a mound called Cārpatra Mudrā in an area of Maināmatī-Lalmai hill range.

A seal is attached to the middle top of the plate. This seal is engraved by a *Dharmacakra Mudrā,* which is flanked by two deer. This type of seal has been found in other Candra plates, e.g. Śrī Candradeva. A single line of inscription is found in the iu seal below the *Dharmacakra Mudrā*. It reads as *"**Śrī Laḍaha Candradevah**"*. Lower portion of the seal has a floral motif. It is a single copper-plate grant inscribed on both the sides. The grant consists of 62 lines of which 31 lines on the obverse and 31 lines on the reverse. The inscription was issued from Vikramapura, located about 40 miles west-south-west of Maināmatī and 24 miles east-south of the centre of Dhaka City.

This grant has mentioned the genealogy of Candra dynasty and its geographical position. The king, Trailokya Candra, the crest jewel of Vaṅga, was the leader over the world. His son, Śrī Candra, the gold of gold, was the shelter of the great rulers of the earth and the possessor of endless resources. His son, Kalyān Candra, sanctified both the families i.e. paternal and thaternal. He was virtuous by nature and whom the good people like the sacred current of the three streams (i.e. Ganges or The Trisrota River) served. His dear wife, Kalyāna Devī was the daughter of a rich merchant and was of uncommon beauty. She gave birth to a son named Laḍaha Candra. The King Laḍaha Candra went to Varanasi. He bathed in the waters of the Ganges to free from sins. The king was designated by the royal title, *Parameśvara Paramabhaṭṭāraha Mahārājādhirāja.* He was a Buddhist but devoted to Hindu Religion.

The donated lands were situated at Paṭṭikeraka in Samataṭa

Maṇḍala under Pauṇḍrabhukt. Three separate pieces of land were granted in the name and to the god Śrī Laḍaha Mādhava by the king Śrī Laḍaha Candradeva. First plot of land, measuring 5¾ dronas, was situated in the village of Phullahada. Campavani called the plot of land. The second plot of land, measuring patakas, 4¾ dronas 5 yaṣṭhi two bindus and 3 kakas, was situated in the village of Vappasiṁhavoraka, relating to (the village) Dollavāyika. The third plot of land, measuring 3 pātakas. 9 dronas and 1 kakas, was situated in the village of Mahādeva together with the market of Dhritipura and relating to (the village) Guptinatana. All together 11 patakas 19.5 dronas 5 yasthi 2 bindus and 4 kakas of land were recorded on 30th day of the month Jyeṣṭha in the 6th regional year of Śrīmad Laḍaha Candradeva, in presence of all royal officers which were approved by *Mahāsāndhivigrahika* and *Mahākṣapaṭalika.* The lands were granted for the increasing of merit and fame of his parents and himself

The language of the inscription is Sanskrit and the characters of the inscription are resembled with the other Candra inscriptions. The king Śrī Candra, grand father of Śrī Laḍaha Candra, was dated in the 10th centuiy A. D. From the analysis of the Caudra copper-plate inscriptions, it appears that Laḍaha Candra may be dated in the beginning of the 11th centuiy A. D.

21. Laḍaha Candra B

The Laḍaha Candra B plate was found accidentally in a mound called Cārpatra Murā, in an area of Mainămatī-Lalmai hill range, associated with the Laḍaha Candra A plate. A seal is fastened on the top centre and resembles closely to the seal of the plate. It is also a single plate engraved on both the sides. This grant consists of 60 lines of which 30 lines on the obverse and 30 lines on the reverse. This grant is also issued from the camp of victory. Vikramapura, generally identified with the ruins of Vikramapura[23].

The genealogical portion of this B plate is similar to the Laḍaha Candra A plate. The 8 patakas and 37.5 dronas of land was granted to Śrī Laḍaha Madhāva Bhaṭṭāraka by the king Laḍaha Candra, in presence of all royal officers and respected persons for increasing merit and fame of his parents and himself. This land is situated at Peranāṭana Viṣaya in Samataṭa Maṇḍala under Pauṇḍrabhukti. The image of Lord Vaṣudeva was erected at Paṭṭikeraka by Laḍaha Candra himself, which bore the name of Śrī Laḍaha Madhava Bhaṭṭāraka. In this plate, the king Laḍaha Candra was designated as *Paramasaugata Parameśvara Paramabhaṭṭāraka Mahārājādhirāja*. He was the devout worshipper of Buddha but he had great devotion to the Hindu Gods. The plates A and B indicate that Laḍaha Candra himself performed more Hindu rites than Candra kings. It is also noted that Laḍaha Candra A and B plates started with the salutation to Lord Vāsudeva while rest of the Candra plates (before Laḍaha Candra) begun with the praise of Buddha, Dharma and Saṅgha.

The land was recorded on 30th day of month Āṣādha in the 6th regional year of King Laḍaha Candradeva. *Mahāsandhivigrahika* and *Mahākṣapaṭalika* approved it. This "B" plate was recorded after two months of "A" plate.

The language of this plate is Sanskrit. Both the plates of Laḍaha Candra were written in verses and prose. The characters are the same as given in other Candra plates[24] . Banerji[25] did the comparative study of these scripts. On palaeographic consideration and discussion with the article of Majumder and Banerji, this plate may be dated in the beginning of 11th century A. D.

22 Govinda Candra

The copper-plate of Govinda Candra was discovered accidentally at Cārpatra Murā of Maināmatī-Lalmai hill range. A seal is attached to the top centre of the plate. It is round in shape but slight projection is also observed to the top of the seal. This seal is described as *Dharmacakra Mudrā* in the inscription. Two deer like other Candra plates flank this *Dharmacakra*. *A* single line of inscription is noticed on the seal. It is read as Śrī Govinda Candra Devah. This is a single plate engraved on both the sides. There was a text of 29 lines on the obverse and 29 lines on the reverse. The plate consists of verses and prose. It was issued from the camp of victory, Vikramapura.

The genealogical informations are found in the inscription. The leader of the kings of the earth, Śrī Candradeva, was born in the family. He was *Paramasaugata* i.e. great devout worshipper of Buddha and was famous by his pure merits that had spread upto the farthest end of the globe including mountains and oceans. His son. Kalyān Candra, was Bali by dint of his sacrifice and was Yudhiṣṭhira by his truthfulness and was mighty Arjun by dint of his heroism. He was very powerful king, made the river Lohitya redoubled by the tears densely dropping down from the eyes of the Mleccha ladies who were agitated owing to the killing of their husbands. The king snatched away the army consisting of elephants, horses and foot soldiers in the battlefield, made the face of the king of Gauḍa bend down under the weight of shame for a long while. His son, Laflaha Candra, lord of the earth, known for morality and who was kind to his people. He went to Varanasi and bathed in Ganges and was donated gold to the Brahmins. His beloved queen, was Saubhāgya Devī, who was dearly loved just as the goddess of fortune is to Hari and the goddess Pārvati to Śiva. She gave birth to Govinda Candra on an auspicious day and in an auspicious moment. He was compared with Mahāsena i.e. Kārttikeya. He was the embodiment of Dharma, the store of forgiveness, the protector of the people, the object of virtue and the abode of Lakṣmī. He was designated as *Parmesvara Paramabhaṭṭāraka Mahārājādhiraja.*

Two pāṭakas of land was donated to Naṭṭeśvara Bhaṭṭāraka at an area of SahaRātalaka in Peranāṭana Viṣaya of Samataṭa Maṇḍala under PauṇḍrabhuktL for the increasing of merit and fame of the king's parents and himself, as long as the Sun, Moon and the Earth endure, according to the law of *Bhumicchidra.* dully touched water, in presence of all royal officers and respected persons.

The plate bears no date but the king Govinda Candra ruled over Samataṭa at least 23 years[26]. The language of this inscription is Sanskrit. The characters of this script are same to the script of the copper-plates of Laḍaha Candra. So the independent king Govinda Candra, most probably, ruled over Samataṭ a in the second quarter of llth century A. D.

23. Harikala Deva

The copper-plate of Raṇavaṅkamalla Harikala Deva was discovered in digging earth for the repair of the highway through the Maināmatī hills in the district of Comilla. The find spot of the plate is about 5 miles to the west of the town of Comilla.

The plate is 11 inches in length and 9 inches in breadth. It bears a symbol of the royal dynasty to the top centre of the plate, measuring 2 inches in height. It was "an abrupt bend allowing room to a figure coarsely delineated and apparently intended to represent a temple" [27]. It consists of an arch and inside, probably, a crown. This is a single plate engraved on one side. It consists of 24 lines, which are composed in verses and last three lines in prose. There is no reference to a centre of issue. The actual endowment was made by Śrī Dhadi-Eba, son of Hedi-Eba, the chief cavalry officer of Harikala Deva, on his own authority. This chief officer of the horses, continuously stationed in the greatness of the supreme element, the master of the worlds, always shines in the politics of charming courses and in the activities of the Sahaja cult. He gave the property to the small monastery dedicated to the goddess Durgottara, a form of the Buddhist goddess Tārā. This monastery was built in the city of Paṭṭikera. It was apparently situated somewhere in the Maināmatī-Lalmai hill range where the plate was discovered. The inscription records a grant of land measuring 20 dronas in a village named Bejakhaṇḍa in the city of Paṭṭikera. The writer of the record, one Medini-Eba makes no secret of the fact that the inscription is in nature of a praise of a family to which probably he himself belonged.

The plate was inscribed in the 17th regnal year of the glorious king Raṇa vaṅkamaila Harikāla Deva in the Śaka era 1141 (i.e. 1220 A. D.), on the 26th day of the month Phālguna.

It was unique for a royal officer to transfer property in his own name without securing his lord's permission. The implication is that Śrī Dhadi-Eba enjoyed the tax revenue from this parcel of land as a hereditary right that could not be resumed by his lord and therefore Śrī Dhadi-Eba was at liberty to dispose of revenue yield as he wished without reference to Harikāla Deva. Also of interest is Śrī Dhadi-Eba's name.

The extraordinary nature of the three names of the grantor 'Dhadi-Eba', his father 'Hedi-Eba' and the writer 'Medini-Eba', all apparently belonging to the same family deserves more than a passing notice. All the three names are entirely unknown in any Indian dialect as far as we know. It appears that a respectable family of Arakanese origin which settled and survived in the 12-13th century A. D. in the District of Tippera, at present Comilla. For, 'ba' and 'ya-ba' (modified to 'e-ba') are not difficult to trace in Burmese names even now 28. Finally, the dedication in favour of a female goddess by a follower of the *Sahajapath* of Buḍḍhism is suggestive of the development in Buddhist practice in the region around the hills.

The language of the inscription is Sanskrit. The grant is dated in 1220 A. D. So, the king Raṇavaṅlkamalla Harikaladeva came to power in the beginning of the 13th century A. D. i.e. in 1203 A. D.

24. Dāmodaradeva A

The copper-plate of Dāmodaradeva was found in the village of Mehar, Sahrasti Police Station of Chandpur district some 18 miles south-south-west from Mainamatī-Mandir. It was found while digging a ditch to a depth of about 8 feet. It was cut partly from its lower edge.

This is a single plate engraved on both the sides. The grant consists of 43 lines of which 24 lines on the obverse and 19 lines on the reverse side. It is 11 inches in length and 9 inches in breadth. The upper edge of the plate was curved upwards, measuring 3 inches in height, to provide room for "A figure of Viṣṇu either riding on Garuḍa, his traditional vehicle, or in the angiy attitude of staying a fallen foe, and on the reverse side, a rayed disc of the sun set upon and inside a crescent"[29]. The images of both the sides are installed on a disposed pedestal. It appears that Viṣṇu is supposed to be in his Purusottama or Kṛṣna-Vāsudeva form. He shows a strong fighting pose. It may be also that the images of obverse side represent a wrestling duel between Kṛṣna and the demon Cāṇura. The representation of Viṣṇu on Garuḍa or of Mādhava over powering Cāṇura is certainly symbolical of the *Vaiṣṇava* faith of king Dāmodaradeva. N. G. Majumdar suggests that this dynasty "professed the *Vaiṣṇava* faith like the Varmanas and the Senas."

The grant mentions the genealogy of the Deva family. Puruṣottama was the progenitor of the Deva family. He is called a "leader of the Deva family" in the plate, It appears that he was not a ruler. His son was Madhūsudana, was "the lord of the earth", "Moon in the ocean of the Deva dynasty'' and famous with having "snatched away the wealth of the enemies in war."[31]

He is designated with Narpati in the Chittagong copper-plate. His son was Vāsudeva, was also called "lord of the earth" and a great "archer". He was a scholar in all the *Śāstras* and foremost in military skill. His son. Damodardeva, was designated with the title of Gajapati and *Arirāja-Cānura-Mādhava.* In the Chittagong plate[32] he was titled "overlord of all kings" and defeated many kings and brought them under subjection. The three plates of Dāmodardeva (i.e. from Mehar, Sobharampur and Chittagong), indicate that his kingdom was extended atleast over the three districts of greater Comilla, Noakhali and Chittagong.

All together 16 plots of land, together with the annual income amounting to 100 puranas were granted to 20 Brahmins in this charter by the donar king Dāmodaradeva. The best Brahmins Kapadi of the *Sāvarṇya gotra* received the Charter from the king Dāmodaradeva. The name of the 20 donee Brahmins are as follows: Śrī Kāpadika, Śrī Saṅkaka, Śrī Sudoka, Śrī Kalemika, Śrī Tārāpate. Śrī Paṇḍoka, Śrī Dedaka, Śrī Sudoka, Śrī Keśava, Śrī Bramoka, Śrī Siroka, Śrī Dharanika, Śrī Panduka, Śrī Sonkoka, Śrī Prajapate, Śrī Nathoka, Śrī Visvarapa, Śrī Madhoka, Śrī Śrīpate and Śrī Śrīvatsa. Some of these mentioned Barhmins are distinguished by the *gotras* to which they belonged and some by villages from which they came. Three *gotras* namely *Sāvarṇay, Bharadvāja* and *Atrey* and villages Kanyāmāla, Purvagrāma, Siddhalago, Dlṇḍisa and Keśarakona are mentioned.

The recorded land of this grant is situated in the village of Mehar belonging to the Vāyiśagrāma Khaṇḍala (sub-division) included in the Pāralayi Vaiṣaya in Samataṭa Maṇḍala under Pauṇḍravarddhanabhukti. The Meharāgrāma of this copper-plate grant may be identified with the Mehar village of the greater Comilla district, at present Chandpur district where the grant was discovered in order to digging the earth.

The grant is also mentioned three nearest royal officers of Dāmodaradeva. The illustrious Gaṅgadharadeva was the honest courtier and resourceful to Damodardeva. Munidasa was *Mahāsāndhivigrahika* and Dalaeva was *Mathakṣapatalika* of the King Damodardeva. were joined with the king in the recorded work of merit.

The date of issue of the grant is the 22nd day of the month Jyaiṣṭha in the 4th regnal year of the king Dāmodara and 1156th year of Saka era i.e. 1234 A. D. So. the king came to the power in 1230 A. D.

The language of the script is Sanskrit. It has close similarity with the other plates of Damodardeva and some of the Sena inscriptions. It is noted that the Senas held suprimacy over the region of Vaṅga including Vikramapura, by that time, the Devas were ruling in Samataṭa. It also appears that the river Meghna was the western boundary of the Samataṭa Maṇḍala. It is also notable from the Maināmatī copper-plate of Ranavankamalla Harikala

Deva that the king Harikala Deva came to the power in some area of Samataṭa Maṇḍala in 1203 A. D. It appears that the king Vasudeva, the father of king Dāmodara Deva, was at least contemporary of Raṇavaṅka Malla. Harikāla Deva.

25. Dāmodara Deva B.

This copper-plate grant of Dāmodara Deva B was discovered in the village of Sobharampur under the Burichong Police Station in the district of Comilla, while digging earth.

This is a single plate engraved on both the sides. It is 10¼ inches in length and 9 inches in width, having semi-circular projection on the top centre of the plate, which is 2 inches in height. This space is depicted by the simple double line disc of the Sun inside the Crescent on the obverse and the human figure on the reverse. This depiction is different from that of the Chittagong[33] and Mehar[34] plate of Dāmodaradeva. In both the plates the human figure is found on the obverse side only. There is no pedestal, below the images of Sun-Moon and human figure, as we find in the Mehar plate. The Sun is also not rayed. The engraved figure of the reverse side is not clear. The inscription consists of 35 lines of which 22 lines on the obverse side and 13 lines on the reverse side.

The very beginning verse is in praises of Viṣṇu's sharp nails, which tore a sunder the chest of the demon-chief (Hiraṇykaśipu). It suggests the Vaiṣṇava faith of the king Dāmodara Deva. This grant is also mentioned the pedigree of the Deva family. The progenitor of the Deva dynasty was Puruṣ ottama. In the Mehar plate, he is called *"Dev-anvayagrāmani"*, i.e. "leader of the Deva family." It appears that he was not a king. His son, Madhunsūdana descrived as lord of the earth and *"Devavams-odadh-indu"*, i.e. "Moonin the Ocean of the Deva dynasty". He snatched away the wealth of the enemies in war. It show' that he was very powerful king in the Deva family. His son was Vasudeva, was the lord of the earth and a great archer. He was also a powerful king. His wife was queen Mitradevi gave birth to a Dāmodara Deva. He was 'well versed in polity', and also bore the title of *Gajapati*. In Chittagong plate, he was designated as "overlord of all kings", and defeated many kings and brought them under subjection. In Mehar plate, he bears the title of Gajapati. In Chittagong plate, both these titles are not mentioned. So, it appears that Damodar Deva may be suffered a setback towards the close of his regin. The minister Gautamdatta, *Mudrādhikarisadva* of the king Dāmodaradeva, devoted to the feet of Śrī Gautama. Śrī Gautama, probably, refers to the Buddha. So, from this idea, Minister Gautama was a devout worshipper of Lord Buddha.

All together 15 dronas of homestead land were granted to two Brahmins named Kauśhika and DevaRāta of the *Agnivesyagotra* by the king Dāmodara Deva. The lands were situated in three villages named **Sundaraya Disaga** and **Vandura** in the **Cāṭihāra Khaṇḍala** within the **Midilli Viṣaya** in the Samataṭa Maṇḍala under Pauṇḍravarddhanabhukti. The village called Sundaram is situated adjacent to the village of Sobharampur where the plate was found. The village Sundaram could be identified with the village Sundaraya one, out of three villages found in the copperplate grant.

The grant was recorded on 15th day of the month Āṣāḍha in the 6th regnal year of his victorius reign and 1158 year of Saka era i.e. 1236 A. D. Threefore. this grant was presented after two years of the Mehar plate of Damodra Deva.

The language of the inscription is Sanskrit. The characteristics of this grant have close similarity to the other plates of Damodra Deva and some of the Sena inscriptions[33]. From Mehar plate and Sobharampur plate of Damodra Deva clearly indicate that Paralayi Viṣaya and Midilli Viṣaya were under Samataṭa Maṇḍala where Damodra Deva was ruling.

26. Dāmodara Deva C

This copper-plate grant was found during re-excavation of a pond at the village of Nasirabad near the Chittagong City.

This is a single plate inscribed on both the sides. It consists of 41 lines of which 18 lines engraved on the obverse and 23 lines on the reverse side. The grant is 7.5 inches in length and 7 inches in width. The toop centre of the plate was curved upwards, measuring 1.5 inches in height to provide room for the figure of a crescent surmounted by a Sun on the obverse and the figure of Viṣṇu riding on Guruḍa on the reverse[36] . This representation suggests the Vaiṣṇava faith of the king.

This grant is also mentioned the genealogy of the Deva dynasty. Puruṣottama was born in the family of the moon. His son was king Madhusūdana. His son was Vāsudeva and Vāsudevas son was Dāmodara Deva. The official seal suggests the representation of Viṣṇu on Garuḍa and the names of all four generations are synonymous of Viṣṇu. In the point of view, Deva dynesty was in *Vaiṣṇava* sect. Majumdra also concluded that they professed the *Vaiṣṇava* faith like the Varmans and the Senas.

Altogether, 5 dronas of land were granted to the **Yajurvedi** Bṛahmana Prthvidharasarman by the king Dāmodara Deva Three dronas of land were situated in the village of **Kāmaṇāpindiyaaka** in **Dambaradama** and two dronas of land were situated in the village of **Ketaṇgapāla in Dambarāḍama**. The village called Ketaṅgapāla may be identified with the modern **Ketahgyapada**[37], forming a part of the village of Hashimpur, P.S. Patiya and bounded on the north by the Maracchara Pukhariya, on the southern bank of the river Sankha.

The language of the inscription is Sanskrit and the characteristics of the inscription are proto Bengali. It has close similarity to the other inscription of Dāmodara Deva and the inscriptions of Varmmans and Senas.

The grant was recorded in the Saka era 1165. It is equivalent to 1243 A. D. . The grant did not mention the day, the month and the regnal year of the ruler king Dāmodara Deva. According to the Mehar plate and the Sobharampur plate, the grant was issued in the 13th regnal year of the king Dāmodara Deva.

27. Daśaratha Deva

The copper-plate grant of Daśaratha Deva was found in the village of Ādāvādi of Vikramapur in the district of Munshigang. This is a single plate mesuring 11¾ inches in length and 8¾ inches in bredth. There is a seal on the top centre of the plate. It bears an image of Nārāyaṇa holding his usual arttributes, conch shell, disc, mace and lotus in four hands. The grant is inscribed on both the sides. It consists of 55 lines of which 26 are engraved on the obvers and 29 lines on the reverse.

The plate was issued from Vikramapura. The income of the land distributed to the Brahmins came to about 500 Pūrāṇas. The names of the donee Brahmins are Sandhyakara, Śrīmakri, Śrī sakra. Śrī sugandha, Śrīsoma, Śrīvadya, Śrīpandita, Śrī mandi, Śrīrama, Śrīledhu, Śrīdakṣā, Śrībhartà, Śrībali, Śrīvasudeva and Śrīmiko. Bhattasali[38] identified some place names, which were mentioned in tin's plate. These are given below.

Antarāvvati is identified with modern Adavadi, Bandikbandi with modern Bainkhada, Nayanava with Nayana, Muladava with mal, Vādāila with Bhaṅgāniya, Gaṇāgrama with modern Ganaisar respectively.

The inscription is dated in the 3rd regnal year of Dasaratha Deva and the 21st day of the month of Kārttika

28. Vīradhara Deva

This copper plate of Vīradhara Deva was found accidentally at Cārpatra Murā in Maināmatī Lalmai hill range. It is 11 inches in length and 9 inches in bredth. A seal is depicted to the top centre and on both the sides of the plate. It is mentioned as Viṣṇucakra Mudrā i.e. the wheel of Viṣṇu. It containts three conncentric circles and 8 spokes like leaf. A pair of conch is on both the sides of the wheel. At the end of the text is engraved the figure of a running dog. This is a single copper plate inscribed on both the sides. It consists of 23 lines of which 11 incribed lines on the obverse side and 12 inscribed lines on the reverse side. The place of issue was not stated, but the regnal year of fifteen was recorded. The grant did not mention the genealogy of the king. Altogether, 17 pāṭakas of land were granted for the illustrious Lord Vāsudeva, in the form of Śrī Laḍaha Mādhava by name, by the king Śrī Vfradharadeva for the increasing of merit and fame of his parents and ownself, up to the time of the Earth, the Sun and the Moon endure, according to the law of *Bhumicchidra,* dully touched water. The first plot out of two plots of donated lands, was situated in the village of Meṣvavarttā and Adhavasā connected with the district of Vāṭagaṅgā in the Division of Samataṭa under the (province of) Pauṇḍravarddhanbhukti. The second plot of land was situated in (the village of) Nāroraka connected with the district of Ganga-maṇḍala. The second plot of land appears to be situated in the same Division and the same Province.

The whole inscription was written in prose and the language is Sanskrit. The grant was recorded on 9th day of the month Karttika in the 15th regnal year of the ruler king Śrī Vīradharadeva. The characteristic of the inscription is proto Bengali.It resembles the scripts of Bodhagaya inscription of Lakṣmana Sena[39] and Gaya inscription of Govinda Pāla of 1175 A.D[40]. According to Majumdar[41], Vīradharadeva is dated to be a later king of Deva family. Later Deva family was ruling in Samataṭa Maṇḍala during the last part of the Sena rule. The date mentioned in this grant is not related to any known era. There is no other information to help for establishing the date of Vīradharadeva. The scripts of Harikāladeva[42] and Dāmodaradeva[43] are closely resembled with the scripts of this plate. Harikāladeva and Dāmodaradeva may be come in to the power in 1203 A.D. and 1230 A.D. accordingly. So, this grant might be dated in the thirteenth century A.D. On palaeographic consideration this plate could be dated to 13th century A. D.

The Chittagong copper-piate[44] and Mehar copper-plate[45]

of Dāmodara Deva and the Pakamoda copper-plate of Daṣarath Deva son of Dāmodara Deva disclosed the genelogy of the Deva famaly. After Daṣaratha Deva, the genealogy of the family is unknown. The grant of Vīradhara Deva did not mention the genealogy of his family. The king avoided the royal titles and epithets used by the kings of extensive domains. He did not acknowledge his subordination to any lord. There was no reference to any governmental officers or procedure for processing the inscription. Therefore, the king Vīradhara Deva was, probablly, a small local ruler in Samataṭa Maṇḍala. It also appeal's that Vīradhara Deva may have assumed his power after Daṣaratha Deva.

TABLE NO -.5
RULERS AND GEOGRAPHIC REFERENCES

SL.	Name of the rulers	Discovering place of the copper-plates	Measurement of the plate in inches	Language	Issuing Place	Total amount of donated lands	Recipient	Datation
1.	Vainya Gupta A	Gunāighar	$10^1/_2 \times 6^1/_2$	Sanskrit	Kripura	11 Pāṭakas	Monastery	6th Century A.D.
2.	Vainya Gupta B	Sālvan Vihāra	$10^1/_2 \times 6^1/_2$	,,	-	-	-	-
3.	Deva Khaḍga A	Āshrāfpur	$10^1/_2 \times 6^1/_2$	,,	Jayakarmanta	9 Pāṭakas, 10 dronas	Monastery	7th century AD.
4.	Deva Khaḍga B	,,	$7^1/_2 \times 6$	,,	,,	6 Pāṭakas, 10 dronas	Monastery	,,
5.	Deva Khaḍga C	Sālvan Vihāra	10×8	,,	-	-	-	-
6.	* Khaḍga D	,,	$7^1/_2 \times 6$	,,	-	-	-	-
7.	Bālabhatta	,,	$13^1/_2 \times 10^1/_2$	,,	-	28 Pāṭakas	Monasteries	,,
8.	Lokañtha	Tippera	$10^1/_2 \times 7^1/_2$	,,	-	The plots of land	Temple and Brahmains	,,
9.	Śrīdhārana Rāta	Kailān	$10^{17}/_{20} \times 8^3/_{20}$	,,	-	The plots of land	Temple and	,,
10.	Ānanda Deva	Sālvan Vihāra	$10^5/_8 \times 8^1/_8$	,,	Vasantpura	$7^1/_2$ Pāṭakss	Temple	7th-8th centuryA.D
11.	Bhava Deva A	,,	-		Devaparvata	3 Pāṭakas	Monastery	8th century A.D.
12.	Bhava Deva B	Tippera	$11^1/_8 \times 8^7/_8$	,,	-	$7^1/_2$ Pāṭakas	Ratnatraya	,,
13.	* Deva (?) A	Sālvan Vihāra	$16^3/_4 \times 10^1/_4$	,,	-	-	-	-
14.	Deva (?) B	-	$5^1/_2 \times 2^3/_4$	,,	-	-	-	-
15.	Śrī Candra A	Rāmpāl	$9^1/_2 \times 8$	,,	Vikramapura	1 Pāṭakas	SarmanPitavasa Gupta	10th century A.D .

TABLE NO -.5

SL	Name of the rulers	Discovering place of the copper-plates	Measurement of the plate in inches	Language	Issuing Place	Total amount of donated lands	Recipient	Datation
16.	Śrī Candra B	Kedarpur	$8^1/_2 \times 7^1/_2$	,,	Vikramapura	-	-	,,
17.	Śrī Candra C	Dhullā	$8^5/_8 \times 7^1/_4$	,,	Vikramapura	19 Halas and Droṇas	Sarman Vgasaganga	"
18.	Śrī Candra D	Edilur	8×7	,,	-	A piece of land	-	,,
19.	Śrī Candra E	Madanpur	$8^1/_4 \times 6^1/_2$	,,	-	more than 8 Droṇas	Brahmin Sukradeva	,,
20.	Laḍaha Candra A	Cārpatra Murā	-	,,	Vikramapura	11 Pāṭakas, $19^1/_2$ Droṇas 5 Yaṣṭhis, 2 Bindus and 4 Kakas	Shrine	11th century A. D.
21.	Laḍaha Candra B	,,	-	,,	-	18 Pāṭakas, $37^1/_2$ Droṇas	-	si
22.	Govinda Candra	,,	-	,,	-	2 Pāṭakas,	-	,,
23.	Harikāla Deva	Maināmatī	11×9	,,	-	20 Droṇas	Monastery	13th century
24.	DāmodaraDevaA	Mehar	11×9	,,	-	$4^{11}/_{16}$ Droṇas	20 Brahmins	,,
25.	-B	Sobharāmpur	$10^1/_4 \times 9$	,,	-	15 Droṇas	2 Brahman	,,
26.	-C	Chittagong	$7^1/_2 \times 7$	,,	-	5 Droṇas	Brahman	,,
27.	Daśarama Deva	Ādāvādi	$11^3/_4 \times 8^3/_4$	,,	Vikramapura	500 Pūrāṇas	Brahmans	,,
28.	Vīradhara Deva	Cārpatra Murā	11×9	,,	-	17 Pāṭakas	Shrine	,,

SECTION-II

DYNASTIC CHRONOLOGICAL ANALYSIS ON THE BASIS OF INSCRIPTIONS; SAMATAṬA

The early history of Samataṭa Maṇḍala is, still not clear to us. There is no epigraphic evidence about the pepole who first ruled or lived in this area. The classical epics and religious treatises refer to it as *Āryans-Pāṇḍava-Varjita-des*. The Purāṇas indicate that the king Suhma, a descendant of Yayāti and son of King Bali, ruled over the kingdom of Suhma named after him. It has been identified with Tippera[47]. The Epic MahābhāRāta describes that Bhim attacked hi the East and "subdued the king of Sukhma and the Mlecchas who dwelt on the shores of the Ocen"[48]. However, the kingdom of Tippera east of the Meghna, was not Mentioned before the 6th century A. D. According to Rajmala written by Babu Kailash Candra Singh, the kingdom of Tippera was founded by Tripura, grandson of Yayāti.

However, now it has come to light from some epigraphic evidences that many dynasties ruled over Samataṭa Maṇḍala from 4th century A. D. to 13th century A. D. We have a number of references about Gupta, Rāta, Khaḍga, Bhadra, Deva. Pāla, Candra, Varman, later Deva and Sena dynasties. Most of them ruled over Samataṭa Maṇḍala directly and some like Pālas ruled indirectly. From the evidences of the copper plate incriptions, in ancient times, Bhukti consisted of Maṇḍalas. Khaṇḍalas. Viṣayas and small unit Grāmas. At present Maināmatī is a village under the district of Comilla. It is situated to west of Comilla town. It appears that Komalā of Vāyu Purāṇa (II ch. v. 369) and Kiamoloṅgkiā of Yuan Chwang[49] refer to the same area. Tliis Kiamolongkia is identified with present Comilla was situated in Samataṭa Maṇḍala.

1. Gupta Dynasty

The name Samataṭa first appeared in the Allhabad Posthumous stone piller inscription of Samudra Gupta[30]- It was mentioned about the middle of the fourth century A. D.

The independent existence of various territoris in Bengal of Gupta Empire in 4th century A. D. came to an end. But the whole of Bengal with the exception Samataṭa was difinitely incorporated in the Gupta Empire by the time of Samudrā Gupta[51]. The northern Bengal formed an integral part of the great Gupta empire down to the end of 5th century A. D- is known to us by the Damodarpur copper-plate of Budha Gupta[52]. The Damodarpur copper-plate inscriptions[53] clearly indicate that there was a powerful ruling Gupta dynasty at Kotivarsa Viṣaya i.e. the tract of contury constituting the northern part of the modern district of Rajsbahi, the southern part of the Dinajpur, Rangpur, Bogra, and the district of Malda under the Pauṇḍravarddhanabhukti from 124 G.E. to 214 G.E. i.e. 443-, 533 A.D. A Gupta copper-plate has been discovered from Gunaighar. It is a village, which is situated to the 18 miles north west of Comilla town. This is the plate of Vainya Gupta. It shows that Vainya Gupta ruled over Eastern Bengal in 508 A.D[54]. The reading of the Gunaighar copper-plate of Vainya Gupta alongwith Damodarpur copper-plate[55] of Gupta dynasty indicates that "south-eastern Bengal was included within the Gupta empire up to the first decade of the 6th century'[06]. The Gunaighar grant of Vainya Gupta was issued from the Kripura. The findspot of the plate is near to Maināmatī-Lalmai hill range. Most probably, the village Gunikagrahara of the grant can be identified with the village Gunaighar. Another copper plate grant of Vainya Gupta was also found in Sālvan Vihāra excavation. But it is highly corroded. Therefore, no information is available from this inscription.

It is unknown to us the history of Samataṭa in the 5th century A.D but it is now clear that latter half of the 5th century A.D and the beginning of the 6th century A.D, North Bengal was under the independent Gupta empire. From the Gunaighar copperplate of Vainya Gupta, it is noted that towards the beginning of 6th century A.D

Gupta Empire showed visible sign of disintegration. This is apparent from the fact that King Vainya Gupta (507-8 A.D.)

succeeded in carving out for himself a virtually independent Kingdom in Eastern Bengal. It is testified by his copper plate grant issued from his "Victorious Camp" at Kripur in Comilla. But no other information regarding the extent of his domain or the length of his reign is available from any other sources.

The famous Chinese traveller, Yuan Chwang, visited Samataṭa in between 637-39 A.D[57]. A number of epigraphical records and the description of Yuan Chawang indicate to the existence of a Bhadra[58] royal family who ruled in Samataṭa in the first half of the 7th century A.D. Yaung Chawang did not mention the rule of Gupta dynasty in Samataṭa Maṇḍala and no epigraphic records of Gupta dynasty have been found from 7th century A.D. The Allahabad inscription of Samudrā Gupta, therefore, indicates political relation with Samataṭa Maṇḍala in the middle of the 4th century A.D.

A number of copperplate grants found from Kotalipada in the present district of Gopalganj and one in Bardwan district (W.B.). A large number of gold coins discovered from Sabhar (Dhaka), and Kotalipada. All the documents testify to the existence of three indenpendent and powerful kings of South-East Bengal, named Gopa Candra, Dharmāditya and Samacār Deva who ruled in the fnst half of the sixth century A.D[59]. The title all these kings assumed *Mahārajādhiraja*. According to Majumdar[60] that Gopcandra was earlier and then Dharmaditya and Samacar Deva. They ruled approxithately between 525 and 575 A.D with the margin of a few year's both at the beginning and at the end. Mahārāja Vijaya Sena was a vassal chief of Gopcandra. So, it seems to appear- that Gopcandra, Vainya Gupta and Vijay Sena were contemporary. But it is not clear that what was the relation between three powerful rulers and Vainya Gupt. Most probably, they ruled over greater portion of Vaṅga and some portion of Samataṭa.

2. KHADGA DYNASTY

Altogether total five copper-plate grants of the Khaḍga dynasty have been discovered, two of them from Ashrapur village, situated in 38 miles north-north-west from Comilla Town and three of them from Sālvan-Vihāra of Mainathatl hill range. These findings support that the western side and the eastern side of the Meghna river i.e. western part of Vaṅga and Samtata were under Khaḍga dynasty.

Ashrafpur grants of Devakhaḍga issued from Jayakarmanta is identified with the modern Badakamta, which is situated in Debidvar Thana of Comilla district, and five miles due west of Maināmatī Mandir of Maināmatī-Lalmai hill range. Jaykarmānta, at least, was the "Camp of Victory" of Khaḍga dynasty.

The Ashrafpur grants and Deulbadi Sarvvam image inscription inform the genealogy of this dynasty to us. The lord of the kings and the founder of the line, Khaḍgodyma, his son Jata Khaḍga, his son Deva Khaḍga, and his son prince Rājāraja (Bhatta) were informed to us. There is no doubt that Rājabhāṭṭa of Seng-Chi, Rājabhadra of Mañjūśrīmulakalpa and Rājarāja bhaṭṭa of the Asharafpur grant, all the three names are of one. He was the son of Devakhaḍga and can be dated in second half of the 7th century A.D. From description of Yuan-Chwang and Seng-Chi, it is strongly suggested that the Buddhist religion had became popular during the rule of Rājarājabhaṭṭa. It is said to the Ashrafpur grant of Rājarājabhaṭṭa that the great lord of the kings[62] donated a piece of land. It indicates the feudatory character of the Khaḍga kings, but it is not clear that who was the great lord of Khaḍga kings.

The copper-plate grant of Bālabhaṭṭa is very badly corroded. The seal, which was attached on the top of the plate, has a similarity with the seal of other Khaḍga plates. The name of Svami Devakhadgea inscribed in line-12 and the name of the donar Rajaputra Bālabhaṭṭa in line-20. Because of the corrosion of the plate it is not clear- that what is the relation between Deva Khaḍga and Bālabhaṭṭa. The study of the Khaḍga plates and the accounts of the Chinese travellers, it is surmised that Bālabhaṭṭa might be identified as a successor of Rājarāja bhaṭṭa. His capital city was ituated at Devaparvata from where the 28 patakas of land were granted. So, it might be suggested that the first capital city of the Khaḍga situated at Jayankarmānta and later on, it was shifted to Devaparvata. Devaparvata might be situated in somewhere of Maināmatī-Lalmai hill range.

It is not clear to us that what was the boundary of the Khaḍga kingdom. But it can be suggested from the epigraphic description and image inscription that the Khaḍgas ruled over both the bank of the river Meghna.

In all probabilites, it appears that Khaḍgas were dated in between the second quarter of the 7th century to an end of the 7th century A.D.

GENEALOGICAL LINEAGE OF THE KHAḌGA DYNASTY

1) Śrī Khaḍgodyama
2) Śrī Jata Khaḍga (Son of -1)
3) Śrī Deva Khaḍga (Son of -2)
4) Śrī Rājāraja (Bhaṭṭa)(Son of-3)
5) SrT Bala:bhaṭṭa (Son of-4?)

3. BHADRA DYNASTY

The famous Chinese pilgrim Yuan Chwang visited Samataṭa in between 637— 639 A.D[63] . He mentioned that the countery Samataṭa was an important kingdom. There were about 30 Buddhist Saṅgharamas (Monasteries) with about 2000 monks. It is also mentioned that Brahmanical temples were also numerous[64]. From his description, we also know that his teacher and head of the Nalanda Mahāvihāra, *Ācāryya* "Śīlabhadra was a scion of the Brahmmlcal royal family of Samataṭa" [65]. He was head of Nalanda Mahā-Vihāra in about second quarter of the 7th century A.D. We find also from the description of Beal Samuel that "South-west of the convent of Gunathati about 20 li. we came to a solitary hill on which is a convent called (the Saṅgharama of) Silabhadra (Shi-lo-po-to-lo), This is the convent which the master of *Śāstras* after his victory caused to be built out of the funds of a village, which were given up. It stands by the side of a single sharp crag like a stūpa. It contains some sacred relices of Buddha. This master of *Śāstras* belonged to the family of the king of Samataṭa (San-mo-ta-cha), and was of the Brahman caste" GG. From this description we can easily understand that Śīlbhadra, the principal of Nalanda University, was Brahman by caste and latter on he converted himself to the Buddhist faith. It is likely to think that after his convert, he became the principal of Nalanda University in about the second quarter of the 7th century A.D and before that he was living in Samataṭa in the beginning of the 7th century A.D. He must have been sufficient advanced in age before he was raised to his exalted position. Sircar says that "there is absolutely no doubt that the typical Buddhist name Śīlbhadra (literally one who is good in regard to the ten Śīlas or Buddhist precepts of morality) was adopted by the Brahman only after he had renounced his original Brahmanical faith and had been initiated into Buḍḍhism"[67] . Some scholar's suggest that the existence of Bhadra dynasty was over Samataṭa in the seventh century. From the references of Yuang Chwang's account, the Mañjūśrīmulakalpa and the Khalimpur plate would go to indicate the existence of three Bhadra Kings in Samataṭa. It is also mentioned in Yuang Chwang's description that there was a king in Samataṭa from the Brahman family of Śīlabhadra. But he did not mention the name of the king. So, it may suggest the feudatory character of the former's position. Paul[68] thinks that the Bhadras and Khaḍgas ruled in Samataṭa at the same time. Bhaltasali mentioned that "Śīlabhadra was a Khaḍga, and those who kept alive the name of Khaḍgas in later times tried in their way to emulate their illustrious predecessor by noble deeds of piety and benevolence"[69]. There is also a possibility, which suggests the identification of the Bhadra kings with the Khaḍgas of Samataṭa. It deserves particular' attention to the Asrafpur plates of the Khaḍgas are surmounted by a seal, which contains in high relief of a bull couchant. We find that the seals of the Pālas and Candras bear the *Dharmacakra Mudrā* but the deals of the Khaḍgas show *Saivite* symbol. The image of the bull on the the copper-plate grants and the covering of the Sarvvani image with gold leaves by the queen of Deva Khaḍga, Pravāvati may be explained by the fact that the Khaḍgas could not forget their association with Śaivism i.e, Brahmanical faith. So, it can be strongly suggested that the Khaḍgas were formerly Brahminical Hindus and became Buddhist later on. From the accounts of Yaung Chwang and the epigraphical records, it is likely that before the visiting of Yuang Chwang Samataṭa was ruled by the Khaḍgas and it was continuing over the 7th century A.D. In all probabilities, it may be suggested that the family was originally known as Khaḍga and when the name and fame of Śīlabhadra was fully well-known in the Buddhist world, the family also become known as Bhadras and due to this Rājabhaṭṭa was called Rājabhadra in Mañjūśrīmulakalpa, in verse 868[70].

From 1-tsing's accounts, it has come to light that fifty-six Chinese pilgrims came to India in the second half of the seventh century. One of them was Shen-chi, found the throne of Samataṭa occupied by the King "Rājabhaṭṭa"[71].

4. NATHA DYNASTY

The Tippera copper-plate grant of Lokanātha[72] shows that the Nātha dynasty ruled over some part of the Eastern Bengal in the second half of the seventh century A.D. From the copper-plate grant of the Khaḍge dynasty, it appears that the Nātha and the Rāta dynasties were feudatories of the rulers of Khaḍga dynasty. From the use of the tittle *nṛpa,* it appears that Loknātha was a local chief not an independent ruler. He was not also designated as *Mahārājādhirāja* like other Gupta and Candra rulers. The learned editor of the *Epigraphia Indica* remarked that "From the oppening words it would seem rather as if the documents were issued from the office of *Kumāramātya* of Lokanātha's overlord and only countersigned by Lokanātha himself '[3]. Basak suggests that "during the Gupta age, the tittle *Kumāramātya* used by officers of state was found to have been applied also to feudatoiy *(Sāmanta)* chiefs, just as the word

Sāmanta generally used by feudatory chief was also sometimes used with other titles by officers of state. So, the word *Kumāramya* in the opening prose portion of this inscription refers to the feudatory chief Lokanātha himself'[74].

The genealogy of the Nātha family was mentioned in the grant of Lokanātha. The first name of the family, mentioned in this plate, is partly defaced and end in the ward Natha. According to Niharranjan Roy, Śiva Nātha was the founder of the family (Bahgalir Itihas: Adiparba, p. 366). Most probably, he was the first king of the Natha family. His son, the next king named Śrīnātha, was a feudatory ruler. He acquired much fame in the field of the battle. His son was Bhavanātha. He was the devout worshipper of the religion. He forshook his royalty in favour of his brother's son who again obtained by his wife Gotradevī a worthy son Lokanātha. Lokanātha's thaternal grandfather, Keśava was a Parasava by caste. The first ancestors of Lokanātha were Brahmanas, but his thaternal grand father had not a pure Brahmana origin. It may be suggestd that his Brahmana father married a *Śūdra* wife and he was, therefore, known to have been parasava. The use of this term in this inscription is veiy important. It sbows that the *anuloma* marriage in Hindu society in the 7th century A.D. was prevalant.

The significant fact mentioned in the plate that the king named Jivadharana made over to Loknatha. This Jivadharaṇa most probably, was the father of Śrīdharaṇa Rāta. If it is correct, then the father of Śrīdharana Rāta was contemporary of Lokanātha. It is also appeared that Jivadharaṇa occupied Lokanātha's kingdom.

Basak read the copper-plate grant of Loknātha[75] and it was dated in the month of Phālguna in the year of 44. On palaeographica! grounds, he suggested that it belongs to the Harṣha era. corresponding therefore, to 650 A.D., i.e., two years after the death of King Harṣha[76]. D.R. Bhandarkar[77] suggests the date of this grant " was at least 144 and not 44", and refers it to the Harṣha era. He pointed out from the use of the letter *"dhika"* before the letters signifying 44. Therefore, it is equivalent to 750 A.D. Both the scholars are referring it to be the Harṣha era. On the remarks of Bhandarkar, Basak again mentions that "it could as well be argued that the date is 344 *"sambat"*, and the reference should in that case be to the Gupta era, as in Vainya Gupta's Tippera plate, and therefore, it is equivalent to 663-64 A.D[78]. But the grant mentions *"Catus-catvārimstsamvatsare"* i.e. the 44th regnal year. There is no doubt that the grant was issued in the 44th regnal year of the king Loknātha. Bhandarkar and Basak, both of them refered it to the Harṣa era. But the grant itself does not mention either the Harṣa era or any other known era.It is well-known that the copper-plate grant of Candras mention only the regnal year of the ruling kings and not any other known era. It is well known that the copperplate grants of Candra rulers mention only the regnal year of the rulsing king and not any other known era in their charter. On the other hand, the copper-palte grant of Raṇavarṅkamall Harikāladeva issued, in the 17th regnal year of the king refers to the Saka era 1141. So, in this case it is easy to calculate the known Saka era 1141, which is equivalent to 1219-20A.D.

On the palaeographic consideration of the copper-plate of Lokanātha and a close study of the Rāta[79] and Khaḍga[80] copper-plate, it appears that the grant may be dated in the second half of the 7th century A.D.

GENEALOGICAL LINEAGE OF THE NĀTHA DYNASTY

1) Śrī Siva Nātha

2) ŚrīŚrīnātha(Sonof-l)

3) Śrī Bhava Nātha (Son of -2)

4)... (Brother's Son of -3), GotraDevī (wife of 4)

5) Śrī Lokanātha (son of "4 and wife Gotra Devī")

6) Śrī Lakṣmī Nātha (son of 5)

5. RĀTA DYNASTY

The history of the Rāta dynasty is known from the Kailān copper-plate inscription of King Śrīdharana Rāta[81]. This grant bore the name of the three rulers of Rāta dynasty named by Sathatatesvara Śrī Jivadharaṇa Rāta founder of the Rāta dynasty his son Śrīdharana Rāta and his son prince Valadharana Rāta.

The name of the king Jīvadharaṇa was mentioned in the copper-plate grant of Lokanātha and he made over a Viṣaya and army without engaging in further battle to Lokanātha. So it is clear that he was the lord of Samataṭa and was the very powerful ruler. There is no room for doubt that Jīvadharana was the contemporary of Lokanātha. So the king may be dated second half of the 7th century A.D. His son Śrīdharaṇa Rāta was designated as *"Prāpta pañca mahāśabda sathataṭeśvara"*. The epithet *"Prāpta pañca mahāśabda"* perhaps indicates his feudatory character. Some scholaras interprets the title as indicating the enjoyment of a combination of five officials possessing desingnations beginning with the word *Mahāt;* they are *Mahāpratihāra Mahāsāndhivigrahika* and *Mahāasvāsāladhikṛta Mahābhaṇḍāgdrika* and *Mahāsādhanika* (c.f. Rajatarangini, IV. verses 140 -43, 680). It is also noted that the king Srīdharaṇa Rāta was not designated as *Mahārājādhirāja.*It is also noted that the king Śrīdharaṇa Rāta was not designated as *Mahārājādhirāja.*

It is difficult to identify the overlord of the Rātas. From the Ashrafpur grants of Devakhaḍga, Sālvan Vihāra grants of Bālabhaṭṭa suggest that in the second half of the 7th century the Khaḍga dynasty was very powerful in Samataṭa Maṇḍala. Ashrafpur grants were issued from Jayakarmanta. It has been identified with the mordem Badakāmta that lies five miles due west of Mainamatī Mandir. So, it can be suggested that Jayakaramanta was the Capitl City of the king Devakhaḍga. The grant of Bālabhaṭṭa was issued from the capital city of Devaparvata wich perhaps located in somewhere in Maithati-

Lalmai hill range. It is probable that the Khaḍgas ruled over Vaṅga and latter Devakhaḍga extended his power over Samataṭa. Some scholars[82] say that Rātas were feudatories of the Khaḍga ruler of Samataṭa.In all probabilities, it appers that Rāta and Nāth rulers were feudatories of the Khaḍga rulers. It is noted that the Khaḍgas were the Buddhist.

The granted 25 pāṭakas of lands were situated in the districts of Guptināṭana and Patalayika under Samataṭa Maṇḍala. The king Laḍaha Candra also doneted land in Guptināṭana area. The 13 pāṭakas land out of 25 pāṭaka lands was granted to a Buddhist monastery. 1 would like to draw attention that the Rāta dynasty was in *Vaiṣṇava* sect. They had great respect to the Buḍḍhism or they were influenced by the poweref.nl Khaḍga kings.

From I- tsings[83] accounts, it is known to us that fifty-six Chinese Buddhist pilgrims came to India in the second half of the 7th century. He came to India in the last quarter of the seventh century. The pilgrim Sheng-chi found the throne of Samataṭa ruled by the king Rājabhaṭṭa. Most probably, the ruler of Samataṭa Rājabhaṭṭa is same to the King Rājarāja or Rājarājabhaṭṭa, a son of Devakhaḍga of the Khaḍga dynsty Sheng-Chi also mentioned that 4,000 Buddhist monks are said to have been living at the capital of Samataṭa during the rule of Rājabhaṭṭa. The famous Chinese pilgrim Yuan chwang visited Samataṭa ahout 638 - 39 A. D. He found only 2,000 Buddhist monks in Samataṭa. The great inerease in the number of Buddhist monks in that country, in the later half of seventh century should probably be explained by the conquest of Samataṭa by the Khaḍgas who were Buddhist. From the above description, it appears that the Rāta king Jivadharana and his son Śrīdharana and the Khaḍga king and his son Rājarāja or Rājarājabhaṭṭā all of them may be dated about the second half of the seventh century A. D.

GENEALOGICAL LINEAGE OF THE RĀTA DYNASTY

1) Śrī Jivadharaṇa Rāta

2) Śrī" Śrīdharaṇa Rāta

3) Śrī Valadharaṇa Rāta

6. DEVA DYNASTY

Altogether, four copper-plates consisting of five grants have known to us, three of them from Sālvan Vihāra of Maināmatī and one from somewhere in Tippera. One of them from Sālvan Vihāra consists of two grants of which one of Ānanda Deva and another one of his son Bhava Deva.

Two plates from Sālvan Vihāra were found in very damaged condition associated with the plate of Ānanda Deva. Association and depection of seal it appears that both of the plates were issued by the Deva dynasty. Epigraphic records _refere to that Deva dynasty ruled over at least Samataṭa before the Candra rulers and after the Candra rulers. Ānanda Deva and his son Bhava Deva were the rulers of the early Deva dynasty.

The four generations of Deva family have come to light from the copper-plates of Ānanda Deva and Bhava Deva. First predecessor was Śānti Deva. But it is not clear to us that what was the royal status of Śānti Deva. From the plate of Bhava Deva, it appears that VFradeva son of Santi Deva, was the first king of Deva family.The king Vira Deva resembled *Acyuta* i.e Viṣṇu in the thatter of subduing mighty foes. His son Ānanda Deva was designated as *Paramasaugata Parameṣvara Paramabhaṭṭāraka Mahārājādhiraja.* His son, Bhavadeva was also designated as the same. From the epigraphs of Khaḍga, Nātha and Rāta, we know that these dynasties " do not bore the desgination as *Paramasaugata Parmaśvara Parmabhaṭṭ āraka Mahārājādhirāja.* So, this title shows the indepedent character of Ānanda Deva and Bhava Deva, In the prose portion of the plate of Bhava Deva- B mentions that the king Bhavadeva was requested by *Mahā-Sāmamtddhipati* Nandadhara to make a grant of 7.5 pāṭakas of land in favour of the *Ratnatraya* of the Vendāthati Vihārikā, and also in the A' plate the king was requested by *Mahāsāmantādhipati* Sn Nandadhara. So, it might suggest that both of them are the same. So, it appears that there were feudatory kings under Bhavadeva. In the grant of Ānandadeva, 7.5 pāṭakas of land were granted to the temple and the grant was issued from the 'Camp of Victory', Vasantapur in the 39th regnal of the king. In the grant of Bhavadeva (reverse side of the plate Ānandadeva), three patakas of land were granted to small monastery from the 'Camp of Victory', Devaparvata in 2nd regnal year of the king. Bhavadeva -B plate was also issued from Devaparvata in the 2nd regnal of the king. It is noted that this plate was issued before 4 months of the Bhavadeva-A plate. Ānandadeva's grant indicates that Vansantapura was the newly constructed capital city. The king Ānandadeva had abandoned the old capital city due to the invansion of the strong enemy force. This fact clearly indicates that the old capital city was situated at Devaparvata, which was regained within a short period either by Ānandadeva himself, or by his son Bhavadeva. The donee of Ānandadeva plate, is Jaybhuti and in the Bhavadeva plate is Jayabhuti. The donees of both the grants are most probably the same person. The donee of the Bhavadeva -B plate is Vibhutidasa.

The charcters of the three grants belong to the East India variety. The characters of the Tippera plate of Lokanātha. the Kailan plate of Śrīndharana Rāta, the Ashrafpur plates of Deva Kṇaḍga and his immediate successor Rajārājabhaṭṭa and Maināmatī plate of Bālabhaṭṭa appear to suggest that all of them flourished in the latter half of the seventh century A. D. On palaeographic consideration, these grants are earlier than the grants of Deva dynasty. It is noted that Samacārdeva (6th century A. D.) of the copper-plate of Ghugrahati[84] and Nalanda, was a contemporary of Somabhuti and Somabhuti's great grandson, Jayabhuti was a contemporary of the doner king Ānandadeva. In all probabilities, it appears that the Deva dynasty ruled over Samataṭa in the 8th century A. D.

GENEALOGICAL LINEAGE AND THE SUCCESSORS OF DEVA DYNASTY

1) Śrī Santi Deva
2) Śrī Vīra Deva (son of-1)   Somadevī (queen of 2)
3) Śrī Ānanda Deva (son of-2)Svamāṅgadevī (queen of 3-?)
4) Śrī Bhava Deva (son of -3)

GENEALOGICAL LINEAGE OF THE DONEE FROM THE GRANT OF ANANDADEVA

1) Śrī Puṣyabhuti
2) Śrī Somabhuti (son of-1)
3) Śrī Śikharabhuti (son of-2)
4) Śrī Ratnabhuti (son of -3)
5) Sn Jayabhuti (son of-4)

GENEALOGICAL LINEAGE OF THE DONEE

FROM THE GRANT OF BHAVADEVA

1) Śrī Āditya Dāsa
2) Śrī Vibhuti Dāsa (son of-1)

7. CANDRA DYNASTY

From the ten copper-plate grants of the Candra dynasty, it has come to light that the mentioned dynasty ruled over Candrdvipa, Harikela, Samataṭa, Vaṅgāla and Vaṅga from last quarter of ninth century to second quarter of eleventh century A.D. Dhaka plate of Kalyān Candra and Pas'cimbhag (Sylhet) plate of Śrī Candra, are not described here because most of the data are found other plates of Candra dynasty, those are mentioned in this chapter.

The Candra dynasty receives prominent mention of the land of Lama Tārānatha, though there is no sufficient evidences to prove its existence from sixth to eighth century A, D. in South-Eastern Bengal. Now, we know that the rulers of Candra dynasty ruled over Arakan region in the seventh century A D. or even earlier. The existence of a line of Candra kings for 19 generations, on a stone piller, found on the platform of the Sitthaung Temple at Morhaung in Arakan[85]. There names end on Candra and an account of nine of them ruling from 788-957 A. D[86]. According to Tārānatha, the Candra dynasty ruled in Bengal before the Pālas and the names of all the mentioned by him prior to Gopala end in Candra. From Tārānatha's account, it has come to light that the five generations of Candra dynasty[8'] ruled over Bengal. Their names are given below.

1) Simha Candra
2) Vāla Candra (son of-1)
3) Vimala Candra (son of 2)
4) Govinda Candra (son of 3)
5) Lalita Candra (son of 4)

It has also said by Tārānatha "Govinda Candra ascended the throne about the time when the great Buddhist teacher Drarmakṛti died. As Dharmakṛti was a disciple of Dharmapāla who was a professor in Nalanda at the time when the Chinese pilgrim Hiuen Trang visited it Govinda candra reign may be seventh century A.D. As his successor Lalita Candra ruled for many years, his death and the end of the Candra dynesty may be placed about 725 A. D.

Some scholars have tried to identify with Candra dynasty of Tārānatha's Account and the Candra dynasty of Maināmatī copper-plate grants. The present copper-plate grants of Candra dynasty indicate that the Candra ruled over Samataṭa aproxithately in between 900 - 1050 A. D[R8].

The historical information of Candra dynasty from inscription is given below. From the copper-plate grants of Śrī Candra, it has come to light that a person named Purṇa Candra was born in the family of Candra rulers. He was the founder and at least a powerful chief of Rohitagiri. Bhattasali identifies the Rohitagiri with the Maināmatī Lalmai hill range. Further discussion about Rohitagiri will be given in the chapte VI. Ganguly remarks that "Purṇa Candra, a sicon of the royal family of Rohitagiri., accompanied by the Pratinaras to Bengal, and got the charge of the administration of the Dacca Division from them[89]. But there is no record in favour of this point that the Candra rulers of Samataṭa i.e. of East Bengal were the feudatoris of Gurjara Pratihāras. Rampal copper-plate of Śrī Candra (V-2) shows that the name of Purṇa Candra was engraved on the pedastals of idols, on Victory Pillers and on copper-plates. So from this evidence, we can tell without any doubt that Purṇa Candra was not only a founder of Candra dynasty but also a king of Rohitagiri region. Dr. Bhattasali suggests that "Purṇa Candra was neither of royal birth nor of pure caste"[90]. But this plate inidicates that Purṇa Candra was borh in the line of Candra kings and was well known on the earth.

From the Rampal, Kedaipur and Madnpur plates of Śrī Candra, we get the information about the illustrious Suvarṇa Candra who was the son of Purṇa Candra and he was the devout worshipper of the hare Jataka of Lord Buddha. Dr. Basak suggests that "Purṇa Candra's illustrious son. Suvarṇa Candra, was the first in the dynasty to embrace Buḍḍhism"[91]. According to Verse 3 of Rampal plate, there is no doubt that Suvarṇa Candra was a wel-known Buddhist in the world. In the light of Rampal plate, Majmudar[92] concludes that unitil Suvarṇa Candra's time the family followed Brahmanical religion but henceforth the family was undoubtedly Buddhist. From the Rampal, Mandanpur, Kedarpur, plates of Śrī Candra, Maināmatī plates of Laḍaha Candra and Govinda Candra. it is undoubtedly true that Suvarṇa Candra, Trailokya Candra, Śrī Candra, Kalyān Candra, Laḍaha Candra and Govinda Candra were the follower of Lord Buddha. But there is no evidence that Purṇa Candra and his forefather came from Brahminical faith. Purṇa Candra and Suvarṇa Candra were not titled with *Parameśvara Paramabhaṭṭāraka Mahārājādhirāja*. Therefore, it is more probable that both of them were the local and small rulers of Rohitagiri region. Hence, R.C. Majumdar[93] took them to be "petty local rulers."

Rampal copper-plate of Śrī Candra shows that Trailokya Candra, son of Suvarṇa Candra, who purified both the families (i.e. paternal and thaternal), was very powerful king, like Dilip, in Candradvīpa. Pascimbhag copper-plate of Śrī Candra indicates that Trailokya Candra was designated with *Paramasaugata Parmeśvara Parmabhaṭṭāraka Mahārājādhirāja.* This designation shows the independent power of the king Trailikya Candra. Sircar suggests that "Trailokya Candra was apparently the ruler of Candradvīpa as a feudatory of the Harikāla king"[94].

Rampal copper-plate of Śrī Candra (V-5) mentions that Trailokya Candra was the support of the royal glories smiling with the royal umbrella having the symbol of the kings of Harikala. Therefore, there is no room for a doubt that Trailokya Candra was the first independent king in south-east Bengal of Candra dynasty. Mr. basak also appeal's that "Trailokya Candra, with his title *Mahārājādhirāja* in all the records became the first independent king, ruling probably from Vikramapura as the capital of his kingdom" [95]. From the study of the plates, it appears that Candradvīpa was the first capital city and most probably Vikramapura was the Capital City of the king Trailokya Candra at the end of his reign. Majumdar[96] and Paul[97] suggest that Trailokya Candra was at first king of Harikela and from there he extended his power to Candradvīpa. Basak[98] seems that Trailokya Candra was at first king of Candradvīpa but later became the ruler over the whole of Harikela.Sircar seems that "Trailokya Candra was not a king of Harikela but was the ruler of Candradvtpa, i.e. Bakla-Chandradvīpa in the present Buckergunje district owing allegiance to or allied with the king of the country called Harikela''[99].

It is a very controversial thatter owing to its unavailable information that Trailokya Candra was at first a king of Candradvīpa or overlord of Harikela king. But from the copper-plate grants of Śrī Candra, it has come to light that Trailokya Candra ruled over Candradvīpa and subjugated Harikela. It is probable therefore, that Purṇa Candra and Suvarṇa Candra was the king of Rohitagiri i.e. Maināmatī-Lalmai area respectively. That is why,-it is comparatively easy to become an overlord of Harikela king first [i.e. According to Kesava's Kalpadmkosa, Harikela or Harikeli was the name of the Sylhet (Śrīhatta) region]. After winning that region, Trailokya Candra became a king of Candradvīpa with help of the king of Harikela. Majumdar[100] indicates that Trailokya Candra and his son Śrī Candra were not only independent but very powerful kings who fought successfully against the Kamboja rulers for a long period and ruling in Harikela and Candradvīpa.

Majumdar[101] suggests that Candradvīpa was the home territory of Candra dynasty. But from the rampal copper-plate and Madanpur plate clearly indicate that Rohitagiri area was the homeland of the Candra dynasty.

The Paścimbhag plate (Shylet) of Śrī" Candra, informs us that Trailokya Candra conquered Samataṭa, where Lālāmvi forest and the glorious city Devaparvata was situated. It is also mentioned that Lālāmvi forest was close to Devaparvata. Lālāmvi may be identified with Lalmai hills which was densely wodded and Devaparvata may be identified with Maināmatī's palace Mound, which, is situated at the northern tip of Maināmatī-Lalmai hill range. This Devaparvata was also mentioned in Deva copperplates. It was the capital city of Deva dynasty.

Bhattasali[102] identifies Rohitagiri with Maināmatī-Lalmai hill range. Rohitagiri could be identified with Lalmai. But Sircar[103] identifies Rohitagiri with Rohtasgrah in Bihar. It appears to be wrong. There is no evidence that the Candras ever ruled in that area.

From the Rampal copper-plate and Sylhet copper-plate of Śrī Candra and Maināmatī copper-plates of Laḍaha Candra indicate that Trailokya Candra was a king of Candradvīpa, conqurered Samataṭa, subjugated Harikela, became the sole ruler of Vaṅga had a contest with the Gauḍas and struggled against the rulers of the Vindhyas and against the Malaya.

From Kedarpur plate (V-5), it is indicated that "Who, possessing desire to win over this earth bounded by four oceans not greedy of worldly objects, extinguished the five of his enemies in the battles by the water of creeper-like sword.

Maināmatī copper-plates of Laḍaha Candra indicate that Trilokya Candra was the leader of the circle of the earth, who was not small had great purity, was dispeller of hunders of terrors, of good character, attratced by good qualities and most auspicious.

The wife of Trilokya Candra bears the name of Śrī Kancana in Rampal plate and Śrī Kanaka in Sythat plate. Parameśvara Paramabhaṭṭāraka Mahārājādhirāji Śrī Candradeva was born by her. Śrī Candra was great both in the field of war and peace.

From Rampal and Madanpur plates of Śrī Candra, be is known as" having put the enimies in jails and having made the earth decorated by a single umbrella". The entire grants praise his fighting genius. From Maināmatī plates of Laḍaha Candra, it is noted that" who made the vow of the shedding of tears for the eyes of the ladies of the lord of Pragjyotiṣ uninterrupted and made the sprouts of the lower lips of the ladies of the harem of the Gauḍa king, with the buds of smiles dropped". This is to show that Śrī Candra was a very powerful and great warrior, who defeated the lord of Prag-jyotiṣ. From the Sylhet plate, we know that he conquered Kāmarūpa and advanced to the banks of the river Lauhitya (Brahmputra) and Puṣpabhadrā and even to the foot of the Himālayas. So it is clear that he had launched a succesful invansion in every direction. From the Dacca copper-plate of Kalyān Candra, we get proper names of the defeated rulers.

Śrī Candra, "who was moist (i.e. soft) in the act of washing away the fear- of Prithavipāla, was hard and enterprising in the churning of Govarnna, was great in the great festivity or re-instating Gopāla was a protector of sacrifices (or vows) in returning the queen of Rātana Pāla , who was easily defeated, and whose arm was the univarsal support of the virtuous and receptacle of various sentiments" [104]. It shows that Śrī Candra was the power of revolt againts. the authority of the Pālas.

The copper-plate inscriptions of Śrī Candra were found in Rampal of Munshiganj, Madanpur of Dhaka, Kedarpur and Edilpur of Shariyatpur, Dhulla of Manikgang, Pascimbhag of Sythat districts. All the grants were issued from the "Camp of Victory", Vikramapura.

It is, therefore, indicated that all the area, where these plates were found, were under the powerful king Śrī Candradeva. From the above discussion, it has come to light that the king Śrī Candra ruled over greater Brishal, Dhaka, Commilla and Sylhet region. He defeated the rulers of Gauḍa and Prāgjyotiṣa, reinstated Gopala II (on the thorne) and re-stored the Captive Pāla queen. He conqured Kāmarūpa and advanced to the banks of the river Louhitya and Puṣpabhadrā and even to the hill of the Himalayas. According to the Madanpur plate, Śrī Candra ruled over that area at least for 46 years.

The long reign of Śrī Candra came to an end with the succession to the throne of his worthy son **Parameśvara Paramabhaṭṭāraka Mahārājādhirāja** the illustrious Kalyān Candradeva. The only one Dhaka copper-plate[103] of Śrī Kalyān Candra was come to our knowledge. The plate is dated in 24th regnal year of King Śrī Kalyān Candradeva. This plate praises only the noble qualities of the king. Maināmatī plates of Laḍaha Candra (V-7) indicate that he was famous for his pure and bright qualities, which were the ornaments of the three worlds and was held on the high heads of the great kings. Verse-8 gives the detail of his fighting glories. It mentions that he "who cre-ated a large flow the mass of tears in the eyes of Mleccha-women, and rendared the moon-faces of the Gauḍa-women bereft of the moon-light of smile, and who spread these eight directions with his never diminishing spot-less fames like the rays of the moon bright on account of the despersal of clouds". This verse clearly mentions that Kalyān Candra faced two enemies i.e., the Mlecchas and the Gauḍas. This fact is further confirmed in the Maināmatī plate of Govinda Candra in verse-VII. It records that he, "who redoubled this great river called Lauhitya by the thick flows of tears shed from the eyes of the Mleccha-women distressed by the killing of their lord; and who made the lord of the Gauḍas low-faced by shame by having forcefully made captive his great army of elephants, horses and foot-soldiers in the battle field for a long time."

There is no room for doubt that the term Mlecchas were the people of Kāmrupa, those were lived on the bank of the river Lauhitya i.e., present Brahmaputra.

Śrī Kalyānadevī, the wife of Śrī Kalyān Candra, was the daughter of a rich merchant. She, the queen, gave birth Laḍaha Candra, the highest of kings. He was the successor of his father, Śrī" Kalyān Candra. There is no record that the king ever invaded any region or kingdom. He was very religious minded and highly popular to his subjects. Maināmatī inscriptions of Laḍaha Candra (V-l 1-15) indicates that he bore all good qualities, attained highest level in various sciences and sub-sciences in a few days only, well-known for rise of his prowess and the hero of the great drama called 'Protection of the world'. Maināmatī three inscriptions of Candras praise his virtuous deed. He went to Varanasi, the abode of lord Śambhu, bathed there in the gangetic waters for removing his sins and gave away gold in the hands of the Brahmins (Maināmatī plate-V-16-17). Laḍaha Candra himself was Buddhist but he was very belive to Hindu God and Goddess. His grants were inscribed with the salutation to lord Vāsudeva and he went to Hindu holy places for removing his sins and all the heroic characters were compared with the Hindu God and goddess and the land was granted for the temple of lord Laḍaha Mādhava-bhaṭṭāraka at Paṭṭikera. Laḍaha is the name of the king and Mādhava means Lord Kṛṣṇa. There is no record that KrisVna (the incarnation of God Viṣṇu) is designated ever as Laḍaha Mādhava. It is probable that Laḍaha Candra, himself, erected the image of lord Vasudeva, therefore, was designated as Laḍaha Mādhava Bhaṭṭāraka.

Śrī Laḍaha Candra himself was designated as *Parameśvara Paramabhaṭṭāraka, Mahārājādhirāja*. He was an independent ruler. Maināmatī copper-plates of Laḍaha Candra indicate that the king ruled at least for 6 years. The Bharella Narṭteśvara image inscription refers that the king ruled at least for 18 years.

Alam suggests that "Mahipala-I (9S8-1038 A.D.) of Gauḍa, his contemporary, after restoring the Pāla rule put a halt upon the military conquest of the Candras. But he did not distrubed Laḍaha Candra considering the help extended to them in time of distress by Śrī Candra" [106]. Laḍaha Candra went to many holy places within the Gauḍa Empire. Therefore, it indicates that there was a good political and socio-cultural relation between the kingdom of Laḍaha Candra and the kingdom of Gauḍa king.

The wife of Laḍaha Candra was Saubhāgya Devī, who gave birth to illustrious Govinda Candra. From the plate of Govinda Candra (V-13) it shows that, "Govinda Candra, himself, was Śaktimān (i.e. Kārttikeya). By the rise of that (king)of great army, this world became reposed, the science were learnt by him with ease in childhood only within a few days and he was well studied in the science of elephants, horses, cariages, and learnt all the arts". In the verse-14. it is also mentioned that "only this single king is praised in every direction, in every house, everyday by the people with joy, with eagerness, with horipilation as Dharma incarnate, as the Ocean of tolerance, as protector of the subjects, as an object of welfare, as the abode of riches, and as unrestrained lustre". In verse-16, he was blessed that "May lord self born produce profuse bliss, may lord Hari bestow steadiness of his body and Lord Hara destroy the opponents''.

The grant opens with three jewels i.e., Buddha, Dharma and Saṅgha. The king was Buddhist but he was great devotion to the Hindu God and Goddess like the king Laḍaha

Candradeva. He and his forth-father compared with the Hindu God and Goddess. The king granted two patakas of land to Natteśvara bhaṭṭāraka (i.e. dancing from Siva). From these evidences, it is not difficult to think that by that time, Brahimanical faith was come to light and Buddhism was going far ahead.

Śrī Govinda Candra was designated with *Parameśvara Paramabhattaraka Mahārājādhirāja.* It shows that he was an independent king. He was the successor of his father Laḍaha Candra deva. The plate is not dated. A Sūrya (Sun-god) inscribed unage was discovered in district of Noakhali. It mentions that the image caused to be made by Lakṣmīdina in 12th regnal year of the Lord Śrī Govinda Candra. Another inscribed image of Vasudeva was recovered in the district of Munshiganj. It indicates that the image of lord Vasudeva caused to be made by Ganga Dasa in the 23rd year of illustrious Govinda Candra. From these evidences, there is no doubt that the king Govinda Candra ruled at least for 23 years. The Triumalai[107] inscription clearly shows that Govinda Candra was ruling over Vaṅgāla-deśa in 1021-23 A. D. But it is uncertain that whether this date refers to his early carrier or later years of his reign. The environmental situation of Southern Bengal is mentioned in Triumalai inscription. Hultzsch says that "Vaṅgāla-deśa, where the rain-wind never stopped, (and from which) Govinda Candra fled, having descended (from his male elephant; elephants of rare strength and treasures of women, which he seized) after having been pleased to put to fight on a hot battle-field Mahipāla, decked (as he was) with ear-rings, slippers and bracelets" . It indicates that Govinda Candra was also contemporary of Mahipala. There is no doubt that this Mahipāla was the Mahipāla-1, who ruled over Varendra (i. e. North Bengal).From theTtriumalai inscription of Rajendra Chola, it has come to our knowledge that Govinda Candra was defeated by him in 1021-23 A. D. It is also clear that the very powerful king Rajendra Chola did not come to invade Vaṅgāl-deśa for ruling but came for winning the victorious glory. After the tough fighting with Mahipāla-I, he went to his kingdom.

From a contemporary hook **Śabdapradip** of Surapala, we know that Rajendra Chola invaded to Vaṅgālades in the early years of Śrī Govinda Candra's reign. On the basis of these evidences, Chowdhury[109] suggests that Govinda Candra was ruling from 1020 A. D. According to the Vasudeva inscribed inscription, Śrī Govinda Candra ruled at least 1020-1043 A. D. The date of previous rulers at Candra dynasty might be calculated in chronological order from the date of Govinda Candra.

According to the Bharella Nartteśvara image inscription, the king Laḍaha Candra ruled at least from 1002-1020 A. D. According to Dhaka copper-plate of Kalyān Candra, he ruled at least from 978-1002 A. D. According to Madanpur copper-plate of Śrī Candra, who ruled at least from 932-978 A. D. For the lack of information, now, it is uncertain to decide the date of three generations i.e. Purṇa Candra, Suvarṇa Candra and Trailokya Candra. From the above mentioned analysis, it has to say that from beginning of the 10th century to first half of the llth century, (i.e. 900 to 1050 A. D.), the Candra rulers ruled over Vaṅga, Vaṅgāla, Candradvīpa, Samataṭa and Harikāla region independently.

How the Candra dynasty came to an end, is not certainly clear to us. But the fact indicateds that the ruling Candras appears to have been destroyed by the invasion of the Kālācuri Karṇa (1041-1070 A. D.). It appears that Kalacuri Karṇa invaded to South-Eastem Bengal and defeated the king of that region. From this fact, most probably, Govinda Candra was the last ruler of Candra dynasty.

TABLE NO - 6

GENEALOGICAL LINEAGE OF THE CANDRA DYNASTY

SL. No.	Name of the Kings	Name of the Queens	At least ruling years	Duration of the rules
1	Sn Purṇa Candra	-	-	-
2	Śrī Suvarṇa Candra (son of -1)	-	-	-
3	Śrī Trailokya Candra(son of -2)	Śrī Kancana Devi	-	900(?)-932
4	Śrī Śrī Candra(son of -3)	Śrī Varnnā Devi	46	932-978
5	Śrī Kalyān Candra (son of -4)	Śrī Kalyāna Devi	24	978-1002
6	Śrī Laḍaha Candra(son of -5)	Śrī Saubhāgya Devi	18	1002-1020
7	Śrī Govinda Candra (son of -6)	-	23	1020-1043

8. LATTER DEVA DYNASTY

The copper-plate grant of Ranavankamalla Harikala Deva was first noticed in 1803 A. D. and due to this, the historical importance of Maināmatī-Lalmai area has come to light to us from that time. The inscription mentioned the name of a city, Paṭṭikera, where the monasteiy was built and dedicated to the Buddhist goddess Durgottara. The name Paṭṭikera is also noticed in the copper-plate grants of Śrī Laḍaha Candradeva who is dated in the beginning of the eleventh century A. .D. Goddess Durgottara is the form of Tārā. It is named in the Sadhanamala as Durgottarini-Tārā (Sādhanamālā, Vol.-I, p. 237-8). The city of Paṭṭikera was apparently situated somewhere in the Maināmatī-Lalmai hill range where this copper-plate grant was discovered- The donated property was situated in the village of Bejakhaṇḍa. It is not definitely identified now. But there is a village named Bejabāḍī near the feet of the hills on the west. It might be identified with the village referred to in the plate[110] .

The Horse officer Dhādi-Eba donated the inscription records a grant of land measuring 20 dronas. It is clear that the gift of the land was made neither by the sovereign monarch nor by a vassal. It was unique for a royal officer to transfer property in his own name without securing his lords permission. The implication is that Śrī Dhadi-Eba enjoyed the tax revenue from this parcel of land as an hereditary right that could not be resumed by his lord and therefore, Śrī Dhādi-Eba was at liberty to dispose of the revenue yield as he wished without reference to Harikāladeva.

The position of the early Devas even as regards their suzerainty over the whole of the district of Tippera is rendered anomalous by the Maināmatī copper-plate grant of Raṇavaṅkamalla Harikāla Deva recorded in the 17th year of his reign which corresponded to the year 1141 of the Śaka era. It is equivalent to 1219-20 A. D. This date of the king shows that he was not a contemporary of both the grand father and the great grand father of Dāmodaradeva.

He was at least a contemporary of Vāsudeva. father of Dāmodaradeva. where precisely Harikāladeva's reign ended or what happened to his line, we can not say now. It also appears from the grant that he ruled a small portion of Samataṭa area. It is also not clear that what was the relation between Harikāla Deva and rulers of Dāmodara's family.

The founder of the Deva family was named by Purṣottama is the synonym of lord Viṣṇu. The plate mentioned that the royal family is claimed to have descended from the Moon. It is not mentioned in the plate that what was the royal status of Purṣottama but it appears that he was the powerful person of the Deva family. His son, Madhusudhana was designated only the litle Nṛpati in the Chittagong plate of Dāmodaradeva. Therefore, it shows that he was the feudatory king of some area of Samataṭa Maṇḍala. His son was Vāsudeva was the lord of earth. He was known to be "Versed in all the *Sastras,* and foremost in military skill. In the Chittagong plate, he is described an one whose feet were rubbed by the foreheads of princes bowing down to him in homage. It appears that king Vāsudeva imposed his authority over the neighbouring cliefs and thus led the way for the rise of his son Dāmodara Deva. In the Mehar plate he bears the title of *Gagapati,* In Chittagonj plate, he is called "over lord of all kings" and in verse 4 and 5 of the same plate he is said to have defeated many kings and brought them under subjection. In Sobharampur plate, he is designated as *Gagapati.He* is also called *Ariraja Canura Madhava.* The Pākamorā copperplate of Dasarathadeva, son of Dāmodaradeva, praised his father as a renovator of his kingdom[111]. From all the designation, it suggests that he was a very powerful king but not an independent king. He never titled in any plate as *Parameśvara Paramabhaṭṭāraka Mahārājādhirāja.*

It is also plausible explanation that when the Deva dynasty was reigning in the Samataṭa area by that time the Sena dynasty held supremacy over the region of Vaṅga including Vikramapura and Navya under Pauṇḍrabhukti. From this inference, it appears that the river Meghna was the western boundary of the Deva kings.

The representation of Viṣṇu on Grauḍa or of Mādhava overpowering Canura is certainly symobolical of the Vaiṣṇava faith of King Dāmodara Deva. Dr. Majumdar identified that the family of Dāmodara professed the Vaiṣṇava faith like the Varmmans and the Senas[112]. It is also noted that all the ending names of Deva family are the synonym of Viṣṇu. It is, therefore, clear that the Devas are the *Vaiṣṇava*.

The Chittagong copper-plate was issued in the Śaka era 1165, in the 13th regnal year of the king Dāmodara. The Sobharampur copper-plate was issued in the Saka era 1158, in the 6th regnal year of the king Dāmodara. The Mehar plate was issued in the Śaka era 1156, in the 4th regnal year of the mentioned king. From these evidences, it is proved that the king Dāmodara Deva came to the power in the 1152 Śaka era. So, it is equivalent-to 1230 A. D. Therefore, the Deva dynasty ruled over Samataṭa in the 13th century A.D.

The illustrious Daśarathadeva was titled of *Parameśvara Paramabhaṭṭāraka Mahārājādhirāja*. He is also designated with *As'vapati-gajapati-narapti-rajatryadhipati, Somavamsapradīpa Pratipannakaranna Satya-vṛātagarṅgeya Saranāgata-vajrapañjara.*

It is mentioned in the plate that the king obtained the kingdom of Gauḍa (Gauḍarājya) through the grace of Nārāyaṇa. Most probably, it was happened after collapse of the Sena power. From his title and the description, there is no doubt that he was the very powerful king and later on, he included Vikrampura area with his kingdom Samataṭa. That is why. he issued the charter from the Vikrampura.

After Daśaratha Deva, the genealogy of the Deva family is incomplete. Another copper-plate grant of Vīradhara Deva was issued in the 15th regnal year of the king. But the grant did not mention any known era and the predecessor of Deva family. Majumdar suggests that the king Vīradhara Deva was a later king of Deva family[113]. From the study of Deva plate, it appears that Vīradharadeva was the successor or a contemporary of Daśaratha Deva. It is noted that the *Viṣṇu Cakra Mudrā* was engraved on the grant and described in the plate of Vīradhara deva. So, he was also a worshipper of Viṣṇu like as other Deva rulers. Bhattacharjee[114] mentioned that total 34 pāṭakas of land were donated. But the grant clearly indicates in line two and in line four on the reverse side that twelve pāṭakas of land were granted in the district of Vataganga and five pāṭakas of land in the district of Gaṅga Maṇḍala in the division of Samataṭa under Pauṇḍravarddhanabhukti. All together 17 pāṭakas of land were granted.

GENEALOGICAL LINEAGE AND SUCCESSORS OF LATER DEVA DYNASTY

1) Puruṣottama . 1) Raṇavaṅkamalla Harikāla Deva.

2) Madhusudhana (son of- 1)

3) Vāsudeva (son of - 2), Mitratdevi (wife of -3)

4) Dāmodaradeva (son of - 3)

5) Dāśarathadeva (son of - 4)

6) Vīradharadeva (successor or contemporary of- 5)

NOTES AND REFERENCES

1. Bhattacharyya, D.C., "A newly discovered Copper plate from Tippera" T.H. Q, Vol.-VI, 1930, p. 52.
2. 2.Ibid, p. 58.
3. Morrison, B.M., P.C.C.R.E.B, Tucson : University of Arizona Press, 1970, pp. 127-41.
4. Ibid, pp. 22-24.
5. Laskar, G.M., "Ashrafpur Copper plate grants of Devakhaḍga", M.A.S.B, Vol.-1, 1906, pp. 85-91.
6. Daniel, H.H., Ingalls, trans, An Anthology of Sanskrit Court Poetry, Cambridge : Harvard University Press, 1965, pp. 59,77, 112-13, 295, 352, 404-5.
7. The plate was illustrated in P. A, Vol.- III, 1966, Plate-41.
8. This plates existence was reported in the same place as the C-plate, and it was illustrated in P. A, Vol.-III, 1966, Plate-40.

9. Bühler, G., "Banskhera plate of Harṣha" E.I, Vol.-IV, Plate facing p. 220.
10. Kielhorn, F., "Madhuban plate of Harṣha", E-I, Vol.-VII, plate facing p. 158,
11. Hultzsch, E., "Plates of the time of Sasanka-Raja", E.I, Vol.-VI, p. 143 and plates.
12. Bhattacharya, Padmanatha Vidyāvinoda, "Nidhanpur copper plates of Bhaskar Varman", E.I, Vol.-XII, p. 65. and plates.
13. Bloch, A.S.R., 1903-04, p. 120.
14. Baṣak, R. G., "Tipperah copper-plate grant of Lokanātha : the 44 th year", E. I, Vol.-XV, 1925, p. 301-315.
15. Sircar, D.C., "The Kailan Copper-plate Inscription of King Śrīdharana Rāta of Samataṭa," I.H.Q, Vol.-XXIII, No.-1, 1947, pp. 222-23.
16. Ibid, p. 223.
17. Laskar, G.M., "Ashrafpur copper plate grants of Devakhaḍga", M.A.S.B, Vol.-1, 1906, pp. 85-91.
18. Sircar, D.C., "The Kailan copper-plate Inscription of King Śrīdharana Rāta of Samataṭa", I.H.Q, Vol.-XXIII, No.-1, 1947, pp. 221-240, and Bhattasali N.K, "The New Kailān Plate of Śrīdharana Rāta", I.H.Q, Vol.-XXII, 1946, pp. 169-71.
19. Basak, R.G., " Tippera copper-plate grant of Lokantha," E.I, Vol.-XV, 1925, pp. 301-315.
20. Khan, F.A., Maināmatī, p. 19.
21. Rashid, Harunur, E. H.S.E.B, with no page reference.
22. Hunter, S. A. B., Vol.-V, p. 224.
23. Cunningham, Alexander, A.S.R, Vol.-XV, pp. 132-33.
24. Dani, A.H., "Maināmatī Plates of Chandras", P.A, No.-3, 1966, p. 23.
25. Banerji, R.D., "The date of Śrīcandra," A.M.S.J.V, 1927, Vol.-III, Pt. 3, pp. 210-22.
26. Bhattasali, N.K., "Betka Vāsudeva image inscription of the 23rd year of Govinda Cnadra," E.I, Vol.-XXVII, 1949, p. 26.
27. Bhattacharya, D.C., "The Maināmatī Copper plate of Raṇavaṅkamalla Harikālādeva (1141 Saka)", I.H.Q, Vol.-Xl, 1933, p. 282.
28. Bhattacharyya, D.C., "The Maināmatī copper-plate of Raṇavaṇkamcalla Harikāladeva: 1141 Saka," V. R. S.M, No.-5, 1934, p. 13.
29. Barua, B.M., and Chakravarti, Pulin Behari, "Mehar plate of Dāmodaradeva" E.I, Vol.- XXVII, Part-3, 1950, p. 183.

30. Majumdar, N.G., "Chittagong Copper plate of Dāmodara", I.B, Vol.-IIT, 1929, p. 159.
31. Ibid, p. 159.
32. Ibid, p. 162.
33. Majumdar, N.G., "Chittagong Copper-plate of Damodara", I.B, Vol.-III, 1929, p. 159 ff. and J.A.S.B, Vol.-XLIII, 1874, Part-1, pp. 318-24, Plate- VIII.
34. Barua, B.M. and Chakravarti, Pulin Behari, "Mehar plate of Damodara deva", E.I, Vol.-XXVII. 1950, p. 182 ff. Plate opposite p. 187.
35. Majumdar, N.G., "Anulia Copper plate of Lakṣmaṇa Sena," I.B, 1929, Plate. Oppisite P. 84.
36. Pandit Prannath, J.A.S.B, Vol.-XLIII, 1874, Part-1, pp. 318-24, and PI. XVIII and Kielhorn. Fronz, List of Inscriptions of Northern India, p. 53, under No.-366.
37. Barua, B.M., and Chakravarti, Pulin Behari, "Mehar plate of Dāmodara Deva", E.I, Vol.- XXVII, 1950, p. 185.
38. Bhattasali N.K., "Adavadi Copper plate of Daśaratha Deva," BhāRātavarṣa, 1332, B.S, pp. 78-81.
39. Vinoda Vihari Vidyāvinoda, "Two Inscriptions from Bodh-Gaya" E.I, Vol.-XII, Pls. opposite- p. 28. and Majumdar. N.G, Patna Museum Inscription of Jayasena", LA, Vol.-48, 1919, pp. 43-48.
40. Banarjee, R.D., "The Pālas of Bengal", M.A.S.B, Vol.-V, No3, pl-XXVIII,
41. Majumdar, R.C., BD.I (Pracin Juga), 1988, pp. 152-53.
42. Colebrooke, H.T., Inscription on a plate of Copper found in the district of Tipura", A. R. T. S. I. B, Vol.-9, 1809, pp. 401-406.
43. Barua, B.M. and Chakravarti, Pulin Behari, "Mehar plate of Damodardeva", E.I, Vol.-XXVI, Part-3, 1950, pp. 186-ff. Plate.
44. Majumdar, N.G., "Chillagong Copper plate of Dāmodara," I. B, Vol.-III, 1929, p. 159.
45. Barua, B.M., "Mehar plate of Dāmodara Deva," E.I, Vol.- XXVII, Part-Ill, 1950, p. 184.
46. Majumdar, R.C., BD.I, (Beng), 1988, p. 152.
47. Khan Nurul Islam, Ed., B.D.G, Comilla, 1977, p. 29.
48. Webster, J.E., E.B D.G, Tippera, 1910, p. 10.
49. Watters, Thomas, "Samataṭa,"Y.C.T.I, 1973, Vol.-II, p. 187 and Bel Samuel, B. R. W. W, Vol.- II, p. 200.
50. Fleet, John Faithful, C.I. I, Vol.-III, 1963, p. 8 and 14 and Cunningham Sir Alexander, Samataṭa, A.G.I, 1924, p. 525.

51. Ahmed Nazimuddin, Mahāsthan, 1975, p. 7.
52. Basak, R.G., "Damodarpur Copper plate Inscriptions," E.I, Vol.-XV, 1919-20, Plate No.-3, 4, and 5. pp. 134-145.
53. Ibid, pp. 113-116.
54. Paul, P. L., "South Eastern Bengal in Ancient Times," I.H.Q, 1936, Vol.-XII, p. 71.
55. Basak, R. G., E.I, Vol.-XV, 1919-20, pp. 113-145.
56. Paul, P. E., I.H.Q, Vol.-XII, 1936, p. 71.
57. Walters, T., Y.C.T.I, Vol.-II, p. 109.
58. Kielhorn F, "Khalimpur plate of Dharmapaladeva," E.I, Vol.-IV, 1896-97, pp. 245-5 I and Jayaswal K.P, I.H.I, in a Sanskrit Text, 1934, p. 60.
59. Majumdar, R.C., "The Kingdom of Samataṭa or Vaṅga", H.B, Vol.-1, 1943, pp. 51-54.
60. Ibid, p.p. 53-54.
61. Bhattasali, N.K., "Some Image Inscriptions from East Bengal," E.I, Vol.-XVII, 1923-24, p. 359.
62. Ray, Niharranjan, Bi. I (Adi Parva), 1402 (Beng). p. 336.
63. Walters, T., Y.C.T.I, Vol.-11, p. 109.
64. Law, B.C., "The Vaṅgas, " L.C, Vol.-1, 1934-35, p. 62.
65. Walters, T., Y.C.T.I, Vol.-II, 1973, p. 109.
66. Beal, Samuel, B. R. W. W, Vol.-II, p. 110.
67. Sircar, D.C., "The Kailan copperplate Inscription of King Śrīdharaṇa Rāta," IH.Q, Vol.-XXIII, 1947, p. 230,
68. Paul, P.L., "Was there a Bhadra dynasty in Eastern Bengal ?", LC, 1935-36, Vol.-11, Pp. 795-97.
69. Bhattasali, N.K., "The Deulbadi Śarvvani image inscription of Mahādevi Prabhāvatī and Queen of Deva Khaḍga." E.I, 1924, Vol.-XVII, p. 358.
70. Paul, P. L., "Was there a Badra dynasty in Eastern Bengal" ?, I.C, Vol.-11, 1935-36, p. 795.
71. Sircar, D.C., "The Kailan Copper plate Inscription of King Śrīdharana Rāta", I.H.Q,Vol.-XXIII, 1947, pp. 230-31,
72. Basak, R.G., "Tippera Copper plate grant of Lokanātha; The 44th year" E.I, Vol.-XV, J925, p. 301-315.
73. Thomas, F.W., Ed., E.I, Vol.-XV, 1925, Foot note in the page -303.
74. Basak, R.G., H. N. E. I, 1934, pp. 195-196.
75. Basak, R.G., "Tippera Copper-plate grant of Lokanātha : The 44th year" E.I, Vol.- XV, 1925, pp. 301-315.

76. Ibid, p. 303.
77. Bhandarkar, D.R., IA, Vol.-LXI, 1932, p. 44.
78. Basak, R.G,, H.N.E.I, 1934, pp. 195.
79. Sircar, D.C., "The Kailān Copper-plate Inscription of King Śrīdharaṇa Rāta of Samataṭa, ¼ I.H.Q, Vol.-XXIII, Nol, 1947, pp. 221-241.
80. Laskar, G.M., "Ashrafpur Copper-plate grants of Devakhaḍga", M.A.S.B, No.-1, 1906, pp. 85-91.
81. Sircar, D.C., "The Kailan Copper plate Inscription of King Śrīdharaṇa Rāta," I.H.Q, Vol.-XXIII, Nol, 1947, pp. 221-241.
82. Chowdhury, A.M., D. H. B, p. 142.
83. I-tsing visited India between 671 and 694 A.D, wrote his book in the period C.700, -12 A.D, Seng -chi visited Samataṭa some time between 650 and 700, Chavannes places I-tsing's stay in India in 673-85.
84. "Ghugrahati Copper-plate of Samacārdeva," E.I, Vol.-XVIII, p. 74.
85. Ghosh, Jogendra Chandra, "The Candra dynasty of Arakan" I.H.Q, Vol.-VII, 1931, p. 37,
86. Ramachandran, T.N., B.C Law Volume. ed.Bhanderkar D.R,Part-II, 1946, p. 217.
87. Majumdar, R.C., "Lama Tārānatha's Account of Bengal", H.B, Vol.-1, 1943, p. 182.
88. Ibid, pp.186-87
89. Ganguly, D.C., "A Side light on the History of Bengal", I.H.Q, Vol.-XVI, 1940, p. 181-82.
90. Bhattasali, N.K., "The Kedarpur plate of Śrī Candra," E.I.Vol.-XVII, 1923-24 p. 190.
91. Basak, R.G., "Madnpur plate of Śrī Candra", E.I, Vol.-XXVIII, 1949, p. 53.
92. Majumdar, R.C., "The Chandras", H.B, Vol.- I, 1943, p. 194.
93. Ibid, p. 194-195
94. Sircar, D.C., "Dhulla plate of Śrīcandra", E.I, Vol.-XXXIII, 1960, p. 135.
95. Basak, R.G., "Madanpur plate of Śrī Candra", E.I, Vol.-XXVIII, 1949, p. 53.
96. Majumdara, N.G., I.B, Vol.-III, 1929, p. 3.
97. Paul, P. L,, "South Eastern Bengal in Ancient Time", I.H.Q, Vol.-XII, 1936, No.-1, in foot note, p. 77.
98. Basak, R.G., "Madanpur plate of Śrī Candra", E.I, Vol XXVIII, 1949, p. 54.

99. Sircar, D.C., "Madanpur plate of Śrī Chandra year 46," E.I, Vol.-XXVIII, 1949-50. p. 338.
100 Majumdar, R.C., "New light on the History of Bengal," J.A.S, Vol.-VII, 1965, pp. 1-4.
101 Majumdar, N.G., I.B, Vol.-III, 1929, p. 3.
102 Bhattasali, N.K., I B.B.S, p. 10.
103 Sircar, D.C., "Dhulla Copper plate of Śrī Candra" E.I, Vol.- XXXIII, 1960, p. 135.
104 Dani, A.H., "Purva-Vanger Chandra Raja-Vamsa", B.A.P, Vol-IV, 1367, B.S, p. 31.
105 Dani, A.H., "Maināmatī plates of the Chandras" P. A, No.-3, 1966, p. 35.
106 Alam, A.K.M. Shamsul, Maināmatī, 1982, p. 16.
107 Hultzsch, E., "Tirumalai Rock Incription of Rajendra Chola I", E.I, Vol.-IX, 1907-8, p. 233 and I.H.Q, Vol XIII, pp. 151-52.
108 Hultzsch, E., "Triumalai Rock Inscription of Rajendra-Chola-1," E. I., Vol.- IX,1907-8, p. 233.
109 Chowdhury, A. M., D.H.B, p. 186.
110 Bhattacharyya, D. C., "The Maināmatī Copper-plate of Raṇavaṅka-malla Harikālādeva : 1141 Saka", V.R.S.M, No - 5, 1934, pp. 10-16.
111 Majumdar, R. C., BD.I (Prācin juga in Beng.), p. 168.
112 Majumdar, N. G., "Chittagong Copper-plate of Dāmodara", I. B., Vol.-III, 1929, p. 159.
113 Majumdar, R. C., BD.I (Pracin Juga in Beng.), pp. 168-70,
114 Bhattacharjee Swapan Bikash, "Maināmatī Copper-plate of Śrī Viradhara Deva", J. A. S. B., Hum, Vol. - 39, No, - 2, 1994, p. 72.

CHAPTER - VI

IDENTIFICATION AND EXPLANATION OF THE PLACES AND THE RIVERS OF THE MAINĀMATĪ COPPER-PLATE GRANTS

Introduction

In an attempt to reconstruct the historical geography of ancient kingdom and different place names, the inscriptions are the most dependable and inforthative source. As documents granting the transfer of property, the plates carry us into the heart of an action, which has a definite learning on the land. Each of the documents records the name of villages, field, mountain, river and limit of the area. Usually, it mentions the administrative jurisdiction within which the land is recorded and mentions its boundary. The most important problem is to identify the place-names that are found in the inscriptions. From the date of the inscription, the place-names, roughly, could be identified. It is also difficult to define exact boundary of the villages, fields, administrative centers and country. I have tried to define the boundaries of the below mention place-names with the help of the identifications made by various scholars earlier.

MENTIONED NAMES OF VARIOUS GRANTS OF MAINĀMATĪ

THE GRANT OF BALABHATTA

Name of the mentioned places	Name of the mentioned river
1.Katakaśīla "	1.Kṣīrodā
2.Devaparvata	
3.Dhanalakṣmitalapāṭaka	

THE GRANT OF ĀNANDA DEVA

Name of the mentioned places

1.Kāmarūpa

2 Śrīkṣetra

3.Vasantapur

4.Peranaāṭana Viṣaya

5.Samataṭa

6.Oḍḍayana

7.Salihrada pattana

8.Magadha

THE GRANT OF BHAVA DEVA

Name of the mentioned places

1.Peranāṭana Viṣaya

2.Devaparvata

THE GRANT OF ŚRĪ LAḌAHA CANDRA DEVA

Name of the mentioned places	Name of the mentioned rivers
1.Prāgjyotiṣa	1.Gaṅga
2.Gauḍa	2. Yamunā
3. Vāraṇasī	3.Buḍḍhi Gaṅginī
4.Vikramapura	
5.Pauṇḍrabhukti	

6.Samataṭa Maṇḍala
7.Paṭṭikeraka S.Phullahdā
9.Campāvani
10.Dollavāyikā
11.Buddha-Nandi Grāma
12.Vallesvara
13.Govindoñcama
14.Oḍa-Godhani
15.Godhani
16.Jayalambha Grāma
17.Vappasimha Voraka Grāma
18.Guptināṭana
19.Karavatti Voraka
20.Vaggurabhoga
21.DhṛtipuraHattika
22.Mahādeva Grāma

THE GRANT OF ŚRĪ LAḌAHA CANDRADEVA

Name of the mentioned places	Name of the mentioned rivers.
1.Prāgjyotiṣa	1.Ganga
2.Gauḍa	2. Yamuna
3.Vāraṇasī	
4.Pauṇḍrabhakti	
5.Samataṭa Maṇḍala	
6.Vikramapura	
7.Peranāṭana Viṣaya	
8.Mawpataka	
9.Brahmanadeva Voraka Grāma	
10.Kaṅsārokaddapolaka Grāma	
11.Paṭṭikeraka 12.SuraVoraka Grāma	

THE GRANT OF ŚRĪ GOVINDA CANDRADEVA

Name of the mentioned places Name of the mentioned river

1. Vaṅga
2. Gauḍa
3. Varanasī
4. Vikramapura
5. Pauṇḍrabhukti
6. Samataṭa Maṇḍala
7. Peranāṭana Viṣaya
8. SāhaRātalāka

1. Lauhitya

THE GRANT OF ŚRĪ VIRADHARA DEVA

Name of the mentioned places

1 .Pauṇḍravarddhanbhūkti
2. Samataṭa Maṇḍala
3. Vātagaṅgā Viṣaya
4. Gaṅga Maṇḍala Viṣaya
5. Adhavaśā Grāma
6. Meśvārvarta Grāma
7. Nārorāka

THE GRANT OF RAṆAVANKAMALLA HARIKALA DEVA

Name of the mentioned places

1. Bejakhaṇḍa.
2. Paṭṭikera.

NAME OF THE MENTIONED PLACES AND RIVERS FROM THE MAINĀMATĪ COPPER-PLATE GRANTS INSIDE OF SAMATAṬA

Name of the Places

1. Pauṇḍrabhukti / Pauṇḍravarddhanabhukti
2. Vaṅga
3. Samataṭa Maṇḍala
4. Peranāṭana Viṣaya

5.Gaṅgamaṇḍala Viṣaya
6.Vātagaṅgā Viṣaya
7.Devaparvata
8.Vasantapura
9.Vikramapura
10.Guptināṭana
11.Paṭṭikera
12.Śālihrada pattana
13.Dhanalakṣmitala pāṭaka
14.Māyupāṭaka
15.Campāvani
16.Phullahada
17.Dollavāyikā
18.Goviiidoñcama
19.Oḍa-Godhani
20.Godhani
21.Katakaśīla
22.SāhaRātalaka
23.Karavatti Voraka
24.Sura Voraka Grāma
25.Brāhmanadeva Voraka Grāma
26.Kaṅsārokadda polaka Grāma
27.Vappasiṁha Voraka Grāma
28. Jayalambha Grāma
29. Mahadeva Grāma
30. Buddha-Nandi Grāma
31. Adhavasā Grāma
32. Meśvāvarta Grāma
33. Vaggurabhoga
34. Valleśvara

35. Nārorāka
36. Bejakhaṇḍa
37. Dhṛtipura haṭṭika

NAME OF THE RIVERS

1. Gaṅgā
2. Yamunā
3. lauhitya
4. Kṣīrodā
5. Buḍḍhi Gaṅginī

NAME OF THE PLACES OUTSIDE OF SATHATAṬA

1. Kāmarūpa
2. Prāgjyotiṣa
3. Śrīkṣetra
4. Oḍḍayana
5. Magadha
6. Gauḍa
7. Vārāṇasī

IDENTIFICATION OF THE PLACE-NAMES MENTIONED IN THE MAINĀMATĪ COPPER-PLATE GRANTS

PAUṆḌRA-BHUKTI

The name of Pauṇḍra-bhukti was found in all the copper-plate grants of Candra dynasty of SouthEast Bengal. The Candra rulers, who ruled in south-eastern Bengal and we do not have any record of their rule in Northern Bengal. All the records of Candra ruler have granted land under Pauṇḍrabhukti. From the internal evidence of the grants, it can be safely generalised that the lands lay in the Dhaka Madaripur, Comilla-Noakhali and Sylhet area of south-eastern Bengal. So, the Pauṇḍrabhukti comprised the south-easterrn Bengal. The full name of the

Paudra-bhukti was Pauṇḍravarddhanabhukti (c.f. Mainămatī copper-plate grant of Viradharadeva). The main city of Pauṇḍranagar indentified with Mahăsthangara in Bogra district of Bangladesh. According to Ray Chaudhuri, "it seems to have learn the biggest administrative division or province of the Gauḍa Empire. It extended from the summit of the Himalayas *(Himăvacchikhără* of a Dāmodarpur plate) in the north to Khādi in Sundarvan region in the south"[1].

We have already referred to the Nalanda inscription of Vipulasrimitra which belongs to the first half of the 12th century A.D. Vipulasrimitra was disciple's disciple of Asokamitra. Asokamitra was a disciple of Maitrisrimitra. Maitrisrimitra was again a disciple of Karunasrimitra, about whom, we are told that he died at Somapura calsping the feet of the Buddha when that place was set on fire by the armies of Vaṅgāla (E.I,Vol.-XXI , p. 97). This Somapura has been identified with Paharpura in the Rajashahi district of Bengal[2]. This Paharpur is not very far from Mahāsthangarh. According to Wilson, the ancient kingdom of Puṇḍra deśa included the district of Rajshahi Dinajpur, Rangpur Malda Bogra and Trihut[3]. According to other authorities the country of Puṇḍra or Puṇḍravarddhana was situated between the rivers Mahānandā and the Karatoya. Farguson has shown that the region of Dinajpur, Rangpur and Bogra formed the ancient Puṇḍravardhana, in short, it was North Bengal. Cunningham has identified the capital with Mahāsthanagad on the Karatoya River, twelve miles south of Barddhankuti and seven miles to the north of Bogra, in the district of Bongra and also with Pabna. According to **Rajatarangini** (Book IV) Puṇḍravarddhana was the capital of Gauḍ in the eighth century A. D. when it was visited by Jayāpiḍa, king of Kasmir during the reign of Jayanta,

VAṄGA AND VAṄGALA

In ancient literature, there is no specific name for the present entire Bangladesh. It consisted of a group of small regions. They were all known by different names. According to the Purāṇas and the great Epic[4], the sage Dīerghatamas had married king Ball's *Śūdra* nurse and had Kakṣivant and other sons; and at Ball's desire begot on the queen Sudeṣnā five sons, Aṅga, Vaṅga, Kaliṅga, Puṇḍra and Suhma, who were called the Baleya Kṣarras and also Baleya Brāhmaṇas and who came as the founders of five respective countries in their names. In the Matsya Purāṇa, Vaṅga and Suhma are included in the list of eastern contries (chap 114, 43-45 and c.f. also Mbh. Bhīṣma Parva. chap- 9. 46), where the Aṅgas, Vaṅgas and Kaliṅgas were mentioned as east Indian peoples (c.f Rāmāyaṇa, Kiṣkindhya Kāṇḍa, canto xlii), the Puṇḍras are mentioned as an Eastern people[3]. Vaṅga, Puṇḍra, Suhma and Tāmralipti mentioned as separate kingdoms (c.f. Mbh Sabhā Parva chap 29). It is also mentioned in the Sabhā Parva that the Pāṇḍavas were credited to have subverted the Puṇḍras and the Vaṅgas and led their victorious army to Suhma (Mbh, Sabha. P, chap. 30, 23-25). The King Jarāsandha was said to have extended his superemacy over the Aṅgas, Vaṅgas, Kaliṅgas and Puṇḍras. (Mbh. XII chap 5, 6607). Karṅa was also once credited to have conquered the Suhmas, Aṅgas and Vaṅgas (Mbh Karṇa P, chap 8, 19). In the Droṇa Parva (Mbh, chap- 10-15), Vasudeva was said to have once routed in battle the Aṅgas, Vāṅgas, Kaliṅgas and Puṇḍras alongwith other peoples. In the time of Vallalasen (12th century A. D.), the present Bangal consisted of four Kingdoms i.e Rāḍhā (west Bengal), Varendra (North Bangal), Vāgadi (present Medinipur district) and Vaṅga

The Kavyamīmāṁṣā of Rajaśekhara (chap 3 and 17) a work of the tenth century A. D, also mentions Aṅga. Vaṅga, Suhma, Brahma, Puṇḍra etc, as Janapadas of the east An almost contemporary reference to the Vaṅga people was made by Kalidāsa in his Raghuvaṁsam where Raghu is credited to have conquered the Vaṅgas[7]. After he had finished his task with the Suhmas and planted his victorious banner in the midstream of the Ganges (canto iv 35-36) Before sometime of Yuan Chwang it is mentioned in Vṛhat Saṁhitā of Varāhamihira that there were separate kingdoms in Vaṅga i.e. Suhma, Samataṭa,

Lohitya, Gauḍaka (Gauḍa), Pauṇḍra, Tāmralipti and Bardhamān[8]. Mostprobably, the name of Vaṅga first mentioned in Aitareya Āranyaka of the Ṛg-Veda. The name of the Vaṅga tribe is certainly found in the Bodhāyans Dharmasūtra (1.1, 14 ; of oldenberg Buddha 394, n). It was mentioned that Vaṅgas were impure alongwtih Puṇḍras, Kaliṅgas, Sauvīras and Araṭṭas[9]. In Jain Prajñapana, which ranks Aṅgas and Vaṅgas, as Aryans. Vaṅga is really the name of the people who inhabited this region from a remote past[10]- It, therefore, appeared that in the period represented by Epics, Purāṇas and from above mentioned references Vaṅga was the important kingdom of Bengal. But it is difficult to define exactly the geographical position of the Vaṅga.

The Vaṅga country is also referred in the Mahākuṭa pillar inscription (E. I, Vol.-V), which tells us that in the 6th century A. D. Kirtivarman of the Chālukya dynasty gained victories over the kings of Vaṅga, Aaṅga, and Magadha, which were three neighbouring countries[11].

The Edilpurr copper-plate of Kesava Sena records the grant of a village called Talapada pataka situated in Vikramapura of Vaṅga under Pauṇḍravarddhana province[12]. It, therefore, appears that Vikramapura, more widely known at present Munshiganj district, was under Vaṅga region. The famous Chinese pilgrim Yuan Chwang visited India in the beginning of the second quarter of the 7th century A. D. He did not mention the name of Vaṅga but mentioned the name of Samataṭa. Hemacandra in his Abhidhana cintamani (IV, 23), mentioned *"Vaṅgāstu Harikeliyāḥ"*. But in Mañjūśrīmulakalpa, Buddhist work mentioned that Harikala, Samataṭa and Vaṅga were separated from each other[13]. Banerji supports Yasodhara's commentary on the Kāmaṣūtra in the Jayamaṅgala (Kāmasūtra Chowkhamba, Sanskrit Book Depot, p. 295), namely *Vaṅga Lohityat purvena; Aṅga Mahānadyah purvena; Kaliṅga Gauḍa - Viṣyad =dakṣīṇena*[14]. According to the Jaina Pannavana. Tāmalitti was included in Vaṅga[15]. Law suggests that "Vaṅga is rougly represented by modern Decca and Chittogong divisions but it seems that the western boundary extended still further"[16]. Paul appears that "at the present state of our knowledge, the rivers Hoogly and Brahmaputra seem to be the western and eastern boundaries and in the north, it was Varendra while in the south it was Bay of Bengal"[17]. Buchanan says that "Baṅga, from which Bengal is a corruption, is applied only to the eastern portion of the delta of the Ganges as Upabanga is to the center of this territory and Aṅga to its western limits"[18]. According to Daji, Vaṅga was the country between the Brahmaputra and the Padma. Bengal was divided in to five provinces: Puṇḍra or North Bengal; Samataṭa or East Bengal; Karṇasuvarṇa or west Bengal; Tamralipta or south Bengal; Kāmarūpa or Assam (Yuan Chwang). According to General Cunningham, the province of Bengal was divided four separate districts after the Christian era. These divisions attributed to Ballala Sena; Barendra and Banga to the north of the Ganges and Rāḍhā and Bagdi to the south of the river (but see J. A. S. B. 1873, p- 211); the first two were seperated by the Brahmaputra and the other two by the Jalingi branch of the Ganges, Barendra, between the Mahānanda and Karatoya corresponds to Puṇḍra, Baṅga to East Bengal, Rāḍhā (to the west of the Bhagirathi), to Karṇasuvarṇa and Bagdi (Samataṭa of Hiuen Tsiang and Bhati of the Akbarnama) to south Bangal[1] . Pargiter suggests that Vaṅga must have comprised the modern districts of Murshidabad, Madia, Jessore, Parts of Rajshahi, pabna and Faridpur[20]. According to George Birdwood, Vaṅga originally included the districts of Bordwan and Nadia. Basak suggests that "during the 7th century A. D. when the Chinese pilgrim Yuan Chwang visited India (629- 48 A. D.) The name Samataṭ a represented these countries, i.e. Vaṅga and itself'[21]. The name of Vaṅga has lastly come to our knowledge from the Maināmatī copper-plate grants of Laḍaha Candra and Govinda Candra.

From above dicussion it is clear- that the name of Vaṅga came in the light from Vedic period. It was famous and prosperous country from the veiy beginning. Samataṭa and Harikāla were just Maṇḍala. Mostprobably, Vaṅga consisted of a group of Maṇḍalas (Divisions). But earlier Samataṭa and Harikṅla had separate political status. According to Yaung Chauang and from the description, it is understood that Samataṭa and Harikela were situated on eastern, side of Lauhitya River (i.e. present Brahmaputra Nada). Therefore, most probably, Brahmaputra River was the eastern boundary of the Vaṅga country.

After the rising of Candra dynasty, the name of Vaṅga used in broader sense. From epigraphic evidences the kings of Candra dynasty, ruled over Harikela, Samataṭa, Candr-dvipa and Vaṅga of which capital city was situated in Vikramapura, in present Munshiganj, district near Dhaka City. These mentioned countries are situated in southeastern Bengal. It is likely that spreading the power over these countries, the name of Vaṅga was used in broader sense. From epigraphic evidences, it is well established that Puṇḍra nagar i.e, Varendra is situated in northwestern side of present Bengal. And present Mahăsthagara is the Puṇḍra Nagar City. So it is understood that the Yamunā was the western boundary, the Brahmaputra was the northern and eastern boundary and Padmā was the southern boundary of Vaṅga in ancient period.

The name of Vaṅgāla is not found in any early records or any religious works. In the 16th century, however, Abul Fazal says " The original name of Baṅga (= Vaṅgāla) was Baṅga (= Vaṅga). Its former rulers raised mounds measuring ten yards in height and twenty in breadth, throughout the province, which were called *al*. From this suffix the name (i.e. Bangala) took its rise and currency"[22] (Jarrett, Ani' .i- Akbari. Trans. II p-120). Paul believes that "Vaṅga and Vaṅgāl can not be regarded as two separate countries. Vaṅgāl seems to be an etymological variation of Vaṅga probably made by the southerners and foreigners"[23]. The Nesari plates of 805 A. D. suggest that "the name of Vaṅgāla (apparently indicating the original territory of the palas in the Buckergunge region) was known even in earlier times though it does not appear to have been popular in the sense of the eastern part or whole of Bengal before the rise of the Candras. This was popularised in the sense first of East Bengal, and then in that of the whole of Bengal by the Muslims" [24].

In Tirumalai Rock inscription of Rajendra Chola mentioned the name of Vaṅgāla-deśa. Hultzsch indicates that Vaṅgāla-deśa, where the rain wind never stopped (and from which), Govinda Candra fled, having descended (from his) male elephant, elephants of rare strength and treasures of women, (which he seized) after having been pleased to put to fight on a hot battle fied Mahipala decked (as he was) with ear- rings, slippers and bracelets"[35]. There is no room for doubt that this Govinda Candra is identical with the Govinda Candra of Maināmatī copper plate. The Tirumalai inscription says about the expedition of conquest by Rajendra Chola. "The king first invaded Takkana ladam and forcibly attacked Ranasura, then turned to Vaṅgāla-deśa from where Govinda Candra fled, afterwards met Mahipala and put him to that fight in a hot battle, and therefore, invaded Uttaraladam as far as the Ganga. This shows Vahagala-desā was situated in southern half of East Barigal and and that the Chola king defeated Mahipal in the northern half thereof'[26]. Bhattasali says " the Tirumalai inscription of Rajendra Chola throws interesting light on the political condition of Bengal during the period of the invision by the Chola Emperor. The invader found one Dharmapala ruling over Dandabhukti, roughly the present district of Midnapur. Daksina Rāḍhā i.e. the district of Howrah and Hooghly was then ruled by a king of the Sura family, named Ranasura. After having destroyed the first and defeated the second, the invader appears to have crossed the Bhagirathi and entered the Vaṅgāla-deśa ruled over by king Govinda Candra. The Vaṅgāla king boldly met the invader. The weather appeal's to have fought in this favour by some heavy showers, as they find particular mention in the Tirumalai inscription. But nothing availed, and Govinda Candra had ultithately to get down from his royal elephant and flee, when the day turned against him. The invader then appeal's to have turned his arms againts Mahipal I, lord of Varendri, north of Gangas. The Pāla army, led by Mahipal in person, met the Chola army and a hot engagement ensued. Mahipala also shared the same fate as the Vaṅgāla king Govinda Candra, and the invader captured a number of women and elephants. He then re-crossed the Padma (Ganges) and entered Uttara-Rāḍhā, present Murshidabad and Birbhum districts, and again reached the banks of the Bhagirathi and returned home by the very route through which he had advanced"[27].

From this fact, it is clear that the Candra kings of south-east Bengal ruled over Samataṭa, Harikela. Vaṅga and Vaṅgāla-deśa (c.f. Copper-plates of Sn-candra, Ladalia Candra Govinda Candra and Tirumalai Rock inscription of Rajendra Chola). From the Tirumalai inscription, it indicates that the location of Vaṅgāla is in southern portion of Bengal. Roychowdhury suggests that " Vaṅga and Vaṅgāla are two separate countries and suggested that Vaṅgāla was probably identical with Candradvīpa 28. The Ablur inscription of Kalacurya Vijjala (1157-67 A.D.) mentions Vaṅga and Vaṅgāla separatly[29]. Hammira Mahākavya of Nayacandra suri (15 th century), which mentions Vaṅga and Vaṅgāla side by side[30]. The Goharwa plates of the Kalachuri King Karnadeva[31], the Tirumalai inscription of Rajendra Chola[32] the Nalanda inscription of Vipulasrimtra[3j] indicate the name of Vaṅgāla.

From the Nesari plates, the name Vaṅgāla has first come to over knowledge. The plate was dated in beginning of the 9th century A. D. From the beginning of the 9th century the name Vaṅgāla was well known and prosperous country. The Candradvīpa is now well established which is identical with Buekergunj district of . . Barishal division. Most probably, the name of Candṛadvīpa had come from the Candra of the Candra dynasty. It is noted that Trailokya Candra of Candra dynasty was first spread his power over that island (c.f.Copper plate grant of Śrī Candra). Mostprobably, from that time that island was named by Candradvīpa. Southern Baṅgāl also consisted of a group of small region in ancient time. It is essential to mention that the greater . - Faridpur and Barishal districts are southern Bengal. Most probably, these greater districts were known as Vaṅgāla. But the name Vaṅgāla was used in broader sense when the Candra dynasty was spread their power over south-eastern Bengal i.e., southern Bengal, Vaṅga, Samataṭa and Harikela.

From the south Indian inscriptions, name Vaṅgāl has come to our Knowledge. At the same time, Maināmatī copper-plates of Laḍaha Candra and Govinda Candra indicated the name Vaṅga. It is also mentioned that at the time of Laḍaha Candra and Govinda Candra, the Vaṅga was gradualy rising to prosperity pre-eminence and peace. So, it is clear that Vaṅga was the whole of south-eastern Bengal.

From the points of view, Vaṅgāla -deśa or Vaṅgāla and Vaṅga are identical in the llth century A. D. From the Vaṅga, Vaṅgāla, Vaṅgāla -deśa, it now presents Vaṅgāla -deśa i.e. Bangaladeśa.

SAMATAṬA

The name of the country, Samataṭa, mentioned for the first time on the Allahabad Posthumous stone pillar inscription of Samudra Gupta[34] as one of the most important among the north-east Indian frontier kingdoms which submitted to the mighty Gupta emperor. It was mentioned about the middle of the fourth century A. D. Samataṭa was associated with Davaka, Kāmarūpa[35], Nepal[36]. It is also mentioned in that plate that the king of Samataṭa giving all taxes and obeying (his) orders and going to perform obeisance. So,it is clear that the king of Samataṭa was a feudatory king under Samudrāgupta in the middle of the fourth century A. D. The Bṛhat Saṁhitā, the work of 6th century, mentioned the name of Samataṭa, was separated from Vaṅga[37]. The river Lauhitya, Samataṭa, Prāgjyotiṣa and the Bhadras are mentioned to the east[38].

Samataṭa is mentioned in the Karmāvibhaga of the Bṛhat Saṁhitā (chap- XIV) as an eastern country and was visited by Yuang Chwang, I-tsing and Seng-Chi, the celebrated Chinese travellers[39]. The famous Chinese travellers Yuan Chwang visited Samataṭa between 637-39 A. D. [40] It was mentioned by Yuang Chwang that from Kāmarūpa, Yuan Chwang went south and after a journey of 1200 li or 1300 li reached the country of Sa- mo-ta-ch. (Samataṭa)[41]. The country, Samataṭa was about 3000 li in circuit and the capital of the country was about 20 li in round. This country which was on the seaside and was low and moist. It was regularly cultivated and was rich in crops and flowers and fruits grew everywhere. The clithate was soft and the habits of the people agreeable. The men were hard by nature and of black complexion. It had more than 30 Buddhist monasteries and above 2000 priests. They were all of the *"Sthavim"* School There were some hundreds Deva temples, in which sectaries of all kinds of live. The naked ascetics called *Nirgranthas* are most numerous. Not far out of the city was a stūpa wich was built by Asokaraja. In this place, *tathāgata* in former days preached the deep and mysterious law for Sevsn days for the good of the Devas. Beside this, were vestiges of a sitting and an exercise place of the four Buddhas. Not far from this in a monastery, was a figure of Buddha of green jade. It was eight feet high showing all the distinctive characteristics and exercising marvelous powers.[42]

The pilgrim then names in succession six countries beyond Samataṭa : these were not visited by him but he gained information about them at Samataṭa. These six countries are 1. Shi-li-cha-ta-lo, the north-east among the hills near the sea, 2. South east from this on a Bay of the sea Kia-mo-laṅg-kia, (3) To-lo-po-ti, to the east of the preceding, (4) East from To-lo-po-ti was I-shang-na-pu-lo (5) To the east of this was mo-ha-chanpo, the lin-yi of the Chinese and (6). To the south west of this was the Yen-mo- na- cheu [J]. For instance" in the Si-Yu-Ki, Hiuen Tsiang (Records II 200) says that to the north east of Samataṭa is the country called Śrīkśetra to the south-east of this is Kamalaṅgka, to the east of this is Darapti (read Dvarapati)"[44]. The capital of Samataṭa (San - mo - ta - cha), is placed at from 1200 - 1300 li or 200 - 217 miles to the south of

Kāmarūpa and 900 li or 150 miles to the east of Tāmralipti or Tamluk[45]. The famous Chinese piligrim, Hiuen Tasang, who came Samataṭa about 635 A. D. speaks of 20 Buddhist monasteries in Puṇḍravarddhana or North Bengal, and 30 more in Samataṭa or south Bengal '. It, therefore, indicates that the kingdom Samataṭa was very famous in the beginning of the second quarter of the 7th century A. D. "Seng -chi a priest, went to India by the southern sea route and arrived at Samataṭa. The king of that country named Rājabhata (or Patu), a Upasaka, greatly reverenced the three objects of worship and devoted himself to his religious duties[47]". The king Rajabhata most probaly, is identical with the Rājarājabhaṭṭa of Ashrafpur copperplate. His main capital city was in Karmanta, which is identified with Badakamta of the Comilla district. Raychaudhuri suggests that "the kingdom of Samataṭa in the 7th century A. D. may be reasonably regarded as having comprised the area bounded by the old course of the lower Brahmaputra River in the north., Chittagong Hills in the east, and the Bay of Bengal on the south. A branch of the old Gangess (Padma) corresponding to modern Gorai and Madhuthati rivers[48] perhaps formed the western boundary. Bhattasali seems that "we remember that natural barriers such as mountains and river marked off one kingdom from another in those days, we can not but accept the plain tract of land bounded by the Garo and the Khasi Hills and the hills of Tippera or the north and east by the Lauhitya or the old Brahmaputra river on the west and by the bay of Bangal on the south as the ancient kingdom of Samataṭ a[49]. Dani suggests that Samataṭa Maṇḍala is generally supposed to include the trans Meghna tracts[50]. According to Law[51], Samataṭa is identical with delta of the Ganges and Brahmaputra and must have comprised, according to epigraphic evidence the modern district of Tipperah, Noakhali, Sylhet (J. A S. B. 1915, pp - 17 - 18) and portions probably of Barishal. According to Watters, Samataṭa is situated to the south of Dhaka in the district of the modern Faridpur[52]. Bbandarkar suggests that "it (Samataṭa) is taken as comprising the delta of the Ganges and

Bramhputra, of which the Jessore District forms the central portion. Its capital Karmmājā has been indentified with Kāmta in the Comilla district by Bhattasali (J. A.B. S. 19]4, P.P.85 f.f.)[S3]. Cunninggham suggests that "Samataṭa must the Delta of the Ganges; and as the country is described as 3000 li or 500 miles in circuit it must have included the whole of present Delta, or traiangular tract between the Bhagirathi River and the main strem of the Ganges'[4]".

From the stone pillar inscription of Samudrāgupta dated in the middle of the 4th century A. D. It has come to light that Samataṭa is situated in the eastern side of Bengal. The Gunaighar copper-plate inscription[33] of Vainyagupta, dated in the beginning of the 6th century A. D. was issued from Kripura (some where in Tripura), and the grant was discovered from a village tank at Gunaighar. The name of the village Gunikagrahara was mentioned in the plate, which might by identified with present Gunaighar. The donated lands of this grant were situated in the Uttara Mandalika. It might be mentioned in the northern side of Samataṭa Maṇḍala. From this fact, it is clear that western part of present Tripura and present Comilla were under Samataṭa Maṇḍala. Another copper-plate grant of Vainya Gupta was also found in the Sālvan Vihāra at Mainămatī. The Ashrafpur copper plate grants[56] of king Devakhadga were issued from the royal residence at Karmanta. It is identified with Baḍakāmtā near Mainămatī. it has come to light from these grants that Vikannpura area of Dhaka Vaṅga and Vaṅgāla were not included in Samataṭa. A gold plated Sarwani image caused to be made by Deva Khaḍga's queen Prabhāvatī was found in Deulbadi about 14 miles to the south of Comilla town. Bhaṭṭasali suggests that "Ashrafpur is near the bank of the old and the real Brahmaputa, the find place of two plates of Deva Khaḍga and Deulbadi sixty miles south east almost at the foot of the hills of Tippera, the find place of the present image mark respectively the western and eastern limits of Samataṭa the kingdom of the Khaḍgas[57]". Chaudhuri says that "The Gunaighar plate does not naturally contain any reference to the

Puṇḍravarddhanabhukti as by it land was granted in the Comilla area of south eastern Bengal[38]. Another three copper-plate grants of Khaḍga dynasty were discovered from Sālvan Vihāra of Maināmatī. From all these evidences, it shows that the Khaḍga kings ruled over Samataṭa Maṇḍala which was situated on the eastern side of Lauhitya i.e. old Bramhputra. The Kailan copper plate of Śrīdharaṇa Rāta was found in the village of Kailan 18 miles south - west of Comilla town and was issued from Devaparvata which was situated on the bank of the river Kṣīrodā. The river Kṣīrodā is identified with the modern Khira or Khirani which is a dried up river and branching of from the Gothati river just west of the town of Comilla. The copper plate grant of Ānanāda Deva was found in Salvn Vihāra excavation. It is known from the plate that Vasantapura was the newly constructed capitalcity of the king Ānanāda Deva. Most probably Devaparvata was the old Capital City. The copper plate grant of Bhava Deva was discovered from Sālvan Vihāra of Maināmatī. This grant was also issued from Devaparvata and dated in eight century A. D. The pascimbhag copper-plate grant of Śrī Candra which mentions Devaparavata situated on the river of Kṣīrodā in Samataṭa. It mentions also the name of the forest of Lālāmvi. There is no doubt that this Lālāmvi is identical with Lamai of Comolla distric.From these facts, there is no room for doubt that greater Comilla region was under Samataṭa Maṇḍala.

Maināmatī copper plate grants of Laḍaha Candra. Govinda Candra, Raṅavaṅkamall Harikala Deva and Vīradhara Deva and Mehar plate of Dāmodara Deva and Sobharampur plate of Dāmodara Deva all of the grant recorded lands under Samataṭa Maṇḍala.

The Samataṭa was just as a Maṇḍala (Division). From epigraphic evidences it shows that a group of Maṇḍala like Samataṭa Maṇḍala under independent ruling dynasties (like Candra dynasty). It does not find the name of Samataṭa Maṇḍala in Indian geography after the 13th century A. D[59].

From the references of Bṛahat Saṁhitā,a description of famous Chinese traveler, epigraphic evidences, it has come to light that from very beginning Samataṭa Maṇḍala was a separate kingdom from Candradvīpa. Vikramapura, Vaṅga, Vaṅgāla and Harikela. It was an easternmost kingdom, which was bounded by the Lauhitya river in the west and north Harikela Maṇḍala on the north east Tripura and Chittagong hills on the east and the Bay of Bengal on the south.

HARIKELA

The name of Harikela was found in the Rampal and Dhulla copper plate grants of Śrī Candra. The lexicographer Hemachandra identifies the Harikela and Harikali contury with Vaṅga and in the passage *"Vaṅgāstu Harikeliay"* in his Abhidhana Cintamam[fi0] (12 th century A. D.). But in Mañjūśrīmulklapa, Budhist work of 8th, century mentioned that Harikela, Samataṭa and Vaṅga were separated from each other but neighbouring century[61]. It is undoubtedly an earlier tradition regarding the location of that country is preserved in Kesava's Kalapadrukosa which says *"Śrīhaṭṭo Harikeliḥ syach = chrihato=pikvachid = bhave[62]"*. In Karpuramanjuri of Rajshekhara (9th century A. D.), which praises the women of Harikela region and also mentions that they were the inhabitants of the east[63]. In Dakarnav[64] it mentioned that there were sixty-four *"Tantrik Pitha"*. One of them was in Harikela and this Harikela was separated from Tikkara Khādi, Rāḍhā and Vaṅgāla-deśa. Thre are two Manuscripts (15th centuiy A. D.) in the University of Dhaka library collection. One is *Rudrākṣa Mahātya* (No.2141B, Folio1) and another one is *Rūpacintamunikośa* (No - 1451 Folio- 15A). Both of the manuscripts mention that Harikela is synonymous with Śrīhatta (Sylhet) adjacent to Kāmarūpa[65]. 7th century A. D. the famous Chinese pilgrim, I-tsing came to Harikela and stayed there for one year. Harikela is reffered to by I-tsing as the eastern limit of Eastern India. From here, he went to Mahābodhi Nalanda and Tiladha[66]. Basak suggests that Harikela was identical with Vaṅga in 10 tli -llth century whose capital was Vikramapura in those centuries[6']. According to a map from Japan, in 18th century A. D., Harikela was situated in the southern side of Tamralipti [68]. From the

Rampal copper plate grant of Śrī Candra, it appears that Purṇa Candra and Suvarṇa Candra were the first and second kings of Rohitagiri. i.e. Maināmatī-Lalmai area and Trailokya Candra, son of Suvarṇa Candra spread his power over Harikela and become a king of Candradvīpa. Paul suggests that "it was contiguous to Candradvīpa and Harikela might have included some portion of Bakerganj and Noakhali districts[69]". But from the present information. Harikela is situated on the northeastern side of Samataṭa and Candradvīpa is situated on the southwestern side of Samataṭa. It,therefore, clear that Samataṭa is situated in between Caudradvīpa and Harikela. Chittagong copper-plate grant of Kantideva™ disclosed the fact that Harikela was a Maṇḍala i.e. Division. So, it is undoubtedly true that Harikela was a separate kingdom from Samataṭa and Vaṅga.

From the epigraphic evidences it appears that present Sylhet division (i.e. Śrīhaṭṭa), was the Harikela Maṇḍala,is situated in the north eastern side of present Comilla district. Before arising the power of Candra dynasty (i.e. up to the beginning of 10th century), Harikela was a separate kingdom. When Trilokya Candra and his son Śrī Candra spread their power over Vaṅga, Vaṅgāla s Candradvīpa, Samataṭa, and Harikela by that time the name of Vaṅga was applied in a wider sense.

CANDRADVĪPA

The name of Candradvfpa was found in the Rampal and Dhulla copper-plate gants of Śrī Candra. The name Candradvīpa, was first noticed from the Rampal copper-plate grant of Śrī Candradeva. It mentions that Trailokya Candra, son of Suvarṇa Candra of Candra dynasty, was like Dilipa became a king of Candradvīpa and was the supporter of the Harikela king. Foucher reads, a manuscript, the work of 1015 A.D. on the obverse side as *"Harikela-dese-Śīla-Lokanātah"*. Or, "the Śīla-Lokanātha in the country of Harikela"and on the reverse side as *"Candradvīpā Bhagavati Tārā"* or, the goddess Tārā[72] in Candradvīpa. Candradvīpa is situated in southern Bengal.

From the Tirumalai Rock inscription of the king Rajendra Chola I, it has come to light that Vaṅgāla- deśa i.e, Southern Bangal was under the Candra King i.e. Govinda Candra. It therefore, seems to appear that the name Vaṅgāla-des'a was used in broader sense and by that time Candradvīpa was under Vaṅgāla-deśa. It is also noted that. Vikramapura was the capital city of Givinda Candra. Sahitya Parishat copper plate of Visvarupa Sena[73], mostprobably, mentions the name of Candraddvipa.The grant mentions the place name Kagharakatti-pataka that was situated in Candradvīpa (Candradvīpa). There is a hazar named Ghaghar-bazar at Kotalipara thana hi Gopalgunj district of south Bengal. This bazaar might be identified with Ghaghara Kaṭṭipāṭka. It is also noted that in that area, there are many villages, which end in Kathi. Paul appears that Candradvīpa and Harikela might have included some portion of Bakerganj and Nokhali districts[74]. But it has discussed in the identification of Samataṭa that Noakhali region was under Samataṭa area not in Bakerganj district. The district of Bakerganj is situated in southern side of Barishal town and the district of Nokhali is situated in the southern side of Comilla district. Sircar suggests that "Trailokya Candra was not a king of Harikela but was the ruler of Candradvīpa i.e. Bakla Candradvīpa in the present Buckergunja district[75],". Mitra belives to appear that "Candradvīpa was another locality in south eastern Bengal and is still a Pargana in the Bakerganj district. It might have included some portion of Khulna district Bagchi indicates that "Candradvīpa might have included some portion of Noakhali district[77]".Majumdar suggests that Candradvīpa was the home territory of the Candra dynasty[78]. Bhandarkar™ says that the kingdom of Candra family was Candradvīpa with its capital at Vikarmpura. Bajpai suggests that Candradvīpa is identical to Bakla - Candradvīpa[80]. Ain-E-Akbari mentions that Bakla Pargana and Candradvīpa both of them is same area[81].Alam seems to appear that "most probably Purṇa Chandra, taking advantage of the declining fortune of the

Pāla power under Narayana Pāla (855-908), conquered portions of lower Bengal in the closing years of 9th century, comprising Patuakhali and Barishal which was later on named Candradvīpa after his family name[82]" . But there is no epigraphic evidence that Purṇa Candra conqueres southern Bangal. From Rampal plate of Śrī Candra mentions that Trailokya Candra was a powerful ruler who ruled over Candradvīpa and was designated with *Mahārājādhirāja*.From the ins crip tion,it is also clear that Purṇa Candra and Suvarṇa Candra,were the local rulers of Rohitagiri region and some portion of present Gopalgongj district.From above mentioned description and the epigraphic evidences, it seems to appear' that Candradvīpa named greater Barishal district and Patuakhli district after the Candras family title.

PAṬṬIKERA AND PERANĀṬANA

The earliest reference to Paṭṭikera occurs in the manuscript of Aṣṭasahasrikā prajñapāramitā preserved in Library of the Cambridge University. This manuscript (ed. 1643 A.D.), copied in the year 1015 A. D. contains the picture of a sixteen armed goddess with label *"Paṭṭikera Cuṇḍāvara Bhavane Cuṇḍā*[83] *"*. The name of Paṭṭkera is also found in the Maināmatī copper-plate grants of Laḍaha Candra and Raṇavaṅkamalla Harikāladeva. The ancient character of Maināmatī area had come to our knowledge from an accidental discovery of the grant of Harikaladeva from Maināmatī area in 1803 A.D. One Śrī Dhādi Eba issued the grant. The inscription records a grant of lands measuring 20 dronas in a village named Bejakhanda, in favour of a Buddhist monastery, dedicated to the goddess Durgottārā. The monastery was built in the city of Paṭṭikera.The donated property was situated in the village of Bejakhanda. There is a village named Bejabādi near; the feet of the hills on the west. It might be identified with the village referred to in the plate.

From this grant there is no room for doubt that Paṭṭikera was a city. Both the copper plate grants of Laḍaha Candradeva mentioned the name of Paṭṭikera. From the second plate of

Laḍaha Candra, it was come to light that Paṭṭikera was under Peranāṭana Viṣaya i.e. the district of Peranāṭana of Samataṭa Maṇḍala under Pauṇḍrbhākti.

A large number of silver coins were recovered from three hoards from Sālvan Vihāra excavation. The coins are inscribed with the legends of Paṭṭikera. Another eight silver coins have already been recovered from Sylhet. The legend on the coins was first real by MacDowall[84] as *Yārikṛtya*. But Dani[85] later on read as Paṭṭikera..Phayre has published the coins of Arakan of Pegu and of Burma[86]. There is a similarity among the coins of Arakan and Maināmatī. In type, fabric and also on some of the coins have close similarity to these of the Arakanese Candra coins. Khan[87] seems to believe that some powerful local rulers issued these silver coins of Maināmatī in 8th - 9th centuries A. D.

It is certain from the epigraphic evidences that the city of Paṭṭikera, flourished around the area of modern Comilla district between 900 to 1050 A. D. and was an important city during the age of Candras whose existence is now definitely established from the evidence of Candra inscriptions. We also have found the history of Candra dynasty from the history of Lama Tārānaths. Though Tārānatha mentions them during the period 6th -8th century A. D. But there is no clear evidence to corroborate this statement, yet the dynasty did exist in. It is learnt from the inscription, coins and Burmese chronicles that they ruled in the Arakan region in the seventh century A.D even earlier . The existence of a line of Candra kings for 19 generations on a stone pillar, found on the platform of the Shittaung temple at Mrohaune in Arakan.[89]

The city of Pattikkera was well known to the 11th -12th century in Burmese and Arakanese chronicles. Anoratha (1044 - 77 A. D.) was one of the most powerful kings in the political history of Burma[90]. According to Hmannan, the kingdom of Anoratha was bounded on west by Patikkara (Arch. Sur. Report of Burma, 1928, p. 31), the country Kalas i.e. foreigners [91] Paul seems to think that in eleventh and twelvth centuries the kings of Burma had important political and social relations with the eastern part of Bengal i.e. the east of Brahmaputra . Burmese chronicles also unmistakably show cultural and political relations of Burma with Pateikara. The same test narrates the romantic love story of the prince of Pateikkara whose love for Shweinthi the only daughter of king Kyanzittha (1084-1112 A.D.) cost him his life[93]. In spite of the wish of the Burmese king, the marriage was impossible between the prince of Pateikkara and the princess of Burma due to the political issue, But Alaungsithu (1112-1187 A.D) the son of princes Shweinth, undoubtedly, had as one of his queens, a priencess of Pateikkara[94]. The king Narathu (1187-1191 A.D.) the son and successor of Alaungsithu, killed this Pateikkara princess, the widow of his father [?]. After hearing the news of the death of the Pateikkara princess, the king of Pateikkara decided to take revenge of his daughter's murder and sent eight faithful and desperate soldiers as disguised Brahmins to Pagan the capital city of Burma. All the Brahmins went into the kings place as if to bless the king and they killed him. All the soldiers killed themselves[96]. Paṭṭikera Princes and Princesses figure in the romances and tragedies, has become subject thatter of some extremely popular- tales, annals, poems and melo-dramas in Burma which are popular even today. It is true that this chronicle shows the political and cultural relation between Burma and Paṭṭikera.

According to Bhattacharya, "the city of Paṭṭikera was apparently situated some where in the Lalmai and Maināmatī hills where the plate was discovered and gave the name to an important paragaṇā in the district of Tippera, still known as Patikara or Paitkara which extends up to the same hills, though the Hills themselves now fall under a separate Pargana named Meherakula. In older documents of the 18th century the name of the Pargana occurs regularly as either Patikera or and Paitkera. leaving no room for any doubt on the identification[97]".

From the epigraphic evidences i.e. copper-plates, coins,

Manuscripts, the find-spot of these documents and the ancient structural monuments and the findings of other artifacts, show that Mainâmatī-Lalmai area was the forgotten city of Paṭṭikera of Samataṭa Maṇḍala.

ROHITAGIRI

The name of the mountain, Rohitagiri has first come to light from the Rampal[98] copper-plate of Śrī Candra.It is also noticed from the Dhulla plate of Śrī Candra[99].From the Candra grants, it is now well established that Purṇa Candra was the founder king of Candra dynasty. Purṇa Candra and his son Suvarṇa Candra, both of them did not titled with *Parameśvara Paramabhaṭṭārakā Mahārājādhirāja*. No invasion of them was recorded in any copperplate grants. It, therefore, shows that Purṇa Candra and his son Suvarṇa Candra were the local ruler of Rohitagiri respectively. Trailokya Candra, son of Suvarṇa Candra, made, first, inversion over Harikela and then Candradvīpa and conquered. Ray remarks that Purṇa Candra ruled in the latter half of the 9th century and came from the Shahabed district of Bihar rests[100]. Sircar suggests that the mountain Rohitagiri, identified with Rohtasgarh in the Shahabad district of Bihar and Trailokya or one of his ancestors migrated to SoutliEast Bengal[101]. Banerjee, identified Rohitagiri with Rotasgarh in the Shahabad district of Bihar[102]. Majumdar remarks that 'The Chandras do not seem to have originally belonged to Bengal. In verse '2' it is stated that they were rulers of Rohitagiri, which is identifiable with Rohitasgadh in the Sahabad district of Bihar. They emigrated to Eastern Bengal, and most probably taking advantage of the weakness of the declining Pāla power carved out a kingdom for themselves[103]". Ganguly remarks that " The names of the kings of the Gahadavala dynasty of Kanauj end in Candra. Nobody, however, thinks that they had any connection with the Candras of East Bengal[104].

But it is undoubtedly clear from the Rampal and Dhulla copper-plate inscription of Śrī Candra that Purṇa Candra founder of Candra dynasty and Suvarṇa Candra son of Purṇa Candra, were the rulers of Rohitagiri. After migration, from one place to another, all on a sudden, nobody can become a king of that new area. It is also noted that no evidences have been found of any Candra kings as ever having ruled in Rohatasgarh of Shabad district in Bihar. But *Rohita* means red or red-coloured and *Giri* means mountain. *Rohitagiri,* therefore, means red-coloured mountain. Pascimbhag copper[105]plate of Śrī Candra states that whose soldiers conquered Samataṭa where was situated the forest of Lālāmvi traditionally said to have been filled with sure medicinal herbs" *Lāl* means red *and Amba or Ambi* means mother. Lālāmbi, means red-mother. In Indian sub-continent, Earth or Bhumi or land is known as mother. The name, Lālāmai, is still survived in Comilla district. *Lal* means red and *mai* means mother. So, Lālāmvi means red-mother. So, there is no room for doubt that Lālāmai is identical with Lālāmbi. It is also noted that the name of the *Lohita (=* Lauhitya) river is situated on the western side of the kingdom of Samataṭa and not far from Maināmatī-Lalmai hill range. *Lohita* means red or red-coloured. There is a village named Rohitar-par still survived in the district of Chandpur, a few miles west from Maināmatī-Lalmai hill-range on the bank of the river present Meghna. Rohitar-par might be meant as bank of the river Rohita (= Lohita). From the map of Phonden-Brook (in 1660 A.D.), it appears that Maināmatī-Lalmai hill rang was very very near to the river Lauhitya i.e. Brahmaputra in ancient time.The geological description of Maināmatī-Lālmai states the colour of the soil is red.From the above discussion, it has come to light that Rohita, Lohita, Lauhitya, Lālāmvi and Lālmai, all are synonymous. Mitra suggests that Rohitagiri is identical with Rangamati in the Hill Tippera[106]. Long ago Bhattasali[107] correctly identified Rohitagiri with the Lālmai range of Comilla district. From all probabilities, it can be concluded that Rohitagiri is identical with Maināmatī-Lalmai hill range.

DEVAPARVATA

The name of Devaparvata was first noticed from the copper-plate grant Śrīdharaṇa Rāta[108]. It is also mentioned in the Maināmatī copper-plate grants[109]. Bālabhaṭṭa, Bhavadeva and Pascimbaga copper-plate grant of Śrī Candra . The entire grant mentioned that Devaparvata was situated in Samataṭa Maṇḍala. It is also noticed that Devaparvata was situated on the bank of the modern river Kṣīrodā. The river Kṣīrodā is the modern Khirā or Khirnāi a dried up river course still traceable as branching off from the Gumati, just west of the town of Comilla. It flows by the eastern side of the Maināmatī hills and skirts the southern end of the hills near the Caṇḍī Murā peak, were another branch of the river meets it flowing by the western side of the hill. The river thus surrounds the southern and of the Maināmatī hills, were the ancient hill fort of Devaparvata seems to have been situated and then runs southwest to fall into the Dakatia river[111].

But Caṇḍī Murā is not to be seemed as an administrative center. The detail description of Caṇḍī Murā has given in Chapter II. The palace and Temple of Queen Maināmatī (ST -1, Local name) is situated on the northernmost limit of the Maināmatī Lalmai hill range. The inscription of Bhavadeva indicates that Devaparvata has a raised mound and a temple that reaches upward as if to touch the sky[112]. Searching for traces of the Kṣīrodā, old river course, nothing was found within a quarter of a mile of the southern tip. However the old Khirā River cut past the northern tip of the hills and drained down the western side of the hills towards the south and extensive deposits of sand were found below this mound in a broad track heading south. About four miles south the track was about one hundred yards in breadth and at least fifteen feet deep (a farmer was digging a well at that point). According to the inscription Devaparvata was the Camp of Victory or the Capital city. The Pakistan Department of Archaeology during 1965-66 excavation season had completed test excavation. From this excavation, it (ST-1) seems to be as an administrative center. So the palace of Queen Mainamatī can be identified with Devaparvata,

BEJAKHAṆḌA

The name of a village Bejakhaṇḍa was noticed from the Maināmatī copper-plate grant of Raṇavaṅkamalla Harikala Deva. There is a village near the feet of the hills on the west which may be identified with the Village Bejakhaṇḍa.

VIKRAMAPURA

The name of Vikramapura was found in the Maināmatī copper-plate grants of Laḍaha Candra and Govinda Candra and all the Candra copper-plate grants. It is identified with the ruins of Vikramapura in Munshiganj district. Now a days, it is known as Vikramapura. It was the Capital City of Candra dynasty of southeast Bengal.

IDENTIFICATION OF THE RIVER NAMES

GAṄGĀ

The name of the holy River Gaṅgā was found in the Maināmatī copper-plate grants of Laḍaha Candra. It is known to all from the very beginning to till today. It is mentioned in the Rg-Veda and Aitareya Brāmaṇa. (Ṛg-Veda, X, 75; Atitareya Brāhmaṇa VIII. 14,4). The course of the Ganges is described with some detail in the Bṛhat Dharma. P. (Madhya. Kli. ch. 22). The main stream[113] of the river originally passed southwards, after leaving Jahnu Aśrama at Sultanganj, through the channal of the Bhagirathi when with the Jellinghi forms the river Hilgli from Shibganj above Boalia. There are six Jahnus which are allegorical representations of changes in the course of the Ganges: 1st, at Bhairavghati below Gaṅgotri at the junction of the Bhagirathi and Jahnavi (Ram. I. 43); 2nd, at Kanyakubja or Kanauj (Viṣṇu-Dharmottara. P. 1, ch, 28); 3rd, at Jahngira in Sultanganj on the west of Bhagalpur (Arch. S. Rep., XV. p. 20 Brahad dharma. P. Purva. kh, ch. 6; J.A.S.B, XXXIII, 360); 4th, at Sibganj above Rampur Boalia; 5th, at Gour near Malda (Martin's Eastern India ; Hamiltion's East

India gazetteer , S.V. Gour III, 81); 6 m, at Jannagar (Brahmanitala) 4 miles to the west of Nadia, (Navadvipa Parikrama, Chaunder's Travels of a Hindu).

The Ganges after flowing past Triveni, Chagda, Goria, Baruipur, Rajganj and Diamond Harbour through Adiganga or Tolly's Nala falls into the sea near Sagar Island (Rev.J.Long's Banks of the Bhagirathi. In Calcutta review vi (1846. P. 403; cotton's Calcutta, Old and New)

YAMUNĀ

The name of the river Yamunā was noticed from the copper-plate of grant of Laḍaha Candra. It is also mentioned in the R g. Veda and the Aitareya Brāhmaṇa (VIII., 14. 4; Ṛg. Veda, x, 75)

LAUHITYA

The name of the river Lauhitya was found in the copper plate grant of Govinda Candra. The river Lauhitya Samataṭa, Prāgjyotiṣa and the Bhadras are mentioned in Bṛhat Samāhitā to the east[114]. The Lauhitya is identified with the Brahmaputra. A tributary of this river is even now called Lohit[115]. It is also mentioned in MarfabaRāta and Raghuvaṁśa (Mbh, Bhīṣma. P, Ch. 9; Raghuvamsa, Ch. IV, V. 81). Parasmima's axe fell from his hand when he bathed in this river, owing to the sin of killing his mother. According to Kālidāsa, the river was the boundary of Prāgjyotiṣa or Gauhati in Assam (Raghuvaṁśa, IV, V. 81)[116]

The Principal River of Assam was also known as Lohitya or Lauhitya (B. Ch. 64; Raghu. IV. 81; Yogini Tantra. 2. 2. 119) which formed the eastern boundery of Prāgjyotiṣa[117].

KṢĪRODĀ

The name of the river Kṣīrodā was found in the copper-plate grant of Bālabhaṭṭa. Bhatasali pointed out that the river Kṣīrodā is the modern Khirā or Khirnāi, a dried up river course still traceable as bruncliing off from the Gothati just west of the town of Comilla.Sircar suggests that it flows by the eastern side of the Maināmatī hills and skirts the southern part of the lulls near the Caṇḍī Murā peak, where another branch of the river meets it flowing by the western side of the hill[118]. But searching for traces of the Kṣīrodā, Old River course, nothing was found within a quarter of a mile of the southern tip, However, the old Khirā River cut past the northern tip of the hills and drained down the western side of the hills towards the south and extensive deposits of sand were found below this mound in a broad track-heading south. About four miles south, the track was about one hundred yards in breadth and at least fifteen feet deep (A farmer was digging a well at that point) So. This Khira could be identified with the Kṣīrodā River.

BUḌḌHI GAṄGINĪ

The name of the river Buḍḍhi Gaṅginī was traced in the Maināmatī copper-plate grant of Laḍaha Candradeva. According to Dani, "This River need not be the modern Buri Ganga, which flows by the city of Dacca[119]". There is a river named Budi Nadi (Old River) flows by the north-western side of the Comilla town. At present, it is known as a small river. There are so many big lakes by the side of this river. It shows that in ancient time, it was a big river in Samataṭa Maṇḍala. Locally it is also known as Budi Ganga Nadi. This Budi Ganga Nadi could be identified with the ancient Buḍḍhi Gaṅginī.

IDENTIFICATION OF THE FOREIGN COUNTRY

KAMĀRŪPA AND PRĀGJYOTIṢA

It was mentioned in his travels by Yuang Chwang that from Kāmarūpa, he went to south and after a journey of 1200 li or 1300 li reached the country of'Sa-mo-ta-ch' (Samataṭa) [120]. He visited Samataṭa between 637-39 A. D. Bṛhat Saṁhitā,the work of 6th century A.D., it is mentioned that the river Lauhitya, Samataṭa Prāgjyotiṣa and the Bhadras are to the east 121 . According to Pargitar, the early kingdom of Prāgjyotiṣa comprised the major part of modern Assam together with the Jalpaguri, Cochbihar, Rangpur, Bogra, Mymensingh, Dhaka and Tippera distrcts and parts of the Pabna district in Bengal and probably also the eastern areas of Nepal . The modern district of Kamarapur extends from Goalpara to Gauhati. Its capital is called Prāgjyotiṣa in the Purāṇa (Kalika. P. Ch. 38), which has been identified with Kāmākhyā or Gauhati (J.R.A.S. 1900 p-25) Kāmākhyā is one of the pithas containing the temple of the celebrated Kāmākhyā Devī on the Nilla hill or Nilakuta- Parvata (Kalika P. ch. 62); it is two miles from Gauhati Raja Niladhvaja found another Capital Komotapura (The modern Kathatapur in Coohbihar, Imp. Gaz. S.V. Rangpur districts). On the opposite or north side of the river Brahmaputra, is situated a hill called Asva Kranta Parvata where Kṛṣṇa is said to have fought with Narākāsura (Brahat Dharma. P. Madhya Kh. ch. 10 and Brahma P. ch. 51; JRAS, 1900, p. 25). The temple of Tamreśvarīdevī or the copper temple called by Buchanan the eastern Kāmākhyā. On the river Dalpani is situated near the north eastern boundary of the ancient Kalmarupa (J.A.S.B, XVII, p. 462). Buchanan suggests that Assam; on the north it included Bhutan on the south it was bounded by the confluence of the Brahmaputra and the Lakhya and Vaṅga and included Manipur,Jayantiya,Kachhar and parts of Mymensingh and Sylhet (Buchanans Account of Rangpur in J.A.S.B. 1838 P. I.). Barua refers to Pargiter's views and suggests that the western boundary of Prāgjyotiṣa was the Kosi River in Bihar and that the Purnea disrict was included in it[123].

The views of Pargitar and Barua, however clearly go against the epic and Puranic tradition regarding Vāsudeva (i.e,Vasudeva,the king of Puṇḍras). Pauṇḍraka, the epigraphic and literary evidence about the location of the land of the Puṇḍras in north Bengal and of Prāgjyotiṣa or Kāmarūpa in the Brahmaputra valley and the Chinese Tang-Shu and the Kalika Purāṇa and Yogini Tantra, stating clearly that the western buoundary of Prāgjyotiṣa-Kāmarūpa was the river Karatoya[124] . According to Kalika Purāṇa (ch. 38) complied in the Assam region during the early medieval period Naraka. Son of the god Viṣṇu and the goddess earth was taken to Prāgjyotiṣa near the temple of Kāmākhyā in the heart of Kāmarūpa. It drove out the Kirāta inhabitants of the country from the area between the Karatoya in the west and the Dikkaravasini and Lalitakanta in the east[125].

According to Yogini-tantra, Kāmarūpa was bounded in the north by the Kanjagiri or Kancanadri (probably the Kaneanjunga) in Nepal in the west by the Karatoya, in the east by the Dikṣu river or Dikkaravasina, and in the south by the Brahmaputra Sangama or the confluence of the Brahmputra and the Lakṣā[126] . The Dikṣu is no other than modern Dikhu falling in the Brahmputra near Śivsāgar in Assam which the Lakṣā is the modern Lakhya, which joins the Brahmputra in the Mymensing district of Bangal[127].

The MahābhāRāta (V. 4. 11; xi. 23. 10) states that Bhagadatta as purva sagarvasin while the Ramāyāṇa (IV. 42.30-31) states that Prāgiyotiṣapura the city of Bhagadattas father Naraka was situated on the Viaraha mountain in the sea. The MahābhāRāta (II. 26. 9; 33. 9-10) also represents Bhagadatta as the leader of the Cinas, Kirātas, Mleccha and Sagaranupavasins. It is, therefore, interesting to note that, in the course of Arjuna's digvijaya in the north, he is said to have defeated Bhagadatta leading the Cinas, Kirātas and Śagaranupavasins (Mabh.l 1.26.9) while Bhima in his expedition in the east is said to have reached the Lauhity a valley and defeated the Mleccha rulers and the Sagarnupavasins (Mbh, II, 30-26-27).

We learn from the Maināmatī copper-plate grants of Candras that they had hostile relations not only with the Gauḍas but also with the Kamarpur. Śrī Candras army entered into the valley of the Lauhitya in order to conquer Kāmarūpa and evidently reached the interior of Prāgjyotiṣa of the country. He is also said to have defeated the king of Prāgjyotiṣa.Bhat suggests that Prāgjyotiṣa is the region around Gauhati[128].According to Raghuvaṁśa (IV.81),it lays on the other bank of the river Lauhitya. Hemacadra tells in his Abhidhānacintāmaṇi (IV.22) that Prāgjyotiṣa is the same as Kāmarūpa.

In all probabilities it might be suggested that Kāmarpura was bounded by the old Brahmaputra on the south, the Karatoya on the west Himalayas on the north and the Dikhu on the east of which the Capital City was Pārgjyotiṣa.

ŚRĪKṢETRA

The name of Śrīkṣetra was noticed from the Maināmatī copper-plate grant of Ānanda Deva of early Deva dynasty. For instance in the Si-Yu-Ki, Hiuen Tsiang (Records ii 200) says that to the north east of Samataṭa is the country called Śrīkṣetra,to the south east of this is Kamalaṅgka, to the east of this is Darapati (read Dvarapti)[129]

OḌḌAYANA

The name of Oḍḍayana was noticed to our knowledge from the copper-plate grant of Ānanda deva. There is difference of opinions about the location of Oḍḍayana or Oḍḍiyana (Uḍḍiyana, Oḍiyana, Oḍyana), region as mentioned in different works and some scholars attempted to located the place in Orissa region others in Kāmarūpa. But in the inscription of Ānanda Deva indicated that Jayabhauti and his forefathers beginning from Pusyabhuti, Pusyabhuti,s son was Somabhuti left his native land Oḍḍayana and at first settled in Magadha from where he again migrated to Bengal. From this fact, it most probably appears that Oḍḍayana is identified with well-known Orissa region instead of Kāmarūpa.

MAGADHA

The name Magadha is known to us from the copper-plate grant of Ānanda Deva. It is the province of Bihar or probably south Bihar (Rāmāyaṇa, Ādi. ch. 2, Mbh, Sabhā P. Ch. 24). Its western boundary was the river Sona. The name of Magadha first appears in the Atharva Saṁhitā, v 22, 14; xv. 2. The ancient capital of Magadha was Girivrajapura[130] (Modern Rajgir) at the time of Jarāsandha who was killed by Bhīma one of the five Pāṇḍavas.

The capital was subsequently removed to Pāṭaliputra,

which was formerly an insignificant village called by the name of Pāṭaligrama enlarged by Ajātaśatru, King of Magadha and contemporary of Buddha, to repeal the advance of the Vrijjis of Vaisali Udayasva the grandson of Ajatasatru is said to have removed the capital from Rajagrah to Patliputra (Vayu P. II ch 37, 369). The country of Magdha extended once south of Ganges from Benares to Monghyr, and southwards as far as Singhbhum. The people of the neighbouring district still call the districts of Patna and Gaya by the name of Maga which is a corruption of Magadha. In the Lalitavistara (ch. 17) Gayasirsha is placed in Magadha. it was originaly inhabited by the Cheras and the Kols who were considered Asuras by the Āryans. After the Andhrabhṛtyas of Pāṭaliputra, the Guptas reigned in Magadha. According to Cunningham, the Gupta era commenced in 319 A.D, when Mahāraja Gupta ascended the throne, whereas according to Fleet[131], it commenced in 320 A.D, when Candra Gupta-1 ascended the throne of Magadha.

GAUḌA

The name of Gauḍa is noticed in the Maināmatī copper-plate grants of Laḍaha Candra and Govinda Candra. It is now well established. The whole of Bengal was denominated eastern Gauḍa from its capital of the same name, the ruins of which lie near Malda at a distance of about ten miles. It was situated on the bank of the Ganges, it was the capital of Pālas, Senas and the Mahammadam rulers. Cunningham says, "Gonda, a suldivision of Uttara-Kosala forty-two miles south of Sravasti, is a corrupt form of Gauḍa[133] .

VĀRĀṆASĪ

The name of Vārāṇasī was recorded in the copper-plate grants of Laḍaha Candra and Govinda Candra. It is now well known to all. It is identical with Benares. Benares is situated at the juction of the river Varna and Asi from which the name of the town has been derived (Vamana. P, ch. III). It was formerly situated at the confluence of the Ganges and Gumti (Mbh, Anuś āsana, ch 30). It was the capital of Kāsi (Rāmāyaṇa Uttara ch

48)- At the time of Buddha, the kingdom of Kāsi formed a part of the kingdom of Kosala. According to James Prinsep, Benares or Kāsi was found by Kasa or Kāsirāja, a descendant of the Pururavas, king of Pratisthana. Benares was conquered by Muhammed Ghouri who defeated Jayachand of Kanauj[134] . "In the 7th century, it was visited by the fampus Chinese traveller Yuang Chwang. He has thus described the city and its presiding god Viśveśvara, one of the twelve Great Liṅgas of Mahādeva. "In the capital there are twenty Deva temples, the towers and halls of which are of sculptured with stone and cut wood. The foliage of trees combines to shade (the site) .... The statue of Deva Mahesvara, made of teou-shin (brass) is somewhat less than 100 feet high". The Padma P. (Uttara. ch. 67) mentions the names of Viśveśvara Bindumādhava and Jnanavapi in Kāsi. Benares is said to be the birth place Kasyapa Buddha, but Fa-Hian[135] says that he was born at Too-wei, which has been identified by Cunningham[136], with Tadwa or Tandwa, nine miles to be the west of Sravasti. According to Buddhaghosha, Kasyapa was born at Banaras and died at Mrigadava or modern Sarnath . In Yuavanjaya Jataka (Jatakas Iv. 75), the ancient name of Banaras is said to have been Surandhana, Sudarsana, Brahmavarddhana, Puṣhpavati and Ramya.

NON - IDENTIFIED PLACE NAMES OF THE MAINĀMATĪ COPPER PLATE GRANTS

1. Gaṅgā Maṇḍala Viṣaya
2. Vatagaṅagā Viṣaya
3. Vansantapura
4. Guptināṭana
5. Salihrada pattana
6. Dhanalakṣmitala pāṭak
7. Māyu pāṭaka
8. Campāvani
9. Pullahadā

10. Dollavāyikā
11. Govindoncama
12. Oḍa-Godhāni
13. Godhāni
14. Katakaṣila
15. ŚāhaRātalāka
16. Karavatti Voraka
17. Sura Voraka Grāma
18. Brāhmaṇadeva Voraka Grāma
19. Kaṅsārokaddpolaka Grāma
20. Vappasimha Vorak Grāma
21. Jayalambha Grāma
22. Mahādeva Grāma
23 . Buddha Nandi Grāma
24. Adhavasa Grāma
25. Mesvavarta Grāma
26. Vaggura bhoga
27. Valleśvara
28. Naroraka
29. Dhṛtipura Hattika

It has come to light from the copper-plate grants of Maināmatī that all the above mentioned name are situated in Samataṭa Maṇḍala. Most probably, all of them are located in the greater Comilla district near the findspot of these plates.

EXPLANTION AND MEANINGS OF THE TECHNICAL TERMS OF THE MAINĀMATĪ COPPER-PLATE GRANTS

The following terms are found in Maināmatī copper-plate grants of various dynasties. Most of the terms denoting officials titles are, at present, obsolate. The explanations and meanings are given here with the help of Kauṭilya Arthaśāstra, the Sanskrit English Dictionary of M.M. Williams and V.S. Apte and rarely devided from the context. The terms are arranged alphabetically. The five terms indicating land measurement units are given at the end, followed by a table of their relations.

1. अध्यक्ष - A departmental head; Director; Superintendent. According to M. M. Williams, preceptible to the sense observable; exrcising supervision; an inspector, superitendent (Col- 1, p. 23). According to Kauṭ iliya Arthaśāstra, the *adhyakṣas* may be clasifed as follows: (1) the assistants of the *samnidhatr* in charge of state goods; (2) those in charge of state establishment, *aśvadhyakśa, hastyadhkśa* and his assistants and the like; (3) Those in charge of mining and industry, *akaradhyakśa* and his assistants, *sutradhyakśa, suradhakśa* and so on; and (4) those who control trade, *panyadhykśa, samsthadhyakśa,* and others. It is to be noted that the writer of *sasanas* or decrees , a subject with which Kauṭilya claims to have dealt with for the first time, is not named as *śāsanādhydkśa;* he is referred to only as *lekhaka* (2.10.3).[138]

2. अमात्य - Minister. According to M.M. Williams, inthate of the same house, belonging to the same house or family, R.V, VII, 15,3; 'a companion (of a king)', minister, M.Bh. (col-2, p. 81); According to Kauṭiliya Arthaśātra, Constitutionally, the state functionary next in importance to the king is the *'Athātya'.* The functions of the *athātya* are stated to be: *mantra,* consultations, *karmanusthana,* execution of under takings, *daṇḍapranayana,* leadership of troops, *Śūnyanivesopacayall,* settlement and development of new territories, *daṇḍakaranugraha,* recovery of fines and taxes and so on (8.1.8,23). In a few places in the text, however, *athātya* seems restricted to the chief minister, who is in charge of the entire administration and is in fact in a position to be a King-maker, as in chapter 5.6. Such an *athatya* is evidently the same as the *mantrin,* who is the most prominent dignitary in the state, as in 9.3.12-13 and other places[139].

3.कोट्टपाल- Protector of a fort. According to M.M.Williams, the commander of a stronghold (Col-3, p. 312). Most probably, it is same as modern *Kotwal* for prefect of city police.

4.गौल्मिक - Military or police officer. According to Williams a single soldier of a troop, M.Bh. X, 359. X. 4.19; the chief of a troop, Inscri (10 th Century) (Col- 2, p. 370); "an overseer or superintendent of forests" -Kielhorn (E. I, Vol.- IV, p. 253) and Fleet (C.I.I, Vol.-III, p. 52).

5.चाट - According to Williams, a cheat, rouge (Col - 3, p. 391). "The head of a *Parganā*" (Vogel's Chamba, pp. 130 32),flatterer (E. I, Vol.- XI, p. 176); rogue (E. I, Vol.- IX, p. 296- 299) and irregular soldiers (E. I, Vol.- XI, p. 19); swindler (V.S. Apte, Col - 2, p. 431), frequently joined *with Bhaṭa* in Inscription.

6.चौरोद्धरणिक - Police official. Accroding to Williams, thief - extirpator; a thief catcher (Col- 1, p. 403); a class of police officers (Vogel's Chamba, p. 129).

7.दण्डनायक - Judge. According to Williams, rod applier, a judge (Col - 3, p. 466). Kangle, describes the meaning of *daṇḍa* in the light of *Kautiliya Arthāśastra.,* "How is the ruler to ensure the protection of the subject ? That is to be done with the holp of *daṇḍa* which is the symbol of the rulers authority (1.4.16) with the help of *daṇḍa,* the ruler is to prevent might from proving right and to enable the weak to hold thire own against the strong. In the absence of *daṇḍa* the strong would swallow up the weak and there would be anarchy everywere (1.4.13-15). It is of course obvious that *daṇḍa* represents the coercive power of the state." [140]

8. दण्डपाशिक- officer entrusted with the punishment of criminals. According to Williams, *Danda Pāśika* means" "a policeman" (Col- 3.p-466 and Col -1 p. 467). According to Apte, "a head police officer" (Col - 1, p. 490). a kind of police officer (Vogels Chamba, p. 130).

9.दुर्गोत्तारा- Buddist goddess. The form of Tārā named in the *Sādhanamālā* as *Durgottārinī Tārā (* Sādhanamālā, Vol.-1, pp. 237 - 8).

10.दौस्साधसाधनिक - Officer in charge of difficult jobs, probably intelligence duties.

11. धर्मचक्रमुद्रा - A Buddhist seal. According to Williams, *Dharmacakra* means, "the wheel or range of the law," M.Bh, Buddha; Jain; (Col- 1, p. 511).

12.नौबलहस्त्यश्वगोमहिषाजाविकादि - Fleet, infantry, elephant, corps, cavalry, Cows, buffaloes, goats, sheep, etc.

13.परम- The great. Accordrng to Williams, most distant, remotest, exterme, last; chief, highest, primary, most excellent, worst; Superior or inferior to, better or worse than, M.Bh; R; highest point, extreme limit, M.Bh. (Col -1, p. 5S8).

14.परमभट्टारक-The great warrior. Accordrng to Williams, *Bhaṭṭāraka* means - a great lord, Venerable or worshipful person (used of gods and of great or learned men, esp. of Buddist teachers and of a partic class of S'aiva monks). (Col-2, p. 745).

15.परमसौगत - The great follower of Saugata i.e. Buddha. According to Williams, *Saugata* means Buddhistic, Kathās; Sarvad; N. of a son of Dhṛltarāṣṭra, M.Bh, (Col -1,p.1252).

16.परमेश्वर - The great lord. - Regnal year.

17.पादीय सम्वत - Regnalyear.

18.भट- A royal servant. According to Williams, a mercenary hired soldier, warrior, combatant, M.Bh; (Col -1, p. 745). Freqquently joined with *Cata* in inscription.

19.भुक्ति- Province a largest administrative Division.

20.भूमिच्छिद्र- In the light of Kauṭiliya Arthaśāstra, Kangle seems to take the expression to mean "Land which can not be used for agriculture because it is unsuited for it is called *bhumicchidra* a weakness in the land, i.e. inferior type of land. It is to be used either for pastures or forests (2.21. ff). Two kinds of forests are distinguished, the *dravyavana* for various kinds of forest produce and the *hastivana* as a sanctuary for elephants. The latter has little economic value, the elephants being mainly intended for purposes of war (2.2.13-14). The principal produce of the *dravyavana* would appear to be timber and wood of all kinds as well as base metals like iron, copper, lead etc. (2.17.4 ff.). There can be doubt that both kinds of forests belong to the state."[141]

21.भूमिच्छिद्रन्यायेन- According to the law of *Bhumicchidra*.

22.मण्डल - Division. It is smaller than *Bhukti* i.e. province e.g. Samataṭa Maṇḍala was under Pauṇḍrabhukti. According to Williams, circular, round; a circle, globe, orb, ring, circumference, ball, wheel; the path or orbit of a heavenly body, sūryas; a halo round the sun or moon, a ball for playing, M.Bh, a circular array of troops, M.Bh; Kam; a district, arrondissement territory , province, country (often at the end of the modern names, e.g. Coro mandala); a surrounding district of neighbouring, state the circle of a kings near and distant neighbours (with whom he must maintain political and diplothatic relations; 4 or 6 or 10 or even 12 such neighbouring princes are enumerated); a multitude, group, band, collection, whole body, society, company; a division or book of the Ṛg-Veda (of which there are 10, according to authorship of the hymps; these are divided in to 85 *Anuvakas* or lessons, and these again into 1017, or with the II additional hymps; the other more mechanical division is into *Aṣhṭakas, Adhyāyas* and Varagas).(Col-3, p. 775).

23. **मण्डलपति** - Head of a division.

24. **महा**- the great.

25. **महाप्रतिहार** - High chamberlain. According to Williams, a chief door-keeper.(Clo-3, p. 797).

26. **महाराजाधिराज**- the over lord of the great king. According to Williams, *Mahārāja* means, a great king, reigning prince, supreme sovereign (Col-3, p. 799) and *Adirāja* meand a supreme king (Col-3, p. 21).

27. **महाव्यूहपति** - The great general. According to M.M.Williams, *Vyūhapati* means -placing apart, distribution, arrangement, orderly arrangement of the parts of a whole, disposition, military array, an army, host, squadron (Col-1, p. 1041).

28. **महाश्वनिबन्धिक**- The chief officer of the horses.

29. **महासर्वाधिकृत** -Chif superintendent. According to Williams, *Sarvā* means 'whole, . entire, all, every (Col-3,p.1184) and *Adhikṛta* means placed at the head of; apointed; ruled, administered; claimed; a superintendent (Col-3,p.20).

30. महासान्धिविग्रहिक-High minister for war and peace or minister of foreign affairs. According to Williams, *Sandhivigrahika* means "a secretary for managing (foreign) affairs in making peace and war, the minister presiding over the above affairs, superintendence over the affairs, of peace and war, a chief foreign minister (Col-1, p. 1145).

31. महासेनापति -The commander in chief. According to Williams, N. of Kārttikeya; of Siva, MBh; of a son of Dhṛitarāṣṭra; the chief commander of an army (Col-3, p. 1246). According to Kangle, " The designation Senāpati is mentioned in the Kautiliy Arthaṣāstra. The *Senāpati* is such a context is to be understood as the commander in chief of all armed forces."[142]

32. महाक्षपटलिक -Accountant General According to Williams, a chief keeper of archives (Col-2, p. 795).Accprding to Kangle, *Akṣapatal* means 'the records and audit office.'[143] According to Stein, *Akṣapatala* means 'Accountant General's office' (Vogel's Chamba, p. 133).

33. राजामात्य-Royal minister. According to Williams, inthate of the same house, belonging to the same house or family, R.V. VII, 15,3; 'a companion (of a king), minister, MBh. (Col-2, p. 81). A minister or councillor attached to a chief (Vogel's Chamba, p. 122).

34. राज्ञी- the queen. According to Williams, a queen, princess, the wife of a king; of the wife of the sun, Pur;(Col- 1 , p. 875).

35. राजपुत्र -Royal prince. According to Williams, prince—a Rajput (who claims decent from the ancient Kṣatriyas). (Col-2, p. 873).

36. राजपुरुष-Royal servants. According to Majumdar N.G ; a state officer; (1.B, p. 187).

37. राणक- A feudal king.

38. विधिवत्- Duly. According to Williams, according to rule, duly (Col-1, p. 968).

39. विधिवदुदकपूर्वकम्- Ceremoniously after doing the water rite.

40. विष्णुचक्रमुद्रा - the seal of disc of Viṣṇu. According to Williams. Viṣṇu's discus, R; a Partic mystical circle (formed from the lines in the hand) (Col-3, p. 999).

41. विषयपति-the head of a district. According to Williams, Viṣaya means dominion, kingdom, territory, region, district Country (Col-1, p. 997) and *Viṣayapati* means the governor of a province (Col-2, p. 997). "Officer in charge of a District". Vogel's Chamba, p. 124, See Fleet, Corp. Ins. Ind, Vol.-III, p. 32.

42. विहार- Buddhist monastery. According to Williams, distribution, transposition (of words) : arrangement or dispositiion (of the 3 sacred fires) ; also applied to the fiers themselves or the space between them); a place of recreation, pleasure ground MBh; (with Buddhist or Jains) a monastery or temple (orginally a hall where the monks met or walked about; afterwards these halls were used as temples); (Col-3, p. 1003).

43. शकाब्द - the Śaka era. According to Williams the Śaka era (beginning A.D. 778, and founded by king Sālivāhana; an expired year of the Śaka era is converted in to the corresponding year A.D by adding to it 78-79; (Col-3, p. 1045).

44. शौल्किक-Customs officer. According to Williams, "relating to taxes or tolls, a superintendent of tolls or customs (Col-3, p. 1093).

45.सहजधर्म- Sahaja cult. According to M.M.Williams, born or produced together or at the same time as (gen), T.S; Congenital, innate, hereditary, original, natural, N.of various kings and other men, M.Bh; of a Tāntric teacher; Buddha; (Col-3, p. 1 193).

46.स्कन्धावार-Camp According to Kangle, An enacampment, a Cantonment, (Kangle R.P, The Kauṭiliya Arthaśāsrra 1960, Glossary, p. 79).

THE LAND MEASUREMENT UNITS

1.पाटक - It was a land measurement unit of South-Eastern Bengal. From the Guniaghar Grant of Vainya Gupta: The year 188 current (Gupta era), it is concluded that "One **Pāṭaka** = 40 **Droṇavāpas.**" [144] But Laskar worked out the equation 1 **Pāṭaka** =50 Droṇavāpas from the Ashrafpur plates (Mem. A.S.B, Vol.-1, p. 87) but this is definitely disproved by the Gunaighar plate.

2. द्रोण- It was a land measurement unit of south eastern Bengal. It is noted that **Droṇa** and **Droṇavāpa** are same unit Sircar remarks that," It is well known that 8 **Droṇavāpas** made one **Kulyavapa** and 5 Kulyavapas were equal to one **Pāṭaka**." Dikshit also suggests that"8 Droṇavāpas of land make one **Kulyavāpa**."[146]

3.यष्ठि - It was a land measurement unit of south-estern Bengal. According to Roy, "Seven Yaṣṭhi make one Poyā."[147]

4. काक - It is also a land measurement unit of south eastern Bengal. According to Roy "Four Kaka make one Uyan."[14S]

5.बिन्दु - It is a land measurement unit of south eastern Bengal. It is a very small unit. No further information has found.

Relations of these and some other units also are given below:

40 Droṇas = 1 Pāṭaka

8 Droṇas = 1 Kulyavāpa

1 Kulyavāpa = 32 Āḍhakas

32 Āḍhakas = 128 Prasthas.

5 Kulyavāpas = 1 Pāṭaka

5 Padas = 1.25 Pāṭakas

3 Krānti = 1 Kadā

4 Kadā = 1 Gandā

20 Gandā = 1 Pan

4 Pan - 1 Rekhā

4 Rekhā = 1 Poyā

4 Poyā= 1 Keyār

12 Keyār - 1 Hala

4 Kāka = 1 Uyān

50 Uyān = 1 Āḍhi

4 Adhi = 1 Droṇa

4 Kuḍava = 1 Prastha

4 Prastha = 1 Aḍha

4 Aḍha = 1 Droṇa.

NOTES AND REFERENCES

1. Raychaudhuri, H.C., H.B, ed.R.C.Majumdar, Vol.-1, 1943, pp. 24, 29.
2. Banerji, Ramesh Chandra, "The Vaṅgālas", I.C, Vol.-II, 1935-36, p. 758.
3. Willson, Viṣṇu Purāṇa, II, pp. 134.170.
4. Vy. P, ch.99, 26-34,47-97; Bnda. P, iii, ch.74, 25-34, 47-100; M.Pch. 48, 23-9,43-89; B.P, IV, chap.18,1; Bhag, P. IX, chap.23, 5; MBh,i, chap.104, 4193-221, with variations: xii, ch.343, 13177-84; cf.Pargiter, A.I.H.Tradition, pp. 109 and 158.

5. Law, B.C., "The Vaṅgas", 1C, Vol.-I 1934-35, Nos-1-4, p. 59.
6. Majumdar, R.C., BD.I (Pracin Juga), 1988, p. 8.
7. Sircar, D.C., 'Bengal'G.A.M.I, 1960, pp. 124-125.
8. Majumdar, R.C., BD.I, (Prachin juga) in Bangali, 1988, p. 8.
9. Roy, Niharranjan, Bi.I, Ādiparba, 1402 Beng., p. 109.
10. Wheeler, R.E.M., F.T.P, 1950, p. 96.
11. Law, B.C., "The Vaṅgas", I.C, Vol.-I, 1934-35, p. 60.
12. Majumdar, N.G., "Edilpur copper plate of Kesava Sena", I.B, Vo-1 III, 1929, p.119.
13. Majumdar, R.C., BD.I (Pracin Juga), 1988, Beng, p. 9.
14 Banerji, R.C., I.C., Vol.-II, 1935 - 36, p. 756.
15. Sen, Prabodh. Chandra, "Some Janpadas of Ancient Rāḍhā", I.H.Q., Vol. Ill, 1932, p. 533.
16. Law, B.C., I.C., Vol.-I, p. 57 and Paul. Pramode Lal, "South Eastern Bangladesh in Ancient Times", I.H.Q., Vol.-XII, 1936, No.-I, p. 67.
17. Paul, P.L., E.H.B, Vol.-I, Calcutta, 1936 p. iii.
18. Buchanana, Francis, "Buchanana Recoard", Calcutta Review, 1894, p. 2.
19. Chunningham, A., A.S.R, Vol.-XV, p. 145 and see also Gopal Bhatta's Ballal charitam, Pūrva. Khaṇḍa, vs. 6,7.
20 Pargiter, "Ancient Countries in Eastern India", J.A.S.B., 1897, p. 85.
21. Basak, R. G., H.N.E.I, 1934, p. 180.
22. Sircar, D.C., Bengal, G.A.M.I, 1960p.124.
23. Paul, P. L., "South Eastern Bengal in Ancient Times, LH.Q, Vol.-XII, No.-1, 1936, p. 78, in Footnote and in the Early History of Bengal, 1939, Vol.-1, p. V.
24. Sircar, D.C., "Vaṅga and Vaṅgāla",G.A.M.I, 1971, p. 140.
25. Hultzsch, E., "Tirumalai Rock Inscription of Rajendra Chola 1", E.I, Vol.-IX, 1907-8, p. 233.
26. Banerji R,C, "The Vaṅgāla's", l.C, Vol.-II, 1935-36, p. 755-56.
27. BhattasaliN.K, E.I,Vol.-XXVII, 1947, p. 24.
28. Paul Pramode Lal, E.H.B, Vol.-1, 1939, p. IV.
29. Sircar D.C, Bengal, G.A.M.I, 1960, p. 124.and E.I,Vo-lV, p. 257.
30. Sircar D.C, G.A.M.I, 1960, p. 124.
31. Hultszsch E, "Goharwa plates of Karna Deva", E.I, Vol.-XI, 1911-12, pp. 139 and f.f.
32. Hultszsch, E., "Tirumalai Rock Inscription of Rajendra Chola I", E. I, Vol-IX, pp. 229 and ff.

33. Majumdar, N.G., "Nalanda Inscription of Viplasrimitra", E.I, Vol.-XXI, 193-32, p. 97 and. ff.
34. Fleet, John Faithful, "Allahabad Posthumous stone Pillar Inscription of Samudrāgupta", C.I.I, Vol.-lII, 1963, p. 8.
35. Bhat, M. Ramakrishana, V. B. S., Part-1, 1981, p. 169.
36. Cuningham, Alexander, A. G. L., 1924, p. 575.
37. Chakravarti, Rasmohan, C. Z. I., 1984, pp. 89-90.
38. Bhat, M. Ramakrishana, V.B.S., Part-1, 1981, p. 168.
39. Law, B. C., "The Vaṅgas", l.C, Vol.-I, 1934-35, Nos. l-4,p.62.
40. Watters, T., Y.C.T.l., Vol.-II, p. 109.
41. Ibid, p. 187.
42. Beal, Samuel, B.R.W.W, (Trans), p. 199-200.
43. Watters, Thomas, Y.C.T.I, Vol.-II, 1973, pp. 187-88.
44. Beal, Samuel, L.H.T., 1973, p. Xiii..
45. Cunningham, Alexander, A.G.I., 1924, p. 574.
46. Wheeler, R.E.M., F.T.P., 1950, p. 97.
47. Beal, Samuel, L.H.T., 1943, p. XT-X1I.
48. Raychaudhuri, H.C., "Kingdom of Vaṅga",in H.B., ed. R.C. Majumdar, Vol.-1., 1943, pp. 85-86 in the foot note-4.
49. Bhattasali, N.K., "The Bhaghaura Narayana Image Inscription", E.I, Vol.-XVII, 1923-24, p. 353.
50. Dani, A.H., "Mainămatī plates of Chandras", P.A, Number- III, 1966, p. 24.
51. Law, B.C., "The Vaṅgas", l.C., Vol.-1, 1934-35, p. 62.
52. Watters, T., Y.C.T.I., Vol.-II, 1973, p. 188.
53. Bhandrakar, D.R., "Identification of the Princes and territories mentioned in the Allahabad Pillar Inscription of Samudragupta", I.H.Q,Vol-1, 1925, p. 256.
54. Cunningham, Alxander, A.G.I., 1924, p. 576.
55. Bhattacharyya, D.C., "A Newly discovered copperplate from Tippera", I.H.Q. Vol.-VI, 1930, pp. 45-60.
56. Laskar, G.M., "Ashrafpur copper- plates grants of Devakhaḍga", M.A.S.B.1906, Vol.-1, p. 85-91.
57. Bhattasali, N.K., "The Daulbadi Sarwani Image Inscription of Mahādevi Prabhavati Queen of Deva Khaḍga", E.I., Vol.-XVII, 1923-24, p. 358.
58. Chowdhury, A.M, "Gography of Anient Bengal: The Pauṇḍravarddhanabhukti", A.S.B, Vol.-XXII, No.-3,1977, p. 184.
59. Sircar, D.C., G.A.M.I, 1971, p. 157.
60. Sircar, D.C., "Madanpur plate of Śrī Candra", E.I,Vol.-XXVIII, 1949-50, p. 338.

61. Roy, Niharranjan, Bi.I: Adiparba, 1402, Beng, p. 112.
62. Sarma, Ramavatara (Editor), Kalpadrukosa of Kesava, G.O.S, Vol.-I, No-42,1928, p. 7, Sloka-26.
63. Raychaudhuri, H.C, H.B., ed. R.C Majumdar, Vol.-1., 1943., p. 17.
64. Roy, Niharranjan, Bi.I: Adiparba, 1402, Beng, p. 112.
65. Paul, P. L., E.H.B, Vol.-1, 1939, p. iii- iv and fn-4. and Roy Niharranjan, Bi.I: Adiparba, 1402, Beng, p. 112.
66. Takakusu, J., "Notes on Geographical names." I-tsing, R.B.R, Trans, 1896, p. XLVL
67. Basak, R. G., "Madanpur plate of Śrī Candra", E.I, Vol.-XXVIII, 1949-50, p. 54.
68. Majumdar, R.C., BD.1, Prachin Juja, Beng, 1988, p. 9.
69. Paul, P. L., The Early History of Bengal, Vol.-I, 1939, p. IV.
70. Roy, Niharranjan, Bi.I: Adiparba, 1402, Beng. p. 1 12.
71. Foucher, M., L' Iconographic Bauddhique de 1 Inde, Vol.- 1, p. 200, No.- 55.
72. Ibid, p. 192, No.-17.
73. Majumdar, N.G., "Sahitya-parishat copper-pate of Visvarupa Sena", IB, Vol.- III, 1929, p. 147.
74. Paul, P.L., E.H.B, Vol.-1, 1939, p. IV.
75. Sircar, D.C., "Madanpur plate of Śrī Candra, year-46", E.I, Vol.-XXWI, 1949-50., p. 338.
76. Mitra, S., J.K.I., Beng. p. 140.
77. Bagchi, P.C., Kalulajnana-Nirnaya, pp. 2.5 ff.
78. Majumdar, N.G., I.B, Vol.-III, 1929,p.3.
79. Dasgupta, Nalini Natli, "Candradvīpa" I.C., Vol.-II, 1935-36, pp. 150-51.
80. Bajpai, K.D., (Editor), G.E.A.M.I., p. 88.
81. Roy Niharranjan, Bi.I., Adiparba, 1402, Beng, p. 113.
82. Adam, A.K.M., Shamsul, Maināmatī, 1982, p. 13.
83. Alfred, Foucher, Iconography, P1-VIII, 4, p. 199 and Majumdar, R.C., "The Kingdom of Paṭṭikera", H.B, Vol.-I., 1943, p. 257.
84. MacDowall, David, W., N.C., Vol.-XX, 1960, pp. 229-34.
85. Dani, A.R., J.N.S.I, Vol.-XXIV, 1962, pp. 141-142.
86. Phayre, A.P., "Coins of Arakan, of Pegu and of Burma", N.O., p. 28-29.
87. Khan, F.A., Maināmatī, Karachi, 1963, p. 23.
88. Ramachandran, T.N., B.C Law Volume, ed. D.R. Bhandarkar, Part-11, Poona, 1946, pp. 216-17.

89. Ghosh, Jogendra, Chandra, "The Chandra dynasty of Arakan," LH.Q, Vol.-Vll, 1931, p. 37.
90. Phayre, A.P., H.Bma, p. 37.
91. Majumdar, R.C., "The Kingdom of Paṭṭikera", H.B, Vol.-1, 1943, p. 257.
92. Paul, Pramode Lal, E.H.B, Vol.-I, 1939, p. VI.
93. Majumdar, R.C., "The kingdom of Paṭṭikera", H.B, Vol.-I 1943, p. 257.
94. Phayre, A.P., History of Burma, 1928, p. 31.
95. Ibid, pp. 49-50.
96. Majumdar, R.C., "Paṭṭikera Rajya", Bangladesher Itihas (Prachin Juga), 1988,p., 155.
97. Bhattacharyya, Dinesh Chandra, "The Maināmatī Copper-plate of Ranavanka malla Harikaladeva: 1141 Saka," V.R.S.M., No.-5, 1934, p. 12.
98. Majumdar, N.G., "Rampal copper-plate of Śrī Chandra", I.B, Vol.-II., 1929, p. 2.
99. Sircar, D.C., "Dhulla Plate of Śrī Chandra", E.I, Vol.-XXXIIl, 1960, pp. 135-140.
100. Ray, H.C., "Baghaura Narayana Image Inscription of Mahipala", LH.Q, Vol.-XVT., 194, p. 632.
101. Śrīcar, D.C., "Dhulla plate of Śrī Chandra", E.I, Vol.-XXXIII, 1960 p. 135.
102. Banerjee, R.D., B.I., p. 233,
103. Majumdar, N.G., T.B, Vol.-III, 1929, p. 3.
104. Ganguly, D.C., "A side light on the history of Bangal", LH.Q, Vol.-XVl, 1940, p. 181.
105. Gupta, Kamalakanta, Copper-plates of Sylhet, Sylhet, 1967, p. 8 ff.
106. Mitra, H.D., LH.Q, Vol.-II, pp. 313, 665.
107. Bhattasali, N.K., BahRātavarsha, Jyaishtha, 1348 B.S, pp. 768 ff.
108. Sircar, D.C., "The Kailan Copper-plate Inscription of King Śrīdharana Rāta of Samataṭa", I.H.Q,Vol.-XXIII,1947,pp. 221ff.
109. Gupta, Kamalalakanta, "Two Maināmatī Copper-plate Inscription of the Khaḍga and Early -Deva Times", B.A, 1979, Number -I, pp. 141ff.
110. Gupta, Chowdhury, Kamala Kanta, "Paschimbhag Copper-plate", N.K B.C.V., Dacca, 1966, P.
111. Sircar, D.C.,"Copper plate Inscription of King Bhava Deva" J.A.S. L, Vol.-XVII,No.-2, 1951, p. 87.

112. Ibid, pp. 83-94.
113. Dey, N.L., G.D.A.M.I, 1971, pp. 61-62.
114. Bhat, M. Ramakrishna, Varahamihira's Bṛhat Samhita, Part-I, 1981, p. 168. 115. Ibid, p. 168.
116. Dey, N. L., The Geographical Dictionary of Ancient and Mediaeval India, 1971, p. 115
117. Bajpai, K.D., G.E.A.M.I, 1967, p. 76.
118. Sircar, D.C., "The Kailan Copper-plate Inscription of King Śrīdharana Rāta", I.H.Q, Vol.-XXIII, 1947, pp. 225-226.
119. Dani, A.H., "Maināmatī Plates of the Chandras", P.A, Number-3, 1966, p. 25.
120. Watters, T., Y.C.T.I., Vol.-II, p. 109.
121. Bhat, M. Ramakrishna, V.B.S., Part-1, 1981, p. 168.
122. Pargiter, J.A.S.B., 1897, p. 106.
123. Barua, K.L., E.H.K., pp. 2-3.
124. Sircar, D.C., G.A.M.I, 1971, p. 161.
125. Ibid, p. 162.
126. E.I., Vol.-XII, p. 68, Sircar.D.C, "The Sakta Pithas", p. 13 and note, of J.A.I.H, Vol.-I, pp. 19-20.
127. Sircar, D.C., G.A.M.I, 1971, p. 163.
128. Bhat, M. Ramakrishna, V.B.S, Part-I, p. 169.
129. Beal, Samuel, L.H.T, 1973, p. X1II.
130. Dey, N. L., G. D. A. M. I., 1971, p. 116.
131. Fleet, C., I.I., Vol.-III, p. 25.
132. Dey, N.L., G.D.A.M.I., 1971, p. 63.
133. Cunningham, Alexander, A.G.I, 1924, p. 408.
134. James Prinsep, Benares Illustrated, Introduction, p. 8, and Vy. P, Uttara, ch. 30.
135. Fa Hian, Legge, ch. XXI;
136. Cunningham, Alexander, A.S.R, Vol.-XL
137. Ghosha, Buddha, Atthakatha, J.A.S.B, 1838, p. 796.
138. Kangle, R.P., The Kautiliya Arthasastra Part - III A, Study, University of Bombay, 1965, p. 133.
139. Ibid, p. 133.
14. Kangle, R.P., The Kautiliya Arthasastra, Part-1, University of Bombay, 1960, pp. 119-20.
141. Kangle, R.P., The Kautiliya Arthasastra Part - III A Study, University of Bombay, 1965, p. 174.
142. Ibid, p. 194.
143. Kangle, R.P., The Kautiliya Arthasastra, Part - I, University of Bombay, 1960, Glossary, p. 3.

144. Bhattacharyya, D.C., "A Newly discovered copper-plate from Tippera", I.H.Q, Vol.-VII, 1930, p. 52.
145. Sircar, D.C., "The Kailan copper-plate grant Inscription of King Śrīdharana Rāta", I.H.Q, Vol.-XXIII, No.-3, 1947, p. 35.
146. Dikshit, K.N., "Paharpur copper-plate grant of the [Gupta] year 159", E.I., 1929, Vol.-XX, p. 61.
147. Roy, Nibarranjan "Bangalir Itihas: Adiparba", Calcutta, 1402. B. S, p. 188.
148. Ibid, p. 190.

CHAPTER-VII

EPILOGUE

Maināmatī, the name of a village and a union, is a very familiar historic place situated in Burichang Thana of Comilla district in Bangladesh. This union consists of 23 villages. Maināmatī is a small strip of hilly land but it is extra-ordinarily rich in transferable and non-transferable archaeological evidences and was one of the most important historical and religious centres in the eastern part of ancient India (at present a part of Bangladesh). The area, located in the centre of the ancient Samataṭa Maṇḍala, was politically very significant in ancient times and gave birth to many popular ballads and folk literature. The greatest assemblage of ancient Buddhist remains lies in the Maināmatī-Lalmai hill range. It extends for 11 miles north-south from Maināmatī village on the Gumati river in the north to Caṇḍī Murā near Lalmai Railway Station in the south and is about 25 miles in circumference. In its widest parts, the ridge is about five miles across and its highest peaks attain a height of 150 feet in a few places, but the average elevation is 40 feet above the plains and 90 feet above sea-level; the highest peaks are Kalir Bazar and Caṇḍī Murā. Like the Barind and Madhupur Tract, this ridge represents a small mass of quasi-lateritic old alluvium. These high lands were formerly thickly wooded with an abundance of wild life, but land-hungry local farmers have now pushed back the forest to the highest points and to the patches of Śrī trees on the slopes. An interesting material found scattered all over the hill range is fossilwood. It shows the ancient characteristic of this area.

This place was named after Mainămatī only a few hundred years back. Till today, no historical or epigraphical evidences for giving this name to this place are found. According to some legends and ballads, Queen Mainămatī gave birth to prince Gopicand. Some scholars have identified Gopicand with Govinda Candra of Candra dynasty of Samataṭa Maṇḍala. But it is strongly contended that Mainămatī did not give birth to Govinda Candra, son of Laḍaha Candra. Most probably the village Mainămatī has come to light from the name of Queen Mainamti, mother of Gopicand, the ruler of Mṛkul.

According to inscriptional evidences the kingdom of Samataṭa was very well-known from 4th century A.D. A number of foreign travellers visited Samataṭa and described its rich geographical details and political and socio-cultural activities. Most probably the area of Kiă-mo-laṅg-kia mentioned by Yuang Chwang (7th century) and Komala of Vāyu Purāṇa, are the same.It is generally accepted that Kia-mo-lahg-kia and Komala are the present district of Comilla. Comilla was under the ancient state of Tripura. A study of the ancient maps by Pargiter, Thomas Walter, John D. Byaros, Svanson D.Ababil,Phon-den Brook and Rennel, indicates the position of the Comilla district which is situated on the northern side of the Bay of Bengal and the eastern side of the River Lauhitya i.e. Brahmaputra.

The geological analysis shows that the existence of Madhupur Clay of Pleistocene Epoch which is observed around the bottom of Mainămatī-Lalmai hill range. The soil of this region is roughly called reddish-yellow coloured clay or sandy soil. From the middle stage of Tertiary era i.e. from the Miocene Epoch, nearly 40,000 feet long alluvium bed has settled in this region forming its bottom as foundation. The bottom foundation of this district is estithated to be nearly 3 crore years old i.e.formed during Miocene Epoch.

Most of the natural environments on geological structural formation of this district are the gift of the river system. From ancient times, numerous rivers and streams are flowing over this district helping the work of its formation. After all, the rivers, from ancient times, have been contributing to the natural land formation.

The line of the Tropic of Cancer passes over the Comilla district. So the entire district is under the influence of the tropical environment. Naturally, tropical monsoonal clithate is observed here. The clithate of this district is comfortable and healthy. Due to this reason, human habitation has come up in this area from very ancient times. No direct evidence has been found of the people who lived in Maināmatī- Lalmai region but the assemblage of the ancient and archaeological sites shows its ancient historic relations with the present. Speaking about its richness in archaeological evidences, it is mentionable that more than fifty sites are traced in this hill range. Out of fifty, thirty-eight are archaeological or ancient brick structures classified into monasteries, large shrines, administrative site, hill-top mound, non-structural sites and water reservoirs. Brief descriptions of these sites are given to show that they cover a span of nearly 8 centuries from 6th to 13th. The remaining 12 sites do not posses any structural evidences or minimal heights required to call them archaeological remains. It is belived that most of these buildings were used for controling the political and socio-cultural activities of south-east Bengal. The large number of such ancient structures indicate that the powerful Buddhist dynasties ruled over this area from 6th to 13th century A.D. A large number of cultural material and artifacts have been exposed from the abondoned sites of this area, which suggests that this area was densely populated. The art and architecture of the artifacts found here represent the characteristic peculiarities of the local artists of south east Bengal.

From the sixth century through the thirteenth century A.D. two major historic phases can be distinguished. The first phase was marked by the establishment and successive enlargement of Buddhist monasteries.The second phase is defined by the structures of small temples.

In the first phase from the 6th to 8th century, a large Buddhist centre had developed in the Maināmatī region. A large number of artifacts were found during excavation in various sites. These include copper plates, silver and gold coins, bronze images caskets and utensils and other metal objects, pottery, terracotta plaques and a number of various minor objects accumulated over the centuries. There are traced seven large monasteries named (l)Army Bunglow Vihāra (St-4) (2) Ānanda Rājā's Pālace(St-12) (3) Rūpbān Kanyā's Pālace (St-15) (4) Bhoj Rājā's Pālace (St-16) (5) Kotbāri Murā (St-20) (6) Rupbān Murā (St-21) and (7) Sālvānpur Mound (St- 24). These seven large monasteries can be dated to 6th to 8th century A.D. when the Buddhist religion, political and socio-cultural relations were flourishing not only in Maināmatī but almost in entire ancient India.

In the second phase, l0th to 13th century, Maināmatī - Lalmai area lost its political autonomy for a short time.As a result, the political support for the monasteries dwindled as Vaiṣṇava shrines gained their place. The copper-plate grants of Candra dynasty donating property in the Samataṭa Maṇḍala were issued from Vikramapura, forty miles to the west from Maināmatī. The Candras were the rulers of Vaṅga, Vaṅgāla, Candradvīpa .Samataṭa and Harikela regions. But their capital was in Vikramapura. It seems that the old capital city of Devaparvata and cities like Kripura, Vasantapura and Karmanta were neglected by Candra rulers. By the time of Candra rulers, the size of the buildings and the budgets were reduced. The amount of the donated lands was also reduced.

The ruins of Maināmatī -Lalmai hill range remind us of the forgotten city of Paṭṭikera, of the capital city- the "Camp of Victory"- Devaparvata, Kripura, Vasantapura and Karmānta, Rohitagiri and Lālāmbivana. From the discussion of the ruins of Maināmatī it has come to light that these structures were mostly used for religious purposes from 6th to 13th century A.D.

Maināmatī excavations have unearthed a large number of artifacts which are valuable for re-constructing the historical co-relation in the time and space of this area. The copper-plate grants discovered from Mainämatī are twelve in all. Out of the twelve copper-plate grants, five are heavily corroded and impossible to deciphered. The remaining seven grants disclose valuable information for reconstructing the historical, geographical and sociocultural relations. Seven other epigraphs three copper plate grants of Śrī Candradeva and four stone image inscriptions which are found not actually from the area under study but from a nearby area are also included because they provide good material for reconstructing the dynastic chronology and historical co-relations of the ruling dynasty of Samataṭa Maṇḍala. On the basis of these evidences the entire thesis presents the geographical, political, chronological lineage and the sociocultural status of various ruling dynasties of Samataṭa Maṇaḍala and the nearby area.

Maināmatī excavations have thrown a flood of light on the history of Samataṭa Maṇḍala. As many as 400 specimens of gold, silver and copper coins of various types and size are found. Except a few, all of them are recovered from an early occupation level of the monastic cells of Sālvan Vihāra. One gold coin has been identified *as Aśvamedha* coin of Samudrāgupta(c.335-375 A.D.) on the basis of its motif and a short legend on its reverse. Out of the three Gupta gold coins, one represents the well-known Lakṣmī and Archer type. This has been identified with a coin of Candra Gupta II (c. 376-415 A.D.). The Lakṣmī and Archer type coins, characteristically Indian in style and design remain an exclusive model for gold currency of eastern India for more than three centuries. Two imitation gold coins belong to one Bālabhaṭṭa, probably a prince of the Khaḍga dyansty. A dozen of post-Gupta era imitation type gold coins are found from Sālvan Vihāra. There is a legend on the coins. It "reads Śrī Vaṅgāla Mṛgāṅka". Most probably these coins were issued by the powerful Deva dynasty of Samataṭa Maṇḍala. These heutiful imitation coins indicate the prosperous condition of the south east area of Bengal under the Devas.

224 silver coins were also found from the interior cells of the Sālvan Vihāra. All of them bear the images of a Trident, the Sun and the Moon on the reverse and an image of crouching bull (most probably Nandi) on the obverse. The portion above the bull contains two type of legends. In some it is Paṭṭ ikera,in others it is **Lalitakera Dharma Vijaya**. It is concluded that the coins were issued try some powerful and prosperous rulers of Samataṭa, probably, Śrī Ānanda Deva of Deva dynasty of Samataṭa. The discovery of various type of coins and some gold ornaments from Mainămatī exacavation indicate the prosperity of the Buddhist Vihāras in those days. It appears that these coins must have been given as donations to the Vihāra by the devotees.

A large number of terracotta plaques in various designs were recovered from Mainămatī- Lalmai hill range. These specimens of terracotta plaques were mostly found in loose conditions from Sālvan Vihāra, Kutilā Murā, Ānanda Vihāra and Cārpatra Murā excavations. These plaques represent the popular folk art of Bangladesh.

The themes of the terracotta plaques are drawn from the daily life of the people. This art shows clearly the popular folk art of that period depicting the motifs of divine and semi divine beings, hybrids, flying Gandharvas, Apsaras, Kinnaras and Yakṣas, mythical creatures and composite animals, men,women and childern either engaged in various activities of life or at rest, warriors, musicians with their instruments, archers, acrobats balancing bodies on their hands, **Makaras** and **Kṛttimukhas,** dancers, sages and ascetics, monkeys and apes, birds, beasts, fish, animal fables, flowers and plants and other such domestic and family studies.They represent their local and ethical characteristics. The exceptionally rich plastic art of Bangladesh reflects a faithful picture of the prevailing social and cultural life of the people. We can get a clear idea about their religious practices, their mode of life, their dress and ornaments etc.

Huge quantity of pottery also was recovered from the archaeological sites of the Mainămatī - Lalmai hill range. Most of them were found from the first and second construction and re-construction level of Sālvan Vihāra. The study of thepottery reveals that the seven large monasteries in this area were built early. The site of the Mainămatī's Pālace Mound had along period of active use and was contemporaneous with all of other structural sites. The large shrines of Cārpatra Murā and Abbas Murā were probably latter in construction and use.A large number of Bronze images and two stone images are also found from this area. The composition of Mainămatī bronze images shows a peculiar local characteristic feature, probably because of the freedom adopted by the local artists. It is also observed that all the sculptures represent Tāntric gods and goddesses. Tāntric Buddhist images, belonging to 8th and 9th centuries, are rare even in the great Buddhist centres like Bodh Gaya, Kukrihar and Nalanda. In view of these images of the Tāntric gods and goddesses, some of the Mainămatī bronze images appear to be earlier in date.

There are no rocks and good stone to be found Mainămatī-Lalmai hill range and all over Bangladesh. Therefore, only two stone images were discovered from the central stūpa of Kutilā Murā. The style, decoration and ornamentation of both the images indicate their close relation with the Gupta art. It is noted that the influence of Gupta art was strong throughout the 7th century A.D. in Bengal. But the local artists of Samataṭa tried to give expression to their own style in their art. A large number of minor objects have also been discovered. These throw a good deal of light on the life style of the contemporary people of this region.

For the historical re-construction, the epigraphs copper-plates, coins, stone image inscriptions etc. are the most dependable and inforthative material. There are a total of 28 inscriptions related to the Mainămatī Lalmai hill range or the adjacent area. They are discussed here for the purpose of corelating their data about the ruling dynasties of Samataṭa Maṇḍala. The early history of Samataṭa Maṇḍala is still not clear to us. There is no proper evidence about the people who first lived in this area. The classical epics and religious treatises refer to it as ***Ārya-Pāṇḍava-Varjita-deśa*** . However, we have some epigraphic evidences that many dynasties ruled over Samataṭa Maṇḍala from 4th to 13th century A.D. We have a number of references to the Gupta, Rāta, Khaḍga, Bhadra. early Deva, Pāla, Candra, Varman, later Deva and Sena dynasties. Most of them ruled over Samataṭa Maṇḍala directly and some like Pāla ruled indirectly.

The name Samataṭa first appeared in the Allhabad posthumous stone pillar inscription of Samudrā Gupta (mid 4th century). The independent existence of various territories of Bengal came to an end under the Gupta Empire in 4th century A.D. The whole of Bengal with the exception of Samataṭa was definitely incorporated into the Gupta Empire by the time of Samudra Gupta. Vainya Gupta ruled over Eastern Bengal in 508 A. D. The study of the Gupta plates reveals that the south eastern Bengal was included within the Gupta Empire up to the first decade of the 6th century A.D. Vainya Gupta's "Camp of Victory" was situated at Kripura somewhere in the Comilla district. He was a contemporary of Vijaya Sena and Gopacandra. Most probably. Vainya Gupta ruled over Vaṅga and some portion of Samataṭa Maṇḍala.

From copper-plate grants, it is clear that five generations of Khaḍga dynasty ruled over Samataṭa. Their camp of victory was first at Jayakarmanta and later on, it was shifted to Devaparvata. The Mainămatī Pālace is generally identified as Devaparvata.

The Khaḍgas are roughly placed in last three quarters of the 7th century A.D. The rule of the Bhadra dynasty over Samataṭa was in the 7th century A.D. It may be suggested that the family was originally known as Khaḍga and when the name and fame of Śīlabhadra spread widely in the Buddhist world, the family also came to be known as Bhadras. There is a strong probability that the Khaḍgas were originally Brahminical Hindus and became Buddhists later on.

The Tippera copper-plate grant of Lokanātha shows that Natha dynasty ruled over some part of the south east Bengal in the second half of the seventh century A.D. We find six generations of the Nātha dynasty ruling in the south eastern Bengal. On the palaeographic considerations of the copperplate of Lokanātha and a close study of Rāta and Khaḍga copper-plates, it appears that Lokanātha may have I belonged to the second half of 7th century A.D.

The history of Rāta dynasty is known from the Kailan copper-plate inscription of King Śrīdharaṇa Rāta. Three generations of Rāta have ruled over Samtata about the second half of the seventh century A.D.

After Khaḍga, Bhadra and Rāta we have the dynasty of Devas. Five grants of Deva dynasty have given good material to re-constouct their lineage. Four generations of Deva dynasty are found mentioned by the grants. They ruled over Samataṭa in the 8th century A.D.

From the ten copperplate grants of the Candra dynasty it has come to light that they ruled over Candradvīpa, Harikela, Samataṭa. Vaṅgāla and Vaṅga from the last quarter of the ninth to the second quarter of the elevnth century A.D. They were the rulers of Rohitagiri i.e. Mainathatl Lalmai hill range and Vikramapura was their "Camp of Victory." They were Buddhists by faith. Seven generations of this dynasty ruled over south east Bengal.

From the copper-plate grants of the later Deva dynasty, we find that six generations of Devas ruled over Samataṭa in the 13th century A.D.

In an attempt to re-construct the historical geography of ancient kingdom and different place Dames, the inscriptions have been our most dependable and inforthative sources. The greatest of the problems was to identify the place names found in the inscriptions. An attempt has been made (in ch. VI) to define the boundaries of the places names of which are listed in 3 separate categories- the 37 places names, five river names and seven kingdom names- with their relevant demarcating areas.

Thus, an attempt has been made here to put together all archaeological data found in the area of Mainãmatī-Lalmai hill range which is relatively very small but archaeologically very rich, also to bring in other relevant data found in the surrounding areas, and to make a systethatic study of them, to attempt to reconstruct a historical overview of the political vicissicitudes of this area and to portray the socio-religious scenes of the area in their bygone ages purely on the basis of the archaeological artifacts consisting mainly of the copper-pl ates (which are all without exception written in Sanskrit) and supported only in a minor way by other archaeological evidences like structural sites, pottery, coins, teracotta plaques, stone images and bronze idols etc. It is expected that the attempt which is made here for the first time will merit a general acceptance.

BIBLIOGRAPHY

Ahmed, Nizamuddin, *Mahāsthan,* Department of Archaeoloy and Museums, Decca, 1981.

Alam A.K.M. Shamsul, *Maināmatī*, Department of Archaeology and Museums, Decca, 1982.

Bagchi P.C., *Kaulajnana-Nir-naya*, Metropolitan Printing and Publishing House, Limited, Calcutta, 1934.

Bajpai, K.D., *The geographical Encyclopaedia of Ancient and Medieval India*, The Indian Academy, Varanasi, 1967.

Banerji, R.D., *Bangalar Itihas Vol-I & II*, Calcutta, 1321 B.S., 1324 B.S.

Bandopadhyaya, Rakhaldas, *Bangalar Itihas : Prathambhag*, Dey's Publishing, Calcutta. 1402 B.S.

Basak, R.G., *The History of North Eastern India*, Kegan Paul, Trench, Trubner and Co. Ltd., London, 1934.

Beal, Samuel, *The Life of Hiuen Tsiang*, Munshiram Manoharlal Publishers Pvt. Ltd., Delhi, 1973.

Beal, Samuel, *Buddhist Records of the Western World (Trans)*, Kegan Paul, Trench, Trubner and Co. Ltd. London.

Bhandarkar D.R. (ed), *B.C. Law Volume Part-II*, The Bhandarkar Oriental Research Institute, Poona, 1946.

Bhattasali, N.K., *The Iconography of Buddhist and Brahmanical Sculptures in the Dacca Museums*, Dacca Museum Committee, Dacca, 1929.

Bhat, M.R. *Varahamihira's Brahat Samhita 2-Parts*, Motilal Banarsidass Indological Publishers, Delhi, 1982.

Chakravarti Roshomay, *Contribution of Comilla to the Buddhist Culture*.

Chakravarti, R.G., *Gauder Itihas*, Malda, 1909.

Chand, R.P., *Gauḍarajamala*, Rajshahi, 1319 B.S.

Chaudhury, A.M., *Dynastic History of Bengal*, Dacca, 1967.

Cuningham Alexander, *Ancient Geography of India*, Chuckervertty, Chatteree & Co. Ltd, Calcutta, 1924.

Dani, A.H. *Indian Pālaeography*, Oxford University Press, Oxford, 1963.

Daniel, H. H., *Ingalls (trans.) An Anthology of Sanskrit Court Poetry*, Harvard University Press Cambridge, 1965.

Das, Ganga (A) Gurunath Vidyānidhi Bhattacharyya (ed), *Chandomanjari*, Sanskrit Pustak Bhandar, Calcutta, 1401 B.S.

Das, Srikrishna (ed), *Markandeya Mahā Puran*, Nag Publishers, Delhi, 1983, *The Brahma Mahā Purāṇa*, Nag Publishers, Delhi, 1985.

Dey, Nundo Lal, *The Geographical Dictionary of Ancient and Medieval India*, Luzac & Co. London, 1971.

Dutt Sukumar, *Buddhist Monks and Monasteries of India*, George Allen and Unwin Ltd., London, 1962.

Foucher, Alfred, *Etude sur L' Iconographie Bouddhique de L'inde*, Ernest Leroux, Editeur, Peris, 1900.

Gangadas, Pandita, *Chandomanjari*, Janakinath Kbytirtha & Bro, Chhatra Pustakalaya, Calcutta, 1934.

Gupta, N., *Vikaramapurer Itihas*, Calcutta, 1316 B.S.

Gupta Kamalakanta, *Copper Plates of Sylhet*, Sylhet by Author, 1967.

Habibullah A.B.M. (ed), *Nalini Kanta Bhattasali Commemoration Volume*, 1966.

Harun-er-Rashid, *East Pakistan*, Lahore, 1965.

Harvey G.E., *History of Burma*, London, 1925.

Hemachandra Vijaya, Dharma Suri (ed), *The Abhidhana-cintamani*, Nathalal Laxmichand Vakil Bhavnagar, 1920.

Hunter, W.W., *Statistical Account of Bengal, Vol-V*, London, 1875-77.

Jakaria A.K.M. (ed), *Comilla Zelar Itihas*, Zela Parishad, Comilla. 1984.

Jayaswal, K.P., *An Imperial History of India in a Sanskrit Text*, Motilal Banarsidass, Lahore, 1934.

Kalhan (A) Durga Prassad (ed), *The Rajatarangini*, The Department of Public Instruction, Bombay, 1894.

Kalidas, (A) Chaudhuri Jogendradas (ed), *Raghuvamsha*, J. Chaudhuri, Calcutta, 1928.

Kangle, R.P., *The Kautilya Arthsastra, Part-II & III*, University of Bombay, Bombay, 1963.

Khan, F.A., *Maināmatī*, Karachi, 1963.

Khan, Nurul Islam (ed), *Bangladesh District Gazetteers*, Comilla. B.G. Press, Dacca, 1977

Kielhorn, Fronz *List of Inscriptions of Northern India.*

Maitreya, A.K., *Gauḍalekhamala*, Rajshahi, 1319 B.S.

Majumdar, N.G., *Inscription of Bengal, Vol-III*, The Varendra Research Society, Rajshahi, Bengal, 1929.

Majumdar, R.C. (ed.), *The History of Bengal,* Vol. I, University of Dacca, Dacca, 193

Majumdar, R.C., *Bangladesher Itihas, Prachin Junga (Beng),* General Publishers and Printers Pvt.Ltd., Calcutta, 1988

Majumdar Sastri S. (ed.), *Ancient Geography of India,* Chuckervertty, Chatterjee and Co. Ltd., Calcutta, 1924

Mitra, S.C., *Jessore Khulnar Itihas,* 2 Vols., Calcutta, 1329 and 1335 B.S.

Mohammed Ali, (A) Nazimuddin Ahmad (ed.), *Archaeological Survey Report Bogra, District,* Department of Archaeology and Museums, 1986

Morrison B.M., *Political Centers and Cultural Regions in Early Bengal,* Tucson : University of Arizona Press, 1970

Muhammad Abdur Rahim, *Bangladesher Itihas*, Nawroze Kitabisthan, Dhaka, 1995

Mookerjee Asutosh, *Sir Asutosh Mookerji Silver Jubilee Vol.-III,* Calcutta University Press, Calcutta, 1927

Pargiter Frederic Edeu, *Ancient Indian Historical Tradition,* Oxford University Press, Lodon, 1922

Paul P.L., *The Early History of Bengal, 2 Vols.,* Indian Research Institute, Calcutta, 1939

Phayer A.P., *History of Burma,* Indian Research Institute, Calcutta, 1939

Qadir M.A., *Paharpur,* Department of Archaeology and Museums, Dacca, 1980

Rabbani Ghulam A.K.M., (ed.), *Village Population Statistics, Comilla,* Bangladesh Bureau of Statistics, Dhaka, 1974

Rajsekhara (A) C.D., Dalal (ed.), *Kavyamimamsa,* Oriental Institute, Baroda, 1934

Rajsekhara (A) Suru, N.G., (ed.), *Karpura-Manjari*, Prof. N.G. Suru, Principal Ruparel College, Bombay, 1960

Roy Niharranjan, *Bangalir Itihas : Adiparb, in Beng.,* Dey's Publishing, Calcutta, 1402 B.S.

Sarma K.V., *The Brahmanda Purāṇam*, Krishnadas Academy, Varanasi, 1983

Sarma Ramavatar (ed.), *Kalpadrumkosa of Kesava,* Vol.-I, Oriental Institute, Baroda, 1928

Sastri Krishna Sankar, *Srimad Bhagavata Purāṇam,* Samsa Press, Varanasi, 1965

Sastri Trambaknath (ed.), *Vayu Purāṇa,* Sri Sayaji Vijay Press, Vadodara, 1814

Sen Benoy Chandra, *Some Historical Aspects of the Inscriptions of Bengal,* University of Calcutta, Calcutta, 1942

Sen D.C., *Bṛhat Banga,* Vol.-I&II, University of Calcutta, Calcutta, 1341-1342 B.S.

Singh Nag Sharma, *The Matsya Mahāpurana*, Nag Publishers, Delhi, 1983

Sircar D.C., *Studies in the Geography of Ancient and Medieval India,* Motilal Banarasidass, Delhi, 1971

Sir Raja Radhakantadeva, *Sabdakalpadruma,* Vol.-II, Motilal Banarasidass, Delhi, 1961

Sukthankar Vishnu S., *The MahābhaRāta,* Bhandarkar Oriental Research Institute, Poona, 1933

Sur. Atul, *Bangla O Bangalir Bibartan,* Sahityalok, Calcutta, 1401 B.S.

Vidyābhusana Satis Chandra (ed.), *Amarakosa,* Asiatic Society, Calcutta, 1911

Vyas Ramakrishana T., *Valmiki Ramayana,* Oriental Institute, Vadodara, 1992

Watters Thomas, *On Yuang Chwang's Travels in India*, 2 Volumes, Munshiram Monoharlal Publishers Pvt. Ltd., Delhi, 1973

Webster J.E., *East Bengal District Gazetteers, Tippera*, Dacca, 1910

Wheeler R.E.M., *Five Thousand Year of Pakistan,* Royal Indian & Pakistan Society, London, 1950

Wilson, H.H., *The Vishnu Puran*, Punthipustak Publishers, Calcutta, 1972

Journals, Reports, Surveys etc.

Archaeological Survey of India

Archaeological Survey Report

Asiatic Researches or Transactions of the Society Institute in Bengal

Asiatic Society of Bengal
Bangla Academi Patrika
Bangladesh Archaeology
Bangladesh Lalit Kala
BhaRātavarsha
Corpus Inscriptionum Indicarum
Epigraphia Indica
Gaekwad's Oriental Series
Indian Antiquary
Indian Culture
Indian Historical Quarterly
Journal of the Asiatic Society
Journal of the Asiatic Society (Letters)
Journal of the Asiatic Society of Bengal
Journal of the Asiatic Society of Bengal (Letters)
Journal of the Numisthatic Society of India
Lalit Kala
Memoirs of the Asiatic Society of Bengal
Memoirs of the Archaeological Survey of India
Numisthatic Chronicle
Numisthatic Orientalia
Pakistan Archaeology
Sahitya Parisat Patrika
Varendra Research Society's Monography.

INDEX